NEWSPAPER MARKETING IN INDIA

NEWSPAPER MARKETING IN INDIA

A Focus on Languages Press

By

Dr. NVR Jyoti Kumar

ANMOL PUBLICATIONS PVT. LTD.
NEW DELHI - 110 002 (INDIA)

ANMOL PUBLICATIONS PVT. LTD.
4374/4B, Ansari Road, Daryaganj
New Delhi - 110 002
Ph.: 23261597, 23278000
Visit us at: www.anmolpublications.com

Newspaper Marketing in India: A Focus on Language Press

First Published, 2003

ISBN 81-261-1556-4

PRINTED IN INDIA

Published by J.L. Kumar for Anmol Publications Pvt. Ltd., New Delhi - 110 002 and Printed at Tarun Offset Press, Delhi.

For

Dr. N. Gangadhara Rao

my mentor, model and also my father

Contents

Preface

Concern for the newspapers stems out of the concern for social and economic development of the mankind through development communication. Historically, newspapers in India were known to have breathed fire in spreading the movements to remove social evils like *Sati*, child marriages and untouchability. Further, newspapers revolutionised the Indian politics and thus emerged the champions of freedom movement. Raja Ram Mohun Roy's *Sambad Kaumudi*, Dadabhai Naoroji's *Voice of India*, Tilak's *Kesari* and Mahatma Gandhi's *Harijan*, to mention a few, are still rememberd even today as though they are achievements of yesterday. Very few products rival newspapers in terms of their all around impact on man and society.

In terms of dailies-to-thousand people, the standing of the Telugu daily was at the rock bottom with only 10 copies against a national average circulation of 29 copies for all languages in India. The Malayalam newspaper of Kerala was the greenest of the oases with 71 copies-to-thousand people. In the backdrop of such a dismal showing of the Telugu newspaper market, there found to be a silverlining too. The phenomenal growth of one newspaper, *Eenadu*, attracted nationwide attention in the industry circles. The paper emerged market leader within four years of its inception, pushing aside a chain newspaper, and a 80 year old pioneer in the field and a champion of freedom movement. From then onwards *Eenadu* not only continued to remain at the top but also continued to grow from strength to strength.

Such of those success stories like *Eenadu* are not uncommon elsewhere in the country. They are hope of newspaper business. They offer definite clues that help flourish the industry. To make it clear, competitive marketing strategies appear to be the key of the business success. The present study addresses to find out and analyse the strategies pursued by the market leader *Eenadu* and also the other competitors in the Telugu newspaper market. Thus the lessons by Telugu dailies from Telugu dailies make the central theme of the study . The survival of the newspaper is its concern.

Newspapers have higher ideals than just making money, responsibility beyond simply keeping their proprietors happy. But newspapers are business that must be managed efficiently and profitably. A financialy failing newspaper cannot shine light in dark corners. A newspaper out of business is no defender of the people's right to know. Newspapers, if revived, may be able to revive hopes and ambitions of the teeming millions of India in rebuilding their nation.

The present book has nine chapters . How communication, development and newapaper are related to each other, the newspaper's product peculiarities, emergence of the marketing era in newspaper business, review of the conceptual framework of the strategic marketing are discussed in chapter One , *The Newspaper and its Marketing*.

Chapter Two begins with the historic relevance of the newspaper in India. Analysis of the comparative growth of the Indian newspapers, overall and language-wise, in terms of circulation forms the central theme of this chapter. Ultimately, this chapter, *The Indian Newspapers* ascertains the status of the Telugu newspapers, the subject matter of this study, compared to its counterparts in other languages.

Chapter Three presents the study design and profiles of the Telugu newspapers under study. The problem and the objectives of the study are clarified therein.

Chapter Four, *The Rise and Fall of Telugu Dailies,* attempts to make a paper-wise analysis of the marketing performance of the Telugu dailies, in terms of their circulation and market share. Though the chapter begins with a summary account of the early players, the special focus is on playing since 1974, i.e., the time marketing started arriving to the Telugu newspaper scene.

Chapter Five is one of the study's most important, marketing strategies being the core of this study. This chapter identifies and analyses such of those strategies, in greater detail, which enabled the market leader *Eenadu* to reach such a predominant position. Further, the strengths and weaknesses of the strategies adopted by the other competitors are dealt in here. Competitiveness of the market leader in Telugu newspaper market compared to the market leaders in other languages, is also examined in *The Competitive Strategies and Achieving Leadership.*

Chapter Six and the one that follows deal with the consumers and their behaviour. They are the causal variables in marketing, making the roots of any strategic design. The socioeconomic bases of the Telugu newspaper consumers and their consumption characteristics are brought out in *The Roots of Strategies.*

Chapter Seven, *Consumers' Evaluation,* turns to find out the buying motives influencing the consumers of Telugu papers and their choicest daily, non-daily and Sunday features from their papers. Comparative evaluation of the select papers, feature-wise, by the multipaper readers also forms part of this chapter.

Chapter Eight treats a crucial subject, crucial for the survival of a newspaper. *Marketing the Space* highlights the space selling strategies emerging in the Telugu newspaper market.

Lastly the book concludes with the summary of the findings and suggestions in chapter Nine. The condensed version of the questionnaire used in the reader survey is given in the Appendix, followed by Bibliography.

Acknowledgements

I am unbelievably fortunate to be initiated into the doctoral research by my beloved Research Director Prof. M. Gangadhara Rao, Director, CMS, GITAM, Visakhapatnam. He was instrumental in shaping my career as a humble teacher and then as a researcher. He has been a towering source of strentgth inspiration and enocuragement from conceptualisation to the completion of this work. I am greatly indebted to him for all this and the parental affection showered on me.

I am highly indebted to Prof. J. Satyanarayana, Emeritus Professor who shaped my career as a humble teacher.

I deem it my good fortune to interact with hundreds of intense Telugu newspaper readers, on the one hand, and many executives representing the Telugu newspapers, on the other. This study could not have become possible but for their spontaneity in providing me invaluable information. I had lenghty and fruitful discussions particularly with Venkataratnam Kanuri and K. Hare Ram of *Andhra Jyoti* and Joydeep Benerjee of *Eenadu*. Earlier, the CEOs of all the newspapers under the study readily consented to provide whatever information is required and whenever they were approached, they rendered me all possible help. I owe all of them a lot.

My long cherished dream of undertaking doctoral research should have remained high and dry but for the support of all kinds received by me from the Management of VRS & YRN College, Chirala, A.P., where I have been teaching since 1985. I consider the opportunity I got to teach there motivated me this far. I express my deep sense of gratitude to my college, the President V.V. Ramachandra Vasu, the Secretary & Correspondent J. Lakshmi Bhavani. I am grateful in equal measure to her predecessors, particularly J. Ramakrishna Prasad and Dr. Y.E.Ch. Vidyasagar and the former Principal P. Jagadiswara Rao and the principals that succeeded him.

I wish to express my gratitude to Andhra Universtiy for bestowing upon me an opportunity to undertake doctoral work on a part-time basis. I am indebted to the University Grants Commission, New Delhi for providing me timely grant under the scheme of Minor Research Projects that has partly enabled me to undertake this study.

I thank Y. Suresh, my College Librarian (PG) and also K. Ramakrishnam Raju, the Labrarian of PG Courses, D.N.R. College, Bhimavaram where I studied, for liberally lending me whatever books and journals required by me.

I am particularly thankful to Prof. K. Rama Mohana Rao and Dr. A. Narasimha Rao of the Dept. of Commerce and Management Studies, Andhra University for making me feel at home whenever I visited Visakhapatnam in connection with my research work.

I thank Prof. V. Venkaiah, Executive Director, GRADE, Dr. B.R. Ambedkar Open University, Hyderabad, Prof. Ch. Ramaprasad Rao of S.K. University, Ananthapur and Prof. G. Anjaneya Swamy of Pondicherry University, Pondicherry for their support and inspiration.

No words can supplement my feelings in expressing my gratefulness to my parents who taught me the value of unconditional love, family and learning.

Finally, I thank Mr. Kripal D. Joshi and his team of Anmol Publications Pvt. Ltd. for bringing out the book in a beautiful way.

N.V.R. Jyoti Kumar

List of Maps, Figures and Tables

Map

Figures

Tables

1
The Newspaper and Its Marketing

The need for news is universal. News-hunger is fundamental in human nature. It is a characteristic of social man, whether he is conscious of it or not. The basic desires are those for food, shelter, clothing and sex. After these are satisfied, other desires crowd forward—for social life, for recognition among one's fellows, for new experience and adventure. These latter desires are greatly stimulated by information or news about others.[1]

There is a desire for news about how other people live and act, not in extraordinary situations, but in common life. There is also often a desire for self-improvement — a zeal for the acquisition of knowledge about the things that are going on in the world. Such desires for news—coming from people of all levels of intelligence, interests and tastes—is significantly satisfied by the "newspaper".[2] And of all the news media, the newspaper has, of course, the premier position.

Basically, the need for news and newspaper arises out of the need for information or communication. In turn, all sorts of communication needs are concerned about bringing prosperity and happiness to the mankind. This chapter intends to begin with an account of the relationship of the newspaper to communication and development. The conceptual framework relating to the newspaper and its marketing is taken up next, since marketing strategies of Telugu newspapers make the central theme of this study.

COMMUNICATION AND DEVELOPMENT

The legendary Adam and Eve were brought together through communication. Shakespeare's drama and Wordsworth's poetry are exercises in communication, that are known the world over. The Voice of America's live coverage of the first ever landing of the man on the moon in 1969 was also an exercise in communication. The world over rejoiced that feat. Cricket lovers everywhere enjoying the sheer batting brilliance of Sachin Tendulkar, played every now and then, that is brought live by a television network into our living rooms is another example of communication. Recently, everyone of us was thrilled when media the world over broke the news that Amartya Sen of India was awarded the Nobel Prize in Economics for the year 1998. It was also communication.

It is communication that brings all organisations to life. It enlivens all forms of human endeavours. Communication informs and inspires, consoles and comforts, motivates and controls, integrates and disintegrates, builds and unbuilds confidence, changes people's attitude, spreads work ethic and so on. Some estimates show that about three-fourth of an active human being's life is spent in communication. It is of even higher proportions of a typical manager's time. In practice, effective communication is a basic prerequisite for the attainment of organisational goals. Communication is an extremely broad topic and, of course, is not restricted to one or few fields of knowledge.[3]

1. Mass Communication

If communication is directed at the masses, it becomes mass communication. And those who monitor such communications at unspecified audiences are known as media of mass communication. Newspaper is one among such media. The stock-in-trade is information called news, which is packed in the form of a daily newspaper. Here the newspaper firm monitors information, the target masses being the receivers. This information that is passed on to the audiences is mass communication. It is a product for the firms in newspaper business intended for outside customers. This is how media products, media businesses and media firms have come into existence. Besides newspapers or magazines, they specialise in products like books and cinema, radio broadcasting and telecasting, dance and drama, song and music and several other forms of this nature.

2. Development Communication

Communication aimed at accelerating development process is development communication. Interest in communication in general and mass communication in particular are the offsprings of concern for development. Development communication is intended to awaken people, mobilise and educate them to be democratic citizens, safeguard national values, preserve unity in diversity, promote developmental and accepted national goals.[4]

The concept of development communication must rest on the meaning of development which can be described as a widely participatory process of directed social change, in a society, intended to bring about both social and material advancement (including greater equality, freedom, and other valued qualities) for the majority of the people through their gaining greater control over their environment.[5] Development encompasses the complicated patterns of economic, social and political changes that take place in a society as it progresses from a traditional to a modern status. These changes include political awareness, urbanisation, industrialisation, migration, literacy, media consumption and a broad general participation in nation-building programmes. Development, therefore, necessarily involves the active participation of the people for whom it is intended. Both development and participation are two-way processes.

According to Singhal and Rogers, development communication refers to the uses to which communication is put in order to further development. Such applications are intended to either further development in a general way, such as by increasing the level of mass media exposure among a nation's citizens in order to create a favourable climate for development or to support a specific development programme or project.[6]

The goals of development communication are very popular. Singhal and Rogers assert, "Who would argue against utilising communication to decrease the number of infant deaths in a country, to improve the health and nutrition of a nation's population, to produce more food so as to decrease hunger, and to overcome the limitations of illiteracy? Though the methods for achieving these goals are often contentious, the goals of this type of directed social change are widely agreed upon.".[7] Thus, development is a multidimensional concept. Besides the economic well-being of the man, the concept includes social development, cultural refinement, educational upgradation, scientific outlook and technological updating, etc., dimensions, the list of which goes on unending and ever changing with the changing values and patterns of living in the society. Media of mass communication such as newspapers, books, cinema, radio and television have a great role in the dissemination of communication aimed at such all round development of the man and society.

Mass communication is considered a powerful and direct force for development. The influential works of Lerner[8] and Schramm[9] led communication scholars to expect the mass media to be a "magic multiplier" of development in developing nations.[10] Jean Dreze and Amartya Sen emphasised that newspapers were instrumental in building up public pressure on the governments in democratic countries to undertake famine prevention measures.[11] Further, Dreze and Sen visualised a great role for the media in general and newspapers in particular: In acting as one of the potential bases of public action not only against standard economic inequalities, but also against social inequalities based on gender, caste, literacy and other characteristics;[12] in highlighting less immediate and less catastrophic deprivations, but more complex to analyse and less easy to remedy problems, such as lack of school facilities or clean water, nonfunctioning of schools and lack of medical care for endemic diseases;[13] in highlighting social marginalisation and psychological hardships from which the widowed women in India suffer, and also domestic violence from which the women in India are suffering;[14] and in activising public participation in all such activities through skills and traditions of investigative journalism.[15]

The media is primarily concerned with bringing in societal development through their impact on the target masses. The development of mass media and the related media firms runs parallel to the development of other institutions of modern society such as schools and industry, and is closely related to some of the indices of general, social and economic growth such as literacy, per capita income and urbanisation. In other words, when a country has reached a relatively advanced stage of mass media growth, we can be quite sure that its per capita income, its proportion of people in cities, its percentage of literates, its industrial products, its proportion of children in schools are also relatively high. When we find a country where income, urbanisation, literacy, industrialisation, school attendance, and other social factors are relatively high, then we can be quite confident that the number of radio receivers, the circulation of newspapers, the number of television transmitters and the flow of information through the country will also be high.[16]

In view of the aforesaid reasons, media have a great social responsibility on their shoulders as vehicles of development communication. The more service they render in that direction, the more acceptance they gain. Wider acceptance results in greater impact on the masses leading to changes in their attitudes and their development. The more the society thus benefited, the more the media are held in high esteem by the society. Besides conferring benefits on society, media firms also flourish in business bringing in satisfactory returns to the investors and fair compensation to the media employees. The entire process, thus results in utilisation of scarce resources of the society more meaningfully.

THE NEWSPAPER

Newspaper is the oldest and the most widely used medium even today. Few technological innovations can compete in terms of impact win, such social inventions like the newspaper.[17] The first man to envisage the modem newspaper was an American. James Gordon Bennet, who founded the *New York Herald*. Bennett brilliantly exploited the twin technological knowledge bases on which a modern newspaper rests: the telegraph and high-speed printing. They enabled him to produce a paper at a fraction of the traditional cost. He knew that he needed a high-speed typesetting, as different from high-speed printing, though it was not, invented until after his death. He also saw one of the two nonscientific bases of a modem newspaper i.e., mass literacy, which made possible mass circulation for a cheap newspaper. But he failed to grasp the fifth base: mass advertising as the source of income that sustains a newspaper. Bennett personally enjoyed a spectacular success; he was the first, of the press lords. But his newspaper achieved neither leadership nor financial security. These goals were only attained two decades later, around 1890 by three men who understood and exploited advertising: Joseph Pulitzer, first in St. Louis and then in New

York; Adolph Ochs, who took over a moribund *New York Times* and made into America's leading paper; and William Randolph Hearst, who invented the modem newspaper Chain.[18]

The purpose for which the newspapers exist is the dissemination of information. In doing so they discharge the obligation to inform the public of latest happenings as and when they happen. Their role is commendable in educating the public and promoting their causes. They persuade, motivate the people and mould the public opinion to be integrated into one community, one nation and one people. They promote peace and harmony, goodwill and prosperity. They fight against injustice and corruption, discrimination and humiliation. They preserve human values and dignity. They promote work ethic and scientific temper. They target reformation, social and cultural. They are the protectors of freedom of the people and nations. They are guardians of democratic fabric and thus acclaimed as the fourth estate. The newspaper continues to retain its pre-eminent position all over the world even in the face of the onslaughts from television.

The newspaper, a semipublic institution is not a public utility subject to government franchise and other regulations, but in certain respects it functions as a utility. In communities where the newspaper has a large circulation and exerts a strong influence for community betterment, it is as important as a telephone exchange, a light and power company, a water company, or a gas service. It is just as necessary for families to receive light on the happenings and issues of the day as to receive light from the community power plant.[19]

Besides producing news, the newspapers produce advertising. Advertising is a force that has revolutionised industry and trade by stimulating competition, which promotes greater efficiency, more and better products, and lower prices. The newspaper builds regional business. By making shopping easy and profitable for its readers through advertisers, the newspaper provides a pleasant and convenient contact between merchants and customers. The reader shops the newspaper's columns, much as the store's customers shop the counters. The difference is that shopping from the newspaper columns may be done without wandering from shop to shop. The reader simply goes to the telephone and orders what he wants.[20] Business and service institutions spend millions of their rupees each year for newspaper advertising. This is enough evidence that the service is valuable to them to promote such products or services.

In the modern living, it is the newspaper which awakens everybody early in the morning. Everyone gives precedence to the newspaper reading to everything else at least for few minutes when the paper is received. It is not simply read and forgotten. The choicest items in it are shared and discussed with others. To make its supply assured, usually, it is subscribed on a monthly basis, which is continued eventually for years together. Thus newspaper addiction is developed in the process.

1. Product Peculiarities

The newspaper, as a product, has a special characteristic —the same product is sold to two different groups of users, namely, readers and advertisers for completely different purposes. It sells news and views to one group i.e, readers and it sells space to the other group i.e., advertisers.

The newspaper, as a product, has an all round impact— social, political, economic and cultural, on the ultimate user of the product as different from that of other consumer products. For example, the quality of textiles, soaps and toothpastes affects us as consumers, but the quality of newspapers affects us as citizens and influence our views on the surroundings and national and international events to a large extent.[21]

The production of newspapers entails much emphasis on speed. Speed is of critical importance because news, the essential ingredient of a daily, is a very perishable commodity. Not only news must be gathered with speed and accuracy but also processed, printed and distributed to readers within the shortest possible time.

The process of producing the daily is initiated without having an idea of how the final product will look like. The only thing known is the number of pages, sometimes not even that. In producing other consumer products, design costs are generally incurred at relatively longer intervals, but in the case of a daily, one has to budget for the cost of product design everyday. In fact, each edition of a newspaper results in additional design and production costs. Resultantly, the argument of the scale of the economies is inoperative in the production of a newspaper. Besides, as mentioned above, the critical importance of making the product for dual market, the quality, the speed at which it should be made, its perishability, etc., result in less than optimum use of production capacity and manpower.

Most of the products cannot be used without possessing them. But one can read a newspaper without buying it. As such, products of this nature are capable of creating time and place utilities devoid of possession utility. If it is some other product, the marketer is not benefited by such unpaid use. But the newspaper is of a different nature. For example, the non-buyer newspaper readers also matter for the marketers. Such a readership, paid or unpaid, creates an increased awareness of the products thereby increased sales to the advertisers on the one hand, and also provides a basis to attract more advertising revenue, through space selling, to the newspapers on the other.

Newspaper is the only tangible product which is sold at a price much lesser than the cost of production. The newspaper industry is a peculiar one in which one group, namely the advertisers subsidises another group namely the readers. And perhaps very few things one can obtain for the price of a newspaper. Its cover price is low and the unit of purchase is one. In the marketing terminology, such products are classified as convenience goods signifying the type of buyer behaviour in relation to such goods. Though newspaper appears to be as simple as convenience goods, in reality it appears the newspaper is nearer to speciality goods. Brand loyalties in newspaper buying are as strong as those in speciality goods like cars and refrigerators. No one asks for just any newspaper for the price he pays, He insists on buying only that newspaper which he wants. Brand loyalties are irrationally strong in the newspaper market. Newspapers are purchased through an unwritten psychological contract for longer periods than what they appear to be. In India, about ninety per cent of newspaper sales are against one month unwritten contracts since they are supplied customarily on credit for a month. But trade practice proves most of the customers continue like that as subscribers at least for few years. Such loyalties and such psychological contracts are unknown in respect of other products. It is not uncommon to find that the thread of continuity of subscription to a specific newspaper cuts across generations of readers.

List of such peculiarities does not end here. All of them influence the marketing considerations and their implications to the marketers.

2. Emergence of the Marketing Era

The central thrust of marketing is to identify customer wants and needs and to satisfy them. This holds true as much for newspapers as it does for manufacturers of a bath, soap. But one important distinction, in the words of Jim Willis is.

"Bath soap does not have the impact that newspapers as purveyors of news and opinion, have on society. About the only harm a bad bar of soap can cause-assuming there are not skin irritants in it—so to leave the user smelling dirty, but a bad newspaper can cause a great deal of harm. The possibilities run from leaving the readers uninformed, to distorting the truth, to serving as a mouthpiece for a demagogue, to ruining some one's reputation.[22] As such, the important additional requirement of the newspaper, from the marketing point of view, is its conformity with sound journalistic standards.[23] Other than that, the imperative of marketing holds as true for newspapers as for any other business.

In fact, any newspaper is an institution, with two different dimensions, social and business. First, a newspaper is a moving and sometimes explosive social force on an altruistic mission to inform and enlighten its readers. Second, a newspaper is a business venture in search of a healthy profit that will act as an incentive for owners to plough even more money back into it. If greater the incoming resources, the better the newspaper has a chance to be. Diminish either of these dimensions and we will no longer have a strong newspaper, either financially or editorially. The challenge then is how to make the two dimensions coexist in the same company and to put both on the same mission in life. That mission is to produce a high-quality newspaper that will reach the breadth and depth of the geographic and demographic market as signified by the Total Newspaper Concept discussed in the subsequent section.

Before independence the Indian newspaper in general had a missionary role and saw itself as a powerful instrument in social reformation and freedom struggle. As of now, newspaper making in India is a multi-crore business. The print medium, in recent years, has been *making* news rather than just reporting the news.[24] Significantly, India is rapidly approaching the UNESCO norm often newspaper copies (both dailies and non-dailies) for 100 persons for the developing nations. There are now more than eight copies (both dailies and non-dailies) per 100 persons although we have to travel a considerable distance before the figure of 10 copies of dailies can become a reality.[25] As revealed by Table 1.1, the circulation of dailies grew by over 12 times, to 35.45 million copies between 1956 and 1995. This table confirms that the Indian daily has advanced at a fast pace. It also shows that after 1976 the growth has been all the more remarkable.

Table 1.1

Growth in Circulation of Dailies in India: 1956-95

(Copies in millions)

Year	*Circulation*
1956	2.908
1966	6.320
1976	9.461
1986	21.849
1995	35.451

Source: Adapted from S.C.Bhatt. *Indian Press Since 1955* (based on RNI figures). Publication Division, Ministry of Information and Broadcasting, Govt. of India, 1997, New Delhi, p. 1.

Traditionally, the functioning of the Indian newspaper as the fourth estate has been more akin either to a mission or to a profession rather than to a business. With the opening up of the economy, the media has grown enormously in size and reach. Its very success has even attracted the attention of foreign investors and media owners. Now the newspaper is viewed more as an enterprise in itself than as a vehicle to air someone's pet views. Except a few instances, there are hardly any newspapers in India which can be said to be belonging to an industrial house having other interests in manufacture or business. Today the newspaper is rather itself an industry and the management wants to make a complete success of it as a media venture. The old concept of a major industrial group running a newspaper as a side business is gone.[26] The newspapers are themselves big business, sometimes with TV and other media interests that will be discussed in subsequent chapters.

The media mix in India is changing rapidly to the point that many newspapers are finding themselves an endangered species. For years the rules of the media game were known to all the players. But things are a-changing, where some business houses are making mega profits, some are finding it difficult even to survive. The six months, from the last quarter of 1996, have been specially marked by news of media outfits crumbling or establishing new profiles. For example, *The Pioneer* of the Thaper group launched and closed its Mumbai edition. Similarly, the high profile Living Media group, publisher of *India Today,* shut down *TV Today,* just seven months after its launch. In New Delhi, the traditional rivals *The Hindustan Times* and *The Times of India* started trading circulation claims against each other, after a period of relative quiet.[27]

The marketing warfare in the segment of Indian language dailies is no less riveting, and in some cases more mind-blowing. For instance, Jaipur city has been the venue of an exciting attack on the long-established *Rajasthan Patrika by* a big Hindi brand from Madhya Pradesh, *Dainik Bhaskur,* launched in the city in 1997. The challenger studied the target reader in extreme depth, evolved a marketing strategy, and launched the paper with a series of innovative reader-baiting maneuvers. It has outstripped the market leader in a short span. Another prominent success in the recent past has been that of *Bartaman,* a Bengali daily which turn market savvy and mopped up thousands of new readers. Similarly, in South India *Eenadu* successfully expanded the readership base by introducing district-wise supplements and reader-interest innovations in early 1990s.

Competition is one reason which is forcing newspapers to change and to react creatively. Competition for audience from TV is the nearest challenge to the newspapers. Before Doordarshan took off in a big way in the mid-1990s, a person's media exposure consisted almost entirely of the press. TV began to occupy that prime slot and readers had comparatively less time for newspapers. Now, with the coming of cable TV, print has begun to occupy an even smaller percentage in a reader's overall media exposure.[28] At the same time, Indian newspapers, just like their American counterparts, are more affected by changes in lifestyle than from any competing medium. Rapid industrialisation and growing urbanisation left people with less time for everything, including reading. Besides, the MODE Survey[29] shows that the coming of cable TV is changing lifestyles across different segments in India. Executives, housewives, traders and students are devoting less time to sleeping, studying, or finishing their domestic chores in order to make space for cable TV. They are also sleeping later than they used to. Following the coming of cable TV to their homes, their overall media exposure has shot up dramatically.

The liberalisation policies of the government have opened many avenues for the electronic media which has resulted in the commissioning of as many as 40-plus foreign and regional channels in India. This along with Doordarshan and video is a major challenge for press advertising as a good part of advertising which otherwise would have gone to the print media is being diverted to the electronic media. The share of the print media in the total advertising budget of Indian advertisers has not only declined between 1985 and 1993 by nine per cent (75 per cent to 66 per cent), but also the total share of TV has increased from 12 to 21 per cent during the same period. DD's own revenue declined by one per cent in 1993. Radio has lost much of its share and has only two per cent of the share, as against four, eight years ago, while outdoor publicity has gone up from six to 11 per cent.[30] Will the newspapers not be affected by the rising trend of TV watching? At what point will a daily become redundant? Even in advanced countries where the literacy level is very high, almost a hundred per cent, the TV habit has led to the closure of many papers, including the big ones. Advertisements and circulation are closely related and if ad revenue falls this would both be an indication of the decline in circulation, and by reducing the resources at the disposal of the newspaper, cause a fall in circulation too.[31]

A newspaper's business, after all, is to sell news to readers, then sell those readers to advertisers.[32] Surely, an industry which serves two consumer constituencies - readers and advertisers—would naturally be consumer-oriented in the true sense of marketing. But that is not true. Even in a well developed democratic nation like the USA, newspapers traditionally have been production-oriented, burdened with a complex manufacturing process that led to business strategies revolving around the newspaper and its problems, not around consumers and their needs.[33] Contrast that with, for example, an American Pillsbury Company, which acknowledges that it was production-oriented when it was formed, way back in 1869, but which became sales-oriented in the 1930s, took as full marketing-orientation in the 1960s, and quickly evolved into what today is a marketing, not production, company.[34] Only recently, decades behind many other industries, are newspapers switching to the marketing concept, looking upon themselves as products that must be tailored to satisfy consumer needs and which must be sold in a competitive marketplace, just like any other product.

Thus, a journalistically outstanding, even superior product will not automatically bring success in the marketplace. The marketing concept enables the management to create a consumer-oriented newspaper whose business philosophy is one of creating customer-satisfaction. Conrad C.Fink suggested some other core characteristics of the marketing approach:

a. The newspaper management have to create *total company focus* on spotting marketplace demand, analysing how it can be met, planning to meet it, then meeting it. In the past, that was what the sales arm of a newspaper did; today, it is what every department—including news—must do.

b. *Research* to identify and measure customer wants and needs must be continual. Whether it is professional assistance from outside or developing an in-house capability, research must guide every department's daily operations and long-range strategy.

c. *Profit*, not volume, is the goal under the marketing concept. Producing and selling more newspapers each day is not necessarily better. Are they being sold to the right readers, those attractive to advertisers?[35]

Realising that newspapers must serve both readers and advertisers has made the view that limited marketing as the mere distribution and sale of goods is obsolete. The main benefit of the modern marketing concept is that every department is working for—and should be an active participant in—its market. This means working together as a team, with news, advertising and circulation personnel sharing ideas and planning together. This concept promotes coordination among departments and enables the newspaper more effectively to anticipate and respond to change. It preserves the freedom of the news department and improves harmony and communication within the newspaper.

Marketing of a typical product like newspaper has its own hazards and problems. Meeting the growing circulation as a result of increase in literacy, more political awareness and economic prosperity, improving further readership by venturing into untapped and potential areas thereby hitting the stands before competitors do, and by having an efficient distribution network -all these need the attention of competent professional managers and call for a strategy to meet, apart from day-to-day matters, problems of the future.

3. The Total Newspaper Concept

The structure of the Total Newspaper Concept developed by the International Newspaper Marketing Association (INMA), rests upon several beliefs, but mainly the following:

1. To be effective and efficient, a newspaper's various departments must communicate, cooperate and coordinate efforts at becoming a superior newspaper ready to meet the challenges of the changing market.
2. To meet these challenges—a newspaper must be concerned about—and respond to the needs of four external target groups: its readers and non-readers, advertisers and non-advertisers. In fact, many newspaper marketers are even more concerned with the infrequent reader and infrequent advertiser than the people not reading or advertising in the newspaper at all. They feel it may be more feasible to try and convert these infrequent customers to steady customers than to try to interest non-readers and non-advertisers in using the newspaper. The best newspaper marketing departments try to go after all these market areas, however. Failure to meet the needs of any one of these groups will mean the newspaper is failing to reach its potential and fulfil its mission.[36]

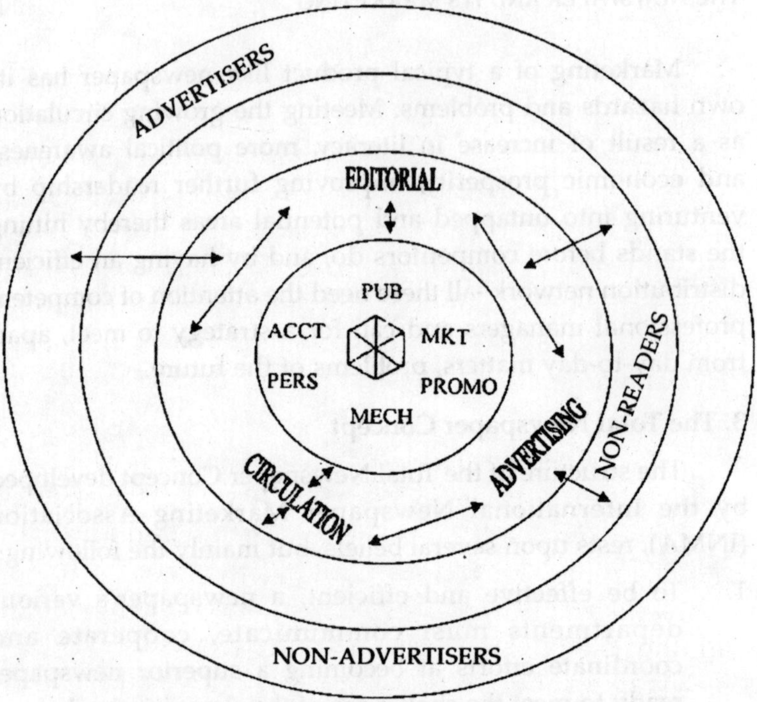

Figure 1.1

The Total Newspaper Concept

The Total Newspaper Concept portrays the fully integrated newspaper interacting with its market of readers, non-readers, advertisers and non-advertisers. In addition to non-readers and non-advertisers, newspaper marketers are becoming more interested in the infrequent reader and the infrequent advertiser.

Source: The International Newspaper Marketing Association. (Taken from: Jim Willis, *Surviving in the Newspaper Business,* Praeger, New York, 1988, p. 11.)

Figure 1.1 shows the importance of the various interfaces between newspaper departments and between the newspaper and the four broad target groups in the market. The departments represented in the case of the figure are the offices of publisher, personnel, promotion, accounting, marketing and the mechanical department. They must constantly interface with the three main newspaper departments: advertising, news-editorial and circulation. These departments, in turn, must coordinate, work with each other and conduct two-way communication with the newspaper's four broad target groups outside the newspaper. It is imperative that the entire newspaper staff realise it is on the same mission: To produce a quality newspaper that will reach the breadth and depth of its geographic and demographic market. With the mission understood, it is easy to see why communication and cooperation are the chief features of the Total Newspaper Concept.

An example of how a newspaper can develop an integrated approach to opportunities in its market was demonstrated by an Illinois daily when it seized its chance in 1981 to capitalise on a high-interest news event which was long awaited by the public. The event was the pending release of the U.S. hostages from Iran in January 1981. The newspaper's management knew the day would come when these men would be released, and they also knew that this would be a wonderful day to spread the news to the far corners of the newspaper's market, to readers and non-readers alike. To take full advantage of this saturation coverage on that day, the advertising department began a campaign to solicit welcome-home ads from businesses that had not advertised with the paper in some time, as well as from the regular advertisers. The circulation department worked out a sampling procedure and had contingency plans for extra carriers in place. The news department worked up special advance side-bars chronicling the history of the hostage incident. The production department was alerted to expect a larger press run that day and had its people in place. Finally the hostages were released, and the entire team, which had met several times in earlier weeks, went into action to implement the plans for saturation coverage. As a result, at least on that one day, this newspaper came very close to reaching its mission and getting out the word to all four target groups.[37]

STRATEGIC MARKETING

The intended study, the design of which is detailed in Chapter-III, is primarily concerned with the analysis of marketing strategies adopted by the Telugu newspapers. In a context as this, this section intends to examine the concepts of strategic planning, strategic marketing and the marketing strategy formulation in general.

One of the major challenges facing today's enterprises is how to build and maintain viable businesses in a fast changing marketplace and business environment. In the West, in the 1950s, the answer was thought to lie in increasing production efficiency. In the 1960s and 1970s, despite the opening up of the Western economies, companies sought growth and profits through vigorous acquisition and diversification programmes. They saw their businesses as constituting an investment portfolio to which they added promising businesses and removed faltering businesses.[38] In the 1980s, however, the agenda shifted to strategic marketing. Market segmentation, market targeting, differentiating and positioning the market offering, etc., dominated the agenda.

The conditions that existed in the developed economies about two decades ago are becoming increasingly relevant in India in 1990s. With the opening up of economy, the survival of any business lies with the successful management of its markets. Thus, a changing environment is a necessary presumption for a strategic marketing context. Discounting certain situational factors, whether it is in the West or in India or elsewhere, environmental change was influenced by:[39]

- A loose regulatory environment leading to free enterprise and resultant fierce competition;

with leadership roles in defining the business mission: analysis of the environmental, competitive, and business situations; developing objectives, goals and strategies; and defining product, market, distribution, and quality plans to implement the business' strategies. This involvement extends to the development of programmes and operating plans that are fully linked with the strategic plan."

Thus, the chief marketing executive's strategic planning responsibility includes: (1) participating in corporate strategy formulation, and (2) developing business unit marketing strategies in accordance with corporate priorities. Since these two areas are closely interrelated, it is important to examine marketing's role and functions in both areas to gain more insight into marketing's responsibilities and contributions.[44] Peter Drucker describes this role:[45]

"Marketing is so basic that it cannot be considered a separate function (i.e., a separate skill or work) within the business, on a par with others such as manufacturing or personnel. Marketing requires separate work, and a distinct group of activities. But it is, first, a central

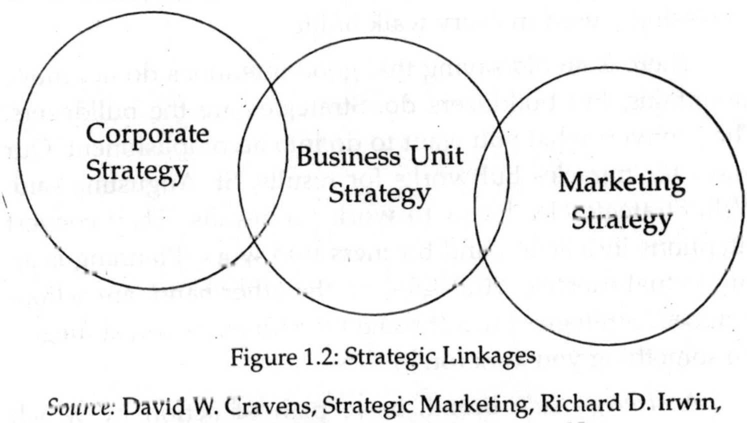

Figure 1.2: Strategic Linkages

Source: David W. Cravens, Strategic Marketing, Richard D. Irwin, Homewood, Illnois, 1987 (2nd ed.) p. 12.

dimension of the entire business. It is the whole business seen from the point of view of its final result, that is, from the customer's point of view."

This perspective of marketing's role in an organisation can be combined with the traditional view of marketing management to define *strategic marketing*—a process of:[46]

Strategic analysis of environmental, market, competitive, and business factors affecting the corporation and its business units and forecasting future trends in business areas of interest to the enterprise.

Participating in setting objective and formulating corporate and business unit strategies. Selecting market target strategies for the product-markets in each business unit, establishing marketing objectives as well as developing, implementing, and managing the positioning strategies of the marketing programme in order to meet market target needs.

2. Marketing Strategy Formulation

The use of the word "strategy" is not limited either to the field of management or marketing. Though it has originated in the field of military science, it has come to be increasingly used in every walk of life.

There is an old saying that good intentions do not move mountains; but bulldozers do. Strategies are the bulldozers. They convert what you want to do into accomplishment. Our prays for miracles but works for results, St. Augustine said. Well, strategies lead you to work for results. They convert intentions into action and business into work. Planning is an intellectual exercise. Strategies, on the other hand, are action-focussed. Strategies are not something you *hope* for; strategies are something you *work* for.[47]

A *strategy* is a broad, basic plan of action by which organisation intends to reach its goal. In military parlance a strategy (from the Greek word Strategia) is a grand plan for winning a battle as a step toward achieving the objective of winning the war.[48]

Let us examine the relationship between goals and strategies, and tactics and strategies, in marketing. Goal (or an objective) is something to be attained. Effective planning must begin with a series of goals that are to be reached by carrying out the plans. A tactic is an operational means by which a strategy is to be implemented or activated. A tactic typically is a more specific, detailed course of action than is a strategy. Also tactics generally cover shorter time periods, are more closely oriented to short term goals - than are strategies. To be effective, the tactics selected must parallel or support the strategy.[49]

Kenchi Ohmae[50] in his *The Mind of the Strategist* defines marketing strategy as "an endeavour by a corporation to differentiate itself positively from its competitors, using its relative corporate strengths to better satisfy customer needs, in a given environmental setting."

According to John O'Shaughnessy[51] "Marketing strategy is a broad conception of how resources are to be deployed to achieve market success. The content of a marketing strategy shows how the proposed key features of the firm's offering (product, price, promotion and distribution) are intended to achieve the firm's objectives." A marketing strategy, as prescribed by O' Shaughnessy, might consist of Statement of objectives; product/market growth options or other investment objective; competitive strategy; core (segmentation) strategy and (brand) support strategies.

Michael Porter uses the evolutionary stages of an industry to suggest suitable strategies.[52] Porter argues that it is industry structure as reflected in the strength of just five forces which are universal that determines the state of competition (both the rules of the game and strategies available) and ultimately the profit potential of the industry. A firm should identify the extent to which it can influence or defend itself against these five forces. Under Porter's concept of extended rivalry, all these forces offer competitive threats to the business. These five forces are: threat of entry; rivalry among existing firms; threat of substitute products or services; bargaining power of buyers; and bargaining power of suppliers.

Porter has condensed many types of strategies that are available into only three generic strategies for coping with the five competitive forces. They are: overall cost leadership; differentiation; and focus (segmentation).[53]

Porter, further, argues that the profit performance of the individual firm depends on: The profit potential of the industry; the profit potential of the strategic group (within the industry) to which the firm belongs; and the firm's advantageous position within its strategic group and competition within the group.

Porter's framework is valuable in drawing attention to the resistances to be overcome in developing an overall competitive stance.

It is useful to mention the results of a survey that attempts to summarise the *practice* of marketing in the 1990s. The Conference Board's comprehensive survey found that more companies have discovered the marketing concept and set their purpose as that of acquiring and satisfying customers rather than producing goods or services. Business plans are more customer and competitive-oriented *and better reasoned and more* realistic than they were in the past. The plans draw more inputs from all the functions and are team-developed. Marketing executives increasingly see themselves as professional managers first and specialists second. Senior management is becoming more involved in making and/or approving marketing decisions. And planning is becoming a continual process throughout the year to respond to rapidly changing market conditions.

However, the survey did find that marketing planning procedures and content vary considerably among companies. The plan is variously called a "business plan," a "marketing plan," and sometimes an "operating plan." Most marketing plans cover one year, but some cover a few years. The plans vary in their length from under 10 pages to over 50 pages. Some companies take their plans very seriously, while others see them as only a rough guide to action. According to marketing executives, the most frequently cited shortcomings of current marketing plans are lack of realism, insufficient competitive analysis, and a short-run focus.[54]

In textbooks devoted to models suggesting strategies, strategies tend to be few. In practice, only the imagination restricts the number of strategies it is possible to consider. Of course, environmental factors impose limits on what is feasible. So the more accurate are management's perceptions of the environment, the more capable they are of selecting suitable alternatives. Practising managers and management consultants are in effect engaging in counterfactual speculations while mentally rehearsing casual hypotheses in relating strategies to possible consequences. In formal mathematical models the relationship between strategy and outcome is set out even if only on a probabilistic basis. In practice, consequences of action are very problematical. With limitless possible alternative and fuzzy endless chain of possible outcomes, it is not surprising that managers are apt to focus on the strategies with which their experience makes them comfortable. Unfortunately, this often means that the cards are stacked against the truly novel and imaginative. Limited resources also affect the search for suitable strategies. Developing a single, adequate solution may be taxing even if that solution does no more than avoid disaster rather than seek major improvements.[55]

Finally, it is to be noted that a clear strategy and a well-thought-out supporting programme may be useless if the firm fails to implement them carefully.[56] Indeed, strategy is only one of seven elements, according to the McKinsey consulting firm, that the best-managed companies exhibit.[57] The first three elements in the McKinsey 7-S framework for business success—strategy, structure, and systems—are considered the "hardware" of success. The next four—style, staff, skills, and shared values—are the "software."

3. A New View of Strategy

Hamel and Prahalad present a radically different way of thinking about strategy and competition in their pathbreaking work *Competing for the Future*. The heart of its message, and, its appeal is hope.[58] They argue persuasively that traditional approaches to strategic planning are unlikely to prepare a firm for industry leadership in the future. They emphasise competition for tomorrow rather than competition for today, thus highlighting opportunity share[59] rather than market share.[60] Their starting premises are simple: "Competition for the future is competition to create and dominate emerging opportunities—to stake out new competitive space. Creating the future is more challenging than playing catch up, in that you have to create your own road map. The goal is not simply to benchmark a competitor's products and processes and imitate its methods, but to develop an independent point of view of tomorrow's opportunities and how to exploit them. Pathbreaking is a lot more rewarding than benchmarking."[61]

Hamel and Prahalad inquired into, in short, what does it take a company to get to the future first. They found, at a broad level, it requires four things: (1) an understanding of how competition for the future is different; (2) a process for finding and gaining insight into tomorrow's opportunities;

(3) an ability to energise the company top-to-bottom for what may be a long and arduous journey towards the future; and (4) the capacity to outrun competitors and get to the future first without taking undue risks.[62]

The New Strategy Paradigm as shown in Table 1. 2 presents Hamel and Prahalad's view of the strategy quite different from what prevails in many companies. They believe

Table 1.2

Hamel and Prahalad's New Strategy Paradigm

Not Only	*But Also*
The Competitive Challenge	
Re-engineering processes	Re-generating strategies
Organisational transformation	Industry transformation
Competing for market share	Competing for opportunity share
Finding the Future	
Strategy as learning	Strategy as forgetting
Strategy as positioning	Strategy as foresight
Strategic plans	Strategic architecture
Mobilising for the future	
Strategy as fit	Strategy as stretch
Strategy as resource allocation	Strategy as resource accumulation and leverage
Getting to the Future First	
Competing within an existing industry structure	Competing to shape future industry structure
Competing for product leadership	Competing for core competence leadership
Competing as a single entity	Competing as a coalition
Maximizing the ratio of new product "hits"	Maximizing the rate of new market learning
Minimizing time-to-market	Minimizing time to global preemption

Source: Gary Hamel and C.K.Prahalad, *Competing for the Future*, Harvard Business School Press, Boston, MA., 1994 (in paperback, 1996), p.26.

that the goal is not to predict *the* future but to imagine *a* future made possible by changes in technology, life style, work style, regulation, global geopolitics and the like. They emphasise there are as many viable futures as there are imaginative firms that can understand deeply the dynamics at work right now which hold opportunities to become the author of the new. For the future is not what *will* happen; the future is what *is* happening. The long term is not something that happens someday; it is what every company is building or forfeiting by its myriad decisions. Future is not a thing to be awaited for, it is a thing to be achieved.[63] There is not one future but hundreds. There can be as many prizes as runners; imagination is the only limiting factor.[64]

References

1. Frank Luther Mott, *The News in Ameirca*, Harvard Univeristy Press, 1952, p. 1.
2. Alvin Silverman, *The American Newspaper*, Robert B. Luce, Washington, DC., 1964, p. 19.
3. Fred Luthans, *Organisational Behaviour*, McGraw-Hill, New York, (7th ed.), 1995, p. 415.
4. P.C. Joshi, "Culture, Communications and Development." *Mainstream*, Republic Day Issue. 1986. pp. 19-21.
5. Everett M. Rogers, "Communication and Development—The Passing of the Dominant Paradigm" in Everett M. Rogers (ed.), *Communication and Development: Critical Perspectives*, Sage Publications, Newbury Park, 1976.
6. Aravind Singhal and Everett M. Rogers, *India's Information Revolution*, Sage Publications, New Delhi, 1989, p. 17.
7. *Ibid.*, pp. 17-18.
8. Daniel Lerner, *The Passing of Traditional Society: Modernising in Middle East*, Free Press, Glencoe, IL., 1958.
9. Wilber Schramm, *Mass Media and National Development*, University Press, Stanford, CA., 1964.
10. Aravind Singhal and Everett M. Rogers, *op. cit.*, p. 20.

11. Jean Dreze and Amartya Sen, *India: Economic Development and Social Opportunity*, Oxford University Press, New Delhi, 1995, p. 75.
12. *Ibid.*, p. 191.
13. *Ibid.*, p. 88.
14. *Ibid.*, pp. 172-173.
15. *Ibid.*, p. 88.
16. P.L.Vishweshwer Rao, *Language Press in India: A Study of Readership, Contents and Language Comprehension with Special Reference to Telugu Daily Newspapers*, Unpublished Ph.D. dissertation, Osmania University, Hyderabad, 1991, p. 5.
17. Peter F. Drucker, *Innovation and Entrepreneurship: Practice and Principles*, First Affiliated East-West Press, New Delhi, 1991, (First published in 1986), p. 31.
18. *Ibid.*, pp. 113-114.
19. Herbert Lee Williams, *Newspaper Organisation and Management*, Surjeet Publications, (The Iowa Slate University Press, 1978), New Delhi (5th ed), 1982, p. 5.
20. *Ibid.*
21. Sunil Kanta Behra, "Newspaper Economics and Management," *Vidura*, April, 1985, p. 90.
22. Jim Willis, *Surviving in the Newspaper Business*, Praeger, New York, 1988, p. 49.
23. *Ibid.*
24. *Business India* editorial, March 24-April 6, 1997, p. 1.
25. S.C. Bhatt, *Indian Press Since 1955*, Publications Division, Ministry of Information and Broadcasting, Govt. of India, New Delhi, 1997, pp. 1-2.
26. *Ibid.*, pp. 138-139.
27. Anupam Goswami, "Message for the Media," *Business India*, March 24-April 6, 1997, pp. 54-55.
28. MODE Survey, "The Clutter of Life," *A&M*, May 1992, p. 58.
29. *A&M* invited MODE Research Private Ltd., to investigate

how the coming of cable TV has affected metropolitan lifestyles and media consumption. The findings of the MODE survey are published in *A&M*, May, 1992.

30. Quoted from: S.C. Bhatt, *op. cit.*, p. 157. These figures on media spend share (percentage) are derived from Doordarshan's 1995 booklet.
31. S.C. Bhatt, *op. cit.*, pp. 158-159.
32. Conrad C. Fink, *Strategic Newspaper Management*, Southern Illinois University Press, Carbondale, 1988, p. 121.
33. *Ibid.*, pp. 121-122.
34. For a fascinating summary of the Pillsbury story, see Eugene J. Kelley (ed.), *Marketing Strategy and Functions*, Englewood Cliffs, N.J., Prentice-Hall, 1965.
35. Conrad C. Fink, *op. cit.*, pp. 122-123.
36. Quoted from: Jim Willis, *op. cit.*, pp. 9-10.
37. *Ibid.*, pp. 10-11.
38. Philip Kotler, *Marketing Management Analysis, Planning, Implementation and Control*, Prentice-Hall of India, New Delhi. (9th ed.), 1997, p. 65.
39. Rakesh Knurana and A.N. Ravichandran, *Strategic Marketing Management: Concepts and Cases—An Indian Context*, Global Business Press, Delhi, 1995, pp. 14-15.
40. Philip Kotler, *op. cit.*, p. 63.
41. *Ibid.*
42. David W. Cravens, *Strategic Marketing*, Richard D. Irwin, Illinois, (2nd ed.), 1987, p. 11.
43. Steve Harrell, in a speech at the plenary session of the American Marketing Association's Educators' Meeting, Chicago, August 5, 1980, (Quoted from: *Ibid.*, p. 12).
44. David W. Cravens, *op. cit.*, pp. 12-13.
45. Peter F. Drucker, *Management: Tasks, Responsibilities, Practices* Harper & Row, New York. 1974, p. 63.
46. David W. Cravens, *op. cit.*, p. 13.
47. Peter F. Drucker, *Managing the Non Profit Organisation*

Principles and Practices, Macmillan India, New Delhi, 1993, p. 59.

48. William J. Stanton and Charles Futrell, *Fundamentals of Marketing*, McGraw-Hill, New York, (8th ed.), 1987, p. 41.
49. *Ibid.*, p. 42.
50. Kenichi Ohmae, *The Mind of the Strategist: The Art of Japanese Business*, Tata McGraw-Hill, New York, 1982.
51. John O' Shaughnessy, *Competitive Marketing: A Strategic Approach*, ELBS, London, 1987, p. 52.
52. See Michael E. Porter, *Competitive Strategy: Techniques for Analyzing Industries and Competitors*, Free Press, New York, 1980.
53. *Ibid.*, Chapter 2.
54. Howard Sutton, *The Marketing Plan in the 1990s*, The Conference Board, New York, 1990.
55. John O' Shaughnessy, *op. cit.*, p. 40.
56. Philip Kotler, *op. cit.*, p. 87.
57. See Thomas J. Peters and Robert H. Waterman. Jr.. *In Search of Excellence: Lessons From America's Best-Run Companies*, Harper & Row, New York, 1982, pp. 9-12.
58. Gary Hamel and C.K. Prahalad, *Competing for the Future*, Harvard Business School Press, Boston, MA., 1994 (in paperback, 1996), p. ix (preface to the paperback edition).
59. Hamel and Prahalad's concept of opportunity share is elaborated in Chapter - IV.
60. Gary Hamel and C.K. Prahalad, *op. cit.*, p. 33.
61. *Ibid.*, p. 24.
62. *Ibid.*, pp. 24-25.
63. *Ibid.*, pp. xi xii (preface to the paperback edition).
64. *Ibid.*, p. 27.

2
The Indian Newspapers
(Trends in their Growth: Overall and Language-wise)

Having outlined the relevance of marketing to newspaper business in the preceding chapter, this chapter highlights the historical relevance of the Indian newspapers. Further, it is intended to analyse trends in their growth, overall and language-wise, in terms of circulation. Such an analysis ultimately enables to ascertain the status of the Telugu newspaper, the subject matter of this study, compared to its counterparts in other languages.

THE HISTORIC RELEVANCE[1]

The origins of the newspapers in India, the troubles and turmoils which they encountered in the hands of the alien rulers; and the social, political and cultural upheavals which they cherished are outlined in this section. The emphasis is on their historic relevance and not on their history or business justification. In a study as this, giving historic account is neither possible nor necessary, since historical research is outside the purview of this study. What is attempted is no more than a rapid looking back into the distant past, rather than immediate past.

Bombay Samachar, a Gujarati daily, published from Mumbai is the oldest existing newspaper in India. It was started in 1822. In all, there are 12 existing centenarian dailies as shown in Table 2.1. This suggests how old is the Indian newspaper. Six of the centenarians are of English. It could be inferred from this that the daily newspaper lives longer in the national markets, compared to newspapers in regional languages whose markets are also regional. It is noteworthy that a quarter of centenarians (three out of 12) represents one regional language i.e., Gujarati.

Table 2.1

Existing Centenarians of the Indian Dailies

Year	*Language*	*Name*	*Place*
1822	Gujarati	*Bombay Samachar*	Mumbai
1832	Gujarati	*Jam-E-Jamshed,*	Mumbai
1838	English	*The Times of India*	Mumbai
1863	Gujarati	*Gujarat Mitra* and *Gujarat Darpan*	Surat
1865	English	*The Pioneer*	Lucknow
1868	English	*Amrita Bazar Patrika*	Calcutta
1875	English	*The Statesman*	Calcutta
1878	English	*The Hindu*	Chennai
1881	Marathi	*Kesari*	Pune
1881	English	*The Tribune*	Chandigarh
1884	Urdu	*Musheer-E-Deccan*	Hyderabad
1887	Malayalam	*Deepika*	Kottayam

Source: Compiled from *Press in India 1996*, Ministry of Information and Broadcasting, Government of India, New Delhi, 1996, pp. 15-16.

The newspaper came to India as one of the benefits of British rule. In the early years it was confined to, and subserved, the interests of the ruling government. While the newspapers in England were gaining in power and influence, the British rulers were from the beginning suspicious of their Indian counterparts and intolerant of criticism.

James Augustus Hicky has the distinction of launching the first newspaper *Bengal Gazette* in January 1780 from Calcutta, as a two-sheet weekly. The paper very soon earned the enmity of Warren Hastings, the governor-general. Within six years of Hicky's venture, five more newspapers appeared in the city of Calcutta, which is known as the birth place of newspapers in India. James Silk Buckingham, came to India in 1818 as the editor of *Calcutta Chronicle.* He was truly the father of Indian journalism just as Alien Octavian Hume, the founder of the Indian National Congress, was the father of Indian nationalism. By deporting him, the British government wanted to warn others but it could not put out the spark he has kindled.

Raja Ram Mohun Roy[2] was also among the earliest champions of press freedom. As a great social reformer he used his pen in the many newspapers he sponsored to achieve a social and cultural renaissance in Hindu society. He founded *Sambad Kaumudi* (the moon of intelligence) in 1821 in Calcutta and Mirut Ul *Akhbar* (mirror of news) in the following year. Lord Bentinck's assumption of the governor-generalship was marked by a significant change in the attitude of the government towards newspapers in India. One of his first acts was to abolish the practice of sati. He was conscious of the fact that more than anyone else Ram Mohun Roy had prepared the ground for the legislation. As Lord Bentinck's liberal attitude towards the press became apparent, a number of newspapers came into existence. In 1830, sixteen Indian language newspapers came into being.

Dadabhai Naoroji,[3] a great nationalist leader, started his own monthly journal *Voice of India* in 1882. In the South, the battle for social reform was taken up by *The Hindu*, through the valiant efforts of its editor, G.Subramania Aiyer. The paper came out as a weekly in 1878 from Chennai. Among the reforms for which the paper campaigned were widow remarriage, raising the age of marriage, abolition of caste and removal of untouchability. *The Hindu's* crusade was so much out of tune with the spirit of the time that it affected its business side and the paper began to lose circulation and advertisements. Subramaniya Aiyer set a personal example in social reforms by solemnising the marriage of his widowed daughter in Mumbai in the presence of leading social reformers of the country.[4]

By the end of the nineteenth century, the Anglo-Indian press had consolidated its position even as its Indian counterpart was struggling hard to stand on its feet. The significant newspapers among them were the *Englishman* and *The Statesman* of Calcutta, *The Times of India* of Mumbai, the *Madras Times* and the *Madras Mail* of Chennai, the *Civil and Military Gazette* of Lahore (now in Pakistan) and *The Pioneer* of Allahabad. The versatile personality connected with the growth of the Anglo-Indian press was Robert Knight[5], founder of *The Statesman* in 1875.

Subrahmaniya Aiyer of *The Hindu* assessed that the Anglo-Indian papers were certainly more powerful, more prosperous and more influential than their Indian counterparts. Newspapers to Englishmen were more or less a trade, a means of livelihood but to Indians they were something more earnest, something more nearly touching the interests of their country.[6] Communication and transport facilities were not fully developed then and newspapers had to be satisfied with publishing old news.

The Indian newspaper owed its vitality, importance and influence to one great factor – its greatest journalists were men with a mission, highly equipped intellectually, powerful writers, able controversialists and men of integrity and courage. Two such journalists in Bengal who revolutionised politics and were the torch-bearers of Indian nationalism were Surendranath Bennerjee and Bipin Chandra Pal. According to them, the Vernacular Press Act of 1878, the most controversial law against the Indian owned language press, was the immediate cause of the awakening of political consciousness and the genesis of the national movement on a countrywide scale. The protests against the Vernacular Press Act during the three years it was in force brought the Indians together in a way they had never been united before. The fight for Indian freedom by the educated masses can really be said to date from the Vernacular Press Act. In Lahore, Bannerjee persuaded Dayal Singh Majithia to start *The Tribune* (which is one of the Indian newspapers to have completed 100 years from Chandigarh).

The first session of the Indian National Congress, formed in 1885 in Mumbai, was closely related to the development of the press because the owners and the editors of some of the leading newspapers were also among the architects of the national political organisation. Of the 72 delegates who attended the first Congress session, a third were journalists. G. Subramania Aiyer of *The Hindu,* Motilal Ghosh of *Amrita Bazar Patrika* and Narendranath Sen of the *Indian Mirror* were among them.

In fact, *The Hindu* was the centre of political activity when the third session of the Indian National Congress was held in Chennai in 1887, when the resources of the press were utilised to the fullest to popularise the session as well as organisation.

Lokmanya Bal Gangadhar Tilak[7], popularly known as the "Lion of Maharashtra" but the British rulers viewed him as "one of the most dangerous pioneers of disaffection", dominated the Indian political scene and newspapers for two decades. Tilak started *Kesari* (means the lion) in Marathi and *Maharatta* (English) in 1881 and they became an immediate success. During the period in which Tilak was in jail, most of the papers propagating his cause had gone out of existence on their editors being sent to jail or heavy securities demanded from them. Kelkar, a staunch follower of Tilak conducted *Kesari* and *Maharatta* with great tact and prudence and steered them clear through troubled waters. To be a subscriber of *Kesari* was then to court great displeasure of the government. Nevertheless, the paper formed the nucleus of all Tilak's future activities.

The revolution in thought and deed came with the arrival of Mahatma Gandhi on the Indian political scene. In the period between 1919 and 1947, the Indian press was permeated with Gandhi's message, and it was like an army marching under the command of the liberator. There was a spurt in language newspapers in all provinces which posed a serious threat to the alien rulers.

Gandhi took over *Young India* in 1919 from Jamnadas Dwarakadas of Mumbai and also started a Gujarati weekly, *Navjivan*. As an editor, Gandhi laid down strict standards for himself which were difficult for others to follow. He would not accept advertisement and he believed that a newspaper or journal had to survive on the revenue from subscriptions. He would not accept any restrictions on the paper and he would rather close it down than submit to the government's invasion of the liberty of the press.[8]

In 1932 while Gandhi was in prison, he started *Harijan*[9] to promote his campaign against untouchability. *Harijan* soon became the Bible of Congressmen and the masses who were led by him. It became the biggest news source for the newspapers and every Saturday news agencies, Indian and foreign, competed with one another in flashing Gandhi's articles to the newsrooms of the press in India and abroad. And every week Gandhi had something important to say and what he wrote became front page stories. He wrote while travelling third class in trains and whenever he could steal time in the midst of his heavy engagements. He was keenly conscious of the deadlines and never missed one.

The Hindustan Times, the first Indian daily in the capital, Delhi was inaugurated by Gandhi and the first issue contained articles by Motilal Nehru, Jawaharlal Nehru and Mohomed Ali. The paper was started in 1923 as an off-shoot of the Akali movement. The paper passed into the hands of G.D. Birla in 1927. It suffered like other nationalist papers during the various Satyagraha movements for supporting the Congress. While the paper has had a great galaxy of prominent editors, its greatest asset was cartoonist Shankar who attained international fame.

The *National Herald* of Lucknow was started by Jawaharlal Nehru in 1938 as an English daily. It had never a moment of peace and its life was full of struggle with the government for its own existence. India became free from the British rule on August 15, 1947 and a jubilant press joined its countrymen in hailing the advent of freedom for which it had fought shoulder to shoulder with the nationalist forces.

Regional newspapers and regional stalwarts looked no different from the national scene, all chasing the service ethic. Newspaper was never a serious business proposition in those days. But the post-independence realities were different. Slowly newspapers started realising that in order to succeed they must first survive.

The Current Scene

Table 2.2 gives a glimpse of the circulation of dailies and non-dailies in India in 1995, in terms of periodicity, their number and circulation. The total number of daily newspapers in India grew to 4,236 by 1995. Their combined circulation was 35.45 million copies per day. The daily newspapers accounted for 44.7 per cent of the total circulation of all the periodicals, whereas the weeklies shared 31.2 per cent. The newspaper scene in India presented a multitude of languages

Table 2.2
Circulation of Dailies and Non-dailies in India, 1995

Periodicity	*Number*	*Circulation (thousands)*	*Per cent*
Dailies	4,236	35,451	44.7
Non-dailies:			
Weeklies	12,695	24,770	31.2
Fortnightlies	5,070	7,246	9.1
Monthlies	10,575	9,598	12.2
Other	7,902	2,218	2.8
Total	40,478	79,283	100.0

Source: Compiled from *Press in India 1996* (RNI data), Ministry of Information and Broadcasting, Govt. of India, New Delhi, 1996, p. 7.

as shown in Table 2.3. The daily newspapers were brought out in 17 principal languages. Thus diversity is the peculiar feature of the Indian newspaper market. It has plenty of marketing implications. Though a foreign language, English being a link language is capable of creating large newspaper markets across the states and throughout the length and breadth of the country. As such the markets for English newspapers are capable of attracting larger advertising revenues. Further, all the English-knowing people in India are literates. Literacy is one of the basis of newspaper sales. Next to English, Hindi language has the advantage of creating large newspaper markets. The Hindi belt of North India covers a stretch of seven states. Four of them are among the large states of India. They are also among the large population segments. For these reasons, the Hindi newspapers enjoy a competitive advantage compared to the newspapers in other Indian languages. Resultantly, a very large proportion of the Indian dailies originated from the Hindi and the English newspaper markets. In contrast, only a handful of dailies originated from several other smaller language segments like

Sanskrit, Manipuri and Assamese. No daily newspaper is published in languages like Kashmiri and Konkani, though they are also among the important languages of India.

Table 2.3

Total Number of Dailies in India, 1996 : Language-wise

Language	*Dailies (RNI 1995)*	*Dailies (ABC)*
English	300	22
Hindi	1,877	25
Assamese	11	3
Bengali	88	6
Gujarati	84	16
Kannada	258	4
Malayalam	199	4
Manipuri	11	—
Marati	256	23
Nepali	2	—
Oriya	56	5
Punjabi	94	3
Sanskrit	3	—
Sindhi	8	—
Tamil	323	3
Telugu	104	4
Urdu	446	4
Bilingual	51	—
Multilingual	14	—
Others	51	—
Total	4,236	122

Source: Compiled from *Press in India 1996*, Ministry of Information and Broadcasting, Govt. of India. New Delhi, 1996, p.19. RNI data relating to 1995 and ABC data relating to July-December 1996.

GROWTH OF THE INDIAN NEWSPAPERS

The growth of any newspaper is often measured by its circulation. Circulation means several things to the newspaper business. It is the basic determinant of profit, though newspapers cannot survive out of the sales revenue of the copies sold. The newspaper mainly sustains on advertisement revenue. But the determinant of advertising revenue is again the newspaper and its acceptance by the customers. The more the circulation, the more the advertisers prefer to buy space in them so that their message can reach more people. The more the circulation the paper enjoys, the more it charges its advertisers. There are agencies to audit and certify the circulation figures of newspapers. Audit Bureau of Circulations is such an example. Besides circulation, one more thing in which the newspaper business is interested is the readership of their newspaper. The more the readership a newspaper enjoys, the more strategically it can position to attract larger advertising revenue. There are agencies to conduct readership surveys. Here again circulation is the basic determinant of readership. However, readership is more an imaginary concept whereas circulation is a hard reality which unfolds most of the things in the newspaper business.

Market shares, market leadership and other top, middle or lower positions of various competitors in the market could easily be ascertained on the basis of circulation figures. To have an inkling of the position of the industry as a whole or a particular newspaper, circulation figures could easily be relied upon if audited.

1. An Overview of Overall Growth

During the last two decades, most of the advanced countries have witnessed a decline in the circulation of daily newspapers. Contrary to that, newspapers in Indian languages have seen a remarkable growth in terms of their number and circulation. The circulation of daily newspapers in all languages have seen a remarkable growth in terms of their number and circulation. The circulation of daily newspapers in all languages trebled between 1976 and 1992—from 9.3 million copies to 28.1 million and the dailies-per-thousand people ratio doubled—from 15 daily newspapers per 1,000 people to 32.[10] Even as early as 1984 such ratio for the USA was 268 copies, which was less than half of Japan's ratio of 562 copies.[11]

No other country in the world has a newspaper industry as complex and highly developed as India's.[12] In 1995, eleven Indian languages (Bengali, Gujarati, Hindu, Kannada, Malayalam, Marathi, Oriya, Punjabi, Tamil, Telugu and Urdu) had a newspaper industry that sold more than a million copies a day.[13] Moreover, the eleven languages, besides English, considered in this section are written in different scripts.[14] In Europe, a literate traveller can decode the headlines from Madrid to Helsinki. In India, a Tamil newspaper may be as unintelligible to a Keralan or a Kannadiga as it is to a Canadian or a Kenyan.[15]

Growth of the Indian newspapers since 1951 in terms of circulation is shown in Table 2.4. Indian newspapers at a glance by the end of 1995 in terms of the number of dailies, non-dailies and their circulations are already discussed. The thrust of this study is dailies. So unless otherwise specified, newspaper means a daily newspaper. It does not include news magazines or any other non-daily periodicals, though the study uses contextually the data and references related to non-dailies in a very limited way. The data used in this chapter originated from the Registrar of Newspapers for India, as different from ABC data.

Table 2.4

Population, Literacy and Circulation of Dailies and Non-dailies in India: 1951-1991

	1951	*1961*	*1971*	*1981*	*1991*	*Growth Index 1991 (Base: 1951)*
			(millions)			
1. Total population	361	439	548	685	846	234
2. Literate population	60	105	161	241	446	743
3. Total daily circulation	2.00[a]	5.25	9.10	15.26	24.29	1,214
4. Total Non-daily circulation	8.00[a]	16.00	20.52	35.84	29.58	370
			(Copies)			
5. Dailies to 1,000 people	6	12	17	22	29	483
6. Dailies to 1,000 literate people	33	50	57	63	55	167
7. Non-dailies to 1.000 people	22	36	37	53	35	159
8 Non-dailies to 1,000 literate people	134	152	127	149	67	-50

Note: [a] The circulation figures represent rough estimates
Source: Census of India for population and literacy (*Statistical Outline of India, 1996-97*, Tata Services, 1996, Mumbai); and Annual reports of the Registrar of Newspapers for India, for circulation figures, Ministry of Information and Broadcasting, Govt. of India, New Delhi.

From a mere two million daily circulation in 1951, the Indian newspaper registered a twelve-fold change, increasing it to 24 .29 million copies in 1991. In terms of such absolute figures, the growth of the Indian newspaper appears to be rosy. As revealed in Table 2.4, and table 2.5 the circulation jump between 1951 and 1961 was really impressive making it 162.5 per cent (from 2 million to 5.25 million copies) increase for the 10-year period. The corresponding increase for the next 10-year period ending in 1971 was only 73.3 per cent, followed by 67.6 per cent by 1981 and 59.1 per cent by 1991. This means, no doubt, circulations were increasing, but at a rapidly decreasing rate. This is only one side of the story.

(i) Circulation Growth By Population

Population in 1991 was 2.34 times to 1951 level at 846 millions. During every 10-year census interval the increase in population was at an increasing rate (ranging from 21.6 to 25 per cent), except during the last 10-year interval ending in 1991 for which the population growth rate was slightly lesser compared to preceding interval. Naturally, such population increases at increased rate and circulation increases at decreased rates did not allow dailies-to-thousand people ratio (DTP) to go beyond 29 copies in 1991 from six in 1951. During the 10-year period ending in 1961 the DTP increased by 100 per cent compared to 41.6 per cent between 1961 and 1971, 29.4 per cent between 1971 and 1981; and 31.8 per cent between 1981 and 1991. On the whole, the DTP ratio was also increasing but at decreasing rate, more or less (Table 2.5).

(ii) Circulation Growth by Literacy

By 1991, more than half of the Indians were literates. Literacy in India steadily increased though sometimes at decreasing rates and other times at increasing rates. In terms of dailies-to-thousand literate people (DTLP), the growth of dailies is more disappointing from 33 copies in 1951 to 55 copies in 1991, which was less than what was it in 1971 (57 copies), implying a negative growth rate (Tables 2.4 and 2.5).

(iii) Non-dailies and the Newspaper Culture

Non-dailies, particularly, weeklies and monthlies in regional languages play a predominant role in initiating and promoting newspaper culture. School-goers when they are still in the lower classes of a high school learn reading habits

Table 2.5

Population, Literacy and Circulation of Dailies and Non-dailies in India: 1951-1991. (Per cent Changes over Previous 10-year Intervals: 1961-1991).

		1961	*1971*	*1981*	*1991*	*Average Annual Growth Rate since 1951 (%)*
1.	Total population	21.6	24.8	25.0	23.5	3.4
2.	Literate population	75.0	53.5	49.7	85.1	16.1
3.	Total daily circulation	162.5	73.3	67.7	59.2	27.9
4.	Total non-daily circulation	100.0	28.3	74.7	-17.5	6.8
5.	Dailies to 1,000 people	100.0	41.7	29.4	31.8	9.6
6.	Dailies to 1,000 literate people	51.5	14.0	10.5	-12.7	1.7
7.	Nondailies to 1,000 people	63.6	23.8	43.2	-34.0	1.5
8.	Nondailies to 1,000 literate people	13.4	-16.5	17.3	-55.0	-1.25

Note: Based on the previous Table 2.4.

scanning through such of those periodicals. They are a matter of irresistible attraction to them and also to the grown up college-goers, men and women at home. In this connection, women are of special importance. Compared to men, their news interest is lesser but their interest in a monthly or weekly in a language of their own is well known, wherever they are, working or nonworking. Such magazines contain less news and more features, particularly some short stories and other features of general interest. Women readers take their own time in completing such a reading rather than rushing through a daily newspaper. As such news magazine is more a she-product and newspaper a he-product. Nevertheless, irrespective of the gender and the age, people thus initiated into reading gradually, graduate themselves into newspaper readers. If one recollects his or her own experience of the younger days of the reading habits, one could easily realise the importance of such periodicals. In this context, such magazines, particularly which are oriented to the needs of the young, the women and everyone in a lighter way act as nurseries of news-interest readers.

Now let us have a look at the circulations of such non-dailies. In 1951, non-daily circulation was four times that of dailies. Even in 1961, it was more than three times, in 1971 and also 1981 more than two times. And in 1991 it was not even one and one-fourth times. (Table 2.4). This relationship between dailies and non-dailies speaks a lot. Non-dailies-to-dailies purchased ratio declined steadily during the 40 years ending in 1991. What does it mean to the marketers? Is it because of the increased circulations of dailies or decrease in the patronage of the non-dailies? Already we have learnt that the circulation of the dailies were discouraging, growing at a rapidly decreasing rate. Perhaps, such a deterioration of the Indian daily had its origin in the ever decreasing patronage of non-daily—a spring board of news habit. It may not be inappropriate to assume that strengthening the Indian non-daily leads to strengthening the Indian daily, in turn. In terms of the DTP, it was 22 copies in 1951 and 35 copies in 1991 which was less than 1961 level of 36 copies. (Table 2.4). Going by the DTLP, in 1991 (67 copies) it was reduced to a half of what it was in 1951 (134 copies). What a misery it is!

To sum up, in terms of average annual growth rates things were alarming both to the Indian daily and non-daily even by 1991. The dailies' DTP grew at an average annual rate of 9.6 per cent and its DTLP is heading for a zero rate growth, placed at 1.7 per cent in 1991 (Table 2.5). The non-dailies' DTP was also like that growing at 1.5 per cent and its DTLP was already in the sub-zero zone at -1.25 per cent. The book lovers the world over are declining which requires no evidence. The book industry has gone already sick. Perhaps, the Indian daily newspaper and the magazine are also poised to move in that direction as in case of book publishing industry. This sort of a fall of the newspaper or magazine cannot be attributed to the increasing invasion of television into Indian homes. By 1991 television invasion was not over. Television started seriously entering into the media scene only just about that time.

The foregoing analysis disproves the inference that increased literacy leads to increased circulation of either dailies or nondailies. Thus literacy and the newspaper culture or magazine culture need not necessarily go together. If it is so book publishing industry should not have gone sick. It is a perplexing paradox. It is both a development paradox and a media paradox in the sense it should concern both the development agencies interested in the country's well being and those involved in media business. Marketers of newspapers should also seriously think of bringing out non-dailies on healthy lines, which in turn may help foster the newspaper culture.

2. Growth by Languages

Language-wise view of the growth of the Indian newspapers is taken up in this section. Here the period of analysis is limited to 20 years (1971-91) instead of 40 years (1951-91) in the preceding section. Robin Jeffrey's series of papers on Indian newspapers evoked a lot of interest on the subject.[16] The tone set in by him and the data used therein provides the nucleus of this and ensuing sections of this chapter, though it is also attempted to draw inferences independently, besides highlighting those of Robin Jeffrey. It appears English newspaper was on top in circulation (2.219 million copies) till 1971 relegating the newspapers in all Indian

Table 2.6

Circulation of Dailies by Language and Population in India: 1971, 1981 and 1991

Language	Population (millions)			Circulation of Dailies (millions)			Dailies-to-1000 people (copies per day)		
	1971	*1981*	*1991*	*1971*	*1981*	*1991*	*1971*	*1981*	*1991*
1. English	(10.9)[a]	(13.6)[a]	(16.9)[a]	2.219	3.355	3.109	204	247	183
2. Malayalam	21.4	25.4	29.0	1.111	1.386	2.061[b]	52	55	71
3. Gujarati	26.7	34.1	41.3	0.683	1.145	1.851	26	34	45
4. Urdu	(28.6)	(35.3)	(43.0)	0.376	0.734	1.440	13	21	33
5. Punjabi	13.6	16.8	20.3	0.073	0.231	0.654	5	12	31
6. Hindi	229.8[C]	290.7[C]	366.8[C]	1.520	3.680	9.310	7	13	25
7. Marathi	50.4 (42)	62.8(52)	78.9	0.910	1.040	2.000	18	22	25
8. Tamil	41.2	48.3	55.9	0.908	0.956	1.20	22	20	22
9. Oriya	22.0	26.4	31.7	0.090	0.178	0.697	4	7	22

10. Kannada	29.3 (22)	37.1 (27)	45.0(33)	0.314	0.556	0.678	14	21	21
11. Bengali	44.3	54.6	68.1	0.597	1.059	0.995[d]	14	19	18
12. Telugu	43.5	53.6	66.5	0.237	0.439	0.664	6	8	10
All-India (incl. others)	548.0	685.0	846.0	9.100	15.260	24.290	17	22	29

Notes: Figures given in the parentheses are of speakers.

a. Estimated at two per cent of total population, b. The RNI's 1991 figure is low due to lower than usual collection of data and therefore the 1992 figure is used. c. Figures relating to the "Hindi states" include: Bihar, Delhi, Haryana, Himachal Pradesh. Madhya Pradesh. Rajasthan and Uttar Pradesh. d. The RNI's 1991 figures seem artificially low. Bengali daily circulations for 1992 had bounced back to 12.42.000, and the same figure is used to calculate the DTP.

Sources: Adapted from Robin Jeffrey's series of essays on Indian Languages-Newspapers published in Economic and Political Weekly between January 4 and March 29, 1997 (The population figures are based on the respective Census of India (*Statistical Outline of India 1996-97*, Tata Services, Mumbai) and the daily circulations are based on the figures of the Registrar of Newspapers for India, Ministry of Information and Broadcasting, Govt. of India, New Delhi.

languages to positions of insignificance as is shown in Table 2.6, arranged in the descending order of DTP ratios, in 1991, language-wise. The Hindi daily was only a distant second with 1.52 million copies. However, by 1981 the Hindi newspaper snatched away the top slot with 3.68 million copies from the English one which was closely behind with 3.355 million copies. From then onwards the English newspaper never recovered and the Hindi newspaper never looked back and raced miles ahead of the English paper. In 1991, the Hindi newspapers' circulation stood at 9.31 million copies representing an unbelievable 152.9 per cent increase during the last 10 years. By then the English newspaper lost its circulation of 1981 marginally.

The Malayalam daily was the unquestioned queen for the third place in circulation since 1971 and even earlier. Other than the English, Hindi and Malayalam, the dailies which crossed one million circulation mark were Gujarati and Marathi (both in 1981 and 1991), Bengali (in 1981), Tamil and Urdu (in 1981). That is how the mountains and deserts of the Indian language newspapers were scattered. The Telugu, Oriya and Kannada daily circulation, for example, looked like deserts far away from a million-mark circulation even in 1991.

Let us have a look at the picture of daily circulation in terms of the dailies-to-1,000 people ratio. No daily in India was as tall as the English daily in terms of DTP ratio (Table 2.6), all through the years. The DTP was 204 copies in 1971, 247 in 1981 reduced to 183 in 1991. Such a reduction by 1991 was attributable to the expanded circulation of dailies in regional languages. For example, the DTP of the Hindi dailies nearly doubled (from 13 copies to 25 copies) between 1981 and 1991. Three-fold increase in the DTP of Oriyan daily (from 7 to 22 copies) is another pointer in this direction. All through the years, the Malayalam daily, placed third in circulation stood second in the DTP ratio, though it is only a fraction of the English daily. Of course, It is inappropriate to compare any daily in Indian languages with the English whose markets are truly national in character, breadth and depth. The Malayalam dailies' DTP stood at 52, 55 and 71 copies in 1971, 1981 and 1991, respectively.

Malayalam was the second smallest of language segments with a population of 29 millions, the smallest being English with 16.9 millions, in 1991. But Kerala, the state of Malayalam speaking people, is the smallest of all linguistic states in India, in terms of geographical area. Thus circulation of 71 copies to —1000 Malayalis made Kerala the daily densest market. In contrast, the English daily, the DTP of which was several times higher compared to the Malayalam daily, represented the thinnest of the daily markets in India as such subscribers are spread over the whole of the length and breadth of India with its characteristics of a sub-continent. Such variations in the market are of far-reaching consequences to the marketer. The newspaper in a wider geographical market may attract more readership per copy and its impact may be truly national in character. This may be one reason for the continued dominance of the English daily in its influence, though not in the number of copies sold. Regional language dailies are in a disadvantaged position in this regard, by their limited geographic reach. Then it occurs why not they start a daily or a magazine to a national market in a truly national language. *The Week* of *Malayala Manorama* and the *Newstime* of *Eenadu* are such examples, the farmer succeeding and the latter languishing. *Malayala Manorama* publishing a yearbook in English is also an attempt to reach the national market successfully. Now that yearbook has become a household name all over India, whatever language they speak.

The opposite is also true. If the publishers in regional languages cannot reach the far-flung markets, the publishers in a national language like English are in disadvantaged position to reach a mass of readers in regional languages. This made some newspaper chains in English to bring out dailies or magazines in regional languages is a step in that direction. For example, the Express group has brought out several dailies in regional languages. *Andhra Prabha,* a Telugu daily, is one among them which was a market leader till late 1970s.

No daily is closely behind the Malayalam daily for a third place in terms of the DTP. It is interesting to note the Gujarati daily occupied that position from far behind all through with 26 copies in 1971, 34 in 1981 and 45 in 1991, respectively. Whatever lower position other dailies might have taken in the DTP rankings in 1991, none of them equalled the Malayalam daily's standing as it was in 1961 with 52 copies.

The DTP ratios of Bengali, Hindi, Kannada, Oriya and Telugu dailies were behind the national average all through the years, at least since 1971. Till 1991, Oriya and Telugu dailies were single digitors in the DTPs. Even in 1991, the Telugu dailies' DTP was only 10 copies compared to 11 copies of Assamese (not shown in the table) and 22 copies of the Oriyan daily.

The foregoing analysis shows the largest language segment need not create the largest circulation. For example, though Hindi is the largest of all language segments, in 1971 its circulation was much behind the circulation of the English daily representing the smallest of all segments. Of course, from 1981 onwards the Hindi daily was in limelight claiming the largest circulation. Malayalam, though the second smallest segment, its daily was firmly saddled for the third place in circulation all through, besides being a topper in the DTP next only to English. It implies newspaper culture is determined not by numbers. May be it is a product of literacy, urbanisation, per capita income, etc., variables.

The dailies in the Indian languages started overpowering the English daily in a small way since 1981. Till then the advertisers considered that the readers of the dailies in regional languages did not have much purchasing power for their goods and services. The surge of the dailies in regional languages in general and the Hindi in particular was a great eyeopener and the keen competition for the advertising pie has come to stay. Till then, the English dailies' predominant position was not seriously challenged. Such an improved standing of the Indian language newspaper in relation to the strongly entrenched English daily is a healthy feature. It is indicative of the spread of a new newspaper culture across the country engulfing all the regional languages by and large. Till then, the advertisers believed the newspaper culture was confined mostly to the English-knowing elite of the populations.

(i) Factors Fostering the Expansion

Such a surge of the regional language daily can be attributed to six factors that have driven the expansion of the Indian newspaper industry in the past two decades. They are:[17]

1. Improved technology which enabled the production and distribution of larger number of more attractive newspapers.
2. Literacy that has expanded steadily.
3. Adequate purchasing power in the hands of a larger proportion of population.
4. Aggressive publishers.
5. Increased political excitement and awareness that has spread to larger sections of population especially in Hindi areas. It has created a desire-to-know which fuels newspaper buying.
6. For a language to flourish, it requires a combination of

government and social support and many Indian languages received such a backing.[18]

Some of them need to be discussed in greater detail.

(a) Technological Innovations

The Indian newspaper industry, particularly the language press, till recently suffered from antiquated printing technology. Moreover, a poor transport network in many regions made the publishers' task of distributing a newspaper into readers' hands early in the morning a difficult one. As the day passes by the newspaper loses its freshness around 9 AM as the readers have to leave for work place. A paper that is delivered late is almost a stale newspaper.

It is to be noted that the transformation of the 1980s has been in printing technology, but not with regard to surface transportation. Even now in most regions, poor roads restrict the transport of dailies. Newspapers, therefore, are not transported more effectively even in the 1990s; but they are produced closer to the readers.

Some of the significant changes that have come about in the print medium in the wake of innovative printing technologies in the recent years include:[19]

Taking advantage of the new technologies and in order to penetrate into the smaller urban areas, multi-centre publishing has become the trend not only with English newspapers but also with language publications, perhaps more extensively in the case of the latter.

Offset printing is fast replacing time-honoured letterpress method. An Indian made offset press like the Orient can turnout 25,000 copies an hour of a 16-page paper. In this regard, the language papers have done even better than some mainline English papers, which were somewhat late in taking to web-offset printing.

Colour in newspaper has finally arrived in a big way and many leading publications offer excellent colour reproduction. Computer graphics are increasingly used.

Important news-bureaus are linked with the control editorial office by means of PC communication using the PSDN. This is many times faster than the teleprinter and helps newspapers improve their deadlines apart from being more efficient.

A handful of newspapers have sought to tackle the twin problem of time and distance by the adoption of page facsimile transmission is now done either through co-axial telephone lines or via satellite. The expansion and improvement of the telecommunications network in our country has also aided the timely transmission of news pictures through the use of easy-to-carry portable photo-facsimile machines.

Two popular methods, however, were identified with regard to the Indian publishers' adoption of technology in their industries.[20] *Malayala Manorama,* India's largest selling daily and *Punjab Kesari,* the largest selling Hindi daily use imported facsimile machines which can transmit a full broadsheet page. News-gathering, editing, type setting, page make-up and paste-up take place in a single centre. Then the full newspaper is sent by facsimile to distant printing centres, equipped with plate-making facilities and offset presses. The printing centre receives from the facsimile machine film which can be made directly into an offset plate for the press. In the case of *Malayala Manorama,* Kottayam in Kerala is used as a central location where from pages by facsimile are being sent to publication centres like Kozhikode, Palakkad, Kochi and Thiruvananthapuram. The same method is employed by *Punjab Kesari* from its principal publication centre Jalandhar to other centres of publication.

Eenadu, the largest circulated Telugu daily, which is published from ten centres found it more effective to adopt a second method, though it has invested in broadsheet-sized facsimile equipment heavily. Under this method, edited and set on a computer at a central location, copy is transmitted to other printing centres by modem, where it is taken of telephone lines in the form of bromides (camera-ready copy) which are ready for paste-up. This requires only personal computers modems and telephones. Regarding page make-up, *Eenadu* gives considerable freedom to its publication centres. Other dailies that follow this option include *Dainik Jagran, Amara Ujala* and *Rashtriya Sahara* (all Hindi) and *Mathrubhumi* (Malayalam).

The technological innovations in printing discussed above enable the publishers to produce slicker newspapers on the large-scale that offer latest news.

(b) Entrepreneurial Support

The expansion of newspapers in terms of circulation depends on the impetus provided by capitalism. Though most publishers proclaim their desire to serve the public, their main goals are power and profit.[21] Those publishers who want to exercise more power and earn more profits need to expand their newspapers further.

The end of emergency in 1977 witnessed hike in newspaper circulations. Few successful vernacular dailies (e.g., *Eenadu* in Telugu and *Aajkal* in Bengali) were started. To hold their ground against, or to steal a march on, competitors, existing newspapers began to improve their printing, distribution and promotion.[22]

By the 1980s, the place of the vernacular press in the scenario of the print medium in India had changed dramatically. Circulations provided the most obvious indicator. For example, in 1961, circulation of Hindi dailies by the most generous estimate was 0.75 million copies; English, 1.3 million copies—in effect, 1.7 English dailies for every one in Hindi. By 1971, little had changed: English daily circulations were 2.2 million copies, Hindi, 1.5 million copies—a ratio of 1.5 English dailies to one in Hindi.[23] But within eight years, Hindi circulations exceeded English (3 million to 2.97 million, according to the RNI), a gap that widened steadily through the 1980s. By 1992, Hindi dailies claimed sales of 11.2 million to 3.9 million for English—a ratio of 2.9 Hindi dailies for each one in English.[24]

Thus, the publishers of the existing newspapers and the new entrepreneurs, in the post-emergency era, began to realise the existence of a thirsty potential readership. Between the first National Readership Survey in 1970 and the second in 1978, people exposed to the print media increased by two-thirds, the largest increase being in provincial towns of fewer than 1,00,000 people. Such towns were largely served by newspapers in Indian languages. In the eighties, the advertisers began to change their perceptions with regard to the language newspapers and realised the market potentiality of the Indian towns with fewer than 1,00,000 people. The language newspapers, therefore, were perceived as an effective media to reach such people.

The Indian languages newspapers began to change their organisation structures and redefine their goals from about this time. The new entrepreneurial publishers like Ramoji Rao successfully brought to their ventures the techniques of capitalist, market-oriented industry with a "product" to sell. Older newspapers convinced that without professional management techniques the newspaper could not flourish and at *Malayala Manorama*, its editor-proprietor K.M.Mathew, called in management consultants in 1979 and reorganised the entire newspaper in 1980. The thrust of such changes has been to bring professional managers into the organisation, with a view to implant a marketing culture. Those dailies who could not do that began to fail. For example, *Andhra Patrika,* the newspaper of the nationalist movement in Andhra Pradesh "could not be brought out on certain days for want of money to buy newsprint."[25] While *Andhra Patrika* closed down in 1991 with less than 20,000 copies of circulation, *Eenadu* reached 3,43,000 copies from six publication centres.

The advent of television in early 1980s added new dimensions to the media scene in India. As a result, competition for advertising rupee became three-folded: the English press Vs. the language press Vs. the television. Very soon the government-sponsored Doordarshan posed a serious challenge to the Indian press. The launch of satellite channels, both foreign and Indian as well, in early 1990s compelled the existing newspapers to improve their printing, distribution and promotion. The language newspapers (for example, *Eenadu* in Telugu, *Malayala Manorama* and *Mathrubhumi* in Malayalam and *Dainik Jagran* and *Aj* in Hindi) have decentralised printing since late 1970s and ensured early supply of newspapers with latest news to draw on a large potential audience. But the proprietors of Bengali newspapers have not followed the road taken by their counterparts in much of the rest of India. In spite of technological possibilities and the apparently increasing wealth and political influence of rural West Bengal, not one major newspaper has even a printing centre outside Calcutta resulting in a lack of penetration of the newspapers into the countryside. All three of the major Bengali dailies sell half of their copies in the city itself, even though Calcutta accounts for only 16 per cent of West Bengal's population and a quarter of the state's literates. Circulation was only useful if it brought influence, and advertisers and Bengali proprietors were not convinced that rural West Bengal would bring either. Poor telephone and road communication and heavy capital costs to establish new production centres added to the discouragement of any attempt to do in West Bengal what was being done in Andhra Pradesh, Kerala or elsewhere.

Aggressive publishers, how rich they may be in commercial acumen and entrepreneurial zeal, alone may not be sufficient to sustain daily newspaper readership. The willingness on the part of the literate people to buy or read a daily depend heavily on local conditions, or level of their politicisation.

(c) Enhanced Political Awareness

The political excitement, as discussed earlier, was created in the post-emergency period which resulted in an unprecedented growth of newspapers, particularly magazines both in terms of number and their circulations. The circulation of the *Illustrated Weekly* touched unsealed heights of 4,20,000 copies in 1978, from a mere 65,000 in 1969. Another major breakthrough in the world of magazine publishing came with the launch *of India Today* in 1974. Many political magazines in major Indian languages followed the footsteps of *India Today.* Prime Minister Indira Gandhi, and Janata Party were incidentally identified as the "causes" of the magazine boom in the country.[26]

In case of Andhra Pradesh, the rise of a regional party, Telugu Desam in early 1980s incited the Telugu people to turn to newspapers. The figures of the Registrar of Newspapers support the suggestion that election excitement over the Telugu Desam Party enhanced circulations. Telugu daily circulation rose from 4,39,000 copies in 1981 to 6,30,000 by 1983, an increase of 44 per cent in two years.[27] With regard to the Hindi speaking North India, three events linked Hindi newspapers with intense political excitement and violence from the late 1980s—the anti-reservation agitation, the Bharatiya Janata Party's leader Advani's rath yatra and the controversy of Ayodhya. In the second half of 1992, which includes the month of December when the mosque at Ayodhya (said to be built on the site of Hindu temple) was destroyed by rioters, audited circulation of *Aj* rose by 41,000 copies; *Amar Ujala* by 25,000; and *Dainik Jagran* by 18,000.

The movements aimed at developing Tamil identity took various forms such as anti-Hindu, anti-brahmin or anti-Hindi. Moreover, Tamil Nadu experienced a kind of competitive politics rare elsewhere. In 1967, the regional party DMK came to power and the Congress party never won a state election thereafter. In the process, Tamil magazines (mostly weekly ones) emerged as the most effective means of a satisfying people's urge for more information relating to films and politics. Elucidating the economics behind the popularity of the weekly magazines in Tamil Nadu, Jeffrey pointed out that the weekly magazine was cheaper than a daily newspaper; it had a life of at least seven days so distribution was less urgent; and its format of fiction, and a little fact, matched the story-lines of films and was simple and less expensive to produce than the news of a daily newspapers.[28]

If one considers the above requirements for growing newspaper circulation against the experience of Kannada dailies, Kannada speakers stand reasonably high in terms of literacy, urbanisation and purchasing power. In 1991, literacy in Karnataka at 56 per cent was higher than the all-India average; and urbanisation, at 30.9 per cent was considerably more than the national average (Table 2.7 infra). But in terms of politics and capitalism, the Karnataka region seems to lag. The intense political competition of Kerala in the 1950s and 1960s, or of Andhra Pradesh and the Hindi heartland of North India in the 1980s, was almost absent. Further, the newspaper publishers were hesitant to expand their business in spite of the arrival of the new technology in the early 1980s. Here lies a key cluster of reasons why the Kannada press appears to be passive. Financial return is one reason for an owner to seek to expand his newspaper; but newspapers have strange effects on their owners: Some seek expansion to extend what they see as their influence or to spread a message. Such passion— notable in the case of Telugu and Malayalam and in the history of Tamil dailies in the 1940s and 1950s—was largely absent, it appears in Kannada.

Such of these developments indicate how fast the profile of the Indian-language daily has been changing. It appears that Indian language newspapers will continue to expand, and advertising revenue and political excitement will continue to shape them. In these circumstances, there seems little doubt the capitalism and consumerism will continue to grow in India. Indian-language newspapers will play a key part in spreading consumerist messages beyond large towns. In so doing, one can expect one—at most two—major newspapers to become dominant in each language region. The diversity and competition that currently characterises most of the language regions seems likely to be obliterated in the next 10 years.[29]

Yet the multiplicity of languages offers some guarantee against a national domination of print media by one or two chains. Neither *The Times of India* nor the *Indian Express* groups has been notably successful in attempts to run newspapers in Indian languages. Regional newspaper groups like *Ananda Bazar Patrika* and *Malayala Manorama* started national weekly publications , in English—*Sunday* and *The Week*, respectively —but neither threatens established English publications. Similarly *Eenadu's* English daily *Newstime* has difficulty holding its own in Hyderabad, much less becoming a national force.

The sheer number of highly developed languages in India ensures against the sort of national chain dominance that afflicts the press in countries like the USA, Canada and

Australia. Similarly the dominance of a "national" press—the Paris press in France or the London press in Britain, for example—is an impossibility. This is not to say that diversity of views and enterprising news coverage will be a consequence. It is conceivable that individual newspapers, overdominant in a language region will stifle competition and indeed promote local chauvinism or even a secessionism. But extreme stances from stabilised newspapers are unlikely.[30]

(ii) Relating Circulation to Literacy, Per Capita Income and Urbanisation

Literacy is considered as one of the bases on which the newspaper grew. Increased per capita incomes and urbanisation are expected to promote daily circulations. The English daily commanding the highest dailies-to-people ratio indicates this. The English-knowing people in India are supposed to be not merely literate and their levels of literacy are also supposed to be high. It may not be illogical to assume that 100 per cent of the English-knowing people in India are literate. Their per capita incomes also might be much higher, though such data is unavailable, compared to the people in other language segments. Similarly such people are supposed to live mostly in urban India. Perhaps, all these things helped the English daily to rise to such a coveted position in terms of dailies-to-people ratio. Next to English, Malayalam is the most literate segment (nearly 90 per cent) in 1991 as is shown in Table 2.7. The English daily is not shown in this table for want of data on per capita income and urbanisation of English-knowing people. For similar reasons Urdu daily is also excluded. This table is also arranged according to the size of DTPs in the descending order, language-wise. Malayalam dailies' position is second only to that of English in DTP as we have already learnt. This leads of the inference that more the literacy rate the larger the newspaper circulations. Let this be verified with reference to other languages(Table 2.7).

Table 2.7

Literacy, Per Capita Income, Urbanisation and Dailies-to-People by Language in India, 1991.

Language	*Literacy (per cent)*	*Per capita income (Rs.)*	*Urbanisation (per cent)*	*Dailies to- 1000 people*
1. Malayalam	89.8	6,242	26.4	71
2. Gujarati	61.3	7,600	34.5	45
3. Punjabi	58.5	12,319	29.5	31
4. Marathi	64.9	10,964	38.7	25
5. Hindi	35.0	7,242	21.0	25
6. Tamil	62.7	7,352	34.2	22
7. Oriya	49.1	4,726	1.3.4	22
8. Kannada	56.0	7,029	30.9	21
9. Bengali	57.7	6,055	27.5	18
10. Telugu	44.1	6,651	26.9	10
All-India (including others)	52.2	7,060	25.7	29

Notes: 1. States where these languages are spoken are: Kerala (Malayalam); Gujarat (Gujarathi); Punjab (Punjabi); Maharashtra (Marathi); Bihar. Delhi, Haryana, Himachal Pradesh, Rajasthan and Uttar Pradesh (Hindi); Tamil Nadu (Tamil); Orissa (Oriya) Karnataka (Kannada); West Bengal (Bengali) and Andhra Pradesh (Telugu).

2. Literacy, urbanisation and per capita income relate to the corresponding linguistic states.

3. The per capita income (provisional) figures relate to 1993-94 of the corresponding states.

Source: The literacy and urbanisation figures are based on the Census of 1991 (*Statistical Outline of India, 1996-97*, Tata Services, Mumbai). DTPs are calculated based on RNI figures (*Press in India 1992*, Ministry' of Information and Broadcasting, Govt. of India, New Delhi).

Next to Malayalam segment, literacy was high in Marathi segment (64.9 per cent). Their per capita incomes were the second highest in the country next only to Punjabi segment. But the daily circulation was only 25 copies to 1000 people in 1991 which was below the national average of 29. In Gujarati and Tamil segments the literacy rates were 60 per cent plus and their per capita incomes were also identical with Rs. 7,000 plus. They were far above the national averages in literacy and marginally higher in per capita incomes. But the Tamil daily circulations to-1000 people were only 22, much lesser than the national average of 29, though the Gujarati daily was next to Malayalam daily with 45 copies. So what holds good in Gujarati segment does not hold good in Tamil segment. In the Hindi belt literacy rate (35 per cent) was the lowest of all segments, though the per capita income was marginally higher to the national average. Still the belt was not the lowest *in* terms of the DTP measure (25 copies). The Telugu segment with much higher literacy rate (44.1 per cent) compared to Hindi was at the bottom of the DTP ratios with only 10 copies.

In essence, there is no relation between literacy and daily circulations and also between per capita incomes and daily circulations. This holds good even between urbanisation and daily circulations. The Marathi segment which was on top in urbanisation (38.7 per cent) traiied in the daily circulation (25 copies) behind the national average. Urbanisation was nearer to the national average in the Malayalam but its circulations were outstanding.

It means that the newspaper culture is neither a consequence of the size of the population, as we have learnt earlier, nor a consequence of the literacy rates, per capita incomes and the degree of urbanisation as is learnt here. This leads to the basic question what creates a newspaper culture resulting in increased daily circulations. Kerala, the linguistic state of Malayalam-speaking people, appeared to be a model to Robin Jeffrey in finding out answers to such of those questions[31] which is taken up last in this chapter.

GROWTH OF THE TELUGU NEWSPAPER

It is interesting to compare the growth of the Telugu daily with the other Indian languages newspapers. The growth of the Telugu daily through the years 1961-91 is depicted in Table 2.8. The story of Telugu daily is a story of the bottoms compared to other Indian language dailies. The two tables referred to earlier i.e., Tables 2.6 and 2.7 show the Telugu daily at the bottom in terms of dailies-to 1000 people. Only in 1991 its DTP reached the double digit, of course, only to remain with the minimum at 10 copies.

Table 2.8

Population Change in Andhra Pradesh and Newspaper Change in Telugu: 1961-96.

	1961	*1971*	*1981*	*1991*
Population (millions)	36.0	43.5	53.6	66.5
Literates (millions)	7.6	10.9	16.1	24.9
Literacy (per cent)	21	25	30	44.1
Urbanisation (per cent)	17.5	19.4	23.3	26.9
Telugu daily circulations (thousands)	158 (1962)	237	439	664
Telugu dailies to 1,000 people in Andhra Pradesh	4	6	8	10

Note: Telugu daily circulations are those of the Registrar for Newspapers of India (RNI), no doubt on the optimistic side (from a proprietor's point of view) but indicative. Circulation figures relating to 1961 are not available; 1962 was the year of the China-India War.Circulations probably rose.

Source: Robin Jeffrey, "Indian Languages Newspapers. 4 - Telugu. Ingredients of Growth and Failure", *Economic and Political Weekly*, February 1, 1997, pp. 192-195.

The state of Andhra Pradesh does not compare that much unfavourably with other states in terms of literacy, per capita income and urbanisation as it appears from the DTP figures. It appears this language segment is condemned to remain at the bottom only all through the years even compared to its Oriyan counterpart (Table 2.6) in 1991. Though the figures relating to Assamese are not shown in the table, they were better than Telugu people with 11 copies to-1000 people in 1988. Increased literacy rates, urbanisation and per capita incomes appeared to be indifferent in creating that much expansion in daily circulations.

1. The Telugu and Hindi Newspapers

An attempt is also made to compare the Telugu daily with the Hindi daily. The status of the Hindi language is not comparable to any other language, being the largest of all language segments. The Hindi belt comprises seven states namely, Uttar Pradesh, Bihar, Madhya Pradesh, Rajasthan, Haryana, Himachal Pradesh, and Delhi. Of them, the first four are large states both in terms of area and population and the last mentioned three states are smaller ones. The three of the four major states namely, Bihar, Rajasthan and Uttar Pradesh had a literacy rate less than that of Andhra Pradesh (44.1 per cent), in 1991 as is shown in Table 2.9. Madhya Pradesh, another major state has a literacy rate (44.2 per cent) more or less equal to that of Andhra Pradesh. In the rest of the smaller Hindi states namely, Haryana, Himachal Pradesh and Delhi the literacy rate was much higher compared to Andhra Pradesh. This means the Hindi belt mostly comprised the populations with literacy rates less than Andhra Pradesh. However, the differences in newspaper circulations between Telugu (the language of Andhra Pradesh) dailies and Hindi dailies are striking. All Hindi states put together had a circulation of 25 copies per 1000 people against 10 copies of Telugu.

Table 2.9

Population, Literacy and Circulation of Dailies, 1991: Hindi and Telugu

Language and States	*Population (millions)*	*Literates (per cent)*	*Circulation of dailies (millions)*	*Dailies to-1000 people*
Hindi	366.8	35.0	9.310	25
Bihar		38.5		
Rajasthan		38.6		
Uttar Pradesh		41.6		
Madhya Pradesh		44.2		
Haryana		55.8		
Himachal Pradesh		63.9		
Delhi		75.3		
Telugu	66.5	41.1	0.664	10

Source: The population and literacy figures are based on the Census of 1991 (Statistical Outline of India. 1996-97, Tata Services. 1996, Mumbai). The daily circulations are based on Press in India 1992, the Registrar of Newspapers for India, Ministry of Information and Broadcasting. Govt. of India, New Delhi.

The comparison of two vast states of Uttar Pradesh and Andhra Pradesh with regard to their total circulation of dailies in all languages against each state's population also exhibits a significant gap between the two. While Uttar Pradesh has a ratio of 28 dailies per 1000 people, Andhra Pradesh has only 16 dailies per 1,000 people in all languages (not shown in the table.)[32]

Such variations between the Hindi belt and Telugu region on the one hand, and between Uttar Pradesh and Andhra Pradesh on the other, suggest that a larger proportion of literate people does not necessarily mean proportionately a higher newspaper sales. Let us try to find out why such variations exist. Even by 1981 the circulations of Hindi dailies were not significant. Their DTP was only 13 at that time (Table 2.6). By 1991 the DTP was almost doubled reaching 25 copies. This could be attributed to much of the political excitement the Hindi belt experienced during the years as discussed earlier. Andhra Pradesh also experienced the phase of political excitement in early 1980s which also triggered off increased newspaper sales. But what happened in the Hindi belt and in the Telugu belt so far as political excitement is concerned appear to be different in intensity and impact. What happened in Andhra Pradesh centred round one regional party i.e., the TDP and its one leader, in 1980s. But what happened in the Hindi belt centred round several issues, several leaders and several parties, depending on the point of time. It appears the excitement and awareness in Andhra Pradesh was shortlived and limited in its impact. On the other hand, the issues in the Hindi belt are alive even through 1990s. The issues assumed increased significance in view of the beginning of the era of coalition governments at the centre, in recent times. This is indicative of good things in store for the circulation of Hindi dailies in the years ahead. In contrast, the prospects of the Telugu daily, which was far behind the Hindi daily even by 1991, appear to be dim in view of reduced political excitement attributable to the reduced importance of the regional party there as a consequence of the death of its supremo, recently. In other words, the present variation in the DTPs of Hindi and Telugu dailies may further widen.

2. The Telugu and Other South Indian Dailies

Let it be examined how the Telugu daily compares with the Malayalam, Tamil and Kannada dailies, all South Indian. A comparison of populations, literacy, circulation and DTPs between Telugu and other three South Indian languages are shown in Table 2.10 relating to 1991, arranged in the descending order of the DTP. Population-wise, Malayalam is the smallest segment followed by Tamil, Kannada and Telugu in that order. All other variables literacy, circulation and the DTPs (not the DTLPs) moved in a direction exactly opposite to the population size. In other words, smaller the population size, larger the literacy, circulation and the DTP. Thus ranking by the DTP, the Malayalam daily was found at the top, the Telugu daily at the bottom, Tamil and Kannada in the middle. But the inter-language variations were vary sharp as were the variations in the literacy and circulations. The Malayalam (71 copies) and the Telugu (10 copies) dailies represent two extreme positions, indicative of two extreme newspaper cultures. Tamil and Kannada appear to represent two identical cultures with 22 and 21 copies each, respectively. On the whole, the inference that higher the literacy rate, the higher the DTP size holds good in respect of all southern languages. It means literacy continues to be a base of circulation. But the question is, how much strong it is?

To find out an answer to this question, let the circulations in terms of copies-to-1000 literate people (DTLP) be examined instead of copies-to-1000 people (DTP). The DTLP figures are shown in the last column of the tables. More or less the same are variances in results, the Malayalam daily on top with 79 copies-to-1000 literate people, the Telugu daily at the bottom with 27 copies, the Tamil and Kannada dailies in the middle with 34 and 37 copies, respectively. This is not to deny the fact that the gap in the inter-language differences was significantly reduced. For example, the difference in terms of the DTP between the Malayalam and Kannada daily stood at 61, 49 and 50 copies respectively. The corresponding difference in their DTLPs stood at 52, 45 and 38 copies respectively. Though differences in terms of the DTLPs no doubt were reduced, yawning differences still existed between one literate segment and another literate segment, by language.

The foregoing analysis leads to the inference that though literacy continues to be a base of newspaper circulation, literate

Table 2.10

Population, Literacy and Circulation of Dailies, 1991: Telugu and Other Southern Languages.

Language	*Population (millions)*	*Literates per cent*	*Literates Population (millions)*	*Circulation of Dailies (millions)*	*Dailies to to 1000 people*	*Dailies to 1000 literate people*
Malayalam (Kerala)	29.0	89.8	26.04	2.061	71	79
Tamil (Tamil Nadu)	55.9	62.7	35.04	1.200	22	34
Kannada (Karnataka)	33.0[a]	56.0	18.48	0.678	21	37
Telugu (Andhra Pradesh)	66.5	44.1	29.32	0.664	10	27

Note: Names of the states where the language is spoken is given in the parentheses. a. Speakers.

Sources: The Population and literacy figures are based on the Census of 1991 (*Statistical Outline of India. 1996-97,* Tata Services. Mumbai). The daily circulations are based on RNI data (*Press in India 1992,* Ministry of Information and Broadcasting, Govt. of India. New Delhi).

language segments are of varying strengths in nurturing newspaper culture. This point can be understood more clearly by striking a comparison between Kerala and Andhra Pradesh. In absolute numbers, Andhra Pradesh had over 3 million more literates than Kerala in 1991 (Table 2.10). However, in terms of the DTLP Malayalam dailies sold nearly thrice as many each day as Telugu daily. Then why should a same proportion of literate population buy daily newspapers disproportionately? Purchasing power and disposable income may provide part of an answer. Robin Jeffrey also probed into this.

(i) Purchasing Power

Purchasing power seems to play a minor role in determining whether a person spends money on a newspaper. Let us have a look at the per capita incomes in 1991 (Table 2.7), language-wise. The per capita yearly income of both Kerala and Andhra Pradesh were nearly equal (Rs. 6,242 and Rs.6,651, respectively) and both of them were below national average. It is estimated that a newspaper costs 12 per cent of yearly per capita income in such states, though it may be only 6 per cent in respect of Punjab, where the per capita income was highest. But the circulations of Kerala (Malayalam) and Andhra Pradesh (Telugu) were poles apart as we have already observed. The same is the case in the states where per capita incomes are much higher compared to Kerala. Maharashtra, one such state with higher per capita income had a circulation of only 45 copies, miles behind Kerala, for example (Table 2.7). Orissa with much less per capita income compared to Andhra Pradesh had a better circulation (22 copies). Of course, Karnataka and Tamil Nadu were identical in per capita incomes and circulations (Karnada 21 and Tamil Nadu 22 copies).

So it appears that the purchasing power and the willingness to spend it on newspapers are not related to each other.

(ii) Urbanisation

Then comes the question of the degree of urbanisation influencing newspaper sales. Compared to Tamil Nadu and Andhra Pradesh, Kerala was less urbanised (26.4 per cent), only marginally higher than the national average (25.7 per cent) as could be seen from the earlier Table 2.7. The rest is the same old story.

To sum up, though literacy is a base of a newspaper sale, literate segments in different languages produced disproportionate sale of newspapers. Though Andhra Pradesh was having as much literate population as of the size of Kerala, it was not reflected in newspaper circulation. Either the per capita income of Andhra Pradesh or its urbanisation which were comparable to Kerala could not produce respectable newspaper sales.

So newspaper sales is not simply literacy plus incomes plus urbanisation. It does not imply newspaper sales could be generated without literacy or incomes or urbanisation. Then what it is? Precisely, trying to find out an answer to this question is understanding the dynamics of circulation in newspaper economics.

The inferences relating to the Telugu daily comparing with the Indian daily on an average, with the Hindi daily, with the other South Indian dailies, in general, and the Malayalam daily, in particular, evoke a lot of interest and strengthen the questions earlier raised relating to newspaper culture influencing the daily circulations. The Telugu daily appears to be neck deep in its fight for a decent survival. Why its going is so hopeless? Besides the death of centenary-approaching *Andhra Patrika* in 1991, the recent years also witnessed the death of *Udayam*, an eleven year old juvenile in the market. It appears things do not stop there. A two-year old infant player *Vaartha* is struggling hard to come out of teething troubles. Meanwhile, *Andhra Bhoomi* is making just a living depending on its chain paper *Deccan Chronicle*, a leader in Hyderabad city. If papers exit like that it does not help the cause of the Telugu daily. Depending on a daily existing in a monopoly or semi-monopoly situation would be an unwelcome feature for the readers and advertisers as well.

In a situation as this, the Telugu daily may be able to draw some useful lessons from the Malayalam newspaper culture-Kerala example, what it is called.

3. The Relevance of Kerala Example

From the beginning of the twentieth century, Kerala[33] was well known for its passion for newspapers.[34] The first reports of the Registrar of Newspapers for India in the 1950s showed Malayalam dailies selling 4,30,000 copies a day, only 84,000 fewer than Hindi, the national language. And *Mathrubhumi* was Kerala's leading daily with an estimated circulation of 19,000 at independence in 1947, which rose quickly to 26,000 by 1952. *Mathrubhumi* came to be known as a Congress newspaper, closely associated with Malabar district and with Nayars, the upper caste group that had largely made up both the gentry and intelligentsia of Kerala.

Commercial competition became visible after the formation of Kerala state in 1956. The other long-established Malayalam daily, *Malayala Manorama* was started in 1888 as a venture of a prospering Syrian Christian family. By 1960, *Malayala Manorama* became the largest selling Malayalam daily with 91,000 copies to *Mathrubhumi's* 78,000. In 1962, *Mathrubhumi* started its second edition in Cochin and recaptured their circulation lead for the next five years. *Malayala Manorama* countered by setting up an edition at Kozhikode itself in 1966, and by 1971 had established a lead in circulation that it has never surrendered. The 1960s ware a decade of striking circulation rises. From 1960 to 1971, both dailies more than trebled: *Malayala Manorama* from 91,000 copies to 3,09,000; *Mathrubhumi* from 78,000 to 2,50,000.[35] In Kerala, the political rivalry between the Congress party and the communists in the post-independence era created news-hungry readers.[36]

Malayalam newspapers have long led India on most statistical measures. By the late 1970s, Kerala seemed a unique state in India. Its growing rate of literacy and falling birth rate caused the label "Kerala Model" to describe its enigmatical economic and social development. Its heavy migration of work force to the Gulf brought foreign exchange that made advertisers of consumer goods eager to reach the Keralans.

Kerala has been the most literate region of India through out the twentieth century.[37] But a flourishing language newspaper industry requires not just literacy. Regions with literacy figures at least as high as Kerala's do not necessarily generate a daily newspaper culture. For example, Thailand in 1967 had a population nearly twice as much as Kerala's, rate of literacy of 70 per cent, yet daily newspaper production was only 3,50,000.[38] Kerala at that time sold above 7,50,000 copies a day.

Today virtually every adult in Kerala is able to read and write. Mass literacy campaigns in the early 1990s were held to have eliminated the last pockets of illiteracy. Indeed, the general editor of *Mangalam* daily claimed that many aged people came to the literacy classes because they wanted to be able to read *Mangalam* for themselves.

During 1971-81, the DTP varied only between 52 and 55 copies. However, this was far higher than the all-India; average of 17 copies in 1971 and 22 copies in 1981. But the big boost was by 1991, when the DTP increased to 71 copies against the national average of 29.

However, the readership has not grown since the 1980s as expected by the managements of Malayalam publications. Although *Malayala Manorama* is the largest circulated language daily in India, the National Readership Survey of 1995 (NRS - 1995) found that no Malayalam daily is placed in the top ten dailies in India in terms of readership. This results from the fact that a number of Malayalam dailies compete so fiercely that no single daily dominates. Similarly, Kerala households appear to want to buy their own newspaper, and the number of individual readers of each copy may be declining in Kerala, even though circulations continue to rise. At *Mangalam*, for example, the editors maintained that some families bought three copies because each member wanted a personal copy to take to work or school.

Transport infrastructure is as important as literacy for the creation of a newspaper culture in a given region. Much of the impact of a daily depends on its reaching readers immediately after its publication. Effective distribution, therefore, is essential, and Kerala has the highest ratio of roads to area of all the states in India, i.e., 268 kms. to 100 sq.kms. area.

Technological innovations which increase the ability to produce large volumes of attractive newspapers fast also influence the growth of a daily-newspaper culture. In this regard, Kerala fascinated European Christians, and by the middle of the nineteenth century, Malayalam type, developed by missionaries, was fairly widely available. Other Indian vernaculars took much longer time to develop effective type style. Further innovations such as computer technology and offset printing allowed the Indian newspaper managements to bring out livelier-looking newspapers. This is especially true in Kerala, which is often described as a vast "urban village" continuous semi-urban, semi-rural settlement running from north to south.

Newspaper must have pages through which the readers come to know more about the stories and practices of their neighbours. Such a newspaper habit creates and reinforces a sense of shared geography and related customs. The Kerala example, therefore, suggests that it is necessary to localise a newspaper in order to expand its circulation.

The Kerala example also suggests that wealth and urbanisation are not essential for the creation of a daily newspaper culture. The per capita income of Kerala as shown in Table 2.7 is nearly 12 per cent lower than an all-India average for per capita income. The 71: 1000 people-to-dailies ratio of Kerala in 1991 may represent as high a consumption of newspapers as India can expect without major increases in wealth. And with regard to urbanisation, by 1981 Kerala was one of the least urbanised - 18.7 per cent against a national average of 23.3 per cent. Even ten years later, the per cent of urbanisation in Kerala was far behind of many states of India, namely, Maharashtra, Gujarat, Tamil Nadu and Karnataka (Table 2.7). But in Kerala, the demand for newspapers has created its own solutions: a wide network of public libraries, reading rooms and schools, all of which subscribe to newspapers. Teashop owners keep at least one daily available for customers. Even agricultural labourers congregate around a community newspaper in their leisure time.

Then it is interesting to find out what makes people eager to read newspapers in the first place. The Malayalam experience illustrates that politicisation is the key factor. An appetite for political news, in Kerala, had arisen by 1920s. A dewan of Travancore, seeking to pass an act to control the press in 1925, lamented that the people were "prone to politics", that "every schoolmaster in our three thousand and odd schools is the centre of a political group" and that consequently the demand for newspapers is great. In the 1940s, the Communist daily, *Deshabhimani,* was reckoned by British authorities to have a circulation of about 8,000 copies and "a most insidious and heartening effect" on communist sympathisers in Kerala. By 1960s, Keralans were so addicted to their 32 dailies that on some days when major political stories broke newspapers were sometimes available only in the black market. Journalists at *Malayala Manorama* date the paper's success in establishing a large following in northern Kerala from 1968 and its brilliant coverage of Naxalite attacks on police stations in the area. In 1966, *Malayala Manorama* had an audited circulation of 1,64,000; by the first half of 1971 it had reached 3,10,000. By the late 1970s, technology was becoming available to allow newspapers to reach even the remote areas in time. Kerala in 1990 had 120 dailies registered with its government public relations department, more dailies than any comparable region of India. The processes of capitalist expansion and technical change worked out more noticeably and dramatically and have not been monopolised by the leading dailies of *Malayala Manorama* and *Mathrubhumi*. The Malayalam newspapers indicate that to maximise readership, it is necessary to localise a newspaper in terms of its geographical coverage and broaden its social coverage. As rightly pointed out by Jeffrey, it would be foolhardy to argue that Malayalam newspapers, because they have long led India on most statistical measures, provide models of the future for other parts of the country. However, the Malayalam experience does underline the impact of capitalist practices and world-class technology, yet the necessity of adapting such forces to local conditions skillfully and continuously.

Lessons to the Telugu Daily

Kerala newspaper culture is deep rooted in its high social development profile measured by high literacy from the early times; small families; intense political awareness and rivalry since independence; intense passion for newspapers even among agricultural labourers; people's willingness to spend money on newspapers irrespective of their incomes and social standing; good network of roads that facilitate transport of papers to the subscribers wherever they live; and the people's habit of reading at commonplaces.

Above all these, there appears to be very healthy competition among the publishers in tailoring the newspapers to suit the needs of their buyers. Kerala newspaper scene is not a one leader and laggards affair. Though the largest circulated Indian language daily *Malayala Manorama,* comes from the smallest linguistic state, it is fiercely contested by several competitors, thus denying a large market share to the leader. Instances of one family buying three copies and instances of buying a newspaper in a black market speak volumes of newspaper culture prevailing in Kerala and how the publishers are reaping a rich harvest of it by accepting the challenges encountered in marketing the newspaper in a big way, realising that it is a concept whose time has arrived in the newspaper business.

The implications of this model are to be analysed carefully and they are worthy of emulation by all other language dailies including Telugu. Bringing newspaper culture of the type of Kerala is a precondition for the success of a newspaper business, whatever the language segment it serves. Culture of any sort cannot just be transplanted into new lands overnight. More so of newspaper culture. Genuine concern for the people's interests and aspirations on the part of the publishers alone may not be able to create newspaper culture. Genuineness of the readers in committing themselves to the purchase of such newspapers is of utmost importance that nourishes the newspaper culture. Affordability is one thing and willingness to spend on newspapers is another thing. It is a matter of people's attitude that germinates newspaper culture. It begins at everybody's home. If the elders read them, children try to emulate them, in return their children's children do it and the chain goes on unending. So also the buying habit.

Nowadays it is pathetic to find elders reading newspapers here and there either at public places or by borrowing and they provide nothing for their children to read, not a book of comics even. It is not of those parents who do not have affordability. It is of those who spend tons of money on their children otherwise.

Malayalis, even with modest means of living, wherever they live in India and whatever they do are known to subscribe for their dailies. Even if the people working in small hotel establishments far away from Kerala are also found to subscribe to their dailies obtaining them through post even. In contrast, Telugu people are notorious for their reading habits without buying. If a traveller in a train is found with a newspaper which he has purchased, in turn, most of the co-passengers are found to be borrowing it and thus ultimately preventing the buyer from reading it. When the destination arrives the buyer passenger finds it a hard time to collect several pages of the newspaper from several passengers that are spread over the whole of the compartment.

Telugu dailies have a responsibility in shaping the attitudes of readers in this direction, if they have serious intentions of creating a newspaper culture of Kerala type. Malayalam dailies problem is one of reduced readership per copy because of the increased number of buyers, whereas Telugu dailies' problem is one of increased readership, but reduced buyers or not so increasing buyers.

The present day Telugu people are less willing to spend on newspapers and magazines, or, the Telugu publishers are unable to bring out quality newspapers. Either of these two things may be true or both. A look at today's Telugu homes reveals they have enough of money to spend on ultra modern two-wheelers (even four-wheelers are also not uncommon), not to speak of the usual two-wheelers. School going boys and girls are found to be spending several times more on clothing than their predecessors. They are found to be living in better houses with modern comforts. More and more of them are found to be living in towns rather than villages. Telephone has started invading the village-homes, not to speak of the town-homes. Few middle class homes are there without refrigerators, TV sets and several other electrical and electronic gadgets that are used in the kitchen. But strangely most of them are found to be spending lesser and lesser on newspapers, magazines and books. This is a commonplace observation, which everybody can witness easily. How can it be assumed that people habituated to spend some money on things like cinema do not have money to be spent on newspapers? How can it be believed the Telugu people who are spending more and more on petrol, electricity and telephone calls do not have money for much cheaper newspaper? This is a serious matter to those interested in marketing the newspapers, the advertisers therein and the communication and development specialists. It is a question relating to the attitudes of the people rather than their affordability. Or, it is a question relating to the media people who are failing to make a product that suits the requirements of the people who are not lagging behind in affordability. Or both of them may be true, to a great extent. The concept of the newspaper culture is inclusive of all such dimensions.

References

1. See S. Natarajan, *A History of the Press in India,* Asia Publishing House, Bombay, 1962; Rangsawami Parthasarathy, *Journalism in India: From the Earliest Times to the Present Day,* Sterling Publishers, New Delhi, 1989; and G.N.S. Raghavan, *The Press in India: A New History,* Gyan Publishing House, New Delhi, 1994.
2. Raja Ram Mohun Roy (1774-1833): Great Social reformer of India; worked for the abolition of *sati;* child marriage

and purdah; founder of Brahma Samaj; and a great scholar of Arabic, Persian and Sanskrit.

3. Dadabhai Naoroji (1825-1917): A great public figure of India during 1845-1917, freedom fighter and educationist; the first Indian to become a member of the British Parliament (1862); President of the Indian National Congress thrice; known as the grand old man of India; and also acclaimed as the father of Indian politics and economics.
4. Rangaswami Parthasarathy, *op. cit.*, p. 56.
5. Knight served for some time as editor of the *Bombay Times.* In 1861, he was responsible in bringing about a merger of the *Bombay Times* and two other Mumbai papers, the *Standard* and the *Telegraph* and renamed it *The Times of India.* Later he started the *Bombay Statesman*, the *Indian Economist* and the *Agricultural Gazette of India.*
6. Rangaswami Parthasarathy, *op. cit.*, p. 75.
7. Bal Gangadhar Tilak (Lokamanya), (1856-1920): Indian Patriot and Statesmen. "Swaraj (means freedom) is my birthright", the revolutionary said. The British called him the father of Indian unrest.
8. Rangaswami Parthasarathy, *op. cit.*, p. 141.
9. *Harijan'* is the name proposed by Gandhi for those who were subjected to untouchability. It means children of the God.
10. Data based on RNI figures.
11. Jim Willis, *op. cit.*, p. 95.
12. Robin Jeffrey, "Indian-Language Newspapers and Why They Grow," *Economic and Political Weekly,* September 18, 1993, p. 2004.
13. *Press in India* 1996, Ministry of Information and Broadcasting, Govt. of India, New Delhi, p. 154.
14. Hindi and Marathi are written in similar script, just as are Telugu and Kannada.
15. Robin Jeffrey, "Indian-Language Newspapers and Why They Grow," *loc. cit.*

16. Robin Jeffrey's series of papers on Indian-languages newspapers published in *Economic and Political Weekly* between January 4 and March 29, 1997. His earlier papers include: "Culture of Daily Newspapers in India—How it is Grown, What it Means," *Economic and Political Weekly,* April 4, 1987; and "Indian Language Newspapers and Why They Grow," referred to earlier.
17. Robin Jeffrey, "Indian-Language Newspapers and why they Grow," *op. cit.,* p. 2004.
18. Robin Jeffrey, "Indian Language Newspapers: 10, Kannada: We fake it There is Competition," *Economic and Political Weekly,* March 22, 1997, pp. 566-570.
19. N. Murali, "Emerging Trends in Media," Keynote address at the seminar in Bangalore on 26 November, 1988.
20. Robin Jeffrey, "Indian-Language Newspapers and Why They Grow," *op. cit.,* pp. 2004-2005.
21. *Ibid.,* p. 2006.
22. *Ibid.,* p. 2007.
23. *Press in India 1972,* Govt. of India, New Delhi, p.47 (Quoted from: Robin Jeffrey, "Indian Languages Newspapers: 2, Hindi, 'Taking to the Punjab Kesari Line'," *Economic and Political Weekly,* January 18, 1977, p. 78).
24. *Press in India 1993,* Ministry of Information and Broadcasting, Govt. of India, New Delhi, p. 37.
25. *Sunday Mail,* August 11, 1991 (Quoted from: Robin Jeffrey, "Indian Language Newspapers: 4, Telugu: Ingredients of Growth and Failure", *Economic and Political Weekly,* February 1, 1997, p. 193.).
26. P.L. Vishweshwer Rao, *op. cit.,* p. 101.
27. Based on RNI data.
28. Robin Jeffrey, "Indian Language Newspapers: 5 Tamil: 'Dominated by Cinema and Politics'," *Economic and Political Weekly,* February 8, 1997, p. 255.
29. Robin Jeffrey, "Indian-Language Newspapers and Why They Grow," *op. cit.,* p. 2009.

30. *Ibid.*, p. 2010.

31. Robin Jeffrey, "Culture of Daily Newspapers in India — How it is Grown, What it Means," *op. cit.*, pp. 607-611.

32. The population in 1991 in the states of Uttar Pradesh and Andhra Pradesh were 138.7 million and 66.3 million, respectively. In 1991, the total circulation of dailies in all languages in Uttar Pradesh was 38.58 million whereas in Andhra Pradesh it was 10.41 million. (Based on Census data and RN1 figures).

33 The demand to bring all the Malayali speaking people under one umbrella was met in two stages, first, with the unification of Travancore and Cochin in 1949 and then with the formation of Kerala state, under the far-reaching reorganisation of Indian states, in 1956.

34. Robin Jeffrey, *Politics, Women and Well-being: Now Kerala Became 'a Model,'* Macmillan, London, 1992, p. 3.

35. Figures are based on ABC reports.

36. The first ever democratically elected Communist government in the world came to power in Kerala in 1957, EMS Nambudripad being the Chief Minister.

37. Robin Jeffrey, "Culture and Governments: How Women Made Kerala Literate (And Why It Happened When It Did)," *Pacific Affairs*, 1987.

38. K.E. Eapan, "Daily Newspapers in India: Their Status and Problems," *Journalism Quarterly*, XLIV, 1967, p. 528.

- -

3
The Present Study

The scenario of comparative growth of the Indian newspapers is outlined in the previous chapter. In such a backdrop, presenting the problem taken up for study is the goal of this chapter. The coverage, the study design and methodology adopted therefore are followed by a section on the players in the market scene.

THE ENQUIRY

The Indian newspaper industry scenario analysed by languages in the last chapter focussed on the bottom position of the Telugu newspaper both in terms of the absolute circulations and dailies-to-thousand people ratio. Such a dismal performance of the Telugu newspaper may imply that the performance of all the players was like that. Alternatively, it may imply that the Telugu people have less inclination to read papers, irrespective of the players' above-average performance in delivering customer satisfaction. Paper-wise analysis alone could answer such questions, satisfactorily. If one or two star performers could be found in such a grossly underperforming market, it could give us certain clues. Probing in that direction may lead to finding solutions to the problems from which the Telugu newspaper industry is suffering.

A cursory look at the circulation data pertaining to the Telugu dailies in Tables 4.2 and 4.3 of the ensuing chapter[1] confirms the existence of one star performer in the Telugu newspaper market. This star performer was not of yester years in a one-seller or a two-seller market. The paper belongs to the contemporary competitive market of several sellers. Further, this player *Eenadu* was not only the extraordinary performer in the Telugu newspaper market but also compared well with many of the market leaders in Indian newspaper markets in other languages.[2] The market leadership of the paper was not for shorter durations of few years, but stretched over an unbroken period of two decades (from 1978 onwards).

During the late 1970s, the Telugu daily has slipped out of the grip of the pioneer *Andhra Patrika* on the one hand and *Andhra Prabha* that belongs to the chain giant *Indian Express* group on the other. The sudden appearance of a new star *Eenadu* made all the difference. *Eenadu*, started in 1974 by a small enterpriser, has emerged as the market leader soon by 1978. Much interesting things followed in later years. *Udayam* which entered the market towards the fag-end of 1984 occupied the market challenger's position soon in 1985 pushing aside *Andhra Prabha*. By 1987, *Andhra Jyoti* emerged as the challenger relegating *Udayam* to the third position.

Early 1990s witnessed the death of two Telugu papers, both the oldest and the youngest. *Andhra Patrika* ceased publication in its 83rd year of existence, in 1991. The ten year young player *Udayam* ended in 1995. Such shocks did not deter the entry of new paper *Vaartha* soon in January 1996 from as many as nine centres—two centres more than the market leader *Eenadu* at that time. And right on entry, *Vaartha* emerged No. 2 player, of course, placed very far behind the leader. In 1998 both *Eenadu* and *Vaartha* are published from 10 centres each, though the former outsells the latter, more than four copies to one and thereby taking a two-thirds of the market share. Only a stupendous marketing effort could have resulted in such an unbelievable superlative market standing of *Eenadu*, even in the face of fierce onslaughts from the new competition.

In essence, the Telugu daily nowadays is found to be in the buyer's market, instead of the seller's market which existed till early 1970s. In the process, the Telugu paper has undergone many changes, in terms of tangible and intangible attributes, over these years. The comparison of a current issue of a daily with an issue published a few years ago would show marked improvements. These include prompt delivery, investigative reportage, better typography, improved layout, "better getup, greater readability, clearer photographic reproduction, use of colour, innovative and increased number of features, better coverage of local news through innovation of district-wise supplements, more pages and more intelligent advertising display. Behind of such improvements lie the adoption of strategic marketing. This sort of situation presents a fit case for an enquiry into the marketing strategies adopted by the Telugu dailies.

Apart from the studies relating to journalistic aspects and readership surveys, the newspaper studies so far focussed much on their historical, political and legal aspects. Several committees and commissions have enquired into mainly the problems of Indian press since independence and its role in a developing country.[3] The studies on sociological[4] and economic aspects[5] are scanty. The studies relating to newspaper business management are still fewer either in English or language newspapers in India.[6]

Nonetheless, the systematic, pathfinding and pioneering studies into the Indian newspapers initiated by Robin Jeffrey deserve a special mention here. The series of essays he has published on the press in the major Indian languages are part of a larger project to map, analyse and try to understand the transformation of Indian-language newspaper industry.

The studies particularly focussed on the changes of the past 20 years that were left out largely unstudied hitherto.[7]

But none of these studies thoroughly examined marketing aspects of newspapers. Precisely, the study of marketing strategies of Telugu newspapers is an attempt to fill this gap.

1. The Problem

The study clearly intends to find out an answer to the question of how to account for the difference in the superlative performance of a particular player on the one hand, and the insignificant performance of all other players on the other, in the Telugu newspaper market. Assuming such successes or failures are attributable to the marketing strategies adopted by the players in the field, this study attempts to identify and analyse them.

Venturing into studying and analysing marketing strategies of newspapers is no easy task. Marketing a newspaper is not comparable to the marketing of a product like toothpaste or a ball pen or a toilet soap. Being a media product, newspaper marketing dwells on the knowledge of various disciplines like journalism, mass communication, communication business management, besides marketing and media economics. Though probing into a problem such as this cannot altogether ignore an inter-disciplinary approach, the focus of the proposed study is mostly confined to the marketing strategies.

2. Objectives of the Study

This study intends, *inter alia:*

1. To bring forth the marketing performance of Telugu dailies in terms of their circulation and market share.
2. To identify the competitive strategies to which the success or failure of the individual papers could be attributed;

3. To enquire into the consumer behaviour of Telugu newspapers; and
4. To examine the emerging space selling strategies in the Telugu newspaper market.

3. The Coverage and Research Design

Telugu newspapers of only local character confining their circulation to few towns or districts are altogether left outside the scope of this study. Such local papers were found to be no serious, not regular and with no significant circulations. Further, papers that are run as organs of political parties, for example, *Visalandhra* of the Communist Party of India and *Prajasakthi* of the Communist Party of India (Marxists) are also left out. Papers whose circulation were limited only to a particular region of the state are also excluded. For example, *Golconda Patrika* which existed till 1966[8] is omitted from this study, since its circulation was mostly confined to Telangana region of the state. It is needless to mention that non-dailies fall outside the purview of this study.

Yet, the study covers all the other Telugu dailies that had statewide circulation at any point of time, irrespective of the fact whether such papers are in existence or not today. Thus, all the seven major Telugu dailies namely, *Andhra Patrika, Andhra Prabha, Andhra Jyoti, Andhra Bhoomi, Eenadu, Udayam* and *Vaartha* which had state-wide circulation are taken up for study.[9] The marketing strategies that were adopted by these major Telugu newspapers during the last two and half decades constitute the main thrust of the study. The traces of marketing arriving to the Telugu newspaper business were not very clear till the appearance of *Eenadu* in 1974. That is why the study particularly focusses on the period since then. Nevertheless, an analysis of the early years is not left out altogether. The detailed examination is to be preceded by a historical and summary account of the early players.

Data Sources

The starting point of a study of this nature is identification of the competitive marketing strategies in the Telugu newspaper business in recent times. Observation is relied upon heavily in doing so.

(i) Observation as a Tool of Strategy Identification

Observation is defined as the process of recognising and noting people, objects and occurrences rather than asking for information.[10] Observation is considered to be a handy tool in marketing research. The strategies a newspaper adopts in relation to its places of publication, contents, distribution, pricing, promotion, space selling, etc., are identifiable from the very product, by observation. A new player's entry in 1974 (*Eenadu*) in a small way, and how it made big news, the paper's changed news-mix, the paper going places, its pre-launch tactics, Sunday supplement in magazine form, district supplements in a tabloid form, positioning of its cartoon, agenda-setting strategies, interest-zoning, ceaseless commitment to deliver the paper at the crack-of-the dawn, novel space selling strategies etc., and the competitors' reaction are all taken from firsthand observation over the years. Similar were also the reflections of the entry of other new players *Udayam* (1984) and *Vaartha* (1996) entering the market and the exit of *Andhra Patrika* (1991) and *Udayam* (1995). Such lists from the memory lane were cross checked either with published articles in reputed journals or magazines or from the concerned paper offices.

(ii) Secondary Data

To find out the impact of such of those strategies identified on circulation etc., the study relied upon the data collected from secondary sources. Annual reports of the Registrar of Newspapers for India (RNI)[11] and the *Half-yearly Reports* of the Audit Bureau of Circulations (ABC)[12] constitute the major sources of secondary data. ABC data is used to analyse the circulations of Telugu papers, paper-wise. Nevertheless, RNI data is used, in the preceding chapter, to analyse the comparative growth of Indian newspapers.

Other sources of secondary data include the reports of National Readership Surveys (NRS)[13] and Indian Readership Surveys (IRS)[14] *Advertiser Handbooks,*[15] *Statistical Outline of India,*[16] *Economic and Political Weekly, A & M* magazine, etc.

Further, data relating to the concerned papers is collected by visiting their offices and by interacting with their people at various levels.

(iii) Reader Survey

Besides observation, the study used reader survey as a tool of collecting primary data. Identifying newspaper consumer bases, consumption characteristics, consumers' evaluation of their own paper and the comparative evaluation of all the papers they read were the goals of this reader survey.

Reader Survey Design

Reader survey was conducted during the months of January-February 1995. *Andhra Patrika* ceasing publication in 1991 and *Vaartha* coming to the scene in 1996, at the time of survey there were only five players in the marketplace, namely, *Andhra Prabha, Andhra Jyoti, Andhra Bhoomi, Eenadu* and *Udayam*. As such, it was intended originally to cover the intense readers of those five papers under reader survey. The intention of the coverage of intense readers weighed high for the reason the survey was aimed at evaluation of the papers, among other things. Comparative evaluation being another goal, multiple newspaper readers were sought after as far as possible. Among the class of intense newspaper readers who are searched for, the readers of *Andhra Bhoomi* could not be easily found as the paper's circulation was getting thinner and thinner even by the time of survey. As such, readers of that paper could not be brought under this survey, thus limiting the readers survey only to four papers.

Nevertheless, limiting the reader survey to four dailies should not be construed as limiting this dissertation only to the marketing strategies of those players. As is already stated, the study design covers all the players, irrespective of the fact whether such papers are in existence or not today. As such, the reader survey is only a part of the study design and not the whole of it. To make it more clear, the strategies of all the marketers are examined, irrespective of subjecting those papers to reader evaluation.

The sample consisted of a total of 480 readers, four of the select dailies representing 120 of them each. Such a sample of readers was drawn equally from four clusters of places. Each cluster comprised one publication centre, one town and two villages, as shown in Table 3.1. The publication centres identified for the purpose of formation of four clusters were: Hyderabad, Vijayawada, Visakhapatnam and Tirupathi. Thus, the cluster-wise sample consisted of 30 readers of each daily, the break-up being 10 from the publication centre, another 10 from the concerned town and the balance from the two villages (five each) included in such cluster. Thus by rural-urban background the break-up was 80 urban readers and 40 rural readers, paper-wise.

In selection of sample places, not more than one place is chosen from each district. It is needless to add 16 places thus chosen are spread over 16 out of 23 districts of Andhra Pradesh. Only such of those towns and villages where all the four selected dailies were available were chosen. Readership experience of five years in case of single paper readers and three years in case of multipaper readers was the criteria for drawing the purposive sample of readers. Such readers are hereafter called intense newspaper readers or consumers, throughout this study.

Table 3.1
Distribution of the Sample Readers by Places

Sample town or village	*Andhra Prabha*	*Andhra Jyoti*	*Eenadu*	*Udayam*	*Total*
Cluster - I					
Hyderabad	10	10	10	10	40
Warangal	10	10	10	10	40
Sarapaka (R)	5	5	5	5	20
Bibinagar (R)	5	5	5	5	20
Cluster-II					
Vijayawada	10	10	10	10	40
Bhimavaram	10	10	10	10	40
Karamchedu (R)	5	5	5	5	20
Duggirala (R)	5	5	5	5	20
Cluster-III					
Visakhapatnam	10	10	10	10	40
Kakinada	10	10	10	10	40
Garividi (R)	5	5	5	5	20
Korlakota (R)	5	5	5	5	20
Cluster-IV					
Tirupati	10	10	10	10	40
Anantapur	10	10	10	10	40
Kovuru (R)	5	5	5	5	20
Dronachalam (R)	5	5	5	5	20
Total	120	120	120	120	480

R = rural

The questionnaire consisted of two parts, first part pertaining to the paper the respondents read as their main paper and the second part pertaining to the comparative evaluation of all the select papers. This made the questionnaire lengthy (see Appendix)[17] thus demanding extra attention and time of the readers. It is proved to be an uphill task to contact 480 readers living in 16 places spread over 16 districts of the state—involving travels of vast distances. Extracting responses to such an elaborate schedule took at least one and half hours of the reader's time. They were mostly contacted at their homes or places of work at their convenience. Although innumerable intense readers were available in urban areas, many a time they could not find plenty of time to spare for this purpose. In rural areas, on the contrary, the reader's time was not that scarce. But in certain villages, the number of intense readers available was small particularly in the case of newspapers having low market shares. However, in many instances group leaders in villages helped the researcher to find out intense readers and their natural interest in newspapers enabled the researcher to surmount most of the problems in data collection.

The primary data collected from the readers is tabulated to make it suitable for further statistical treatment. Simple statistical devices such as percentages and averages are extensively used to interpret and analyse the data collected. Buying motives influencing the readers, the extent to which they liked specific features of a newspaper, etc., are measured by rank order rating scales. For evaluating the newspaper around selected value premise a combined 13-point rating scale is used.

THE PRELUDE

The study begins with the paper-wise analysis of the growth of Telugu papers, in the next chapter. Before getting on to it, it is thought appropriate to present here the profiles of the players in the Telugu newspaper market scene. The coverage of this section is not merely limited to the papers that are surviving today. It is intended to give a brief account of all the major players that existed now or before. They are: *Andhra Patrika, Andhra Prabha, Andhra Jyoti, Andhra Bhoomi,*

Eenadu, Udayam and *Vaartha*. *Andhra Patrika,* the earliest of the players was started in 1908 and *Vaartha,* the youngest of them in 1996. Death of *Andhra Patrika* and *Vaayam* left the play field only to the remaining five players as on today.

1. Andhra Patrika

With the beginning of the twentieth century, Telugu journalism made strident progress. *Andhra Patrika* means the paper of Andhras or Telugu people was the grand old newspaper in Telugu. It was founded in Mumbai by Kasinadhuni Nageswara Rao Pantulu as a weekly in 1908. Later it was shifted just before the First World War to Chennai where it was soon converted into a daily. Nageswara Rao Pantulu, a patriot of the first-rank and an untiring benefactor of many public causes, made *Andhra Patrika* an organ of Indian nationalism and Andhra sub-nationalism. This paper always stood for robust nationalism and played a leading part not only in the struggle for independence but also in the struggle for the creation of a separate Andhra state. During the days of non-cooperation movement it wrote stirring articles appealing to the people to join the struggle, emphasising that it is a fight for dharma (means righteousness) and as such it could never be defeated.

Initially *Andhra Patrika* office consisted of two small rooms in the city of Mumbai. The eight-page weekly newspaper was published every Wednesday. The annual subscription of the weekly was Rs.2-00. This included the postal charges of 13 annas[18] and the publisher got the residual amount of one rupee and three annas for meeting all the costs.[19] Kasinadhuni Nageswara Rao was a successful manufacturer of patent medicines, particularly Amrutanjan, a balm for headaches and body pains. The self advertisement published in the leaflet of Amrutanjan created 2,000 subscribers for *Andhra Patrika.* It reached the Telugu people in the nook and corners of the country. By the time the weekly moved to Chennai in 1914, it had 7,000 loyal subscribers.[20] *Andhra Patrika* played an important role in creating the upsurge of feeling of nationalism among the Telugu people who were scattered all over the country. In view of the close affiliation of Kasinadhuni Nageswara Rao with the popular leaders of the Indian National Congress, the British government deputed one special officer to inspect the news and editorial contents before they go for publication in *Andhra Patrika*.

Aravapalli Narayana Rao who served earlier as the editor for the popular newspapers of *Desopakari* and *Krishna Patrika* has earned the distinction of the first editor of *Andhra Patrika*. Kotamraju Punnaiah[21] was its assistant editor. Kasinadhuni Nageswara Rao faced stiff problems in running the newspaper. To quote him: "Publishing a language newspaper is a highly difficult path. Managing an Andhra (Telugu) newspaper in non-Andhra region is a herculean task. Generally, owners of the language newspapers do not get any profit. No respect for them. Great risk is involved. These things naturally create frustration...".[22]

Another significant move made by Kasinadhuni Nageswara Rao was starting the publication of special annual Ugadi[23] issues from 1910. These annual issues were published uninterruptedly for about 80 years till the closure of *Andhra Patrika* in 1991. The annual issues which were initially given free of cost to the subscribers of *Andhra Patrika*, played a notable part in the general spread of knowledge and culture in Andhra.[24]

The World War I (1914-18), the beginning of Gandhi's nationalist movement, the upsurge of sub-nationalism among the people of Andhra and their movement for separate state for Andhras, and the spread of the library movement in Andhra region are among the main factors responsible for the creation of readership among the Andhras. In 1914, *Andhra*

Patrika weekly was shifted to Chennai and a daily with the same name was born in that year. The objectives and philosophy behind the publication of a new daily were well reflected in its first editorial.[25]

> "...The daily intends to reflect the public opinion .... Achieving the fruit of nationalism among Andhras which will contribute to the accomplishment of the Indian nationalism is the main endeavour of the publisher. The upsurge of Andhra nationalism is not against the Indian nationalism. At times of conflict between the two philosophies, we shall not behave against the Indian nationalism. We are for the progress of Andhra and we have no hatred for others ... Spreading the flavour of friendship and feeling of unity among all the people cutting across the lines of sub-castes, castes, religions and regions is our motto ... we shall promote the Andhra language and culture and support the establishment of a university for Andhras[26] and cause of separate Andhra province ...".[27]

Andhra Patrika helped to shape both modern Telugu language and an identity that resulted in the creation of the state of Andhra Pradesh.[28] The newspaper itself wandered over the territories in which the Telugu language was spoken. Besides giving news in Telugu, *Andhra Patrika* published the Reuters' (an international news agency) war news and telegrams in English during the First World War.[29] Gaining a reputation even among the British as "the most evil influence in the Telugu country",[30] it supported the freedom struggle from 1920. For two decades 800 copies of the newspaper were supplied free to the libraries in Andhra. In 1931, in the heat of the civil disobedience movement against British, the circulation of *Andhra Patrika* reached 10,000.[31] At the time of independence, it was the largest best known Telugu daily. *Andhra Patrika* became the member of the Audit Bureau of Circulation (ABC) formed in 1948.

The greatest appreciation to *Andhra Patrika* came from none other than Mahatma Gandhi. Acknowledging the dedicated efforts put by Nageswara Rao in enlightening the people of Andhra, Gandhi compared the paper with Bala Gangadhar Tilak's *Kesari* in Maharashtra.

Gadicherla Hari Sarvothama Rao served as the editor of *Andhra Patrika* daily for three years (earlier, he underwent the rigorous imprisonment for opposing the British Government). He is succeeded by Challa Seshagiri Rao who played a notable role in the movement for separate Andhra Province. Nageswara Rao had been succeeded by his nephew and son-in-law, Sivalenka Sambhu Prasad followed by Sivalenka Radha Krishna . The story of *Andhra Patrika* came to an end in April 1991 when it stopped its publication.

2. *Andhra Prabha*

Ramanath Goenka, the doyen of the Indian newspaper industry started *Andhra Prabha* (means the glory of Andhras) from Chennai in 1938. Its second editor Nyapati Narayanamurthi, the first being Khasa Subba Rao,[32] had made it rather spicy with his Pansupari column in its toddling days. Its later position of supremacy and stability was entirely due to Narla Venkateswara Rao who had built it up with his toil, team and sweat, over a period of 17 years. In the expert hands of Narla, the newspaper assumed the full fledged form of a first-rate modern daily comparable to its counterparts in English, Bengali and Tamil. Telling headlines, bright page make-up, vigorous leaders and effective cartoons are some of the elements that had gone into its success.[33]

Narla's association with *Andhra Prabha* (as a sub-editor, news editor, and then editor) had been epoch-making in the history of Telugu newspapers. He had taken up a non-descript paper and left it a first-rate instrument of political education and general enlightenment. The revolution that he effected in headline and caption-writing, in news display, in page make-up and in framing of action photos is now taken for granted, having been adopted by all the other newspapers in course of time. As a leader-writer, Narla had succeeded in evolving a limpid style of the utmost simplicity, which has an instant appeal to the readers. He has some beauties that come with no straining for effect. One of the best-read among the Telugu editors, with a close familiarity with a variety of intellectual disciplines through the English language, he not only managed to wear his learning lightly but succeeds in evolving a native Telugu idiom, pure and undefiled, that can adequately convey the gist of an idea contained in an English sentence. His political restraint, shrewd judgement of men and affairs, and intellectual maturity mark him out in a class by himself among the Telugu editors of his and the earlier generations.[34] Narla has a style of his own in Telugu which is at the same time precise, original and forceful. He coined scientific Telugu terminology to suit the dynamic needs of the society.

Goenka and Narla believed in the freedom of expression. They even temporarily closed down *Andhra Prabha* during the Quit India Movement for a few months to protest the British Government's attempt to impose censorship on press. *Andhra Prabha* strongly opposed anarchic and feudal governments of Nizam and Mysore provinces. Consequently, these governments banned the entry of the newspaper into their provinces. At that time *Andhra Prabha* was said to be sold in black market in the Nizam region and its circulation rose to 72,000 copies.[35]

While inaugurating the Narla's felicitation function, P.V. Rajamannar said, "*Andhra Prabha* means Narla, Narla means *Andhra Prabha*."[36] His journalistic excellence in Telugu reached the highest watermark in his editorship of *Andhra Prabha*. Through the newspaper, he played an important role in shaping public opinion in Andhra Pradesh.[37] Narla was jockeyed out of editorship for his sympathy with the workers in the press that led to a prolonged strike in Chennai.[38] Later Narla was succeeded by Neelamraju Venkataseshaiah, Panditharadhyula Nageswara Rao, Kuchimanchi Satya Subrahmanyam, A.B.K.Prasad and Potturi Venkateswara Rao as the editors of *Andhra Prabha*. At present, the paper is being edited by V. Vasudeva Deekshitulu.

Andhra Prabha along with *Indian Express* has published a series of the investigative reports that were a landmark in Indian journalism.

3. *Andhra Jyoti*

In anticipation of the birth of a new paper *Andhra Jyoti* (means the light of Andhras) in Vijayawada in 1960, then market leader *Andhra Prabha* moved there all the way from Chennai in 1959 itself. Thus the market expectations of *Andhra Jyoti* at that time were that high, considering Narla Venkateswara Rao till about that time the editor of *Andhra Prabha* was to assume the founder-editorship of the new paper. Yet another reason for sensation was the arrival of newspaper business into the heartland of Telugu people i.e., Vijayawada. Once Narla came out of *Andhra Prabha,* K.L.N. Prasad conceived the idea of giving shape to the new paper, both of them originating from Kavutaram village in Krishna District.

K.L.N. Prasad, a Congress politician and a business magnate with interests in businesses like banking and film distribution and financing founded *Andhra Jyoti*. *Andhra Jyoti* has made remarkable progress, after getting over its teething troubles. It has justly earned a name for itself as a quality newspaper, with a sober outlook on men and affairs, marked by reason, commonsense and a scientific temper in every respect. By its special features and centre-page articles, its newsletters and topical write-ups, its frequent book-reviews and political profiles, it was striving to find a niche for itself in the marketplace. This is no small achievement, in view of its limited resources and the competition from older and more powerful institutions.[39]

Narla Venkateswara Rao, who was nominated to the upper house of the Parliament twice in 1958 and 1964, relinquished his editorship in 1977. Nanduri Rama Mohana Rao, a popular writer, who served *Andhra Jyoti* in different capacities succeeded Narla as the editor. He was there for more than 15 years. Presently the paper is edited by I.Venkata Rao.

4. Andhra Bhoomi

Of the seven market players that are covered by the present study, two of them were born in the same year. One of them was *Andhra Jyoti*, as mentioned earlier, the other being *Andhra Bhoomi*. *Andhra Bhoomi* (means Andhra land) was launched in 1960 from the publishers of *Deccan Chronicle*, Hyderabad, which was in existence since 1938. At the time of launching *Andhra Bhoomi*, K.R. Pattabhiraman was at the helm of affairs of the group. The support from K.R. Nandagopal came in handy in initiating the Telugu daily. Govinda Rama Sastry, widely known as Gora Sastry, the editor of *Deccan Chronicle* at that time, also assumed the editorship of *Andhra Bhoomi*. Earlier Gora Sastry edited *Swatantra* (Telugu) weekly which was earlier edited by Khasa Subba Rao along with *Swatantra* (English) weekly.[40]

The ownership of the group changed hands in 1977, T. Chandrasekhar Reddy, taking it over.[41] Presently, T. Venkatrami Reddy is at the helm of its affairs, M.V.R. Sastry being its editor.

The paper also brought in Gajjela Malla Reddy and A.B.K. Prasad as its editors for brief spells in quick succession during the late 1980s. Those two editors who caused ripples during their stints as editors in other papers made no impact on the readers of *Andhra Bhoomi.*

Irrespective of *Andhra Bhoomi* is published from four places, the main stay of the publishers continues to be the *Deccan Chronicle,* all through the years. The Hyderabad city edition *of Deccan Chronicle* alone commanded a circulation of over one lakh copies in 1995.[42]

5. Eenadu

The launch of *Eenadu* (means today) in 1974 from Visakhapatnam by Cherukuri Ramoji Rao was a turning point in the history of language newspapers in India. Ramoji Rao hailed from a middle class, agrarian family in a small village—Pedaparupudi of Krishna District. He had his primary education in his native village. Graduated in science from A.N.R. College, Gudivada, he left his home town in the late fifties because he could not stand the feuds there. He was an unsuccessful applicant for a job at the steel plant at Bhilai and finally made it to Delhi where he started working in an advertising agency. There a tremendous liking for advertising developed in him and as a result learnt more and more. But ultimately he realised that he had to start something on his own because he was uncomfortable working there.[43] While in Delhi, an addiction to newspapers also developed in him because of the rich newspaper culture there. He was then unable to live without a clutch of morning newspapers.[44]

Then Ramoji Rao received an offer from a multinational company for the position of a regional officer. This was the turning point in his life. On the one hand he had a lucrative job offer, and on the other the itch to start off on his own. Chit funds were becoming very popular during those days and even though he was a bit sceptical in the beginning, he decided to take the plunge.[45]

After working in the advertising agency for five years, Ramoji Rao shifted to Hyderabad in 1962 to set up Margadarsi Chit Funds. His second project was a hotel Dolphin, in Visakhapatnam taken up in early 1970s. He used to travel to Visakhapatnam frequently during these days, mainly to sort out the problems at Dolphin. One day he realised that there was no newspaper published in the city and all the Vijayawada editions used to reach in the afternoon. The state of Telugu newspapers during those days was pathetic, as most of them were four page affairs with half the space devoted to advertisements. The readers were not getting their money's worth. Ramoji Rao decided to give it to them.[46] Launched in 1974 from Visakhapatnam with a print run of 4,500 copies, *Eenadu* took just four years to become the largest selling newspaper in the state of Andhra Pradesh. As the newspaper became popular, a Hyderabad edition was launched in 1975 with a print run of 15,000 copies. For this purpose a 1932 model 8 unit Albert Rotary was acquired and physically divided, distributing four units each to Hyderabad and Visakhapatnam. It was not until 1978 when the Vijayawada edition was started that a new rotary was acquired. However, Rao's *Newstime*, an English daily from Hyderabad has been struggling hard to survive right from its launch in early 1980s.

6. Udayam

The first issue of *Udayam* (means morning) saw the light of the day on December 29, 1984. Never before a Telugu paper was simultaneously published from two centres, right on entry. *Udayam* did it, making its maiden appearance from Vijayawada and Hyderabad. Dasari Narayana Rao,[47] a famous film director and Kondapalli Ramakrishna Prasad, a grandson of veteran freedom fighter Gottipati Brahmaiah were the firm's chairman and managing director, respectively. Dasari hailing from Palakollu of West Godavari district migrated to Chennai in 1967 in search of a film career. Ramakrishna Prasad had a print media background of publishing a Telugu monthly Sneha in late 1970s. The monthly brought out a novel authored by Dasari Narayana Rao as a serial. Such association ultimately resulted in the birth of a Telugu daily, A.B.K. Prasad being its founder editor.

It was a big bang entry into the industry with preparations for inaugural circulation of two lakh copies. The paper launched its third edition from Tirupati in 1986. But A.B.K. Prasad continued there as editor only till May 1986 and one of the founders Ramakrishna Prasad also parted ways with the paper soon in early 1988.[48] Then Dasari became its chief editor. Undeterred by the partings of its founder associates, Dasari continued to put up a brave fight in the marketplace. Its initial success was not insignificant, the paper climbing to the second position soon. However, it could not sustain the enthusiasm for long.

In the face of such continued drift, the paper could not withstand the financial strain. The firm was sold away to Magunta Subbarami Reddy. The new proprietor could hardly run it for a year thereafter and the paper closed all its operations in May 1995. Nevertheless, the paper's new proprietor had the serious intentions of reviving the paper at any cost. He was prepared for a massive financial commitment even. Then the newspaper lovers were expecting such a dream of *Udayam's* new proprietor coming true. All such dreams were unfortunately shattered with the brutal murder of Subbarami Reddy subsequently.

7. *Vaartha*

Vaartha (means news), the youngest of all the players under study, was inaugurated by the prime minister P.V. Narasimha Rao on January 25, 1996. Several years of hard work and planning have gone into the making of *Vaartha*.

The project was conceptualised by A.B.K.Prasad. In his own inimitable style, A.B.K at one time or the other helped the spruce up the image of each of the major dailies in Telugu. Anne Bhavani Koteswara Prasad hailed from a small village Uppaluru in Krishna district. As is already learnt, he was the founder editor of *Eenadu* and *Udayam*, and editor of *Andhra Bhoomi*. For some time he associated himself with Andhra Pradesh, a government monthly and on contract edited *Andhra Prabha* for two years. He started his career as a sub-editor in *Visalandhra* in 1959.[49] He has never stuck to editing a paper for more than three years since starting *Eenadu*. ABK is known to have developed differences with all the managements he worked for.

After attaining 58 years of age and when he stopped editing Suprabhatam, the Telugu fortnightly, it was widely believed that he had retired from active journalism. At such a time, he started thinking on his new venture *Vaartha* by floating ABK Publications Ltd. His initial plans were going for a public issue to part finance the project. Had it happened like that, *Vaartha* could have become the first newspaper in the country to get started on a public issue. But things did not move in that direction. At such a critical juncture, the financial support from the Sanghi group of industries of Hyderabad came in handy to ABK Publications Ltd. A Telugu paper receiving such a big support from a non-Telugu business group was a shot in the arm to the newspaper industry. The paper was given a final shape, Girish Sanghi of the group becoming the managing director and ABK Prasad remaining the chief editor.

Vaartha brought with it the latest satellite technology into the industry. *Vaartha's* entry was unusual in several ways. They had grand designs of invading the total market in a giant leap forward style. Such high ambitious intentions of ABK could be given a trial with the real impetus he received from the Sanghi group, assuming all-out financial responsibility. The costs and stakes involved were extremely high, considering the paper was launched from nine centres at a time the market leader *Eenadu* was published from only seven centres. There was a lot of pre-launch fanfare over the press, radio, TV and outdoor media even several months earlier. Though not succeeded, they intended to inaugurate their paper with 4,00,000 registered subscribers. But the ground level realities of the grand design operations were disappointing.

What was in store to ABK - the paper's founder and founder editor, was one and the same as before. AGA Publications Ltd., of the Sanghi group taking over the ABK Publications, the paper's creator ABK was edged out. In place of ABK, K. Ramachandra Murthy became the paper's editor in April 1998.

References

1. See Chapter IV.
2. See Table 5.3 in Chapter-V, for a comparative standing of the market leader in Telugu with others.
3. A sample of them includes: *Report of the Press Commission,* Govt. of India, New Delhi, 1954; Report of the Study Team on Five Year Plan *Publicity,* Govt. of India, New Delhi, 1963; *Report of the Mass Communication Study Team,* Ministry of Information and Broadcasting, Govt. of India, New Delhi, 1963; and *White Paper on Misuse of Mass Media during the Internal Emergency,* Govt. of India, New Delhi, 1977.
4. A sample of them includes: S.C. Dube, *Communication, Innovation and Planned Change in India,* East-West Centre Press, Honolulu, 1964; Y.V. Lakshmana Rao, *Communication and Development,* University of Minnesota Press, Minneapolis, 1966; Paul Hartman, B.R. Patil and Anita Dighe, *The Mass Media and Village Life: An Indian Study,* Sage Publications, New Delhi, 1989; and P.L. Vishweshwer Rao, *Language*

Press in India: A Study of Readership, Contents and Language Comprehension with Special Reference to Telugu Daily Newspapers, Osmania University, Hyderabad, unpublished Ph.D. dissertation, 1991.

5. A sample of them includes: *Report of the Study Group for Newspaper Industry,* National Commission on Labour, New Delhi, 1968; Ashok Desai, *Economic Aspects of the Indian Press,* Press Institute of India, New Delhi, 1971; IENS, *Newspaper Distribution Costs: Case Study of a Delhi Newspaper,* New Delhi, 1974; and *Report of the Fact Finding Committee on Newspaper Economics,* Ministry of Information and Broadcasting, Govt. of India, New Delhi, 1975.
6. A sample of them includes: IENS, *Problems of Newspaper Industry in India,* New Delhi, 1957; Sindhwani, Trillet N., *Newspaper Economics and Management,* Ankur Publishing, New Delhi, 1958; *Report of the Enquiry Committee on Problems of Small Newspapers,* Ministry of Information and Broadcasting, Govt. of India, New Delhi, 1965; Lingam, *Circulation Problems in Indian Newspapers,* The Press Institute of India, Delhi, 1968; Arun Bhattacharjee, *Indian Press: Profession to Industry,* Vikas Publishing House, New Delhi, 1972; and IENS, *Impact of Newsprint Shortage on Indian Newspapers,* New Delhi, 1974.
7. Robin Jeffrey's series of 11 essays that were published in the *Economic and Political Weekly* in 1997 (January 4 through March 29) and some of those during the earlier years referred to in the previous chapter.
8. *Golconda Patrika* was revived in 1974 and continued publication for three years. It reappeared in 1979 as an evening paper which lasted for a little more than a year (P.L.Vishweshwer Rao, *op. cit.*, p. 57).
9. Table 4.1 in Chapter-IV gives an idea of the extent of the statewide circulation these papers commanded in terms of the number of publication centres wherefrom they were published. Some papers had the record of their publication even from outside the state.

10. H.W. Boyd Jr., et al., *Marketing Research: Text and Cases*, All India Traveller Bookseller, Indian edition, Delhi, 1990, p. 249.
11. On the recommendation of the First Press Commission, the office of the Registrar of Newspapers for India, RNI, was created as a government agency from July 1, 1966. One of the functions of RNI is to compile an annual report on the press in India. Allocation of newsprint is also a statutory responsibility entrusted to it.
12. Set up in 1948, the ABC has among its members newspaper publishers, advertisers and advertising agencies. The ABC certificate is issued to the publication every six months, if the Bureau's own auditor confirms the figure claimed by the paper and certified by its auditor.
13. Readership surveys were introduced in India by advertising agencies and consumer good marketers. The National Readership Surveys provide a comprehensive databank on media patterns among India's urban adults. So far, six National Readership Surveys have been carried out in 1970, 1978, 1982, 1989, 1995 and 1997.
14. Pioneered by Media Research Users Council (MRUC), the Indian Readership surveys cover both urban and rural India. So far, two Indian Readership Surveys have been carried out in 1995 and 1998.
15. *Advertisers Handbook* is a reference annual for marketing, advertising and media professionals published for Indraprastha Prakashan, New Delhi.
16. *Statistical Outline of India* is annually published by Tata Services Ltd., Mumbai.
17. See Appendix for a condensed version.
18. One sixteenth part of a rupee was one anna.
19. V. Lakshmana Reddy, *Telugu Journalism Avatharana—Vikaasam* (Telugu), Gopichand Publications, Vijayawada, 1985, p. 381.
20. *Ibid.*, p. 381.
21. Later he became popular as the editor of *Sindhu Observer*.

22. V. Lakshmana Reddy, *op. cit.*, p. 384.
23. *Ugadi* is the New Year's day of the Telugu people.
24. V. Lakshmana Reddy, *op. cit.*, p. 380.
25. *Andhra Patrika*, April 1, 1914.
26. Andhra University came into existence in 1926.
27. Andhra state was formed in October 1953, comprising the Telugu speaking Coastal and Rayalaseema regions, with Kurnool as its capital. Till then these regions were part of Madras state.
28. Andhra Pradesh was formed on 1st November, 1956 when the Indian states were reorganised on linguistic basis, thus merging Telugu speaking districts of the erstwhile Hyderabad state with Andhra state. Hyderabad became the new capital.
29. V. Lakshmana Reddy, *op. cit.*, p. 391.
30. Robin Jeffrey, "Indian Languages Newspapers: 4 Telugu: Ingredients of Growth and Failure", *op. cit.*, p. 112.
31. *Ibid.*
32. Khasa Subba Rao was also joint editor of the *Indian Express* at that time.
33. Chronicler, "Telugu Journalism—Leaders and Landmarks," published in *The Golden Book*, (n.d.), pp. 120-125.
34. D.Anjaneyulu, "Some Telugu Editors", in K.R. Seshagiri Rao (ed.), *Studies in the History of Telugu Journalism*, Narla Shashtyabdipurti Celebration Committee, Delhi, 1968, pp. 141-146.
35. Rapolu Ananda Bhaskar, *Journalism Charithraa—Vyavastha* (Telugu), Udayam Publications, Hyderabad, 1988, p. 61.
36. V. Lakshmana Reddy, *op. cit.*, p. 397.
37. K. Subbarao, "Narla's Impact on Telugu Journalism", in K.R. Seshagiri Rao (ed.), *op. cit.*, p. 148.
38. P. Rajeswara Rao, "Telugu Dailies" in K.R. Seshagiri Rao (ed.), *op. cit.*, pp. 101-111.
39. D. Anjaneyulu, "Telugu Journalism: A Summary", in K.R. Seshagiri Rao (ed.), *loc. cit.*

40. Rapolu Ananda Bhaskar, *op. cit.*, pp. 97-98.
41. *Ibid.*, p. 98.
42. The ABC figures relating to July-December, 1995.
43. S.N. Vasuki, "The Ramoji Rao Phenomenon", *Business India*, April 23-May 6, 1984, pp. 87-94.
44. Robin Jeffrey, "Indian Languages Newspapers 4: Telugu: Ingredients of Growth and Failure," *op. cit.*, p. 193.
45. S.N. Vasuki, *loc. cit.*
46. *Ibid.*
47. An entryholder in the *Guinness Book of World Records* for directing a record number of films.
48. Rapolu Ananda Bhaskar, *op. cit.*, pp. 115-117.
49. Stanley Theodore, "Making News," *The Week*, May 16, 1993, p. 24.

4
The Rise and Fall of Telugu Dailies

Chapter - II ended focussing on the growth of Telugu dailies as a lot, compared to those of other Indian languages, in terms of their circulation, over the years. Now it is time to have a close look at the Telugu newspaper market scene. This chapter attempts to make a paper-wise analysis of the marketing performance of the Telugu dailies, in terms of their circulation and market share. The seven Telugu dailies, the profiles of which are given in the preceding chapter, in the market are taken up for analysis. It is needless to add that the ABC data is used here, unless otherwise specified, in contrast to the RNI data used in Chapter - II. During the years of nonmembership, claimed circulations are used.

Market Share

Besides circulation, market share is used as another criterion to analyse the competitive position of the Telugu dailies in this chapter. Market share means the share of an individual firm in the total sales of that product by all the sellers during a stated period of time in a stated market.[1] Here the product is Telugu daily newspaper and the market being the buyers of such dailies. Sales in the stated period usually refers to average daily sales of the newspapers in a year. The Strategic Planning Institute of the USA sought to identify the most important variables affecting the profits by launching a study called Profit Impact of Market Strategy (PIMS). For the purpose, it gathered data from hundreds of business units in a variety of industries and identified the most important variables associated with the profitability. Market share is one among the key variables thus identified affecting profitability.

According to a PIMS report, "The average return on investment (ROI) for business with under 10 per cent market share was almost 9 per cent .... On the average, a difference of ten percentage points in market share is accompanied by a difference of about five points in pretax ROI." The PIMS study shows that business with market shares above 40 per cent earn an average ROI of 30 per cent, or three times that of those with shares under 10 per cent.[2] Market leaders can improve their profitability further through increasing their market share. In many markets, one share point is worth tens of millions of dollars. For example, in the USA, a one-share-point gain in coffee is worth $ 48 million and in soft drinks $ 120 million![3]

In a newspaper business, market share as a variable affecting profitability assumes greater importance. A firm commanding a high market share in newspaper sales usually attracts a much larger share in the advertising revenue.

Despite strategy researchers and practitioners focussing much attention on the problem of getting and keeping market share, it is not without its limitations. Hamel and Prahalad highlight the drawbacks of market share. They argue, "... what is the measure of market share in markets that barely exist? How can one maximize market share in an industry where the product or service concept is still underfined, where customer segments have yet to solidify, and customer preferences are still poorly understood?" Further, they emphasised competition for tomorrow is more important rather than competition for today. Competition for the future is competition for opportunity share rather than market share. It is competition to maximize the share of future opportunities a company could potentially access within a broad opportunity arena.[4]

A PREVIEW

In 1998, there were five serious players in the Telugu newspaper market, namely, *Andhra Prabha, Andhra Jyoti, Andhra Bhoomi, Eenadu* and *Vaartha*. The five papers were published from 16 towns or cities spread over the whole of the state of Andhra Pradesh and two of them located outside the state, one in Chennai and the other in Bangalore, as are shown in Table 4.1. The break-up of publication centres was: *Eenadu* and *Vaartha* 10 each, *Andhra Prabha* five, *Andhra Jyoti* and *Andhra Bhoomi* four each. The paper-wise average daily circulations in 1997 were: *Eenadu* 6,54,000; *Vaartha* 1,63,000; *Andhra Jyoti* 1,15,000; *Andhra Prabha* 32,000 and *Andhra Bhoomi* 20,000,[5] thus generating a total circulation of 9,84,000 copies.

These circulation figures present an interesting picture of the competitors in the market for Telugu newspapers. *Eenadu,* aged 23 years then, claiming 66.5 per cent of the market share, just then born *Vaartha* occupying the No.2 slot (16.5 per cent market share) and the senior-most existing player *Andhra Prabha* finding itself in an unimportant position are worth-noting. If one looks beyond these figures, the Telugu newspaper scene was more startling considering the death of the oldest of the Telugu newspapers *Andhra Patrika* in 1991 and a ten year old *Udayam* also meeting the same fate in 1995. The centres from which these two dailies were published are also shown in the table.

Till 1959, major Telugu newspapers enjoying statewide circulation were published only from Chennai, Vijayawada and Hyderabad were brought on the Telugu newspaper map with major players only in 1959 and in 1960, respectively, though much of the publishing activity in the state was confined to Vijayawada. Till the advent of *Eenadu* in Visakhapatnam in 1974, publication of Telugu dailies in Andhra Pradesh outside Vijayawada and Hyderabad was unknown, though *Andhra Prabha* was published for a brief spell at Chittoor in early 1960s, which was ultimately shifted to Bangalore in 1966. Presently all the five major dailies are published from Vijayawada, Hyderabad and Visakhapatnam. Tirupati became the fourth publication centre of newspapers in the state in 1982 with the presence of *Eenadu* there. Tirupati and Rajahmundry emerged as important publication centres bringing out three of the five dailies from those centres, though the latter town became newspaper centre only in 1992 beginning with *Eenadu*. Of the 16 publication centres, 10 of them originated only in 1990s, including five of them in 1996 and two in 1998. Nellore was the youngest of all centres wherefrom *Eenadu* is published. Much of the geographic expansion is attributable to *Eenadu* going new places and the advent of *Vaartha* in 1996 from many new centres. Of the 16 towns and cities wherefrom Telugu dailies are published, *Eenadu* was the first entrant in eight places and *Vaartha* in four places.

Ten centres publish only one newspaper each. Thus Chennai and Bangalore each bring out only *Andhra Prabha*, Karimnagar, Suryapet, Guntur and Nellore bring out *Eenadu*, and Cuddapah, Ongole, Nizamabad and Warangal bring out only *Vaartha*. Centres wherefrom Telugu dailies under study are published are shown in Map 4.1.

This analysis shows that by and large Telugu dailies are making a herculean effort to come closer and closer to the readers. In the process, instead of bringing out larger number of copies from fewer centres, they are bringing out fewer

Table 4.1

Towns and Cities Wherefrom Telugu Dailies are Published, 1998.

Town or City	*Andhra Patrika*[a] (1908-1991)	*Andhra Prabha* (1938)	*Andhra Jyoti* (1960)	*Andhra Bhoomi* (1960)	*Eenadu* (1974)	*Udayam* (1984-1995)	*Vaartha* (1996)	*Total*
				Year of the Entry				
1. Chennai	1914	1938	—	—	—	—	—	1
2. Vijayawada	1965	1959	1960	1988	1978	1984	1996	5
3. Hyderabad	1975	1977	1986	1960	1975	1984	1996	5
4. Bangalore	—	1966[b]	—	—	—	—	—	1
5. Visakhapatnam	—	1985[c]	1991	1986	1974	—	1996	5
6. Tirupati	—	—	1987	—	1982	1986	1996	3
7. Anantapur	—	—	—	—	1991	—	1998	2
8. Karimnagar	—	—	—	—	1992	—	—	1
9. Rajahmundry	—	—	—	1994	1992	—	1996	3
10. Cuddapah	—	—	—		—	—	1996	1
11. Ongole	—	—	—	—	—	—	1996	1
12. Nizamabad	—	—	—	—	—	—	1996	1

13. Warangal	—	—	—	—	—	—	1996	1
14. Suryapet	—	—	—	—	1996	—	—	1
15. Guntur	—	—	—	—	1996	—	—	1
16. Nellore	—	—	—	—	1998	—	—	1
Total	Closed	5	4	4	10	Closed	10	33

Note: Years of establishment and closure (if so) of the newspaper are given in the parentheses.

a. Published from Mumbai till 1914 as a weekly newspaper, b. Formerly at Chittoor. c. Formerly at Vizianagaram.

Map 4.1

Telugu daily going places: 1914-98

1. Chennai (1914)	2. Vijayawada (1959)	3. Hyderabad (1960)	4. Bangalore (1966)
5. Visakhapatnam (1974)	6. Tirupathi (1982)	7. Ananthapur (1991)	8. Karimnagar (1992)
9. Rajahmundry (1992)	10. Cuddapah (1996)	11. Ongole (1996)	12. Nizamabad (1996)
13. Warangal (1996)	14. Suryapet (1996)	15. Guntur (1996)	16. Nellore (1998).

The daily also exsisted at Chittor and Vizianagaram briefly.

copies of newspapers from larger number of centres, thus denying themselves the economies of scale of operation. The market leader *Eenadu* taking a lion's share in total circulation, all other competitors in the market appear to be operating at sub-optimum level sharing paltry circulations among them originating from a still large number of centres.

The Telugu newspaper market existed for nine decades. However, till about mid-1970s the Telugu newspaper continued to be production-oriented. The market scene till about that time is analysed in the section that follows.

THE EARLY PLAYERS

Andhra Patrika, then a news weekly, was shifted to Chennai as a daily from Mumbai in 1914 to get closer to a large number of Telugu speaking people, as is already learnt.[6] The paper was a labour of love for Kasinadhuni Nageswara Rao. He ran it in a spirit of service and sacrifice. On his own admission its circulation was about 5,000 copies till 1930. Because of the impact of the Salt Satyagraha and the Quit India movement in 1942, public interest in the day-today developments increased and its sales doubled. Nageswara Rao displayed wisdom and vision in utilising the services of stalwarts such as G. Harisarvothama Rao,[7] K. Siva Rama Krishna Rao and Challa Seshagiri Rao, who were closely associated with the Andhra movement.[8] *Andhra Patrika* has had an unbroken tenure of public service. which was practically unaffected by the ups and downs in the newspaper market, receiving the required financial support from Amrutanjan.

Andhra Patrika was in an unquestioned monopoly market for nearly a quarter century till the commencement of *Andhra Prabha*. in 1938. It was under the "imaginative stewardship"[9] of Narla Venkateswara Rao that the *Andhra Prabha* quickly grew to be the premier Telugu daily. At the time of independence. *Andhra Prabha.* was a well-known Telugu daily along with *Andhra Patrika*.

During the freedom struggle, the justification for running a newspaper, and its attractiveness to readers, were often the same: to fight against the alien rule. People like Nageswara Rao had to struggle in the early days to make their papers forge ahead financially and otherwise. After 1947, however, all governments were Indian governments, and a newspaper's foes as well as its friends were Indians, not foreigners. Newspaper ownership then needed other rewards—profit or power - as well as a sense of "serving the people". To pay the bills and survive after 1947, nationalist newspapers had to conduct their affairs more like the long established English language newspapers which were already well-connected to the few sources of existing advertising.[10]

Once the struggle against the British ended, the nationalist newspapers like *Andhra Patrika* enjoyed certain advantages. Being the leaders in their language, such newspapers had the support of the readers who were emotionally and politically attached to them. Further, the freedom fighters whom the newspapers had supported before independence were often in positions of political power, for example, membership of legislative assemblies and parliament, and ministerial berths after independence. As such they could effortlessly get the support of the government in the form of advertising, concessions and licenses.

Andhra Patrika remained in Chennai, which continued to be the centre of Telugu publishing even though a separate state of Andhra Pradesh for Telugu people was formed in 1956 with Hyderabad as its capital. In 1957, the total circulation of Telugu publications, including non-dailies, published from Chennai city was estimated at 3,67,000. as against the total circulation of only 2,16,000 of all publications within Andhra Pradesh.[11]

Andhra Prabha, with its English counterpart in the chain *Indian Express* moved to Vijayawada in 1959, the rich commercial centre of the state. Later it brought out another edition from Chittoor to cater the needs of Rayalaseema and Karnataka. The second edition of *Andhra Prabha* was subsequently brought out from Bangalore in 1966 consequent on the closure of the centre at Chittoor. Thus, *Andhra Prabha* was the first daily to be published from two places simultaneously. On the other hand, *Andhra Patrika* could not commence its second edition until 1965 when it started an edition from Vijayawada in addition to the one at Chennai. Even five years earlier, by 1960, *Andhra Prabha* stole a march over *Andhra Patrika* and became unassailable. At that time, the circulation of *Andhra Prabha* was 53,000 copies for its two editions from Vijayawada and Chittoor, whereas *Andhra Patrika* sold 48,000 copies from its single edition of Chennai.[12] Ten years later in 1971, *Andhra Prabha,* then publishing from Vijayawada and Bangalore, reached 1,16,000; *Andhra Patrika* still remained at 48,000.[13]

After getting out of *Andhra Prabha,* Narla Venkateswara Rao, along with an industrialist K.L.N.Prasad, succeeded in founding *Andhra Jyoti* in 1960 at Vijayawada. Narla accepted to be its editor. Soon it made remarkable progress. Commencing from Hyderabad in 1960, *Andhra Bhoomi* commanded only a meagre circulation.

The depressing state of newspaper readership in Andhra is revealed in a survey[14] conducted in the late 1950s. According to it, a little over 16 for every thousand of population in Andhra were known to read any newspaper, while in the neighbouring Tamil Nadu the corresponding figure was about 38 and the Indian average was 32. According to the Registrar of Newspapers for India in 1967, there were eleven Telugu dailies published in Andhra, while there were 27 in Tamil Nadu, nearly 30 in Karnataka and over 40 in Kerala.[15] The overall circulation of the dailies published from the state showed a declining trend from 3.04 lakhs in 1962 to 2.52 lakhs in 1967. Overall circulation of the papers published has never touched the level attained in 1962 and a declining trend prevailed till 1965. The position had, however, improvised by 16 per cent in 1966 in comparison with the preceding years and the trend continued during 1967. One of the obvious reasons for the low circulation of papers published in the state was the persisting low literacy percentage (23.3) in the state.[16] The sharp rise in circulation in 1962 and again in 1965-66 was evidently attributable to the public interest in news in the context of the Chinese and the Pakistani invasions during those years.

In the mid-1960s, the newspaper situation in Andhra Pradesh was characterised by two other factors. First, the largest number of dailies or other categories of papers circulating within the state were published from the state capital, Hyderabad, followed by papers published from the second largest city Vijayawada and, second, the higher circulations enjoyed by the latter than by the former. The major proportion of the dailies and periodicals published in the state were, naturally, in the Telugu language (269) followed by papers in Urdu (84), English (77) and others (56)[17] In 1967, Telugu papers also commanded the largest share of circulation (62.5 per cent), English papers coming next with 18.7 per cent, while papers in other languages shared the balance of the circulation. The highest circulation was commanded by nine Telugu dailies (1,55,000) followed by Telugu monthlies (1,08,000), English dailies coming next with a circulation of 74,000, while 20 English monthlies had a circulation of 20,000. Urdu occupied the third place with four Urdu dailies having a circulation of 26,000 followed by 12 Urdu weeklies with a total circulation of 23,000.[18]

The "poor" and "underveloped"[19] state of Telugu newspapers existed as there was not an increase in the number of newspapers (including periodicals) in Telugu in the same proportion as in Gujarati or Marathi despite Andhra Pradesh was the fifth largest state in area and the fourth largest in population.

Evaluating the Early Players by Competition

It may not be justifiable to evaluate newspaper firms of yesteryears in terms of their competitive strengths and weaknesses in the marketplace. Making a newspaper was not a commercial proposition at that time. Profit never loomed large in the minds of the marketers in those years. The goal of the newspapers was clearly a social gain rather than a profit margin. Newspapers then were a mission, an upheaval and a movement. Certainly it was not just another marketable commodity. Awakening the masses against the oppressive rule of the alien powers, removal of superstitions and social disparities, creation of linguistic states and literacy and the language reformation drive, etc., causes were uppermost in the minds of those who brought out newspapers.

Nevertheless, marketplace compulsions cannot altogether be ignored. Though *Andhra Patrika* lived in a monopoly market till the advent of *Andhra Prabha* in 1938, it was never known to take advantage in such a situation. Instead, *Andhra Patrika* depended for its survival more on the profits of *Amrutanjan.*

Realising the precarious situation as this in running a newspaper, the *Indian Express* group took advantage of the innovation in a chain newspaper to bring out *Andhra Prabha* in 1938. Thus *Andhra Prabha* stood in the position of competitive advantage even at the time it was created: As such *Andhra Prabha* could think in terms of competing with *Andhra Patrika.* On the whole, both the dailies were instrumental in spreading the newspaper culture among the

Table 4.2

Audited* Circulation of Telugu Dailies: 1970-97

(Copies in thousands)

Year	*Andhra Patrika (1908-91)*	*Andhra Prabha (1938)*	*Andhra Jyoti (1960)*	*Andhra Bhoomi (1960)*	*Eenadu (1974)*	*Udayam (1984-95)*	*Vaartha (1996)*	*Industry Total*
1970	44	104	28	18				194
1971	45	116	27	18				206
1972	39	113	27	16				195
1973	49	112	31	17				209
1974	40	101	24	15	5[a]			185
1975	39	103	27	16	35[a]			220
1976	40	89	34	15	54			232
1977	51	110	44	19	73			297
1978	47	117	52	20	127			363
1979	42	127	46	15	185			415
1980	39	122	54	15	205			435
1981	37	106	48	14	197			402
1982	36	100	48	14	240			438
1983	40	111	57	17	342			567

1984	41	119	77	21	356	e		614
1985	31	115[b]	72	11	295	200[a]		724
1986	25	94[b]	69[c]	14[a]	292	130		624
1987	21	82	122	14[a]	267	127		633
1988	21[a]	80	176[d]	18[a]	283	125[a]		703
1989	20[a]	78	173[d]	24[a]	311	124[a]		730
1990	20[a]	70	135	18[a]	301	121[a]		685
1991	18[a]	51	169	12[a]	326	120[a]		696
1992		55	140	12[a]	339	118[a]		664
1993		53	132	15[a]	423	119[a]		742
1994		56	130	20[a]	517	118[a]		841
1995		52	132	20[a]	557	110[a]		871
1996		38	118	24[a]	595		175	950
1997		32	115	20[a]	654		163	984

Notes: Years of establishment and closure (if so) of the newspaper are given in the parentheses.

*. During the years of non-membership of the ABC, claimed circulations are taken into account.

a. Claimed circulation.

b. Excluding the Vizianagaram edition commenced in 1985.

c. Excluding the Hyderabad edition commenced in 1986.

d. Data relating to the period of July — December 1988 and 1989.

e. The paper was brought out only for three days during the fag end of 1984.

Source: Compiled from ABC half-yearly reports (figures for both the half-years are averaged), Audit Bureau of Circulations, Mumbai.

Telugu people faster, though both of them were positioned in Chennai, very far away from the heartland of Telugu districts. Soon they have become household names, though *Andhra Patrika* was better known in the towns and *Andhra Prabha* even in the villages. In a way the healthy competition between them supplemented each other in satisfying the news-hunger of Telugu readers to a great extent. Besides, their weekly magazines were among the most widely read periodicals.

Andhra Prabha was the first to realise the necessity of publishing nearer to the readers. This made them starting their publications from Vijayawada in 1959. Even in the face of such competition, *Andhra Patrika* could not start its centre at Vijayawada till 1965. *Andhra Patrika* had to face competition from *Andhra Jyoti* and *Andhra Bhoomi* since 1960 from Vijayawada and Hyderabad, respectively. All these things resulted in *Andhra Patrika* losing its foothold and *Andhra Prabha* emerging as the unquestioned leader which commanded a circulation of 70,589 copies (51.9 per cent of market share) followed by *Andhra Patrika* (31,603 copies or 23.2 per cent of market share), *Andhra Jyoti* (22, 310 copies or 16.4 per cent of market share), and *Andhra Bhoomi* (11,542 copies or 8.5 per cent of market share) in 1967. Thus competition in a small way had come to the Telugu newspaper market from the time they were published from the centrally located Vijayawada, allowing the chain publication *Andhra Prabha* to be the front-runner. No doubt, more number of newspapers were available to the customers, but the publishers were not found to be increasingly competing with each other in providing them more and more want-satisfaction benefits. In other words, the differences in products they have offered to the customers were negligible, leaving the industry in production-orientation stage rather than moving towards marketing-orientation.

PLAYING SINCE 1974

The last quarter of this century witnessed significant happenings in the Telugu newspaper market. The era of marketing has started taking roots into the Telugu newspaper business. The competitions in the Telugu newspaper market started competing with each other in customer want-satisfaction. The marketers succeeded, in a big way, in creating hitherto non-existing customers. Of course, some papers have also failed in retaining the hitherto existing customers. All this process resulted in the emergence of star performers and the exit or near-exit of poor performers, howsoever long-standing they may be.

1. An Overview

Paper-wise circulation of Telugu dailies under study are shown in Table 4.2 for the years 1970-97. During the years 1970-75, the total circulation looked very placid, without not much of either an uptrend or a down trend. During the period, the total circulation ranged from 1,85,000 copies (1974) to 2,20,000 (1975) copies. During these years (1970-75), the paper-wise circulation ranged from: *Andhra Prabha* 1,01,000 to 1,16,000 copies; *Andhra Patrika* 39,000 to 40,000 copies; *Andhra Jyoti* 24,000 to 28,000 copies; and *Andhra Bhoomi* 15,000 to 18,000 copies. *Eenadu*, entered into the newspaper business only in 1974, became a member of the ABC soon in 1976.

Table 4.3 shows the market shares. In 1975, paper-wise market shares in circulations, were (per cent): *Andhra Prabha* 46.8; *Andhra Patrika* 17.7; *Eenadu* 15.9; *Andhra Jyoti* 12.3; and *Andhra Bhoomi* 7.3. *Eenadu* sprang a surprise in occupying No.3 slot in the second year of its existence. *Andhra Prabha* continued to be the market leader.

Sea-changes swept the Telugu newspaper market during the five years that followed i.e., between 1976 and 1980. Year after year, there were jumps in the total circulation. Compared

Table 4.3

Market Share of Telugu Dailies in Circulation: 1970-97.

per cent

Year	*Andhra Patrika* (1908-91)	*Andhra Prabha* (1938)	*Andhra Jyoti* (1960)	*Andhra Bhoomi* (1960)	*Eenadu* (1974)	*Udayam* (1984-95)	*Vaartha* (1996)
1970	22.7	53.6	14.4	9.3			
1971	21.9	56.3	13.1	8.7			
1972	20.0	58.0	13.8	8.2			
1973	23.5	53.6	14.8	8.1			
1974	21.6	54.6	13.0	8.1	2.7		
1975	17.7	46.8	12.3	7.3	15.9		
1976	17.2	38.3	14.7	6.5	23.3		
1977	17.2	37.0	14.8	6.4	24.6		
1978	13.0	32.2	14.3	5.5	35.0		
1979	10.1	30.6	11.1	3.6	44.6		
1980	9.0	28.0	12.4	3.5	47.1		
1981	9.2	26.4	11.9	3.5	49.0		
1982	8.2	22.8	11.0	3.2	54.8		

1983	7.0	19.6	10.1	3.0	60.3		
1984	6.7	19.4	12.5	3.4	58.0		
1985	4.3	15.9	9.9	1.5	40.8	27.6	
1986	4.0	15.1	11.1	2.2	46.8	20.8	
1987	3.3	13.0	19.3	2.2	42.2	20.0	
1988	3.0	11.4	25.0	2.6	40.3	17.7	
1989	2.7	10.7	23.7	3.3	42.6	17.0	
1990	2.9	10.2	22.6	2.6	44.8	17.7	
1991	2.6	7.3	24.3	1.7	46.9	17.2	
1992		8.3	21.1	1.8	51.0	17.8	
1993		7.2	17.8	2.0	57.0	16.0	
1994		6.7	15.4	2.4	61.5	14.0	
1995		6.0	15.2	2.3	63.9	12.6	
1996		4.0	12.4	2.5	62.7	—	18.4
1997		3.3	11.7	2.0	66.5	—	16.5

Note: Based on Table 4.2

to what it was in 1975, the total circulation nearly doubled by 1980 (from 2,20,000 to 4,35,000 copies). The market never experienced such broad jumps. The figures in the table establish such jumps in total circulation were mostly caused by the presence of the lone new daily *Eenadu*. During the years 1976-80, if the circulation of *Eenadu* is subtracted from the total circulation of the respective years, the story remains more or less the same old one, implying stable circulation. To put it differently, there were not notable changes in the paper-wise sales of other dailies during these years. It means *Eenadu* virtually succeeded in creating new customers in the real marketing sense, instead of weaning them away from the old firms. This implies total sales of Telugu dailies grew with sales of *Eenadu*, by and large. A fantastic achievement by the new paper indeed! Let it be illustrated with reference to the year 1980. Out of the total circulation of 4,35,000 copies, *Eenadu's* circulation was 2,05,000 copies. What all other competitors achieved through the ages was nearly achieved by the new daily in just five years. It appears as though the new paper targeted at the opportunity share, emphasised by Hamel and Prahalad referred to earlier, and achieved it. To gain a disproportionate share of future opportunities it is necessary to possess a disproportionate share of the requisite competencies.[20] New paper might have possessed and fully exploited such of those competencies. Resultantly, there was a reversal in the showing by market shares in 1980 (per cent): *Eenadu* 47.1; *Andhra Prabha* 28; *Andhra Jyoti* 12.4; *Andhra Patrika* 9; and *Andhra Bhoomi* 3.5. In fact, *Eenadu* became the market leader in 1978, four years after the entry and two years after becoming an ABC member, pushing aside the then market leader *Andhra Prabha* to a second place. *Andhra Patrika* till then a player in the second place was pushed into the fourth place, *Andhra Jyoti* occupying the third place. All these things happened in one stroke—the presence of the new competitor *Eenadu*.

More or less a similar trend continued during the next five years, 1981-85. Total circulation continued to gallop but at a marginally decreasing rate compared to the preceding five years. The total touched seven lakh mark in 1985. Even during that live-year period, there were no drastic changes in the circulation of competitors other than the leader *Eenadu* and presence of the new daily *Udayam*. Nevertheless, the down trend in the circulation of *Andhra Patrika* and *Andhra Bhoomi* commenced in 1985. There was an uptrend in the circulation of *Andhra Jyoti, Andhra Prabha's* circulation remaining stable. *Eenadu's* sales were a near three lakh copies in 1985, though they were around three-and-half lakhs in the earlier two years. This implies *Eenadu* continued to create new customers and the old dailies started struggling to retain their existing customers. *Eenadu* losing its customers in significant numbers in 1985 (61,000 copies) compared to 1984 is attributable to the entry of yet another new paper *Udayam*. Performance standings in terms of market share in 1985 were (per cent) : *Eenadu* 40.8; *Udayam* 27.6; *Andhra Prabha* 15.9; *Andhra Jyoti* 9.9; *Andhra Patrika* 4.3 and *Andhra Bhoomi* 1.5. Circulation cake was growing. *Udayam* emerged No.2 player right on entry. Resultantly, all other competitors' share steeply declined. *Eenadu's* market share which was raced to 60.3 per cent in 1983, was slashed to 40.8 per cent in 1985. However, *Andhra Jyoti's* loss in market shares as minimum (9.9 per cent in 1985 compared to 12.4 in 1980).

What happened during the next 10-year period 1986-95 is not comparable to what happened during the preceding 10 years. The industry started declining in 1986, the total circulation falling below 7,00,000 copies. The industry could regain the 1985-level of circulation only in 1989. Nevertheless, the total circulation fell below seven-lakh mark in the very next year only to be regained in 1993. From then onwards, the industry never looked back, touching 8,41,000 in 1994.

Paper-wise, the older the competitor, the quicker they lost their circulation during those 10 years, by and large. *Andhra Patrika's* circulation was a mere 21,000 copies in 1987, ceased to be an ABC member later, and closed in 1991. The next oldest competitor *Andhra Prabha* not only conceded its second place to the youngest daily *Udayam* in 1985, its circulation dwindled rapidly to a mere 52,000 copies in 1995. *Andhra Bhoomi* remained a nominal non-serious competitor as before. *Udayam* was closed in 1995, losing its second place to *Andhra Jyoti* in 1988.

During this spell of 10 years, *Andhra Jyoti* improved its market standing remarkably in terms of circulation. Its sales were more than doubled in 1988 and 1989, compared to 1985. An all time record circulation of 1,76,000 copies in 1988, a near repeat performance in the following year and a one-and-half lakh plus copies circulation in 1990 and 1991 were the significant achievements *of Andhra Jyoti. Andhra Jyoti*'s market share in 1988 was 25 per cent, the largest ever for that paper. The market share hovered around 23 per cent during the next three years. However, in 1995 its circulation stood at 1,32,000 copies, representing a market share of 15.2 per cent.

Focussing on the market leader, there were ups and downs in the circulation of *Eenadu*. The circulation falling below three-lakh mark in 1985, the paper struggled to regain it only in 1989 and the paper never looked back later, touching a four-lakh mark in 1993 and a five-lakh mark in the next year. *Udayam*, the new competitor and *Andhra Jyoti* placed No. 2 might have gained the temporary losses in the circulations of *Eenadu*. In 1995, *Eenadu's* market share was 63.9 per cent.

Coming to 1996, *Vaartha* entered the market straight away taking the second place, pushing *Andhra Jyoti* to the third place with a claimed circulation of 1,75,000 copies.

Competitive Evaluation

An attempt is made to examine the implications of the foregoing analysis to the competitors in the market be examined. A tremendous potential for Telugu dailies exists in the market. Reluctance of the people to buy the existing dailies is no indication of this potential. Such a reluctance may signify the rejection of such dailies, as they are, by the prospective customers. But whenever publishers came out with a new daily, keeping in mind the ultimate goal of satisfaction of the customer's wants, there was overwhelming response and enthusiasm in receiving such products. This is what happened to *Eenadu* since its appearance in the marketplace, keeping on attracting new customers in the beginning and for longer years that followed, without taking away many of them from the existing dailies, emphasise the potentiality of the Telugu newspaper market. This drives home the importance of researching into the non-readers of the newspapers. Non-readers are never a non-factor in newspaper business. Inquiry into the causes of their indifference, if not aversion, to the newspapers brings to light the weaknesses of the existing newspapers and the inabilities of their publishers. If such of those weaknesses are corrected, the market may be able to transform the latent sales potential into a newspaper boom. After all, with few exceptions here and there, non-readers are in a great majority in the Indian conditions. They should not be written off, particularly those with enough of literacy levels, incomes, and willingness to spend, as the nonlovers of the newspapers. If the newspaper business realises this and if it unravels what is in the mind of such a non-reader then it looks as if the sky is the limit for the growth of the newspaper. It is not to neglect the research into the present readers. It is the other side of the same coin. Newspaper business enjoys certain natural advantages. From the view point of customer, the unit of purchase and unit price are small in newspaper business. The trade usually offers a facility of one month credit to the customers in India. Very few consumer products enjoy such advantages which make the new product adoption process easier. This was also reflected in the large inaugural sales of *Udayam* and *Vaartha,* besides *Eenadu.* So to say, newness is one thing which the non-readers like most on their initiation into newspaper buying. This is a boon to those venturing into this business line.

However, the analysis of Tables 4.2 and 4.3 did not establish that the readers dislike easily the newspapers they were buying already. Even in the face of fierce competition from *Eenadu,* the old papers retained their customers nearly for a decade, though their market shares declined drastically in view of the galloping sales of the new competitor. This is a unique advantage for the existing firms in newspaper business. The older the firm, the longer is its staying power, during which time it could regroup its resources in effectively meeting the competition. But if the staying power is mistaken as the firm's enduring strength it borders on complacency leading to the onslaught of competition and ultimate disaster. *Andhra Patrika* ended like that and *Andhra Prabha* and *Andhra Bhoomi* also appear to be sailing dangerously. Because *Udayam* existed for a brief period its staying power withstanding competition also remained short, ultimately resulting in its closure sooner. *Andhra Jyoti,* though slept over competition initially, did not keep quite later. As such it is existing with greater respectability compared to the other runners-up.

Winning customer confidence by gaining product acceptability on a wider scale on launching a newspaper and occupying a coveted position in performance standings are not games of chance. They are the fruits of years of strategic planning and hard work that are put into the marketing efforts. But such initial successes alone do not automatically bring continued patronage of customers to a newspaper. *Eenadu's* experience is a pointer in this regard. Six-year time lag to reach a two-lakh plus sales mark in 1980, a nine-year time lag to reach a three-lakh mark in 1983 and a nineteen-year time lag in reaching a four-lakh mark in 1993 amply demonstrate this. At the same time, there were also several patches of reduced circulations, as was observed earlier. What the daily did to increase its sales will be taken up later in this section. In the absence of such continued marketing efforts *Udayam* faded away, despite its initial success. Even if the young players succeed in pushing up their paper's circulation considerably in initial years, that alone may not be adequate for its long run survival. So what is equally important to the runner-up firms as in case of the market leader is their advertising revenue. As such one should be cautious in jumping to the conclusions basing on circulation figures in such cases.

2. Transition to Customer-Orientation

Hitherto we have learnt what changes occurred in the market for Telugu newspapers. Let us know now how these changes took place during the last 25 years. The process of transforming the Telugu newspaper market into customer-orientation in a significant way was initiated from the precincts of *Eenadu* by its founder Ramoji Rao, a small name then, whether he really intended it or not, at that point of time.

It is interesting to examine how Ramoji Rao, the founder of *Eenadu* turned his paper into Andhra Pradesh's most popular daily. Hailing from an agricultural family in the Krishna district, he drifted into advertising, in the late 1950s in Delhi "like a fish to water".[21] As noted earlier, in the preceding chapter,[22] he became an addict of Delhi's rich newspaper culture, unable to live without a clutch of morning newspapers. In 1962, Ramoji Rao shifted to Hyderabad, the new capital of Andhra Pradesh where he established a chit fund firm, Margadarsi. Margadarsi Chit Funds eventually became the base for an array of other businesses along with

Eenadu including pickles, hotels, shipping and film production and distribution. In 1969, Ramoji Rao started *Annadata*, a monthly magazine on farming in Telugu. During his frequent business trips to Visakhapatnam in the late 1960s and early 1970s in connection with the construction of a star hotel, he had noticed that the only newspapers available in the city were the so-called "dak" or evening editions of Telugu dailies published in Vijayawada, 350 kilometres away, which reached Visakhapatnam nearly a day after they had gone to press. Thus Visakhapatnam was a place peculiarly ill-suited to satisfy Ramoji Rao's addiction to newspapers. But its geography attracted him. Being a centre of a rich rural hinterland, Visakhapatnam was fast emerging as an industrial city with a growing naval base.

At that time (1974), the newspaper capital of Andhra Pradesh was Vijayawada. While *Andhra Prabha* was published from Vijayawada (90,000 copies) and Bangalore (15,500 copies), *Andhra Patrika* (41,900 copies) and *Andhra Jyoti* (24,900 copies) were published from Vijayawada. *Andhra Bhoomi* was published from Hyderabad (15,300 copies).[23] Explaining the rationale behind this situation, C.V.H. Rao, a veteran journalist and editor commented, "... Newspapers published from places such as Vijayawada can command convenient and easy transport facilities for distribution in different districts inevitably secure the larger share in circulation. These facilities are not enjoyed even to a smaller extent by papers published even from the state capital.[24]

Daily newspaper, however, is a highly perishable product which needs to be delivered to the news-hungry reader at the earliest with the latest news. Here the creative marketer in Ramoji Rao "smelt an opportunity".[25] He suggested his friend K.L.N. Prasad, the founder *of Andhra Jyoti* to launch an edition from Visakhapatnam. But Prasad ridiculed the idea by saying "This is a newspaper business, not a chit fund business.[26] Then Ramoji Rao decided to go ahead and in 1974, he started a newspaper from Visakhapatnam with a print order of 4,500 copies. Ramoji Rao coined a distinct brand name for the paper —*Eenadu,* thereby deviating from his predecessors who inevitably put the word "Andhra" in the brand names of their papers. The readers of Visakhapatnam delighted to receive a new newspaper that would reach their doorsteps by the crack of the dawn. Its emphasis on local news, its language and get-up made it the most popular daily in the region. The paper started with hand composing of type and was printed on an ancient flatbed rotary press bought secondhand from Kerala.[27] *Eenadu* launched its second edition in 1975 from Hyderabad "in spite of Vijayawada being a more potential town"[28] *Eenadu* enrolled itself as a member of the ABC in the very next year (1976). And *Andhra Prabha* which was publishing from Bangalore and Vijayawada started its third edition from Hyderabad in April 1977. *Eenadu's* third edition was launched from Vijayawada in May 1978, thereby "entering Andhra's largest market from an established position of strength.[29] By 1978, *Eenadu* was the largest selling paper (1,27,000 copies) in the state, registering a market share of 35 per cent followed by *Andhra Prabha* with 32.2 per cent of market share (1,22,000 copies). *Andhra Jyoti* established a lead over the pioneer *Andhra Patrika.*

The early 1980s provided a much needed boost to the circulation of Telugu dailies. The political excitement among the Telugu people following the formation of the Telugu Desam regional party in 1982 by N.T. Rama Rao created a tremendous interest in newspaper reading. For the last six months of 1981, the combined circulation of the five Telugu dailies, namely, *Eenadu, Andhra Prabha, Andhra Jyoti, Andhra Patrika* and *Andhra Bhoomi* was 3,95,730 copies.[30] For the same period a year later it was 4,72,704 copies, a rise of 19.45 per cent.[31] By the end of 1983, it had reached 5,66,756, an increase of 43.2 per cent (or 1,71,026 copies) in two years.

Interestingly, it was *Eenadu* which capitalised most on the political excitement among the Telugu people as it accounted for over 81 per cent (or 1,39,724 copies) of such increased circulation.

Further, *Eenadu* brought on Triupati to the Telugu newspaper map when it started its operations in June 1982 therefrom. This step enabled the paper to cover both the Rayalaseema region and neighbouring Tamil Nadu, with its large Telugu population.

The launch of *Udayam* on December 29, 1984 from two publication centres of Vijayawada and Hyderabad simultaneously is a noteworthy feature in the history of Telugu newspaper business. Founded by a popular film director Dasari Narayana Rao, the new paper was edited by Anne Bhavani Koteswara Prasad (A.B.K.Prasad) who is known as "the man with the golden touch"[32] in industry circles. Interestingly, he served *Eenadu* as its founder editor and hence was instrumental in its success. After *Eenadu* had been quickly established, he moved out in 1977. Then followed a succession of jobs until 1983 when he found an opportunity to edit a new daily, *Udayam*. Once again, the abilities of A.B.K. Prasad were well-reflected in the initial circulation of *Udayam* when it was more than two-lakh copies.[33] In fact, *Udayam* is accredited as the first news daily in the country which achieved a phenomenal circulation of two lakh plus copies soon after its inception. The marketing executive of *Andhra Jyoti*, confessed that the new daily did what the other long-established papers could not think of as *Udayam* ventured to position itself directly against the market leader, *Eenadu*.[34] *Udayam* commenced its third edition at Tirupati from July 1986 and with its three publication centres, it became No.2 newspaper in Telugu with 1,30,000 copies (20.8 per cent of market share), pushing aside *Andhra Prabha* (94,000 copies or 15.1 per cent of market share) to the third spot. Following a dispute with Dasari Narayana Rao, A.B.K.Prasad, taking along with him his team of followers moved to *Andhra Jyoti* in mid-1986 and he took over the editorial reigns of *Andhra Jyoti*, which until then had been published only from Vijayawada. He was instrumental in the paper commencing edition from Hyderabad (1986) and Tirupati (1987). So dramatic was *Andhra Jyoti's* upsurge that it overtook *Udayam* for No.2 spot within a year of A.B.K.'s taking over. Its circulation rose by 2.34 times to 1,56,767 copies in 1987 from a mere 66,962 copies a year ago.[35] The circulation of *Udayam* stood at 1,23,639 copies at the close of 1987.[36]

Meanwhile *Andhra Prabhas* sales slashed by 18.3 per cent in just one year in 1986 (circulation: 94,000 copies). Thereafter *Andhra Prabha* had been showing consistency in losing sales on continuously despite commencement of two more new publication centres in Vizianagaram (later it was shifted to Visakhapatnam) in 1985 and Chennai in 1988. During the period 1985-90, the circulation of *Eenadu* fluctuated between 2.67 lakh (1987) and 3.11 lakh copies (1989). During the period its market share ranged from 40.8 to 46.8 per cent.

A.B.K. Prasad, after serving *Andhra Jyoti* about two-and-half years, left it in November 1988 to join *Andhra Bhoomi*. The 28 year old daily then had been languishing, and over the last couple of years, its circulation had been limited to only 14,000 copies. A.B.K. galvanized this sleepy Telugu daily into the launching of Vijayawada and Visakhapatnam editions in 1988. Until then the paper was publishing only from Hyderabad.

In 1988, the publishers of *Eenadu* revamped the week-end Sunday supplement by offering a 32 page demy sized magazine which was of general interest rather than political in content. By 1988, *Eenadu* commanded 40.3 per cent of market share but its circulation started dwindling from 3,56,000 copies in 1984 to 2,83,000 copies in 1988, thereby registering a fall of 20.5 per cent between the years. On the other hand, *Andhra Jyoti's* increased circulation of 1,76,000 copies in 1988 speaks of the narrowing gap between the No. 1 and No. 2 newspapers. Perhaps this motivated Ramoji Rao of *Eenadu* to think in terms of expanding his market. Then he conceived the idea of district supplements in tabloid size which would be given for every district along with the main newspaper. The district supplements carry only district news. The state, national and international news are carried in the main newspaper. In addition to 23 districts of Andhra Pradesh, separate supplements are launched to cover the Telugu-speaking border areas of Tamil Nadu, Karnataka and Orissa as well as city supplements for Vijayawada, Hyderabad and Visakhapatnam. One big advantage of the district or city supplement is that advertising in *Eenadu* is now within the reach of almost every potential advertiser. The content of *Eenadu* has been continually upgraded. In 1990, a business page was introduced - for the first time in a Telugu newspaper - and this was expanded to two pages by 1992. *Eenadu* further started a cinema page in 1991 and an exclusive women's page *Vasundhara* in 1992. It has also features on educational and career counselling *(Pratibha)* and computers (computer chitchat). And mostly these features appear regularly on every day in *Eenadu* nowadays. The details of all these new features as market segmentation strategies are further elaborated in the next chapter.

But such content upgradation alone may not suffice to expand a newspaper's market. The newspaper should reach the reader fast with the latest possible news. Till 1991, *Eenadu* had been publishing from four centres; *Andhra Prabha* five; *Andhra Jyoti*, *Andhra Bhoomi* and *Udayam* three each and *Andhra Patrika* two. All these 20 editions were coining only from seven cities of Vijayawada (6), Hyderabad (6), Visakhapatnam (2), Tirupati (3), Vizianagaram (1), Chennai (1) and Bangalore (1). Ramoji Rao realised that this leaves large areas of the state uncovered. To carry the newspaper closer to readers and create new readers *Eenadu* started as many as six more publication centres, in 1990s, from different strategic locations of the state. The fifth edition of *Eenadu* was launched from Ananthapur on 24th February 1991, which was the first ever daily from Ananthapur. This consolidated its hold over Rayalaseema, along with the Tirupati edition. Then *Eenadu* started its sixth centre from Karimnagar on 30th March 1992 for the sole benefit of its north Telangana readers.[37] At that time, *Eenadu* commanded 72 per cent of the total readership of all the Telugu newspapers.[38] Within six months of launching the Karimnagar centre, *Eenadu* commenced its seventh one on 24th September 1992 from Rajahmundry which is located in the rich coastal region. Understandably, it is from this day, *Eenadu* started offering an exclusive daily page Vasundhara for the Telugu women. *Eenadu* further commenced three more new centres at Suryapet and Guntur in 1996, and at Nellore in 1998. The Suryapet edition covers the districts of Khammam and Nalgonda of the Telangana region, the Guntur edition covers the coastal districts of Guntur and Prakasam and the Nellore edition covers the neighbouring areas of Nellore district.

The ultimate test of any newspaper is the circulation it generates. In this, *Eenadu* is far ahead of the competition (see Tables 4.2 and 4.3). While *Eenadu* remained as the tallest market leader since 1978, the other dailies have been struggling under its shadow.

How the sweat and toil of *Eenadu*'s marketing efforts bear fruit in terms of circulation is depicted, *inter alia*, in Table 4.4 for selected years, along with average annual percentage changes in Table 4.5. Such condensed data enables to identify the paper-wise circulation trends that were emerging broadly, instead of a microscopic view of year-by year trends of 6.54 lakh copies of sales it captured by 1997, 31.3 per cent of them (2,05,000 copies) were netted even by 1980 i.e., by the sixth year of its existence. Such initial instant successes are unusual. Between the initial years 1976 and 1980 the average annual percentage change in circulation was as high as 69.9 per cent. The subsequent circulation fetes were nowhere near this mark. Retaining the market wrested in the initial years on the one hand, and keeping on improving it year after year on the other, require strategic planning and canny marketing sense. Phenomenal successes in the marketplace require phenomenal marketing efforts. For example, *Eenadu* took five years time to sell 90,000 copies extra between 1980 (2,05,000 copies) and 1985 (2,95,000 copies). Further, the average annual percentage change in circulation was lowest for the years between 1985 and 1990 (0.4 per cent). However, the years 1993 and 1994 received big circulation jumps of 24.7 and 22.2 per cent, respectively. During all other selected years, such a change varied between 3.9 and 9.9 per cent.

The aforesaid Tables 4.4 and 4.5 further show comparative standings of the dailies in their circulation and also where they stand in comparison with the industry's performance in marketing. The former table gives the circulations in absolute figures, whereas the latter table shows the average annual percentage changes in circulation for the corresponding years. These two tables, particularly Table 4.5, very clearly shows *Eenadu* as a distinctive mountain with peaks high and low in the Telugu newspaper market compared to all its competitors in the selected years. There the average annual percentage change in circulation did never go to a sub-zero level. As is already learnt, such changes were as high as 69.9 per cent that too for a stretch of four years (1976-80) and it was 20 per cent plus for certain years. Now let *Eenadu*'s marketing performance be compared with the total performance of Telugu newspaper business.

Table 4.4

Circulation of Telugu Dailies in Selected Years: 1970-97

(Copies in thousands)

Year	*Andhra Patrika*	*Andhra Prabha*	*Andhra Jyoti*	*Andhra Bhoomi*	*Eenadu*	*Uday-am*	*Vaar-tha*	*Industry Total*
1970	44	104	28	18	—	—		194
1975	39	103	27	16	54[a]	—		230
1980	39	122	54	15	205	—		435
1985	31	115	72	11	295	200		724
1990	20	70	155	18	301	121		685
1991	18	51	169	12	326	120		696
1992		55	140	12	339	118		664
1993		53	132	15	413	119		742
1994		56	130	20	517	118		841
1995		52	132	20	557	110		871
1996		38	118	24	595	—	175	950
1997		32	115	20	654	—	163	984

Note: 1976 figures, a member of the ABC only since then.
Source: Compiled from *ABC Half Yearly Reports* (figures for both the half years are averaged). Audit Bureau of Circulations, Mumbai. (Condensed from Table 4.2)

The industry as a whole experienced a decline in sales in tenns of selected years twice, once in 1990 covering a stretch of the previous five years and second time in 1992, thus recording a negative change in average annual sales. Even during such years the sales of *Eenadu* showed positive signs. Further, the average annual percentage changes of *Eenadu* were miles ahead of such changes in the total industry, comparing favourably in all the years. For example, 17.8 per cent average annual change in the industry's sales by 1980 corresponds to 69.9 per cent change in *Eenadu*. All other papers

Table 4.5

Average Annual Changes in Circulation of Telugu Dailies during Selected Intervals: 1970-97

Year	*Andhra Patrika*	*Andhra Prabha*	*Andhra Jyoti*	*Andhra Bhoomi*	*Eenadu*	*Udayam*	*Vaartha*	*Industry Total*
	Average annual change in circulation (per cent)							
1970	—	—	—	—	—	—		—
1975	-2.3	-0.2	-0.7	-2.2	—	—		3.7
1980	0.0	3.7	20.0	-1.3	69.9[a]	—		17.8
1985	-4.1	-1.1	6.7	-5.3	8.7	—		13.2
1990	-7.0	-.7.8	23.1	12.7	0.4	-7.9		-1.0
1991	-10.0	-27.2	9.0	-33.3	8.3	-0.8		1.6
1992	—	7.8	-17.2	0.0	3.9	-1.6		-4.6
1993	—	-3.6	-.5.7	25.0	24.7	0.8		11.7
1994	—	5.7	-1.5	33.3	22.2	-0.8		13.3
1995	—	-7.2	1.5	0.0	7.7	-6.8		3.5
1996	—	-26.9	-10.7	20.0	6.8	—	—	9.0
1997	—	-15.8	-2.6	-16.7	9.9	—	-6.8	3.5

Note: a. Based on 1976 figures.

Source: Based on Table 4.4.

looked like valleys of varying depths on the whole. For most of the years, their average annual percentage changes in circulation were in the sub-zero zones. Sometimes the negative changes were as high as 27 per cent (*Andhra Prabha* in 1991 and 1996) or 33 per cent (*Andhra Bhoomi* in 1991). Among the runner-up firms, *Andhra Jyoti* was better of the lot in circulation changes compared to the industry's standing with more peaks.

To sum up, drastic changes took place in the Telugu newspaper market since 1974. Those days of Telugu readers receiving their dailies only from places outside the state like

Chennai or Bangalore, or from one or two centres within the state like Vijayawada or Hyderabad were gone where the industry was heavily localised. Those days of receiving their daily around noon or late hours in the evening were over, even in the farthest corners of Visakhapatnam and beyond. Their news-mix started slanting towards less of international stories and more of state and local news. The era of either the old players or a chain newspaper dominating the market came to an end, thus the market opened up for new players. Regional newspapers started competing with the English dailies in expanding sales or attracting advertising revenue. Telugu dailies gave up their hesitation to expose the misdeeds of the parties or people in power.

Decisively a new newspaper culture had started taking roots. Newspaper as a business started transforming into customer-orientation from production-orientation. Marketing thus has started arriving to the boardrooms of Telugu newspapers, marking a beginning of the era of competition. For the first time the publishers had started realising that unless they compete with others in customer want-satisfaction, there is no survival. New competitors were there in their wings ready to plunge into the market on a full-scale to try their chances even in a frontal attack even with the established giants. Any competitive position for any player could never be taken for granted as settled. Such a process resulted in the death of two dailies, *Andhra Patrika* and *Udayam,* the former one was the oldest and the latter one though very young, but well-entrenched to fight well.

The sweeping changes in the marketplace augur well to the Telugu newspaper business. A daily started playing only since 1974 soaring to meteoric heights and some too young dailies willing to compete with such a giant are symptoms of good things in store for the Telugu newspaper. Such of those marketing efforts may improve the standing of a Telugu daily vis-a-vis others in terms of circulation and DTP in future. More than a five-fold increase in the total circulation between 1974 and 1997 gives rise to this hope.

Yet, a long way to go, considering even all such improvements in the Telugu newspaper business could not help it to raise from the bottom. What is needed is not just a superlative performance from a lone or very few performers and an eclipse of others. What is further needed is a Malayalam type of market situation, wherein the market shares of top performers were close to each other, as is dealt in the next chapter.[39] Business purpose and marketing sense should seep deep into the minds of all competitors. Marketing battles are fought inside the mind. The mind is the battleground. A terrain that is tricky and difficult to understand. The entire battleground is just six inches wide. This is where the marketing war takes place. One tries to outmanoeuvre and outfight his competitors on a mental mountain about the size of a cantaloupe. A marketing war is a totally intellectual war with a battleground no one has ever seen. It can only be imagined in the mind, which makes marketing warfare one of the most difficult disciplines to learn.[40]

THE FALL OF TWO DAILIES

Hundreds and thousands of business firms come into existence into the world around us, day in and day out. Some firms influence the society in a big way and the others in a small way. For example, if a bank fails, it makes headline news the next day. But the failure of innumerable firms in several lines of business remain unnoticed and unfelt by the society. Viewed in this sense the impact of the newspaper, particularly the one that existed for a long time successfully is immeasurable and if such a newspaper is closed down it is remembered for years to come by several generations of people. As such the death of the newspapers should not be viewed lightly. This section intends to analyse what happened at *Andhra Patrika* and *Udayam*. Obviously, business or product failures are as important an area as their success in the field of management and marketing.

1. Andhra Patrika

Andhra Patrika, the grand old newspaper of the nationalist movement; the lone Telugu daily till 1938; the market leader till 1960, the year in which that position was conceded to *Andhra Prabha;* the No. 2 player till 1976, the year in which that position was lost to *Eenadu;* also lost the No. 3 place to *Andhra Jyoti* in 1978. By then the circulation was 47,000 copies but the market share reduced to 13 per cent. At the time of independence and even by 1960 the circulation was stagnated around that figure. Nonetheless, its market share steeply declined. This implies *Andhra Patrika* lacked the will to improve its sales.

Its Hyderabad edition (1975) could not arrest its declining market share. While the size of the circulation cake of Telugu dailies has been significantly growing, *Andhra Patrika* could not cash on new market opportunities. Its circulation touched an all-time low since independence of just 18,000 copies (2.6 per cent of market share) from two centres in 1991. Its owners stopped paying their dues to the ABC since 1988 and sold the indebted newspaper in 1989. A dispute then arose over whether the purchaser had acquired full legal control of the company. Law suits and questions in the assembly followed, and employees were no longer paid. On certain days the paper even could not be brought out for want of money to buy newsprint. The owners of the paper had left with no choice except to exit from the marketplace in the year 1991.

Although *Andhra Patrika* earned the appreciation of general reading public and media experts as well, for setting up high journalistic standards in Telugu and also for playing a notable role in India's freedom struggle, the paper could not escape from meeting its death in the absence of able management and skilful marketing. Losing market leadership as early as in 1960 while selling 48,000 copies and still retaining the circulation around 40,000 copies till 1984 speaks of the high esteem the subscribers had for *Andhra Patrika*—once a synonym for a newspaper. Irrespective of market share slashing from a near 50 per cent to a mere 6.7 per cent, it should be remembered that the paper could retain its customers in absolute numbers even in the face of massive invasion of the market by the new paper, *Eenadu* since 1974. May be the longer the standing of a paper in the market, the stronger the loyalties of the customers to their newspaper. This enhances the staying power of the firm while encountering competition from the new paper. Such a breathing spell could be utilised to regroup its resources in effectively meeting the competition. The paper failed to exploit such an advantage and after serving the Telugu people for more than 80 years, the era of *Andhra Patrika* came to an end in 1991, living through an era of political movements or social upheavals tougher compared to its survival in the marketing era. *Andhra Patrika*, a star performer of early times, failed in adapting itself to the marketing era, unfortunately. It appears it lost all the marketing wars either with the chain daily *Andhra Prabha* or new papers *Eenadu* or *Udayam* by default rather than by defeat. Defaulting in designing appropriate marketing strategies defensive or offensive spelt disaster to *Andhra Patrika*.

2. *Udayam*

The story of a ten year old *Udayam* reveals how an initially successful daily could lose its grip over the market very quickly, in the absence of proper management. The paper was simultaneously started from two publication centres of Vijayawada and Hyderabad by a popular film director Dasari Narayana Rao in 1984, under the editorship of A.B.K. Prasad, who has "a history of successes".[41] The phenomenal success of *Udayam* is well reflected in its initial circulation figures when the paper achieved the claimed circulation of 2,00,000 copies. Nevertheless, by 1986, ABC confirmed its No. 2 position with only 1,30,000 copies, and the paper began to challenge the market leader *Eenadu* from three publication centres, Tirupati being the new one. In 1988, its standing in the market was reduced to No. 3 position. The paper could not sustain the market expectations for a long period. An undesirable conflict crept in between the publisher Dasari Narayana Rao and the editor A.B.K. Prasad. ABK parted company with Dasari.

Mounting losses as a result of improper management forced Dasari to sell away the paper to Magunta Subbarami Reddy, the chairman-cum-owner of a Rs. 550 crore Balaji group of industries. Subbarami Reddy was elected as a member of the Parliament in 1991 general elections. However, Subbarami Reddy's taking over the reigns of *Udayam* management could not prevent the paper from losing its sales. Its claimed circulation in 1990 was 1,21,000 copies and the down trend continued in the subsequent years.

In an open letter, in 1990, to the reading public, the marketing manager of *Udayam* confessed that the paper is not up to the expectations of its readers in the recent past. In his letter, S.Vijayakumar, marketing manager, honestly confessed the deficiencies of his paper. In his own words, "... It is true. Your *Udayam* has not been reaching your doorstep on time for the past few days. Printing is not clear. Photos are not visible. News is coming late. Some of the features which impressed you in earlier days were stopped. The paper engrossed itself in the circle of problems...".

The letter further elaborated the on-going efforts of the management to give *Udayam* totally a new look and better value for the customer's rupee. They include: an effective news collection network, news analysis by prominent journalists, special pages for specific interest groups such as women, students, businessmen and so on, and, above all, multicolour printing every day.

Subbarami Reddy, the new owner realised that a mere content upgradation was not enough to capture circulation and advertising. Perhaps this prompted Subbarami Reddy to conceive an expansion programme which was estimated to cost Rs. 15 crore. His modest goal was to make *Udayam* regain its No. 2 position. As its name means, he intended his paper reach the nook and corners of the state by the crack of the dawn every day. Apart from the three editions, he planned to launch *Udayam* from seven more centres namely, Visakhapatnam, Rajahmundry, Ongole, Ananthapur, Kurnool, Khammam and Karimnagar.[42] Subbarami Reddy further revealed his plans to acquire *Andhra Patrika* which was closed in 1991 and to launch an altogether new regional English daily *State Express*.[43]

Subbarami Reddy, however, could not translate his dreams into a reality. *Udayam* was closed in 1995. To quote Reddy, who achieved tremendous success in many other fields of business, "Running a newspaper is not an easy job. I have burnt my fingers in this affair and I learnt many lessons from this *(Udayam)* experience."[44]

Udayam's exit leads to some useful inferences. Customers welcome new papers. But if their expectations are not met in want-satisfaction they do not hesitate to give them up. Customer loyalties to a new paper do not last longer as in the case of established papers. Such factors naturally cut short the staying power of the new competitor. This proves the hypothesis that retaining a coveted position is not as easy as attaining it for a new competitor in the market-place. Failure of the attempts of reviving *Udayam* leads to the belief that starting a new paper is easier than that.

The tale of two dailies *Andhra Patrika* and *Udayam* do tell us about the conditions to be fulfilled to produce successful newspapers. Obviously, entrepreneurial acumen and managerial expertise are crucial. Newspapers, as observed by Robin Jeffrey, are thought to influence people: to make them exponents of social reforms or followers of Mahatma Gandhi or, after independence, of particular political parties are goals, like the creation of an Andhra state or prohibition of alcohol. Newspapers also provide a vehicle for protecting one's own interests and menacing the interests of one's adversaries. Newspapers are risky but exhilarating business; but above all they must be business.[45]

VAARTHA MAKES NEWS

By 1995, while two of *Eenadu's* rivals *Andhra Patrika* and *Udayam* had collapsed, the other competitors *Andhra Jyoti* and *Andhra Prabha* were struggling with a low circulation of 1,32,000 (from four centres) and 52,000 (from five centres) copies, respectively. *Eenadu* commanded 63.9 per cent of circulation of Telugu dailies.

No doubt, the size of the circulation cake of Telugu dailies has been growing over the last quarter century (Table 4.4). This is a healthy sign indeed for the industry. At times the average annual change in circulations was as high as 17.8 per cent i.e., during the years 1975-80. Annual changes were also significant in the years 1985, 1993 and 1994 with 13.2, 11.7 and 13.3 per cent, respectively. Negative annual changes were exceptional and insignificant, though the positive changes for most of the years did not exceed 4.6 per cent. Newspaper sales nearing one million copies in 1997 from 1.94 lakh copies in 1970 indicates, that the sales of the Telugu newspapers are significantly responding to the marketing efforts of the industry as a whole.

The audited circulation rose by 40.2 per cent to 7,46,000 copies in 1995 from 5,32,000 copies in 1990, despite the closure of two popular dailies *Andhra Patrika* and *Udayam* during that period. However, as is evident from the ABC figures, while *Eenadu* captured 2,56,000 additional subscribers during the period 1990-95, its competitors *Andhra Prabha, Andhra Jyoti* and *Andhra Bhoomi* lost a total number of 42,000 subscribers from their fold during the same period.

Obviously, more Telugu people were reading newspapers than ever before. In some ways, there is no surprise in it. In fact, the transformation in technology allowed the production of faster and more attractive newspapers. The state of Andhra Pradesh experienced striking educational changes in the 1970s and 1980s. Between 1971 and 1991, the number of people in Andhra Pradesh who could read a newspaper more than doubled - from 10.9 million to 24.9 million. Thus by 1990s, Telugu newspapers had a potential audience 30 per cent greater than the population of Australia.[46]

Population alone, however, does not determine whether people can afford the price of a newspaper. But in the 1980s, slender improvements in living standards, reducing those living below a miserable poverty line to an estimated 30 per cent of India's total population, also occurred in Andhra Pradesh. According to an estimate, the number of households with an annual income of more than Rs. 36,000 grew from 3,09,000 in 1988 to 19,35,000 in 1993, an increase of six-fold, or from two per cent of all households to 13 per cent.[47] Even if these figures seem too high to be, purchasing power unquestionably increased.[48]

Realising the untapped market potentiality for a Telugu newspaper, A.B.K. Prasad conceived an idea of starting a totally new paper. Interestingly, over the last many years, the strongest opposition to Ramoji Rao and *Eenadu* has come not so much from a newspaper group as from a journalist, A.B.K. Prasad.[49] In 1993, ABK felt the need for a new newspaper.[50] He noticed that the five leading dailies in the state with their 19 editions had a combined circulation of only 6.5 lakh at that time. Even if the readership is put around 65 lakh, it was only about 25 per cent of the literate population in the state. In other words, three quarters of the literates were not serviced by any Telugu newspaper.[51] Besides, all the dailies together cover only 500 of over 1,100 revenue mandals[52] in the state in terms of reportage and circulation. A solid chunk of 600 mandals remains to be tapped. "It depends on how well we can create the market. The ability to wean readers of other publications comes much later," felt ABK.[53]

In its pre-launch campaign for *Vaartha*, the ABK publications described the peculiar condition of the Telugu newspaper industry: "While only one paper is dominating, the others are losing their ground and one or two papers are even collapsing .... In such a monopoly situation, people are left with no choice except to buy one particular paper that has no competition..." After much fanfare, the new daily *Vaartha* was launched from nine publication centres of Andhra Pradesh simultaneously in January 1996 (see Table 4.1). The paper earned the distinction of the first daily in the country that was started from so many centres. Thus, *Vaartha* was aggressively positioned against the market leader *Eenadu*. At that time *Eenadu* was publishing from seven centres with a combined circulation of 5,67,798 copies, *Andhra Jyoti* from four centres with 1,34,034 and *Andhra Prabha* from five centres with 52,636.[54] Countering the challenger *Vaartha's* strategy, *Eenadu* had started two more publication centres in 1996 at Suryapet and Guntur, and their tenth centre in the next year at Nellore. Earlier in the same year *Vaartha* started its tenth edition at Anantapur. Even by adding up two more centres, *Eenadu* could increase the additional circulation of only 36,314 copies (6.3 per cent gain) by the end of 1996.[55] At the same time, *Andhra Jyoti*[56] and *Andhra Prabha*[57] lost 15,704 (11.7 per cent loss) and 18,645 (35.4 per cent loss) copies, respectively. These figures suggest that the new daily *Vaartha* did affect the circulation of existing dailies including that of *Eenadu*. In other words, the paper soon emerged as No. 2 daily as the industry sources confirmed its claimed circulation of 1,75,000 copes.[58] But *Vaartha's* management is not happy over its circulation performance, as 10 publication centres produce not more than 1,75,000 copies, the average circulation per centre being less than 20,000 copies, compared to *Eenadu's* circulation of 67,000 copies per centre. However, growing circulation, in the absence of desired advertising support, means inviting further losses. The new comer has to go a long way to bridge the circulation gap between it and an established, strong market leader *Eenadu*. The paper is still suffering from its teething problems.

THE FUTURE OF THE RUNNER-UP PAPERS

With the exit of *Andhra Patrika* in 1991 and *Udayam* in 1995, it may be of relevant to analyse what is in store for the other runner-up firms in the Telugu newspaper industry. The term runners-up in the marketing terminology is used to include all the competitors in the market other than the market leader.

The Arthur D.Little management consulting firm sees firms as occupying one of six competitive positions in their industry:[59]

Dominant: This firm controls the behaviour of other competitors and has a wide choice of strategic options.

Strong: This firm can take independent action without endangering its long-term position and can maintain its long-term position regardless of competitors' actions.

Favourable: This firm has a strength that is exploitable in particular strategies and has more than-average opportunity to improve its position.

Tenable: This firm is performing at a sufficiently satisfactory level to warrant continuing in business, but it exists at the sufferance of the dominant company and has a less than-average opportunity to improve its position.

Weak: This firm has unsatisfactory performance but an opportunity exists for improvement and it must change or else exit.

Nonviable: This firm has unsatisfactory performance and no opportunity for improvement.

Every firm or business unit can recognise itself in one of these competitive positions. The business unit's competitive position, along with its stage in the product life cycle, will help it decide whether to invest, maintain, harvest or exit from the industry.[60] Accordingly, it is needless to add that the runner-up firms of the Telugu newspaper industry fall into one of the five categories last mentioned, the leader occupying the dominant competitive position.

Classification of competitive positions such as this or a different classification that suits other industries may not exactly suit the newspaper industry, in view of the added dimension of advertising revenue. It is further complicated considering that market shares in advertising revenue are not comparable to their corresponding market shares in circulation usually.

Advertising revenue is a high-low business as it is related to circulation. The winner or the leader takes away a very large chunk of the advertising cake, leaving a relatively small slice to No. 2 competitor and a very paltry proportion to be shared by the rest of the competitors. Nevertheless, such a classification may help to analyse the strengths or weaknesses of the Telugu newspaper firms in the present study. But one should be very cautious in labelling the competitors by their competitive positions they are currently occupying. Labels signify their current status as in any other game-in-progress. For example, in a tennis match a player may be behind two sets, also trailing in the third set, may still turn the tables to snatch a victory by winning the last three sets to make it a five set thriller. Such reverses are also natural in business games. *Andhra Patrika* has the longest innings as a dominant competitor first and a strong competitor later, but never attempted to stage a comeback. *Andhra Prabha* was also found in similar positions for long. It can try to stage a comeback to such positions of glory. Nothing is impossible. New competitor *Eenadu* so soon coming to the dominant position proved it. Such a feat could be repeated by a runner-up firm or another new firm.

What is significant is competitors' attitudes and their reactions to what happens in the market place in the years ahead. What matters most is how they perceive and what they do tomorrow, not what their competitive strengths were yesterday. As at the end of the 1997, *Andhra Bhoomi's* competitive position was deteriorating faster in terms of market share, despite its stagnant circulation more or less (Tables 4.2 and 4.3). It appears its competitive position at best may be described as weak, if not nonviable considering the publisher's main interest in *Deccan Chronicle. Vaartha* though youngest, appeared to be the strongest of all runner-up firms on the basis of its circulation of 1,63,000 copies in 1997. Considering its heavy investment within a short time in establishing ten publication centres, its sales potential appears to be more than its actual circulation figures. If it could transform its potentiality into a reality, *Vaartha's* competitive position could be classified either as strong or at least favourable. By and large, its competitive position looks like hope of tomorrow.

Let us examine the prospects of *Andhra Prabha,* another runner-up firm. A 40-year old daily then, *Andhra Prabha* lost its market leadership to the 4-year prodigy player *Eenadu* in 1978 itself (Tables 4.2 and 4.3). Things did not stop there. It further lost its No. 2 position in 1985 to the newly born *Udayam* and in 1987 *Andhra Prabha* even lost its No. 3 position to *Andhra Jyoti* when the latter achieved a circulation of 1,22,000 copies, compared to 82,000 copies of the former.

Despite *Andhra Prabha* losing its market leadership in 1978, it continued to maintain its circulation of one lakh plus copies till 1985 through several jerks. The fall in sales was steeper and steeper through 1990s, ultimately reducing to a mere 32,000 copies in 1997. *Andhra Prabha* has started losing its market share with the entry of *Eenadu.* A circulation of 1,04,000 copies of *Andhra Prabha* meant 53.6 per cent of market share in 1970. More or less the same circulation of 1,03,000 copies in 1975 meant a market share of 46.8 per cent and 1,17,000 copies of circulation in 1978 meant only 32.2 per cent market share, the year in which it lost its leadership to *Eenadu* having 35 per cent of market share. A similar circulation of 1,15,000 copies in 1985 meant only 15.9 per cent of the market share. This speaks how complacent *Andhra Prabha* was for such a long period in the face of the market leader growing from strength to strength. This also speaks of *Andhra Prabha's* customers staying with it undisturbed by other temptations in the market. But the publisher did not realise that unless they put in the extra effort to satisfy their customers they could neither retain them nor attract new customers. And *Andhra Prabha* paid the penalty. Since 1986, there was a steep decline in circulation. In 1991 they could sell only 51,000 copies, making a market share of 7.3 per cent. For such a complacency of this, *Andhra Patrika* faced death in that year. In 1997, *Andhra Prabha*'s sales were a mere 32,000 copies from five centres, market share being 3.3 per cent. In other words, *Andhra Prabha* sold just one copy for every 20.4 copies of *Eenadu*. Where it leads to is anybody's guess. It cannot be said with confidence that its competitive position is tenable. At best, it is in a weak position, implying the firm has unsatisfactory performance but an opportunity exists for improvement and it must change or else exit.

Being a member of India's largest chain newspaper group, *Andhra Prabha* is backed with tremendous resources—technological and financial. But a newspaper to flourish in today's customer-oriented environment requires more than physical resources. The future of *Andhra Prabha* depends on the mindset of its top management and the degree of their commitment in delivering value for their target markets better than their competitors.

Finally, let us analyse the competitive position of *Andhra Jyoti*, another runner-up firm placed at No. 3. The circulation trends of *Andhra Jyoti* suggest that this paper's position is not as pathetic as that of *Andhra Prabha*, still commanding a circulation of one lakh plus copies in 1997. In the 15-year period till 1975 (Tables 4.2 and 4.3), *Andhra Jyoti* was poorly pushed away by the largest selling daily *Andhra Prabha* and the oldest daily *Andhra Patrika* in No. 2 position. For example, in 1975, while *Andhra Jyoti's* circulation was 27,000 copies (12.3 per cent of market share) from only one centre Vijayawada, *Andhra Prabha's* circulation was 1,03,000 copies (46.8 per cent of market share) with two editions from Vijayawada and Bangalore; and *Andhra Patrika*'s was 39,000 copies (17.7 per cent) also with two editions from Vijayawada and Hyderabad. *Andhra Jyoti* took more than 15 years time to start its second publication centre in Hyderabad in 1986 and the third one at Tirupati in 1987. Its fourth centre was set up in 1991 in Visakhapatnam.

By and large, competition from new entrants in 1974 (*Eenadu*) or in 1984 (*Udayam*) did not deter *Andhra Jyoti's* circulation in numbers. Over the years the paper went on to increase its sales steadily. Resultantly, its market share did not slide down as it happened in case *of Andhra Prabha*. Its market share of 14.4 per cent (28,000 copies) in 1970 was retained more or less in 1978 (52,000 copies or 14.3 per cent of market share). Despite the competition from *Eenadu* and *Udayam* in the years that followed, circulation was never below 46,000 copies. In 1985 its circulation was 72,000 copies, market share being 9.9 per cent. To this, one lakh copies were added three years later in 1988 thereby increasing the total to 1,76,000, an all time high for the paper and its market share also touched an all time high of 25 per cent. The paper became No.2 player in that year and retained that position till the entry of *Vaartha* in 1996. In 1997 *Andhra Jyoti* sold one copy for every 5.6 copies of *Eenadu*. But its circulation started declining since 1989. So also the market share, making it 11.7 per cent in 1997 with 1,15,000 copies. This record of the paper publishing from four centres is far from discouraging. The paper appeared to have been fighting not only to retain its customers but also to attract new subscriptions. Though started declining in recent years, such a steady circulations are expected to bring respectable share in advertising revenue. The publishers confirmed that though *Vaartha's* entry made them No. 3 player since 1996, still they lead in the advertising revenue among the runner-up firms. It may be inferred that the advertisers of *Andhra Jyoti* seem to be convinced about the quality of its audiences in terms of their socio-economic characteristics. New competitors usually are denied of such an advantage despite their doing well on circulation front.

Such of these strengths of *Andhra Jyoti* make one to believe that the paper is in a favourable competitive position. It implies this firm has a strength that is exploitable in particular strategies and has more than average opportunity to improve its position. If its publishers also perceive its strength like this, great prospects are in store for this 38-year old paper. On the other hand, if they assume that they are occupying a tenable competitive position much cannot be expected. Thus improvement is a matter of top management's perception to *Andhra Jyoti.*

To sum up, at *Andhra Jyoti,* marketing appears to be a neglected area even today. Its top management lacked vision as well as long-term strategic planning and thus could not succeed in narrowing the wide gap between it and the market leader, particularly since 1990. *Andhra Jyoti* need to plan and implement suitable turn-around strategies in the interest of its long run survival in the marketplace.

References

1. William J. Stanton and Charles Futrell, *op. cit.,* pp. 172-173.
2. Robert D. Buzzell, Bradley T. Gale, and Ralph G.M. Sultan, "Market Share—A Key to Profitability", *Harvard Business Review,* January-February 1975, pp. 97-106. For a summary of the more recent findings, see Robert D. Buzzell and Bradley T. Gale, *The PIMS Principles: Linking Strategy to Performance,* Free Press, New York, 1987.
3. Philip Kotler, *Marketing Management: Analysis, Planning, Implementation and Control, op. cit.,* p. 382.
4. Gray Hamel and C.K. Prahalad, *op. cit.,* pp. 33-34.
5. Includes ABC figures of 5,000 copies in respect of Hyderabad edition and the claimed circulation of Vijayawada, Visakhapatnam and Rajahmundry editions may be on the high side.
6. See Chapter-III.
7. He was the first to court imprisonment for sedition in Andhra area during the *Vandemataram* movement of 1906.
8. P. Rajeswara Rao, "Telugu Dailies", in K.R. Seshagiri Rao (ed.), *op. cit.,* pp. 107-108.
9. D. Anjaneyulu, "Telugu Journalism: A Survey", in K.R. Seshagiri Rao (ed.), *op. cit.,* p. 135.

10. Robin Jeffrey, "Indian Languages Newspapers: 4. Telugu: Ingredients of Growth and Failure", *op.cit.*, p. 192.
11. *Annual Report of the Registrar for Newspapers in India*, Govt. of India, 1958, pp. 91, 251.
12. *A Preliminary List of Circulations Certified for the Six Monthly Audit Period Ended, December 31, 1960*, Audit Bureau of Circulations, Mumbai, p. 2.
13. *A Preliminary List of Circulations Certified for the Six Monthly Audit Period Ended June 30, 1971*, Audit Bureau of Circulations, Mumbai, p. 3.
14. D. Anjaneyulu, "Telugu Journalism: A Survey", in K.R. Seshagiri Rao (ed.), *op. cit.*, p. 132.
15. *Ibid.*
16. C.V.H. Rao, "The Press in Andhra" in K.R. Seshagiri Rao (ed.), *op. cit.*, p. 43.
17. Out of 56, 46 were bilingual papers and 10 multilingual papers.
18. C.V.H. Rao, "The Press in Andhra" in K.R. Seshagiri Rao (ed.), *op. cit.*, p. 41.
19. M. Chalapathi Rau, *Press in India*, Allied, Mumbai, 1968, pp. 144-145.
20. Gary Hamel and C.K. Prahalad, *op. cit.*, p. 34.
21. Robin Jeffrey, "Indian Languages Newspapers: 4, Telugu: Ingredients of Growth and Failure", *op. cit.*, p. 193.
22. See Chapter — III.
23. Circulation figures relate to January-June 1974.
24. C.V.H. Rao, "The Press in Andhra" in K.R. Seshagiri Rao (ed.), *loc. cit.*
25. Mitali Kar, "Meteoric Rise", *A & M*, 15 June, 1994, p. 65.
26. Interview on 25 May, 1990, Appa Rao, Managing Director, Dolphin Hotel, Visakhapatnam.
27. Robin Jeffrey, "Indian Languages Newspapers: 4, Telugu: Ingredients of Growth and Failure", *op. cit.*, p. 193.
28. *Eenadu's* promotion material.

29. *Ibid.*
30. The ABC figures relating to July-December, 1981.
31. The ABC figures relating to July-December, 1982.
32. K. Sai and Brij Bhushan Sahni, "Telugu Press-Colourful Battle", *A & M*, October 1989, p. 28.
33. *Udayam* enrolled itself as a member of ABC in 1986 and continued its membership till the next year only. Except for 1986 and 1987, such of those circulation figures were used as claimed by the paper.
34. Interview dated August 20, 1997, K. Hareram, marketing executive, *Andhra Jyoti*, Vijayawada.
35. ABC figures relating to July-December, 1987 and July-December, 1986.
36. ABC figure relating to July-December, 1987.
37. *Eenadu'u* promotion material.
38. National Readership Survey IV (Quoted from *Eenadu's* promotion material).
39. See Chapter — V.
40. Al Ries and Jack Trout, *Marketing Warfare*, Mcgraw-Hill, New York, 1986, p. 44.
41. Stanely Theodore, "Making News", *The Week*, May 16, 1993, p. 24.
42. *Udayam's* promotion material.
43. Amarnath K. Menon, "*Udayam*—Patrika Rangamlo Kotha Samaram", *India Today* (Telugu), May 21-5 June, 1994, p. 44.
44. *Ibid.*
45. Robin Jeffrey, "Indian Languages Newspapers: 4, Telugu: Ingredients of Growth and Failure", *op. cit.*, p. 193.
46. *Ibid.*, p. 194.
47. S.L. Rao and I. Natarajan, *Indian Market Demographics: The Consumer Classes*, Global Business Press, New Delhi, 1996, p. 77.
48. Robin Jeffrey, "Indian Languages Newspapers: 4, Telugu: Ingredients of Growth and Failure," *op. cit.*, p. 194.

49. K. Sai and Brij Bhushan Sahni, *op. cit.*, p. 28.
50. Stanley Theodore, *op. cit.*, p. 23.
51. *Ibid.*, p. 24.
52. Mandal is a revenue segment of a district.
53. Stanley Theodore, *op. cit.*, p. 24.
54. ABC figures relating to July-December, 1995.
55. The figure represents the circulation gain between July-December, 1995 and July-December, 1996.
56. Its circulation data relating to July-December, 1996 period was not received by the ABC. Hence, the figure represents the circulation loss between July-December, 1995 and January-June, 1996.
57. Its figure represents the circulation loss between July-December, 1995 and July-December, 1996.
58. The paper was not a member of the ABC at that time.
59. See Robert V.L. Wright, *A System for Managing Diversity,* Arthur D.Little, Cambridge, MA, 1974.
60. Philip Kotler, *op. cit.*, p. 374.

5
The Competitive Strategies and Achieving Leadership

The effect of the free play of market forces on the making and unmaking of market leaders through the years, in the Telugu newspaper market, is brought out in the previous chapter. In the process, new players entered the market. Some papers faced death and for some others survival in the newspaper business is still a problem, howsoever undesirable such consequences may be. *Eenadu* ultimately emerged at the top reigning as the market leader since 1978, while others were languishing. This chapter intends to identify and analyse the marketing strategies, in greater detail, which enabled this newspaper to reach such a predominant position in the market. It is also intended to analyse the strengths and weaknesses of the strategies adopted by the other competitors.

(A) Strategies to Conquer

Only such of those strategies that are discernible to an outsider as evident from the product form, its features and contents, the distribution system, market expansion, etc., are taken up for consideration, as stated earlier.[1] A list of the major strategies identified like that is presented in Table 5.1, in chronological order, as far as practicable. *Eenadu's* strategies are given on one side of the table and its competitors' strategies on the opposite side. But they need not necessarily be viewed rigidly as strategies of the market leader and the counter strategies of its competitors, or *vice versa.* Because what is done by the competitors need not be a counter to the leader's strategies. The competitors might have developed their own strategies independent of the leader's actions. Similarly the leader's strategies need not necessarily be a counter to those of the others. It should be remembered that today's market leader *Eenadu* was not the leader from the beginning.

Table 5.1

Marketing Strategies of *Eenadu* and its Competitors since 1974

Eenadu's Strategies	*Its Competitors' Strategies*
1	2
1. Venturing into newspaper business in 1974 from Visakhapatnam, a fast growing industrial centre in the state but a place never before a publication centre, 350 Kms. away from Vijayawada.	1. *Andhra Prabha,* then market leader, entered Visakhaptnam very leisurely in 1985, to launch their edition, losing its leadership to *Eenadu* by 1978. Still late entrants were *Andhra Bhoomi* (1988) and *Andhra Jyoti* (1991).
2. Launched their second edition in 1975 from Hyderabad, the capital city of the state but a place less known for Telugu newspaper business wherefrom *Andhra Bhoomi,* a weak competitor, was playing before.	2. *Andhra Patrika* also entered Hyderabad in the same year. *Andhra Prabha* then also market leader entered in 1977 and *Andhra Jyoti* in 1986 to launch their editions from Hyderabad.
3. After becoming No.2 player in 1976, *Eenadu* further advanced to launch its third edition from Vijayawada in 1978, the nerve centre of Telugu newspapers and	3. Having lost the battles of Visakhapatnam and Hyderabad already, this time they lost the war, by default rather than defeat.

1	2
thereby wresting market leadership the same year.	
4. Having won a decisive war earlier, initiated its fourth edition in 1982 from Tirupati with a determination to come closer to its readers in Rayalaseema and the neighbouring Tamil Nadu.	4. A new player *Udayam* ventures to counter the onslaughts of the market leader by simultaneously entering into Vijayawada and Tirupati in 1983 and thereafter from Hyderabad in 1986, the year in which *Andhra Jyoti* also entered there. *Andhra Jyoti* also appeared in Tirupati in 1987. *Andhra Bhoomi* entered Vijaya-wada and Visakhapatnam in 1988.
5. Markets a wave capitalising on the political excitement that generated on NTR entering into politics in 1982, thus setting the people's personal agenda. The excitement continued in 1984 with the dismissal of democratically elected NTR government. Though the entire press backed NTR and the statewide mass agitation, *Eenadu* was in the forefront. Spearheaded the anti-liquor agitation in 1994, thus once again performing the people's agenda-setting function, particularly of womenfolk. This led the new government after 1994 assembly elections, prohibiting liquor.	5. Others competitors never relised the gravity of the situation and were either indifferent to the political situation or misread the people's mood. Despite the competitors stoutly protesting the dismissal of NTR government, *Eenadu* outclassed them in improving the newspapers sales. Never took the issue so seriously.

1	2
6. In 1988, Sunday supplement was revamped to give it the shape of a magazine, in content and appearance.	6. Competitors remained late and poor imitators in this regard; However, *Vaartha* made a good imitation of it on its entry into the market in 1996.
7. Introduction of 28 tabloid size district or city supplements in 1989.	7. Competitors were several years behind once again to remain as poor imitators. However, *Vaartha* on its entry in 1996 straight away imitated this feature.
8. Interest-zoning was initiated in a big way, keeping in mind varied interests of various groups of readers and advertisers: business page (1990), cinema page (1991), women's page (1992), and several features like career counselling, computer chit chat and several others in the subsequent years.	8. Needless to add the competitors reacted slowly and poorly. But *Vaartha* introduced all such features on its entry in 1996.
9. After consolidation, yet another phase of expansion began, by entering Anantapur (1991), Karimnagar and Rajahmundry (both in 1992), places hitherto unknown for newspaper publication.	9. Me-too appearance by *Andhra Bhoomi* (1994) and maiden appearance of *Vaartha* in Rajahmundry (1996). *Vaartha* also entered Anantapur in 1998.
10 Expansion unending, *Eenadu* entered Suryapet and Guntur (both in 1996), and Nellore (1998) he places new to newspaper publishing.	10. Though *Eenadu's* strategies were countered by several competitors several times in several ways, a major offensive worth the name was initiated by a new

1	2
	player *Vaartha* in 1996 by launching simultaneously from nine places on entry and from 10th place subsequently.
11. Other strategies: Exploiting the use of colour in printing, effective use of the cartoons, investigative reportage, credibility, effective presentation of news in a sweet language etc.	11. In matters such of these, the competitors are generally influenced by the trends set by the leader or other better competitors in that matter.

Some of the major marketing strategies employed by *Eenadu* are analysed, one by one, in the six sub-sections that follow. Further, what the other competitors did is also analysed in the corresponding sub-section.

1. Gateway of the Entry: Flanking Attack (1974)

Let us look into item No. 1 in the aforesaid table. As is already learnt, Ramoji Rao chose to launch his paper *Eenadu* in 1974 from Visakhapatnam, located in the north-eastern region of the state that was totally neglected by the long-established dailies like *Andhra Prabha, Andhra Patrika* and *Andhra Jyoti.* Those old players never thought of starting a new edition in the state beyond their base centre Vijayawada. The new paper's avowed objective was its delivery at the crack of the dawn, with a particular emphasis on state and local news. This is how *Eenadu* made a very small beginning in the newspaper business with a print order of a mere 4,500 copies.

In the warfare terminology it is a flanking attack or strategy. An enemy's army is necessarily less severe in its flanks and rear. Its weak spots (blind sides), therefore, are natural targets for attack by the enemy. The major principle of modern offensive warfare is concentration of strength against weakness. The aggressor may attack the strong side to tie up the defender's troops but will launch the real attack at the side or rear. This "turning" maneuver catches the defending army off guard. Flank attacks make excellent marketing sense and are particularly attractive to the aggressor possessing fewer resources than the opponent.[2]

So also the strategy was followed by *Eenadu*. How the "dak" editions of the newspapers were received in the late hours of the evening, thus Ramoji Rao's dismay at it and his putting a suggestion to the founder of *Andhra Jyoti* to start an edition from Visakhapatnam were already narrated in the previous chapter.[3] That is how *Eenadu* was born.

(i) Crack of the Dawn Sensation

Soon it became a sensation. What a sensation it was to hear the thud of a newspaper as early as 5 o'clock in the morning, even in the premises of the households located in the farthest comers of Visakhapatnam city, typically sprawling over a very wide area compared to its size of the population. At that point of time, even people living in the neighbourhood of Vijayawada were not known to receive their morning newspaper that early in the morning, though they were published even in the vicinity of their households. Understandably, the news of *Eenadu* entering Visakhapatnam spread like a wildfire across the whole of the state, irrespective of the fact the people away from Visakhapatnam had no chance to see it themselves. People occasionally visiting Visakhapatnam city or neighbouring areas used to take pride in bringing a copy of it on their return journey. A news-hungry reader is eager to receive his newspaper early in the morning. But the Telugu dailies till 1974 were taking their readers for a ride on this count. *Eenadu's* flanking strategy spotted this ill-served market need. And right from the outset, *Eenadu* was positioned in all its promotional campaigns as a paper—that pleasantly awakens the readers by knocking the door at crack of the dawn (*Ushodayam*, in Telugu). Never before a newspaper in any language in India was prominently positioned like that on entry and lived true to such marketing philosophy.

(ii) A New Package of News

Further the adequate coverage of the state news and the news stories relating to the local issues and people was a special attraction for the readers in the neighbourhood of Visakhapatnam city. By that time, all other Telugu papers were filled with news from Delhi, Mumbai and the major metropolitan cities that were datelined by national news agencies. News of local relevance was hardly given any importance. *Eenadu* virtually changed the basic perception of news. A reader's natural urge to know the local news events was strategically exploited by *Eenadu* right from its launch. News is gathered, written, edited and published not from the view point of the supplier (news agency or reporter) or even editor but from the view point of the user (reader). Emphasising the local news does not necessarily mean giving the news relating to the readers' locality alone. It is, in fact, looking at, and analysing of the news events, including international and national happenings through the eyes of the reader. A newspaper reader is not only curious to know the news but he is also keen to assess the likely impact of such news events on his personal life and community. To put it simply, with the entry of *Eenadu*, marketing-orientation entered into the news or editorial rooms of a Telugu daily. For the first time, a Telugu newspaper with a new face was available to him which was very relevant.

(iii) Three-Dimensional Flanking

What happened at *Eenadu* has three strategic dimensions

—all part of a flank attack: (1) Entering the newspaper market from far-flung Visakhapatnam where competitors were underperforming is a geographical flanking; (2) delivering the newspaper before the sunrise is flanking with distribution —bringing a change in the distribution network to provide a better service; and (3) changing the news mix to the liking of the readers is an example of flanking with product form.

Flanking requires a knowledge of the principles involved. They include: (1) A good flanking move must be made in an uncontested area. Traditional marketing theory might call this approach segmentation, the search for segments or niches. This is an important qualification. To launch a true flanking attack, one must be the first to occupy the segment. Otherwise, it is just an offensive attack against the defended position. (2) Tactical surprise ought to be an important element of the plan. The most successful flanking moves are those that are totally unexpected. (3) The pursuit is as critical as the attack itself. Marketing history is filled with the stories of flanking attacks that are initially successful, yet ultimately went nowhere because of lack of resources to follow through.[4] In both a marketing and a military sense, flanking operation is a bold move, the most innovative way to fight the competitors. It requires detailed planning on an hour-by-hour, day-to-day basis.[5] Yet *Eenadu* succeeded in effectively using it. Flanking leads to a fuller coverage of the market's varied needs. Flanking is the best tradition of modern marketing philosophy, which holds that the purpose of marketing is to "discover needs and satisfy them." Flank attacks are more likely to be successful than frontal attacks.[6] *Eenadu* might have succeeded in fully exploiting the flank attack, having understood all its implications.

Ralph Biggadike examined what strategies best suited for entering markets held by incumbent firms. He found, *inter alia,* that out of 40 of such firms, 28 claimed superior quality, and five matched incumbents' quality. He also found

21 entered at a high price. The modal marketing mix of the entrants thus consisted of higher prices and higher quality, narrower market segments and superior service, among other things[7]. What happened at *Eenadu* corroborates with such findings. Their flanking was found to be fully loaded with the elements of such a modal marketing mix of entrants. *Eenadu's* price is not known to be less than the price of any daily in India, since its launching.

What the Other Competitors Did?

Other competitors' strategies are also chronicled alongside those of *Eenadu* in Table 5.1. The competitors were *Andhra Prabha,* then market leader which sold 1,12,000 copies the year before in 1973, followed by *Andhra Patrika* (49,000 copies), *Andhra Jyoti* (31,000 copies) and *Andhra Bhoomi* (17,000 copies), the total market size being 2,09,000 copies.[8] Those circulation figures suggest how strong the competitors were. As such their egos stood on the way of blocking the insignificant attack from an insignificant quarter on an insignificant front. So they did not like to see what was happening in the flank. Their egos were either so strong or they were so indifferent to the happenings around them. Many leaders refuse to block because their egos get in the way. Even worse, they knock the competitors' development until it is too late to save the situation.[9] Thus they slept over dangerously.

Ultimately *Andhra Prabha, Andhra Bhoomi* and *Andhra Jyoti* appeared in Visakhapatnam in 1985, 1986 and 1989, respectively. In 1984, *Eenadu's* circulation was 3,56,000 copies, the total circulation of all its competitors put together was much less than this.

Thus another factor contributing to the success of flank attack of *Eenadu* was the failure of the competitors to defend themselves. It looked like a very petty battle to its competitors, in terms of *Eenadu's* very meagre initial sales. But they failed to read that such circulation was only a tip of an iceberg. They have failed to measure the iceberg of psychological impact of the new entrant on the minds of the readers and non-readers of newspapers, the latter target group being more important than the former. Perhaps they might have brushed aside the keenly felt psychological upsurge created by *Eenadu* then in the market, as a mere euphoria.

2. Yet Another Flank Attack (1975)

This time the flank under attack was Hyderabad (item No.2 in Table 5.1), yet another area where the readers of Telugu newspapers were ill-served and wherefrom *Andhra Bhoomi* was publishing with 15,000 copies the year before. Success breeds success. *Eenadu* tasted the blood of success in Visakhapatnam. Success not in terms of the copies they have sold and the geographical area they served. The success was not in terms of quantity. It was in terms of both product and service quality. The response they got from the readers of Visakhapatnam was immeasurable, as is already learnt. This made them to make a move so swiftly, again with an element of surprise, to the new centre. The objectives did not differ from those of the earlier centre. The earliest delivery of the paper loaded with regional and local news was still their pet theme. This time the flank was from the capital city of the state, making their presence more emphatic and felt more. This attack has brought them a trophy for the first time in 1976. They emerged as No. 2 player with 54,000 copies or 23.3 per cent of market share. The strength of a flank attack lies in its pursuit. *Eenadu's* experience of continued flanking in Hyderabad was a lesson in pursuit.

What the Other Competitors Did?

Andhra Patrika, then No. 2 player, was quick to react by

entering the playfield in the same year. This did not help it to retain its No. 2 position. *Andhra Prabha* brought out its new edition from this place in 1977, and *Andhra Jyoti* in 1986. Except *Andhra Patrika,* the other competitors then lost the second opportunity of blocking the strong competitive move from *Eenadu.*

Most players have only one chance to win, but leaders have two, assert Al Ries and Jack Trout. If a leader misses an opportunity to attack itself to provide better products, the company can often recover by copying the competitive move. But the leader must move rapidly before the attacker gets established.[10] *Andhra Prabha* still the unquestioned leader then failed to make either of such moves, thus letting down the second chance even.

The importance of the defender improving the product, *inter alia,* was earlier emphasised by Hauser, Shugan and Gaskin in a model they have built and tested called Defender. The defender should improve its strong product features even more rather than try to improve along the lines of attacker's strong product features.[11] Expansion or protection of the market shares was not in the dictionary of either the defender *Andhra Prabha* or other competitors. They were merely contented with the size of their circulation remaining either stationary or increasing marginally, unmindful of product improvement.

Decreasing market share in the face of expanding market size spells danger to the defender. Increasing market implies the ability of the attacker to create new users of the product. The ability to create new users here means the ability to convert non-readers into customers, which presents a great opportunity to all the players to enhance their sales. If the leader fails to take cognizance of such positive signs in the marketplace, it is playing the game blindfold.

3. Frontal Attack: The Challenger's Battle Royal (1978)

This time the attack was not from the flanks as on the earlier two occasions (item No. 3 in Table 5.1). The attack was heads-on. The battle was confined to almost all the players - really a battle royal. The battlefield was none other than Vijayawada, the citadel of Telugu newspapers.

It was 1978. Having become the improved challenger in 1977 with 24.6 per cent of market share or 73,000 copies, it has picked up the courage to indulge in the luxury of frontal attack with its third edition in so quick a succession. By that time the combined circulation of all other competitors from Vijayawada stood at 2,05,000 copies and *Andhra Prabha* continued to be the leader with 37 per cent of the market share.

(i) Taming the Lion

This resulted in another bout of success. The success was so large that *Eenadu* became the largest selling newspaper within just six months (by the end of 1978) with 35 per cent of market share (1,27,000 copies) pushing aside *Andhra Prabha* which commanded market leadership for about two decades in the Telugu newspaper market. Thus soon after reaching Vijayawada the copies of *Eenadu* started reaching more and more households of the Telugu people. Whether *Eenadu* reached the households or not, its impact was felt almost everywhere. Its pre-launch tactics were so effective that people felt the paper was around them even before the paper actually reached Vijayawada. They have erected large hoardings in all the towns of the future market which attracted the attention of the people most. The backs of rickshaws and autos used to carry their placards. Never before a newspaper employed such tactics. As a matter of fact, prospective customers awaited in great enthusiasm to receive the newspaper, known for the new values it has created both to the reader and advertiser. Its cartoons, its sweet language, its attractive layouts and its investigative reportage became matters of discussion at commonplaces as well as in most of households, wherever people interested in news gathered. Such of those strategies resulted in the expansion of *Eenadu's* market share, growing to 44.6 per cent (1,85,000 copies) in 1979, 47.1 per cent (2,05,000 copies) in 1980 and touching a nearly 50 per cent (1,97,000 copies) in 1981.

(ii) Taming the "False Leader"

A market challenger (Philip Kotler's description of No. 2 player)[12] before exercising its choice of a strategy, must first define its strategic objective. The military principle of objective holds that: "Every military operation must be directed toward a clearly defined, decisive and attainable objective."[13] Given clear opponents and objectives the starting point is known as the *principle of mass*, which holds that "superior combat power must be concentrated at the critical time and place for a decisive purpose."[14] The strategic objective of most market challengers is to increase their market shares, thinking that it will lead to greater profitability. Chasing such an objective, attacking the market leader is one of the options available to the market challengers, Philip Kotler asserts. This is a "high-risk" but potentially a "high-payoff strategy and makes good sense if the leader is a "false leader" and not serving the market well. The "terrain" to examine is consumer need or dissatisfaction. If a substantial segment is unserved or poorly served, it provides an excellent strategic target. The alternative strategy is to out-innovate the leader across the whole segment.[15]

The assertion of Philip Kotler has come true in *Eenadu's* case. It could win the battle so easily because the market leader *Andhra Prabha* was a false leader without caring for customer needs. The alternative strategy of out-innovating the leader across the whole segment was already initiated by *Eenadu* in the segments of Visakhapatnam and Hyderabad much earlier than reaching Vijayawada, thus reducing the high-risk element in it.

For a pure frontal attack to succeed, the aggressor needs a strength advantage over the competitor. The principle of force says that the side with greater manpower (resources) will win the engagement. The military dogma is that for a frontal attack to succeed against a well entrenched opponent must deploy at least 3:1 advantage in combat firepower. If the aggressor has a smaller force or poorer firepower than the defender, a frontal attack amounts to a suicide mission and makes no sense.[16] But the attack on the false leadership made the job easy for *Eenadu*. Pure frontal attack implies attacking the opponent's strengths rather than its weaknesses. But the false leader's weaknesses were a plenty in terms of its customer's dissatisfaction, despite its plentifulness in all other resources (considering *Andhra Prabha* was a member of a chain).

A challenger rarely improves its market share by relying on only one strategy. Its success depends on combining several principles to improve its position over time.[17] While realisation as this started taking roots deeper and stronger at *Eenadu*, its route to the market leadership became clearer and nearer.

What the Other Competitors Did

There was no semblance of either the then market leader *Andhra Prabha* or other competitors defending themselves in the face of such devastating blows into their faces. They remain contented since they were not losing much of their circulation. But they were blind to the fast growing market size that was triggered at the initiative and advances of the new player *Eenadu*. It appeared—their fastly melting out market share did not bother them at all, though everyone of them was uprooted from their earlier standings in the marketplace. Either it was a case of continued complacency, or an example of chronic ego ultimately developing into a crisis of confidence, or both. Any way they have lost not only a crucial battle but also the whole of the marketing war.

Maintaining market leadership in the face of repeated attacks from able challengers requires remarkable ability. Leaders' success is based not on doing one thing well but on doing everything well. They do not allow any weaknesses to develop.[18] It appears things were moving in the opposite direction in respect of *Andhra Prabha* despite repeated attacks from *Eenadu*. Perhaps they might have grossly underestimated the ability of the challenger, paying a very high price for it.

4. Setting the People's Personal Agenda: A Windfall

Item No. 4 and 5 of Table 5.1 are the subject matter here. Market share steadily growing to 50 per cent of the size of the market, *Eenadu* was growing in stature and along with it in self-confidence. At a time of such an upbeat, political excitement was erupted, N.T.Rama Rao plunging into politics, surprising everybody. What happened later is vividly described in the previous chapter.[19] In this context *Eenadu* jumped into the fray to make use of such a political excitement by performing the agenda-setting function.

If the media content influences the people and thus sets people's personal agenda, that is what is known as agenda-setting function.[20] The media cannot tell audience members what to think. They are not very successful persuaders. But the media do tell audience members what to think about. That is how media content sets people's agenda of what is important. For all practical purposes the issues people report as significant match the issues that have appeared prominently in the mass media. Those issues people name as the most important are the ones likely to have received most extensive coverage in the mass media. Additionally, the research confirms issues reported in the media show up on the public agenda later. This last finding means the mass media set the public agenda rather than the other way around.[21]

(i) Marketing a Wave

What all Rama Rao did during his historic nine-month long stop-whistle tour of the state received the most extensive coverage in *Eenadu*. N.T.Rama Rao was a great crowd-puller, the state has ever known, whatever the reasons might be. Besides his film glamour, his touring on a van fitted with a public address system with all staying facilities inside was an innovation. Whatever N.T.Rama Rao did naturally attracted the attention of the common man and the media. *Eenadu* just reported back all such happenings to the masses who admired him most thus further fuelling their desire for news-hunger. Almost *Eenadu* monitored a blow-by-blow account with lots of photos, interesting comments and cartoons. *Eenadu's* interest and commitment to the agenda was so much that it conducted a prepoll survey which predicted a landslide victory to the TDP. Agenda's dream coming true, the paper celebrated it in a novel way. In jubilation, thousands of *Eenadu*'s copies were rained into the streets of Vijayawada on the day the election results were out. Like rain, they were free for all. Thus NTR's TDP came to power in January 1983, to be the first non-Congress government in the state after three and half decades.

Even today people are found to be discussing whether it was NTR creating the TDP wave or *Eenadu* making it. Such was the impact of the paper in influencing the people's personal agenda. As a consequence, there was an unbelievable surge in the circulation of *Eenadu,* raising its market share from 49 per cent (1,97,000 copies) in 1981 to 60.3 per cent (3,42,000 copies) in 1983.

The political excitement and the agenda-setting function of *Eenadu* continued in the year 1984, covering events of dismissal of democratically elected chief minister NTR and his reinstatement within a month. Its circulation in 1984 was 3,56,000 copies though market share was reduced to 58 per cent.

Nonetheless, high risks are involved in the agenda-setting strategy for a leader. Sometimes it may not be able to persuade the people in the direction of its agenda. Then there is a danger of the paper losing its image. Yet *Eenadu* came out with windfall gains thus succeeding in marketing a wave.

Keeping in view the pro-TDP image the paper was acquiring slowly, this agenda was abandoned in the years that followed.

But the paper took up a new agenda in spearheading the antiliquor agitation in 1993 and 1994 thus influencing the new government after the assembly elections in 1994 to prohibit liquor. But it is difficult to come to a conclusion on the impact of such an agenda on *Eenadu's* sales.

Item No.4 in the table relates to *Eenadu* starting its fourth edition from Tirupati in 1982. After consolidating itself as the market leader, the expansion began with an eye on further expansion of the market share, quite justified as a leader's strategy.

(ii) Then, the Market Leader Declines (1984-92)

This is of its decline, not its defeat. Windfalls are windfalls. Their impact does not last longer. The euphoria of the TDP dying down, the decline in the circulation of *Eenadu* was set in. Its market share started declining from 1984, though the circulation started declining from the next year. The market share which was 60.3 per cent in 1983 steadily declined to 42.2 per cent in 1987, gradually improving to 51 per cent only in 1992. Circulation that was 3,56,000 copies in 1984 declined to 2,67,000 copies in 1987 which gradually increased to 3,39,000 copies only in 1992, still short of 1984-level.[22]

New entrant *Udayam's* frontal attack since 1985 and *Andhra Jyoti's* improved performance since 1987 partly accounted for such a decline. This was also a period of decline or stagnation in market size.

What the Other Competitors Did?

So far as the political excitement in 1982 was concerned the competitors were either indifferent or misread the people's mood. Nevertheless, their sales also marginally increased in the heat of the political excitement. Though the entire press was in sympathy with NTR when he was dismissed as the chief minister, only *Eenadu* was able to gain significantly in sales.

Reverting to item No. 4, *Udayam* was in frontal attack with the market leader on its entry by launching Vijayawada and Hyderabad editions simultaneously in 1984. Further, the paper launched its third edition from Tirupati in 1986. Thereafter *Andhra Jyoti* reached Tirupati in 1987. *Andhra Bhoomi* entered Visakhapatnam in 1986 and Vijayawada in 1989. Thus for the first time things started hotting up on a wider scale in the competitors' camp, outside *Eenadu*. *Udayam* succeeded in entering the market and becoming No. 2 player sooner in 1985 (27.6 per cent of market share), though it could not retain that position later on. After a long interval *Andhra Jyoti* succeeded in improving its market share to 25 per cent in 1988, an all time high for that paper. Such of these developments lead to the decline of the leader as is already learnt, despite *Andhra Patrika, Andhra Prabha* and *Andhra Bhoomi* continued to lose further ground.

Comparing *Udayam* and *Eenadu* on Entry

Udayam met with initial successes as in case of *Eenadu* on its entry. People were eager to try new papers. *Eenadu's* entry resulted in the increased market size thus creating new customers in the long run. In contrast, *Udayam's* entry resulted in the expanded market size only to a limited extent, that too during the initial year. It could only wean away the customers of other papers to its fold by and large. *Eenadu's* entry strategy was flank attack, whereas *Udayam* depended on frontal attack. It means *Eenadu* entered where the competitors were weak whereas *Udayam* entered where the competitors were strong. Events that occurred at *Udayam* in subsequent years proved the paper chewed more than it can swallow.

5. The Leader's Defensive Strategies to Recover, Consolidate and Expand

Only the market leader should consider playing defence. This is one of the basic principles of defensive warfare.[23] While the market size expanding, the dominant firm must continuously defend its current business against rival attacks. The leader is like a large elephant being attacked by a swarm of bees. The largest and nastiest bee keeps buzzing around the leader. Sometimes there are several other large dangerous bees. Clearly the leader cannot defend all its territory and needs to decide where to draw the battle lines. Twenty centuries ago Sun Tzu told his warriors: "One does not rely on the enemy not attacking but relies on the fact that he himself is unassailable." In marketing warfare the most constructive response is *continuous innovation*. The leader refuses to be content with the way things are and leads the industry in developing new product ideas, customer services, distribution effectiveness and cost cutting.[24]

After a decade of unmatched successes, *Eenadu* was on the defensive losing circulation and market share in the face of new competition from *Udayam* and the old competitor *Andhra Jyoti* consolidating. To stage a retrieval *Eenadu* once again resorted to innovation.

Continuous innovation was high on the agenda of *Eenadu*. Even after getting firmly established as the market leader, it was striving hard to continually improve its newspaper. Let it be examined what happened at *Eenadu* in the direction of continuous innovation.

Item Nos.6,7,8,9 and 10 may broadly be classified into two defensive strategies adopted by *Eenadu*. They are geographic segmentation and interest-zoning.

(i) Geographic Segmentation

As is already learnt, *Eenadu's* philosophy to serve the specific local news-interest segments and thereby giving the paper a distinctly local flavour received tremendous response. In an attempt to give a new shape to its philosophy the paper launched 28 district or city supplements in tabloid size in January, 1989. Presently these supplements are published from their respective 10 publication centres.

The number of pages of district supplements range from 8 to 16 depending upon the size of each district or city in terms of its geography and demography. With a separate editorial desk having three or four editorial staff for each district and over 1,500 stringers across the state, the technology, money and managerial ability involved in bringing out such tabloid editions is stupendous. In the words of Ramoji Rao, "It is like producing a broadsheet newspaper of more than 124 pages every day."[25]

What possibly compelled *Eenadu* to opt for such a risky, though innovative, exercise? The dailies in Andhra Pradesh just like their counterparts in many regions in India were targeted at the upmarket reader for many years. Geographically, till early eighties the Telugu newspaper's reach was restricted mainly to the urban areas and rural conglomerations having well-connected roads and rails. As observed earlier, the political excitement in 1982 created intense interest among the Telugu people in local politics. Consequently, the newspaper in Andhra Pradesh has become a much sought after product in 1980s. A study of a village, in Srikakulam district, the most northerly and one of the most remote districts, found six newspaper subscribers before the state elections of 1982. But once N.T.Rama Rao began his campaign, three villagers and the panchayat office started subscribing to *Eenadu*, brought each day by high school students returning from a neighbouring town. It was estimated that a single copy had upto 50 readers. Interviews showed that readers liked *Eenadu* because of its "detailed coverage of the regional news", especially about election candidates.[26] Election excitement created by the Telugu Desam Party and people's political involvement expanded the Telugu newspaper market from 4,38,000 copies in 1982 to 6,14,000 copies by 1984, an increase of 402 per cent in two years. On *Udayam's* entry, the uptrend in the market expansion continued during 1985, total circulation increasing to 7,24,000 copies, implying 17.9 per cent change compared to 1984. Nevertheless the down trend in the market was set in, losing 13.8 per cent circulation in 1986. The industry could regain 1985-level of circulation only by 1989.[27] This suggests that the larger urban areas like Hyderabad, Vijayawada, Visakhapatnam and Tirupati can no longer provide the extent of new readership they have in the past. Hence, the growth will have to come from the smaller towns and large villages.

Moreover, *Eenadu* has been losing circulation or market share or both since 1984 as observed earlier. Although *Eenadu* continued to be the undisputed market leader, the narrowing gap between *Eenadu* and the runner-up *Andhra Jyoti* or *Udayam* was another factor for concern from the former's point of view.

Ramoji Rao himself says that the idea of the district supplement struck him when he began realising that a lot of local news simply could not find place in the paper.[28] The idea of offering district supplement can be described as an extreme form of serving the reader who wants to know what is happening in his own countryside. To quote Lynn de Souza, media director of Trikaya Grey, "When it came to providing consumer satisfaction, there are few publishing groups in the country that I know of that have done better than *Eenadu.* The publication's philosophy, as outlined in their presentation to advertisers, sounds pompous and trite: *to ceaselessly innovate, upgrade and add value for the reader and the advertiser.* But unlike so many corporate mission statements that exist only for framed glass, *Eenadu* has shown us time and again that they mean it."[29] In fact, it is not only the reader who is benefitted from a tabloid supplement that gave him news at the absolute grassroots level, but also the advertiser. Such implications are to be taken up in greater detail in Chapter-VIII.

Eenadu's idea of giving 28 tabloid supplements - daily in colour - was summarily dismissed by many media people as commercially not viable. For example, in 1989, the owner of the rival publication compared with Ramoji Rao's ambitions to that of "a long jumper trying to do the pole vault."[30]

The expenditure involved in providing eight additional tabloid pages and 16 in case of the city supplements is enormous. At the time of launching the tabloid supplements in 1989, the additional daily costs on ink and newsprint alone amounted to Rs. 2 lakh. Further, in the initial months there had also been production problems because, as Ramoji Rao says, "It is like producing 28 newspapers simultaneously." Ramoji Rao who has clear vision about his venture further declared: "Success goes to those who dare and act. I am prepared to wait. The day those district supplements stabilise, I will have a fantastic weapon in my hands."[31]

Eenadu's concept of offering district supplement in tabloid form, in addition to the main edition in the usual form, everyday to the reader is perhaps first of its kind in India. However, the amazing success of such district supplements furnish sufficient evidence of the demand for the presentation of local news and advertisements in a format approximately half in size of the standard newspaper.

The readers' acceptance of tabloid supplement was well-reflected in *Eenadu's* circulation figures. Its circulation grew by 18.68 per cent from 2,89,000 copies in second half of 1989 to 3,43,000 copies in the first half of 1990.[32] The greatest compliment to Ramoji Rao came from his competitors who subsequently emulated *Eenadu's* strategy. *Udayam* and *Andhra Bhoomi* started similar supplements in 1992 and *Andhra Jyoti* in 1994. *Andhra Prabha* which is known for its slumberous way of looking at the things has also launched the district supplements in September, 1997. *Vaartha*, the latest entrant in the Telugu newspaper market has been offering tabloid editions from the day of its commencement.

No doubt, the tabloid supplements enabled the publishers to penetrate into new markets particularly rural areas and thereby new readership is created.

However, critics voiced against the concept of district supplement for they have totally cut off the people from each other. Even news of neighbouring districts is blanked out in the name of giving the detailed coverage to the events of a particular district. For example, the residents of Chirala town are naturally interested in knowing the important news events that would happen in its neighbouring town Bapatla which is just 15 kms away. But the citizens of Chirala are being denied news relating to Bapatla as these two towns fall under two different districts. Many a time, a curious newspaper reader has to look at an English daily for detailed news coverage relating to the rest of the state. For example, *The Hindu* which is published only from Hyderabad and Visakhapatnam in the state has increased its regional pages to four to cater to the news needs of the reader interested in native state.

At times, news of minimal news values is published to fill up the space, particularly when there is no sufficient advertising. The district supplements could have another fall out: They could very well spell the death of small newspaper confining to towns or districts as they cannot withstand the well established papers. From industry's point of view, district supplements serve as an entry barrier to potential competition. As such, the monopoly of the big papers is then likely to spread to the grassroots level which is no good for the freedom of the press.[33] Though "minies" (tabloid editions are often called so in industry circles) created a vast network of news reporters, the quality of reporting has been a major casualty since most of the stringers are not professionally trained.

Eenadu launching their editions from six more centres (bringing the total to ten) in early and late nineties was complementary to its launching district supplements earlier. Together, they formed part of geographic segmentation, making two sides of the same coin. They complemented each other in taking newspaper closer to the customers with the desired news mix, at the same time, creating desired audience to the advertisers.

(ii) Interest-Zoping

After segmenting the Telugu newspaper market on the basis of geography, *Eenadu* went for segmentation by demographic and psychographic variables. *Eenadu's* interest-zoning strategy called for discovering and satisfying the specific interest groups of readers by adding exclusive features or pages for them. For example, introduction of a 32-page weekend Sunday supplement in a magazine form (1988), regular features of a business page (1990), a cinema page (1991), an exclusive women's page (1992), career counselling and matrimonial advertising, and a column on computers once in a week are some of the contents innovated at *Eenadu*. Their women's page deserves a special mention.

The National Readership Surveys show that reading habits among Telugu women have not improved between 1983 and 1990. Literacy rate among urban adult women in Andhra Pradesh was 50 per cent and that women readers comprised a quarter of the readership of any newspaper, including *Eenadu*[34] By launching a special page-*Vasundhara*, what *Eenadu* described as India's first women's page, as a daily feature, the paper attempted to bring the women folk into its fold. No other newspaper in India had a special colour page for women every day of the week earlier.[35]

When the women's page was being planned by *Eenadu*, there was no clear information on what the typical Andhra woman was like. Was she traditional or modern? Housewife or a career women? *Vasundhara* (means mother earth) was launched with much advertising fanfare—a four-part teaser campaign in press followed by a series of four colour spreads, with an audiovisual campaign on television and cinema. One showed a college girl, the second a housewife, the third a career woman, and the fourth an elderly woman. The ad aimed at the college girl spoke of fashion, education and job interviews and how *Vasundhara* was going to help her with them, while the ad for the elderly woman said how it would help her cope with her life now that her children had grown up and gone away. The success of *Vasundhara* was reflected immediately in the circulation figures of *Eenadu* when circulation had shot up by 25,000 copies within three weeks of *Vasundhara's* launch in September 1992.[36]

Drawn closer to the customer in physical terms through geographic segmentation, interest-zoning was thus intended to get much closer to the interests of the readers by their demographic and psychographic variables. Closeness to customer was uppermost in the priorities of *Eenadu* throughout its existence as a new player, a challenger, a market leader and a defender. Research into America's best-run companies by Thomas Peters and Robert Waterman Jr., revealed "close to customer" was one among the eight attributes[37] of such excellent, innovative companies. " ... The excellent companies *really are* close to their customers. That is it. Other companies talk about it; the excellent companies do it."[38] It appears *Eenadu* is equally fanatical about it. The attribute includes, *inter alia*, service, quality, reliability and values.[39]

To put it differently, geographic segmentation and interest-zoning put together worked like a pre-emptive defence at *Eenadu*. Pre-emptive defence is an aggressive defence manoeuver to launch an attack on the enemy before it states its offence against the company. Pre-emptive defence assumes an ounce of prevention is worth more than a pound of cure.[40] It could assume the proportions of grand market envelopment as happened at *Eenadu* with as many as 28 district supplements and a great variety in its other features. The best defensive strategy for the leader is the courage to indulge in self-attack. Because of its leadership position, the defender owns a strong point in the mind of the prospect. The best way to improve the leader's position is to constantly indulging in self-attacking. Competition continually struggles trying to catch up. A moving target is harder to hit than a stationary one.[41] Precisely, this was practised at *Eenadu*. The implications of geographic segmentation and interest-zoning in space marketing are to be taken up in chapter - VIII.[42]

What the Other Competitors Did?

As in case of district and Sunday supplement, all the other competitors in subsequent years mostly imitated the market leader's interest-zoning strategies. The new daily *Vaartha* looked like a replica of the market leader *Eenadu* in almost all its product features from the first day of its launching in 1996. May be, competitors' captions were different, contents of the features remaining the same. May be, competitors had extra features as different from the leader. But such variations were only a few and certainly not of major consequence in terms of their impact on consumers.

However, every innovation in the Telugu newspaper ıarket was not the brain child of *Eenadu's* Ramoji Rao. KNY Patanjali, who edited *Udayam* sometime back claims: "The concept of district supplements originated here (at *Udayam*). We went in for it because we could provide greater and more meaningful coverage of events in the districts."[43] *Andhra Bhoomi,* on the other hand, claims to have been the first to emerge with a district supplement for its Visakhapatnam edition in November, 1988. Even assuming that these conflicting claims are valid, what cannot be denied is that it is *Eenadu* which took the idea to its logical end.

Vaartha's Encirclement Attack

Vaartha simultaneously launching from as many as nine centres on entry in 1996, while well-entrenched leader *Eenadu* was operating only at seven centres, was an encirclement attack. Indian newspaper industry never knew such a grand scale operation exercise on entry.

The encirclement manoeuver is an attempt to capture a wide slice of the enemy's territory through a comprehensive "blitzkrieg" attack. Encirclement involves launching a grand offensive on several fronts, so that the enemy must protect its front, sides and rear simultaneously. The aggressor may offer the market everything the opponent offers and more, so that the offer is unrefusable. Encirclement makes sense where the aggressor commands superior resources and believes that a swift encirclement will break the opponent's will.[44]

Vaartha's, dream of encircling the enemy did not

materialise, despite the added advantage of using satellite technology, superior resources or greater willingness to invest. A Rs.50 crore plus investment from a Rs.1000 crore Hyderabad based Sanghi group speaks of *Vaartha's*, bold bid of toppling *Eenadu*'s hold over Telugu newspaper readers. Nevertheless, any competitive advantage could not be harvested out of its strategies.

An input of resources alone is not sufficient to guarantee success. If the company is to be successful, the resources have to be allocated in the way that produces strategic excellence positions.[45] A strategic excellence position may be defined as a capability which enables an organisation to produce better-than-average results over the long term compared with its competitors. Corporate strategy must aim to identify and occupy strategic excellence positions, because they are the only basis for superior profitability.[46] Michael Porter asserts, "Attacking a leader that is aggressively pursuing a cost leadership or differentiation strategy will usually require that a challenger conceive of a major strategic innovation ...if it is to mount a successful challenge".[47]

Consequently, the grandeur in attack could bring *Vaartha* only a limited success, leaving it to be a far distant No. 2 player. But this was achieved on entry straight away. Though *Vaartha* claimed to have launched with four lakh plus registered subscribers, it had to be contented with an average daily circulation of 1,75,000 copies in the initial year 1996. It appeared *Vaartha* seemed to be weaning away more customers from other competitors compared to *Eenadu*.

Comparing *Vaartha* and *Eenadu* on Entry

Eenadu secured a competitive advantage on entry, putting its limited resources to the best use by moving into an uncontested area concentrating on as narrow a segment as possible, employing a tactical surprise that too facing a false or underperforming leader. One at a time was *Eenadu's* approach in marketing warfare. It had no faith in waging more than one battle at a time. Winning a battle, gaining confidence, consolidating and moving to the next battle was its approach. In contrast to *Eenadu's* entry, *Vaartha* chosen to open war on all fronts against the well entrenched vigourously performing market leader. Instead, had it entered into one or two segments to begin with, the story would have been different by now. Ad revenue besides circulation success sustains a newspaper. Any attempt to promote circulation boost without adequate ad revenue is contrary to the principles of newspaper economics. Building up ad revenues takes a lot more time compared to building up circulation. Besides, research shows newspaper loyalties are irrationally strong as in case of tooth paste. It took *Eenadu* over two decades to build up a clientele of over 6.5 lakhs. *Vaartha's* dreaming of such a fantastic catch of customers overnight or a short period of two or three years seemed to be an overambitious and unrealistic game plan. Added to such inherent weaknesses, *Eenadu's* defensive strategies were a great entry barrier to *Vaartha*. Because the other competitors were not so aggressive in defending themselves, they could easily be overtaken by *Vaartha*.

6. Leader's Other Strategies

It is not an easy task to identify and enlist the strategies even though that are discernible. It is also not intended here to analyse all these strategies. Only most important of them are taken up earlier. Omitting some of the other strategies from detailed discussions does not signify that they are less important. Some of them may be more important than any of the strategies discussed earlier. For example, credibility is the most important attribute of a newspaper. It is its very life. Other important strategies of the leader *Eenadu* include: investigative reportage, printing in colour, pre-launch tactics, the effective use of cartoon, effective presentation of news in a sweet language (item No. 11 in Table 5.1).

Such of those strategies permeate through all other features and they are ceaselessly pursued. As such, they are included in the last item of Table 5.1, disregarding the chronology. *Eenadu* was found to be second to none in exploiting such of these strategies all through the years. How *Eenadu* exploited the use of colour in printing, the positioning of its cartoon; increased use of investigative reportage, above all, the paper's credibility have become a matter of envy and example to its competitors. Consumers evaluation of such of these strategies will be taken up in the chapter-VII. *Eenadu's* pre-launch tactics which do not form part of such an evaluation deserve a special mention here.

Pre-launch Tactics

Right from *Eenadu's* launch from Visakhapatnam, its marketers looked for innovative ways to launch the newspaper. At that time Visakhapatnam offered few possibilities for advertising. So when they started *Eenadu* they spoiled many walls by hiring scores of wall painters to paint the new daily's name all over the city. When *Eenadu* began publishing from Hyderabad, its marketers divided the city into target areas, recruited delivery boys three months before publication began and gave the paper away free for a week.

Indeed the most innovative of the *Eenadu's* launches was the strategy used for the launch of Rajahmundry edition in September 1992. The rich East Godavari district was earlier served by Visakhapatnam and Vijayawada editions of *Eenadu, Andhra Jyoti* and *Udayam*. Over 15,000 copies of *Eenadu's* Visakhapatnam edition, 9,000 copies of *Andhra Jyoti's* and another 6,000 of *Udayam* made this region a 30,000 copy market, which *Eenadu* felt deserved an edition of its own. Squarely targeting itself at the 15,000 circulation that the other papers enjoyed in the district, *Eenadu* distributed free copies of Rajahmundry edition to *non-Eenadu* homes every morning for the first week. Nothing new there. But then they did not just leave it at that. Every afternoon these *non-Eenadu* homes also received a free tabloid called *Visleshana* (means analysis). And all that *Visleshana* did was to put together the coverage of all the newspapers that morning, comparing the coverage in *Eenadu* with that of the other papers. The tack used was simple: "See for yourself." *Eenadu* claimed to be very happy with the outcome.[48] With the addition of Rajahmundry edition in September 1992, *Eenadu*'s overall circulations rose by 43,370 copies in the second-half of 1992 from 3,17,177 copies in the first-half of 1992.[49] During the same period, *Andhra Jyoti's* overall circulation was slashed by 8,825 copies, to 1,35,522 copies in the later-half of 1992.[50] These figures suggest that *Eenadu,* with its Rajahmundry edition not only attracted the subscribers of its competitive papers into its fold but, at the same time, created a large number of new customers too.

What the Other Competitors Did?

In matters such as those, it is not easy to clearly distinguish between what the leader and the other competitors did . Competing and winning on every front is not possible for any competitor. For example, it is not easy for any competitor to make a match with those of Sridhar's cartoons in *Eenadu.* So it may not be appropriate to strike comparisons on every front. Sometimes the other competitors may be ahead of the leader on a particular front. For example, it was not the market leader *Eenadu* but *Andhra Jyoti* which triggered the current trend of colour war, but only to lose it to the well-entrenched leader.

(B) Leadership Through Building Customer Satisfaction

What is discussed in the earlier section brings home two things very clearly, one, the unquestioned ascendancy of *Eenadu* to the throne i.e., market leadership and two, the listless performance of all its competitors put together. Becoming a market leader so soon (within four years) is one thing and retaining that position for twenty years so far, speaks volumes. Table 5.2 sums up and contrasts how *Eenadu's* superior customer-oriented philosophy prevailed over those of their rivals. Even a cursory look into the details of this table enables one to arrive at some useful inferences - useful to the marketers of newspapers. *Eenadu's* every encounter with the rivals was laced around the customer and the product as perceived by him or her. That is how the publishers of *Eenadu* perceived the customer as the hero of the marketing show. For them product is not simply a newspaper. A product is its benefits aimed at customer want-satisfaction.[51] A product is a set of both tanigle and intangible attributes. Eenadu kept in mind creating all possible of such of those want-satisfaction benefits to the customer. That is how they started delivering the newspaper at the earliest. In fact, this sort of innovation in enhancing time and place utilities forced the rivals, including English dailies, to follow the example of the new player but this did not help them to improve their old image. Thus *Eenadu* brought a new newspaper culture into everybody's home.

Table 5.2

Achieving Leadership Through Building up Customer Satisfaction

What the rivals offered earlier	What *Eenadu* offered
1	2
1. A newspaper at a time convenient to the publisher or their agents, not earlier than 6 AM and till 3 PM and beyond.	1. Not just a newspaper but its want satisfaction benefits, more than a set of physical attributes, delivering between 5 AM and 6 AM and at any cost not later than 6-30 AM.
2. News whatever they could receive, mostly international and national.	2. News for which the customers craved for, mostly regional, local and national.
3. Published the newspaper from a place convenient to the publisher.	3. Published it from a place that suits the customer most, entrenched in 10 centres and

1	2
	in 8 of them *Eenadu* was the first player.
4. Gathering and transmitting the news as they are received.	4. Trying to be the first in receiving them and reaching the customer.
5. Delivering the same paper, whoever and whatever their customers are one edition to all the people.	5. Delivering not a readymade shirt, but a tailor stitched one and that suits customers' size and taste—28 different sets and not just one newspaper.
6. Short-gun approach in capturing the readers aiming at everybody in a haphazard way.	6. A rifle approach in creating different sections to different interest groups in a systematic way for example, Sunday supplement in a magazine form.
7. Contented in passing on the routine old news stories.	7. Concentrated on investigative reportage to bring forth to light the misdeeds of people at high places. Even the routine stories were presented in attractive layouts, spiced in pointed criticism and sweet language.
8. Though one of them was first to go colour, it never exploited seriously.	8. *Eenadu* did that.
9. Never took the onslaughts of the enemy seriously and lost all the battles one by one. Two players ceased to exist - *Andhra Patrika* and *Udayam*.	9. Never complacent in winning a battle. Went on to open new battles and won all of them. Ascended to the position of leader very soon and never looked back.
10. Never tried to minimise the war losses. Instead poorly imitated the leader's strategies and lost much more ground.	10. Believed in preemptive defence and self-attacking through continuous innovation. Even battles with a new player were fought

1	2
	seriously and successfully, for example, battle with *Vaartha.*
11. Never saw the possibility to compete with the English dailies.	11. Did so successfully.
12. Kept themselves as mute spectators to the people's impulses.	12. Sensing the moon of people, indulged in agenda-setting function.
13. Contented in using the cartoons as just another weapon.	13. Used it as a main weapon. Sridhar's cartoons have become a household topic.
Sold the steak	Sold the sizzle.
Sold the product.	Sold the customer-want satisfying benefits.

Selling benefits, instead of product, just started like that to be unfolded into many more dimensions. *Eenadu* started publishing from centres closer to their customers unlike their competitors who had no such thoughts. *Eenadu* did several things in the direction of extending customer want-satisfaction benefits instead of delivering just a newspaper, as are listed in Table 5.2. And whatever *Eenadu* did enabled the customers to receive such benefits. By the time the competitors poorly imitated the new player's strategies, everything was over to find themselves in defeat and dismay.

What happened at *Eenadu* is just the translation of customer-oriented marketing philosophy into action. Product is a basic profit determinant for a firm and what is basic to a product is customer need-satisfaction. The social and economic justification for the existence of a business is its ability to satisfy its customers. *Eenadu* attempted to do this with all seriousness it deserves. Elmer Wheeler, an author and sales training consultant, said, "Do not sell the steak, sell the sizzle".[52] So did *Eenadu* and thus shot into national fame. According to Peter Drucker, there is only one valid definition of a business purpose: to create a customer.[53] Because it is its purpose to create a customer, any business enterprise has two -and only these two—basic functions: marketing and innovation. They are the entrepreneurial functions.[54] And whatever *Eenadu* did looked like the performance of such functions in letter and spirit. It is a worthy example to be emulated by others. One should not forget that the centrepiece of all their activities is their customer and it is with whom they tried and still trying to match their product, not merely the newspaper, its benefits.

But finding out customers in as many number as possible is not the dead-end for media firms. What advertisers need is the circulation of a newspaper among the audiences they chase most. This demands interest-zoning of the newspaper. This is also well realised by *Eenadu* and as such created things of special interest to women, cinema lovers, youth and the like in the spirit of all the tilings to all the people, so that it results in maximisation of advertising revenue - the backbone of a newspaper.

The competitors of *Eenadu* attribute the amazing success of the paper to the innovative and visionary entrepreneurship. *Eenadu* had imagination and determination lavished on it. Its proprietors were able to deploy as much money as needed at any given time. By the 1980s, Ramoji Rao's investment in the newspaper far surpassed that of any competitor. The revolution in technology both made such investment necessary and led to spectacular outcomes. While the training and conditions of many languages-newspapers' journalists are generally poor across the country, *Eenadu* set up its own school of journalism in Hyderabad to train and retrain its journalists. Even the newsrooms of large languages dailies are often primitive with not even a reference book, but *Eenadu* has established an outstanding library - Research and Reference Group in Hyderabad. A few language newspapers such as *Sakal* and *Malayala Manorama* have such libraries.

Eenadu's competitors confessed that the success of *Eenadu* is attributable to their inherent weaknesses. Except the new dailies *Vdayam* and *Vaartha,* the other established dailies like *Andhra Prabha* and *Andhra Jyoti* never attempted to challenge or attack head-on *Eenadu* since its inception. By the time, its competitors initiated retaliation, everything was over. *Eenadu* has always aspired to achieve what its competitors would dismiss as impossible. When it was launched in 1974 from Visakhapatnam, the established publishing houses laughed at the idea that how a two-bit paper from there could compete with their papers in Vijayawada. Similarly the idea of offering district supplements was summarily dismissed by its competitors as well as many media watchers as commercially unviable. Suitably chastened, competitors later acknowledged that they had underestimated the paper and its innovation. Jagadish Prasad of *Andhra Jyoti* said, "He (Ramoji Rao) was prepared to take risks and enter virgin markets; the district editions cost a lot of money, but he was willing to take his chances. All that hard work has paid off."[55] Ramoji Rao owned multi-diversified business units and there is no doubt about where his priorities lie. "Most of my time and energy is devoted to *Eenadu.* That's my first love; everything else is just business," he clarifies.[56] His canny marketing sense is well-hidden by a serene altruism: "The fact that *Eenadu* has a considerable lead over the other newspapers has never been taken into account while planning my strategies," he says. This is because *Eenadu* has always strived to deliver value to its readers and there can never be a ceiling on this.[57]

(C) *Eenadu* and Other Market Leaders

Comparative standing of *Eenadu* with the market leaders of other languages is depicted in Table—5.3. The average

Table 5.3

Comparison of *Eenadu* with the Market Leaders of Other Languages, 1996.

Market Leader	*Language*	*Circulation (copies in thousands)*	*Market Share (per cent)*	*No. of publication centres*	*Average circulation per publication centre*	*Number of ABC number in each language*
1. *Eenadu*	Telugu	604	63.5[a]	9	67	4
2. *Asomiya Pratidin*	Assamese	82	60.2	1	82	3
3. *Malayala Manorama*	Malayalam	829	48.7	7	118	4
4. *Daily Thanthi*	Tamil	444	47.0	12	37	3
5. *Ajit*	Punjabi	165	46.9	1	165	3
6. *Prajavani*	Kannada	94	46.7	2	47	4
7. *Ananda Bazar Patrika*	Bengali	480	41.8	1	480	6
8. *Saisat*	Urdu	44	39.8	1	45	4
9. *Gujarat Samachar*	Gujarati	718	37.6	5	144	16
10. *Samaj*	Oriya	127	24.5	1	127	5

11. *The Times of India*	Englis	989	22.9	6	165	22
12. *Lokmat*	Marathi	400	19.8	6	67	23
13. *Punjab Kesari*	Hindi	671	15.9	3	224	25
Total		5,647	—	62	91	122

Median average circulation per centre of 62 centres: 67,000 copies.

Note: a. For determining this claimed circulation of rivals are also included.

Source: Compiled from ABC data relating to June-December. 1996, Audit Bureau of Circulations, Mumbai.

daily circulations of market leaders, in 1996, in 13 major language segments of the Indian newspaper industry ranged from 44,000 copies (*Saisat*, Urdu) to 9,89,000 copies (*The Times of India*, English) copies.[58] The median of the leaders' average daily circulation stood at 4,44,000 copies. Circulations, market shares, number of publication centres, average circulation per centre, etc., details are shown in the table, leader-wise. Thirteen market leaders brought out their editions from as many as 62 centres. The median of average circulation per centre of 62 centres stood at 67,000 copies.

In such a scenario of the market leaders, let the competitive strengths and weaknesses of *Eenadu* be examined. Only four of the market leaders commanded a higher circulation than *Eenadu's* 6,04,000 copies. Of such four leaders, two belonged to much larger and widespread language segments, namely, English *(The Times of India)* and Hindi *(Punjab Kesari)*. Nevertheless, the other two leaders belonged to smaller language segments compared to Telugu, namely, Malayalam *(Malayala Manorama)* and Gujarati *(Gujarat Samachar)*. Of the leaders, *Eenadu* stood second in terms of the number of editions, publishing from nine centres,[59] with an average circulation of 67,000 copies. *Eenadu* was on top of all other market leaders with the highest market share of 63.5 per cent. *Eenadu* was found to be playing where there were fewer serious players (five in all, including *Vaartha* which was not a member of ABC in 1996 but a member since 1997), compared to other languages. In some segments, the serious players were three or four times to that. For example, in Gujarati newspaper market, there were 16 ABC members and in Marathi 23 players. Now it is pertinent to find out which of these market factors contribute to the strengths or weaknesses of *Eenadu* in particular, and to the competitive structure of Telugu newspaper market, in general.

A large market share need not necessarily signify the

market leader's strength. Rather it may signify the weakness of the leader's competitors. Similarly the leader's low market share may signify its competitors' strength rather than the leader's weakness. As such, it appears that *Eenadu* was operating with unusually large market share, taking advantage of its weak competitors. But such a conclusion is hasty and incorrect, considering the number of centres from which it is published. They speak of the paper's herculean efforts in getting closer to the customers. This is in addition to the paper building up customer satisfaction, brick by brick through its innovation in product and distribution forms, as discussed earlier. Thus, *Eenadu's* strength is attributable to its own inherent strengths. Enormous strength of this sort saved it from the encirclement attack of *Vaartha*. Nonetheless, the presence of such a competitor literally at every doorstep of the market leader operating from more centres at times is good for the industry. If the challenger could outperform the already well performing leader, such a situation may lead to creation of a very large number of new customers, thus taking the industry to new heights of growth.

Hence, what is desired is the emergence of a competitive industry. The wider the gap between the leader and its challenger in their market shares, the lesser the competition and vice versa. The yawning gap in the market shares of *Eenadu* (63.5 per cent) and *Vaartha* (18.4 per cent) signify almost a two-paper market and yet a one paper show. This might be one reason for the lowest dailies-to-thousand-people ratio of Telugu papers, as observed in Chapter II.[60] At a particular point of time the same two players might not be in existence. Despite changes in players, the two-player predominance continued for long in the Telugu market, historically.

In a closely contested market, the leader commands a low market share facing more stiff competitors. The differences in the market shares between the leader and the challenger and also between the challenger and other competitors tend to be lesser. Such a competitive scene attempts to provide better products thus enlarging the industry's size. For example, in Marathi newspaper market, there were 23 competitors, though Maharashtra state is comparable to Andhra Pradesh in area and population. The leader's (*Lokmat*) market share was only 19.8 per cent against the challenger's share of 17.1 per (*Loksatta*) and No. 3 player's share of 16.5 per cent (*Sakal*), resulting in larger industry size and higher DTP ratio.[61]

More than the number of competitors, the quality of the competitors decides the competitive structure of an industry. In the Malayalam market, the competitors were only few. But the market leader's share was not more than 48.7 per cent as against the challenger's (*Mathrubhumi*) 36.9 per cent, resulting in the largest industry size and the highest of the DTP ratio among all Indian languages.[62]

As noted earlier, average circulation per centre of *Eenadu* (67,000 copies) is on par with the median of the average circulation per centre of 62 centres of all the leaders (also 67,000 copies). This indicates that *Eenadu's* publication centres may not be working at sub-optimum level, on the whole.

Competitive Advantage in Trade Terms

The average trade terms offered by the paper to its distributors are chosen to measure the competitive advantage of that paper compared to others. Trade terms mean the percentage of commission to which the distributor is entitled, on the cover price of the paper. Newspaper is a type of business where there is no scope for directly selling the paper to the customer, but for paltry postal subscriptions. The paper has to totally depend on its distributors or agents. The trade terms that are allowed to the distributors by the papers also form part of the ABC reports. Such data relating to a sample of 43 dailies, including those of the leaders, representing 12 languages is perused.

The average trade terms of the aforesaid 43 dailies ranged from 18.3 to 39.9 per cent in 1996.[63] The median of the average trade terms offered by those papers was 29.4 per cent. The paper that has offered the lowest of the trade terms in India was none other than *Eenadu.* In view of such top standing of the paper, in trade terms, in the Indian newspaper industry as a whole, it is not particularly attempted to compare this paper with the market leaders elsewhere. Of course, the trade terms of other leaders were far higher to those of *Eenadu,* to say the least.

Eenadu achieving this unique competitive advantage is attributable to the pull strategy it has employed in its promotional mix. A pull strategy involves marketing activities (primarily advertising and consumer promotion) directed at end-users. The purpose is to induce them to ask intermediaries for the product and thus induce the intermediaries to order the product from the manufacturer. Pull strategy is especially appropriate when there is high brand loyalty and high involvement in the category, people perceive differences between brands and people choose the brand before they go to store.[64] *Eenadu* very cleverly exploited this strategy.

To ensure that the editions reach readers first in the morning, *Eenadu* built-up a highly efficient network of 4,800 agents across the state under the banner of Margadarsi Marketing, an associate company. The company also look on the distributorship of a number of other publications including national magazines such as *India Today* and *The Week,* besides other Telugu periodicals of their own. This was done to strengthen the finances of their agents. The more publications they sell, the more money they make. In return, the paper earned the staunch loyalty of its vendors.[65] But the strength of *Eenadu's* pull strategy is mostly drawn from the inherent strengths of the product.

In contrast to *Eenadu's* pull strategy, the most of the papers in India are found to be adopting a push strategy. A push strategy involves manufacturer marketing activities (primarily sales force and trade promotion) directed at channel intermediaries. The goal is to induce the intermediaries to order and carry the product and promote it to end-users. Push strategy is especially appropriate where there is low brand loyalty in a category, brand choice is made in the store, the product is an impulse item and product benefits are well understood.[66] Nevertheless, the push strategy obviates offering minimum of trade terms.

(D) Future of the Telugu Daily

The future of the Telugu daily depends on finding out solutions to the problems faced by it. The multiplicity of the problems encountered in the Telugu newspaper market include: (1) Unwillingness of the trailing firms to revitalise; (2) the challenger's grossly misdirected attacks on the leader, thus leaving large underutilised capacity, despite huge financial commitment; (3) the threat of TV; (4) the unprecedented non-buyer readership; and (5) the imbalances in the social composition of the population of Andhra Pradesh consisting of 40.9 per cent of agricultural labourers.

Table 5.4 gives an idea of the extent of Telugu newspaper industry's underutilised capacity, compared to other language segments. 308 centres in 13 languages produced a total audited circulation of 18,950,000 copies in 1996.[67] Thus the average circulation per centre stood at 61,525 Copies. The Telugu newspaper industry's average circulation per centre was about half of that (31,000 copies), the lowest average next only to Urdu, of all the language segments. If the Telugu industry is made to perform on par with the national industry in terms of average circulation per centre, it can double its sales. The industry should redesign its plans to achieve such a realistic goal. Much of the initiative is expected from the challenger firm, *Vaartha,* which was grossly underperforming by bringing out only 19,400 copies per centre from nine centres at that time. Besides, concerted action by all the players, including market leader, to fill in the expectancy-performance gap as perceived by the paper consumers will go a long way in improving the performance of industry as a whole. The extent to which such gaps exist is taken up in chapter-VII.[68]

Table 5.4

Average Circulation per Publication Centre, 1996: Language-wise

	Language	*Total Circulation (thousands)*	*No. of centres*	*Average circulation per centre (thousands)*
1.	Bengali	1,149	6	192
2.	Punjabi	353	3	118
3.	Oriya	518	6	86
4.	Malayalam	1,702	20	85
5.	Kannada	629	8	79
6.	Gujarati	1,909	25	76
7.	Hindi	4,217	62	68
8.	English	4,313	75	58
9.	Marathi	2,015	40	50
10.	Assamese	136	3	45
11.	Telugu	951	31	31
12.	Tamil	945	24	39
13.	Urdu	113	5	23
	Total	18,950	308	61.52

Source: Compiled from ABC data relating to July-December 1996, Audit Bureau of Circulations, Mumbai.

The threat of TV is not limited to the Telugu newspaper market alone. The problem is so threatening that some major Indian newspaper houses started diversifying into television in recent times. *Eenadu* is also one among them, indulging in such cross media ownership. The desirability of such cross media ownership is debatable, considering that 93 per cent of newspaper readers in Andhra Pradesh are already *Eenadu* readers.[69] This is not to say that print and electronic wings of the *Eenadu* group will necessarily play favourites, or show bias, but to point to the danger inherent in such a situation.[70] This scenario raises the prospect of Telugu people becoming as dependent for their information on Ramoji Rao as Australians are on Rupert Murdoch and Kerry Packer.[71]

But in certain circumstances, TV may be good for dailies. People who watch TV for headline news may eventually turn to the next day's morning papers for details and analytical coverage of events. The prospect of TV becoming a threat or an opportunity to the newspaper depends upon how the latter firms react and reorient to the ever changing media scene. Still the first generation TV viewers i.e., the viewers since their childhood have not yet attained the age of reading the newspapers. Then only the impact of TV on newspaper could be clearly known.

The issue of unprecedented non-buyer readership among Telugu people is one relating to their attitudes. Attitudes are not that easy to be changed. It is the problem of problems of underdevelopment. All sorts of underdevelopment stem from the underdeveloped attitudes. People who are aged, well-educated and better employed with higher incomes are reluctant to buy papers. And at the same time they are over enthusiastic to read them, by borrowing or otherwise. This speaks of the lack of self-esteem building up in the minds of the Telugu people. It is a thing to be really ashamed of. Only some sort of social reformation promoting buyer readership, particularly among those who can really afford it, can bring in the attitudinal change. Here again, the newspapers have to play a crucial role in ushering in such a reformist movement of converting the non-buyer readers into the graceful buyer-readers. Buying newspaper should not be viewed as an exercise in spending money wastefully. It is a family product influencing and shaping the destinies of every family member and through them their friends and relatives, thus spreading the message of development to the society at large.

Agricultural labourers forming part of two-fifth of the state's population,[72] their low incomes and low literacy levels together is a major deterrent to the newspaper growth. No other state in India has such a high proportion of farm labourers, including a very backward state of Bihar. Besides, Andhra Pradesh has a poor ratio of roads to area: 56 kms of road per 100 square kms., inferior even to Uttar Pradesh (76: 100), making the newspaper penetration into far-flung rural areas cumbersome and slow.

References

1. See Chapter — III.
2. Philip Kotler, *op. cit.*, pp. 389-390.
3. See Chapter IV.
4. Al Ries and Jack Trout, *op. cit.*, pp. 84-88.
5. *Ibid.*, p. 83.
6. Philip Kotler, *op. cit.*, p. 390.
7. Ralph Biggadike, *Entering New Markets: Strategies and Performance*, Marketing Science Institute, Cambridge, 1977, pp. 12-20.
8. Cf. Table 4.2 Chapter IV.
9. Al Ries and Jack Trout, *op. cit.*, p. 58.
10. *Ibid.*, p. 58.
11. John R. Hauser and Steve M. Shugan, "Defensive Marketing Strategy", *Marketing Science*, Fall 1983, pp. 319-360; John

R. Hauser and P. Gaskin, "Application of the 'Defender' Consumer Model", *Marketing Science,* Fall 1984, p. 327.

12. Philip Kotler, *op. cit.*, pp. 374-375.
13. *Ibid.*, p. 385.
14. *Ibid.*, p. 388.
15. *Ibid.*, p. 385.
16. *Ibid.*, p. 389.
17. *Ibid.*, p.393.
18. *Ibid.*, p. 386.
19. See Chapter IV.
20. Gerald Stone, *Examining Newspapers: What Research Reveals about America's Newspapers*, Sage Publications, Newbury Park, 1987, p. 134.
21. *Ibid.*
22. Cf. Table 4.1, Chapter — V.
23. Al Ries and Jack Trout, *op. cit.*, p. 55.
24. Philip Kotler, *op. cit.*, p. 377.
25. Mitali Kar, *op. cit.*, p. 6.
26. P.L.Vishweshwer Rao, *loc. cit.*
27. Cf. Table 4.2, Chapter - IV.
28. Vinay Kamath, "The Making of Media Moghul", *Business World*, 15th June 1994, p. 102.
29. Lynn de Souza, "Horoscopes and Hustle", *A & M*, July 1993, p. 22.
30. K. Jagadish Prasad, managing director, *Andhra Jyoti* (Quoted from: Vinay Kamath, *op. cit.*, p. 103).
31. Vinay Kamath, *op. cit.*, p. 103.
32. *ABC Half Yearly Reports* for the respective periods, Audit Bureau of Circulations, Mumbai.
33. P.L.Vishweshwer Rao, *op. cit.*, p. 153.
34. Mitali Kar, *op. cit.*, p. 60.
35. Lynn de Souza, *op. cit.*, pp. 22-25.
36. ABC report for the period.

37. The eight attributes are: 1. a bias for action, 2. close to customer, 3. autonomy and entrepreneurship, 4. productivity through people, 5. hands on, value-driven, 6. stick to the knitting, 7. simple form, lean staff, and 8. simultaneous loose - tight properties (*In search of Excellence: Lessons from America's Best-run Companies*, Thomas J. Peters and Robert M., Waterman Jr., (An Imprint of Harper Collins Publishers India), 1993, New Delhi, pp. 13-15).
38. *Ibid.*, p. 156.
39. *Ibid.*, pp. 170-172.
40. Philip Kotler, *op. cit.*, p. 380.
41. Al Ries and Jack Trout, *op. cit.*, p. 56.
42. See Chapter - VIII.
43. K. Sai and Briz Bhushan Sahni, *op. cit.*, p. 28.
44. Philip Kotler, *op. cit.*, p. 390.
45. Cuno Pumpin, *The Essence of Corporate Strategy*, Jaico Publishing House, Mumbai, 1995, p. 39.
46. *Ibid.*, p. 19.
47. Michael E. Porter, *Competitive Advantage: Creating and Sustaining Superior Performance*, The Free Press, New York, 1985, p. 516.
48. Lynn de Souza, *op. cit.*, p. 25.
49. *ABC Half Yearly Reports* for the respective period, Audit Bureau of Circulations, Mumbai.
50. *Ibid.*
51. William J. Stanton, *op. cit.*, p. 190.
52. Quoted from: William J. Stanton, *op. cit.*, p. 190.
53. Peter F. Drucker, *The Practice of Management*, Pan Books, London, 1968, p. 52.
54. *Ibid.*, p. 53.
55. Vinay Kamath, *op. cit.*, p. 103.
56. *Ibid.*
57. Mitali Kar, *op. cit.*, p. 66.

58. Circulation relating to July-December, 1996, *ABC Half Yearly Reports,* Audit Bureau of Circulations, Mumbai.
59. Published from 10 centres, in 1998.
60. Cf. Table 2.7, Chapter - II.
61. *Ibid.*
62. *Ibid.*
63. ABC data relating to July-December, 1996.
64. Philip Kotler, *op. cit.*, pp. 587-88.
65. Vinay Kamath, *op. cit.*, p. 102.
66. Philip Kotler, *op. cit.*, pp. 587-88.
67. ABC data relating to July-December, 1996.
68. See Chapter - VII.
69. As per National Readership Survey, 1997.
70. N. Bhaskara Rao and G.N.S. Raghavan, *Social Effects of Mass Media in India,* Gyan Publishing House, New Delhi, undated, p. 71.
71. Robin Jeffrey, "Indian Languages Newspapers: 4, Telugu: Ingredients of Growth and Failure", *op. cit.*, p. 195.
72. *Statistical Outline of India, 1996-97, op. cit.*, p. 10.

6
The Roots of Strategies
(Consumers and their Consumption Characteristics)

The earlier two chapters dealt with the market position of Telugu dailies in terms of their circulations, the market shares and the strategies employed therefor, in that order. But marketing begins and ends with the customer. This chapter intends to analyse the socio-economic profile of the Telugu newspaper consumers and their consumption characteristics. Their evaluation of what they buy and read is deferred to the next chapter. In essence, the consumer behaviour of Telugu papers that shapes the marketing strategies is the core of this chapter and the one that follows.

The market players' performance with respect to product, price, distribution and promotion results in perceptions held by buyers and prospective buyers. Perceptions, in turn, affect purchases and the market share. Market share is the single best measure of a firm's market position. But it is the result and not the cause of the market position.[1] The consumers and their behaviour constitute the causal variables in marketing, making the roots of any strategic design

All marketing plans embody myriad assumptions about the buyer. Whether we are trying to retain customers, to convert buyers from rivals, to attract new users, or simply to increase sales with existing customers, marketing strategy seeks to influence the buyer. The more we understand *why* people want a product, *how* they go about choosing a brand and *what* induces them to buy or not buy, the more likely we are to design an effective marketing strategy.[2]

This chapter, along with the next one, is based on the reader survey of select Telugu dailies. The details of the survey design and the methodology employed are given in Chapter-III.[3] As already mentioned, the select dailies are only four namely, *Eenadu*, *Andhra Jyoti*, *Andhra Prabha* and *Udayam*. Others could not be included for various reasons given in Chapter - III.

Table 6.1

Respondents' Classification into Buyers and Non-buyers: Paper-wise

Newspaper	*Number of*		*Total*
	Buyers	*Non-buyers*	
Eenadu	97	23	120
Andhra Jyoti	95	25	120
Andhra Prabha	79	41	120
Udayam	81	39	120
Total	352	128	480

Classification of the Respondents

Of the 480 total respondents, 352 were buyers and the on remaining 128 were non-buyer readers as shown in Table 6.1. Further, on the basis of the number of newspaper readers. Table 6.2 shows that 328 of the total 480 readers were multipaper readers and the remaining 152 were single newspaper readers. Each of the four select dailies were read by 120 respondents as their main newspaper. It should be remembered the sample of the respondents was not a random one. It was a purposive sample. Intense newspaper readers, preferably those reading more than one select paper were searched for as the study sought the evaluation of the newspapers by such readers, as is already mentioned.

Table 6.2
Respondents' Classification into Single and Multipaper Readers: Paper-wise

Newspaper	*Number of*		*Total*
	Multipaper readers	*Single paper readers*	
Eenadu	71	49	120
Andhra Jyoti	87	33	120
Andhra Prabha	76	44	120
Udayam	94	26	120
Total	328	152	480

THE SOCIO-ECONOMIC BASES

The socioeconomic origins of the newspaper consumers have marketing implications. Marketers are naturally interested in finding out which of the socioeconomic groups are capable of generating more of newspaper buyers or readers. This section intends to identify the intense newspaper readers by their age, educational level, rural-urban background, occupation and income.

The ensuing Tables 6.3 through 6.6 show the socioeconomic origins of the Telugu newspaper readers, namely, age, educational level, occupation and income, paper-wise. However, a close examination revealed there was no significant association between the brand of a newspaper and the socioeconomic origins. It does not mean that such association is ruled out altogether. If the sample of the readers chosen was a random one, it should have exhibited the tendencies of the association between a particular socioeconomic variable and a particular brand of the paper.

But the sample of readers was a purposive one confining only to the intense newspaper readers, preferably multipaper readers. Considering they read more papers with more involvement, they were indifferent to brand loyalties. As such paper-wise analysis amounts to repetition of inferences of the aggregated analysis. Hence the latter course is resorted to.

1. Age

Age is a significant variable influencing newspaper readership. Since Schramm and White[4] did their landmark study of newspaper-item readership and the age level, research has always documented that youngsters and teenagers begin the newspaper reading habit through the comics. Interest in sports and news broadens with age.[5] Let it be examined now the association between age and intense newspaper readership.

Age-wise, over three-fifth of the consumers under the study were of 20-40 years young, as could be seen from Table 6.3. The middle aged consumers in their 40s comprised about one-sixth. And as many as 13.8 per cent of the consumers were in the age group of 50 years and above.

Table 6.3

Readers of the Four Telugu Dailies by Their Age

Age (years)	*Eenadu*	*Andhra Jyoti*	*Andhra Prabha*	*Udayam*	*Total*	*Per cent*
	No. of readers					
Below 20	11	9	10	10	40	8.3
20 -30	39	33	34	42	148	30.8
30 -40	42	39	25	39	145	30.2
40 -50	17	21	26	17	81	16.9
50- 60	6	11	15	7	39	8.1
60 and above	5	7	10	5	27	5.7
Total	120	120	120	120	480	100

These findings confirm that the newspaper reading habit begins even among the people in their teens or even earlier when they were in a high school or a college. Probably the newspaper habit of their parents or the reading habit at common-places might have influenced them in becoming newspaper readers so young. 8.3 per cent of the sample readers following newspapers even in their teens evidences this. The higher the proportion of readers representing the lowest age group, the greater will be the prospects for newspaper business.

Today's readers of comics are likely to become tomorrow's buyers and serious readers of newspapers. Children, when they grow older after completing their college studies secure jobs, get married and finally set up their own households. The households still continue to be the major base of newspaper consumption everywhere in the world.

Over three-fifth of the serious newspaper readers were in their 20s and 30s. This speaks of the importance of the households that generates newspaper sales. The association between age and intense newspaper reading appears to be getting weaker and weaker as the age advances beyond 40 years. Thus intense newspaper readers in their 40s were only 16.9 per cent compared to 30.2 per cent of their counterparts in their 30s. Readers in their 50s and 60s comprised of only 8.1 per cent and 5.7 per cent of the sample, respectively. Thus, it makes no sense if the interests and aspirations of the young and middle aged consumers are given a goby in designing the newspaper. The lifestyles and values are found to be changing continuously. Youth and middle aged are found to be fast in catching up with the changed values. The newspapers which do not reflect such changes will have to remain as poor marketable products. Accordingly, even some renowned national newspapers failed to predict the opposition of the people to the oppressive measures of the government in the name of internal Emergency during 1975-77. Further, they failed to predict the Janata party wave that followed under the leadership of Loknayak Jayaprakash Narayan. After the election results were out in 1977, such newspapers that misread the people's aspirations have to cut a sorry figure. Such misreading results in serious marketing miscalculation. Loss of credibility results in loss in newspaper circulation not in thousands but in lakhs, not on a short-term basis but for the years to come, thereby ultimately denying a lot of ad revenue.

2. Educational Level

The association between the attribute of education and the newspaper's sales is clearly brought out in Chapter-II,[6] in terms of literacy levels. The relation between educational level and intense newspaper readership is the subject matter here. Table 6.4 reveals that the undergraduates (56.1 per cent) far outnumbered the graduates and postgraduates (43.9 per cent) put together among the serious readers of Telugu newspapers. Postgraduates formed the smallest group (8.9 per cent). Perhaps these people prefer to subscribe to an English daily.

Table 6.4

Readers of the Four Telugu Dailies by Their Educational Levels

Educational level	*Eenadu*	*Andhra Jyoti*	*Andhra Prabha*	*Udayam*	*Total*	*Per cent*
			No. of readers			
Below X Class	15	17	17	24	73	15.1
X class	22	30	30	22	104	21.6
Intermediate	23	22	27	21	93	19.4
Graduate	48	42	34	44	168	35.0
Postgraduate	12	9	12	9	42	8.9
Total	120	120	120	120	480	100.0

Spread of literacy and increased educational levels enlarge and strengthen the base of newspaper sales. Nevertheless, the foregoing analysis reveals the increased educational levels need not necessarily result in increased newspaper sales in regional languages. A great majority of the consumers representing the undergraduate segment leads to this inference. Strengthening the newspapers in the regional languages along the lines of the English newspapers at the national level may improve the situation in favour of language dailies.

By rural-urban background, graduates and postgraduates put together were more in urban areas (52.8 per cent) compared to rural areas (35 per cent) among the intense readers. Such details are not shown in the table.

3. Occupation

Occupation, rather than the income is a determinant of one's social class, lifestyle and buying behaviour. Table 6.5 relates newspaper consumption to the readers' occupation. It is not surprising to find that a majority of them were either white-collared employees or self- employed workmen (51.9 per cent). White-collared employees were nearly one-third of the Telugu newspaper readers. Such employees included clerks, teachers, officers, etc. Self-employed workmen comprising one-fifth of the readers were mechanics and small businessmen. Traders and students were significant among the other readers, representing nearly one-sixth, each.

Though India lives in villages and despite sea-changes taking place on the agricultural front in the name of green revolution, it is distressing to find that the newspaper was not within the reach of the average Indian farmer. Agriculturists making only ten per cent of newspaper consumers supports this view point. This is indicative of the failure of development planning of the last 50 years. As such the options of newspaper marketers appear to be limited on the rural front. Only a paltry 2.5 per cent (12 out of 480) of the intense newspaper readers were women (housewives). As such, Telugu newspaper continued to be predominantly a male product as is elsewhere. General women readership may not be that low. Telugu papers in the recent years were found to be competing with each other in devoting a full page everyday for women.

Table 6.5

Readers' Occupation of the Four Telugu Dailies

Occupation	*Eenadu*	*Andhra Jyoti*	*Andhra Prabha*	*Udayam*	*Total*	*Per cent*
			No. of readers			
1. Agriculturists	13	15	11	9	48	10.0
2. Traders	18	19	18	20	75	15.6
3. Employees	42	34	38	42	156	32.5
4. Self-employed	21	22	26	24	93	19.4
5. Students	19	23	17	18	77	16.0
6. Others*	7	7	10	7	31	6.5
Total	120	120	120	120	480	100.0

* Includes unemployed 14, housewives 12 and professionals 5.

4. Income

The association between income and newspaper sales is already discussed in Chapter-II,[7] in terms of levels of per capita income in different language segments. The impact of reader's household income on intense newspaper readership is to be examined here. Income and intense newspaper reading moved in the same direction as revealed in Table 6.6. Only about a third of the Telugu newspaper readers originated from a segment of less than Rs.25,000 annual income, the rest of two-thirds representing still higher income segments.

Table 6.6

Readers of the Four Telugu Dailies by their Family Income

Annual Income (Rs.)	*Eenadu*	*Andhra Jyoti*	*Andhra Prabha*	*Udayam*	*Total*	*Per cent*
		No. of readers				
Below 25,000	40	37	46	41	164	34.2
25,000-50,000	40	32	42	42	156	32.5
50,000-75,000	30	26	23	33	112	23.3
75,000- 1,00,000	9	10	5	4	28	5.8
1,00,000-and above	1	15	4	—	20	4.2
Total	120	120	120	120	480	100.0

On the whole, it is found that age, education, occupation, income and rural-urban background are closely linked demographics, having a chain relationship among them. Educational levels grow with age of individuals. Better education leads to better employment opportunities, higher income and urban living, ultimately resulting in more newspaper sales. Indian newspaper marketers are yet to face the first real television generation - people who had television since their infancy. Consequently, the young adults, people under 40 years constituted the largest base of newspaper clients, accounting for nearly 70 per cent of intense newspaper readership (Table 6.3, *supra*).

(B) Newspaper Consumption Characteristics

In marketing terminology, products and production have characteristics depending upon the classification of goods into natural, agricultural and manufactured goods. Again between one and another of innumerable products of each class, there are innumerable differences in such characteristics. Similar are also the differences in their consumption characteristics. Marketing strategies are designed on the tripod of the product, production and consumption characteristics.

The habitual aspect of newspaper reading is one of the neglected themes of newspaper research in India. Origins of the newspaper habit; what paper they buy and read as their main newspaper; how frequently they buy and read; how eagerly they await to receive their newspapers; their prime tune preferences; the number of rounds in which they complete their reading; what other newspapers they read, besides their main newspaper; etc., consumption aspects of Telugu readers are taken up for analysis in this section.

1. Impact of Parent's News Interest

Stone and Wetherington surveyed a small sample of college students in California and found that even college students were bound by the newspaper reading habits they established at home ten years earlier.[8] The present survey also attempted to find out whether the present readers were influenced by their parents' news interest.

A majority of the sample readers (55.6 per cent or 267 out of 480) revealed that their parents exhibited keen interest in the newspapers during their (respondents') childhood, as shown in Table 6.7. 60.9 per cent of such urban readers appreciated their parents' interest in newspaper reading, whereas only 45 per cent of the rural readers acknowledged so. Thus a strong correlation existed between parent's news interest and that of their children.

Means of gratification of such parents' news interest are shown in Table 6.8. The major gratification source was subscribing to a daily on a regular basis, followed by its occasional buying. As many as 60.5 per cent of the urban parents and 54.2 per cent rural parents purchased the Telugu newspapers regularly. The incidence of occasional buying was more among rural parents (36.1 per cent) and less among urban parents (22.1 per cent). Borrowing was yet another means of gratification of parent's news interest. The incidence of borrowing was more among urban parents (15.9 per cent) and less among rural parents (9.7 per cent). However it should be remembered borrowing includes reading at community places like library, panchayat office, street corners, coffee houses, besides borrowing from friends or neighbours.

Table 6.7

Parent's Newspaper Interest during the Reader's Childhood

Parent's Newspaper interest	*Urban*	*Rural*	*Total*	*Urban*	*Rural*	*Total*
	No. of readers			*Per cent*		
Yes	195	72	267	60.9	45	55.6
No	108	82	190	33.8	51.2	39.6
Cannot say	11	3	14	3.4	1.9	2.9
No response	6	3	9	1.9	1.9	1.9
Total	320	160	480	100	100	100.0

n = 480

Table 6.8

How Parent's Newspaper Interest is Gratified during the Reader's Childhood

Means of gratification	*Urban*	*Rural*	*Total*	*Urban*	*Rural*	*Total*
	No. of readers			*Per cent*		
Subscribing to a daily	118	39	157	60.5	54.2	58.9
Buying Occasionally	43	26	69	22.1	36.1	25.8
Borrowing*	31	7	38	15.9	9.7	14.2
No response	3	—	3	1.5	—	1.1
Total	195	72	267	100	100	100.0

n = 267 Readers whose parents had newspaper interest.

* Includes borrowing from friends or neighbours, reading at community places like library, panchayat office, street corners and coffee houses.

In this context the findings of Stone and Wetherington mentioned earlier are worth noting. Their findings showed, among other things: (1) If the parents had a special time to read a newspaper, so did students; (2) if the parents had a special place to read a newspaper, so did students; (3) students were likely to read the newspaper at the same time of the day their parents did; and (4) students were currently likely to read the newspaper in the same room they remembered their parents having read it.[9] Such of those findings are indicative of the strength of a household as a major base of the current and future readers of the newspaper.

2. Time Sense and Newspaper Use

It is the newspaper which greets everybody early in the morning. Despite several television channels telecasting news bulletins every hour - 24 hours in a day, newspaper reading is considered as one of the joyous and indispensable activities of human life. Newspaper readers seldom think that reading a daily is a chore or a waste of time. The paper boy is often considered as an important visitor to the house and his delayed arrival even by half an hour is very much felt by

Table 6.9

Distribution of Readers by Their Reading Habits

Type of reading habit	*No. of readers*	*Per cent*
Awaiting impatiently to receive the newspaper	56	11.7
Reading soon after waking up	196	40.8
Reading at convenience	212	44.2
No response	16	3.3
Total	480	100.0

news-hungry readers. Time sense related habits of the readers in newspaper use often give some clues about the reader's intensity of desire for his newspaper.

Table 6.9 discloses the eagerness of the Telugu readers in receiving and reading their dailies. For a majority of them (52.5 per cent or 252 out of 480), the day essentially began with the newspaper reading. They include 11.7 per cent of readers who were in the habit of awaiting to receive their morning newspaper with a little bit of curious impatience. This finding suggests how these readers were addicted to the newspaper reading. 44.2 per cent (212 out of 480) read the daily at their convenience. Availability of the borrowed newspaper and leisure time were two important factors that could affect one's access to a daily. This shows how important the time of delivery to the marketers. The earlier chapters adequately illustrated how *Eenadu* on its entry in 1974 capitalised on the weakness of other competitors in not adhering to timely delivery. Nowadays, it is a common phenomenon in the Telugu newspaper market to find various publishers racing with each other to deliver the paper at the earliest. Similar competition exists even between Telugu and English dailies in this regard. Instances of switching over to another daily, in case of delays, are not uncommon. Multieditions from multicentres, dependence on private distribution network, instead of the public transportation system, use of the latest printing technology by the marketers are all aimed at achieving the goal of prompt delivery. Even those who are not interested in scanning the daily soon after delivery are found to be upset, if it is not received in time. As such, even those reading at their convenience cannot be taken for a ride. Thus timely delivery of a newspaper had come to stay as the essence of contract between the subscriber and the publisher in the Telugu newspaper market.

Table 6.10

Number of Rounds in which the Readers Complete Their Reading the Newspaper

No. of Rounds	*No. of Readers*	*Per cent*
One rounds	194	40.4
Two rounds	201	41.9
Three rounds or more	67	13.9
No response	18	3.8
Total	480	100.0

Newspaper reading is not necessarily a one-time affair. A reader who looks at the news headlines in the morning might prefer to go through the contents in detail after the day's work is over. Table 6.10 reveals the number of rounds in which the readers completed the reading of the newspaper. 82.3 per cent of the respondents completed the paper reading in one or two rounds. It required three sittings or more for 13.9 .per cent of them. The number of rounds in which the reader completes the reading of his newspaper is no indication of either the size of the newspaper or the amount of time devoted for reading the newspaper.

It should be remembered that the number of rounds related to the reading of their main newspaper to which they subscribed to or borrowed. Findings such as these suggest that Telugu newspapers are not able to sustain reader interest beyond one or two rounds. Readers who are habituated to follow both the Telugu and English dailies were found to have a feeling that usually the former newspapers did not last for more than one round. In contrast, they were emphatic in stating at least three or four rounds were needed to complete an English daily. A situation as this poses a serious challenge to the marketers of Telugu papers. It could be one reason for the underperformance of Telugu dailies in particular and language dailies, in general, compared to their counterparts in English in terms of the DTP ratio. However, analysing the performance of Telugu dailies in terms of adequacy of news etc., is deferred to the next chapter.

Table 6.11

Prime Time Preferences of the Urban and Rural Readers

Prime time preference	*Urban*	*Rural*	*Total*
	No. of readers (per cent)		
Before 6 am	7.2	1.9	5.4
6 to 8 am	52.1	60.0	54.8
8 to 10 am	16.3	20.6	17.8
10 to 12 noon	8.4	5.0	7.3
12 to 2 pm	6.6	5.0	6.0
After 2 pm	6.6	5.0	6.0
No Response	2.8	2.5	2.7
Total	100.0	100.0	100.0

n=480

Commencing earlier than 6 o'clock in the morning, the prime time reading of Telugu dailies appeared to end by 10 AM (Table 6.11). As many as 82.5 per cent of the less busy rural readers and 75.6 per cent of the more busy urban readers completed the newspaper reading by 10 AM. The peak of the prime time was between 6 and 8 AM during which time 52.1 per cent of the urban readers and 60 per cent of the rural readers preferred to do their paper reading. It is worth noting that 7.2 per cent of readers in urban areas were habituated to read their newspaper before 6 o'clock in the morning, as against not even 2 per cent of such readers in rural areas. Closeness to the publication centres enabled the urban reader to get his newspaper earlier than his rural counterpart.

Paper-wise prime time preferences are given in Table 6.12. Of the one-fifth of the readers completing their reading beyond 10 o'clock for all the papers put together, the readers *of Andhra Prabha* constitute the largest segment (27.5 per cent), followed by *Udayam* (21.6 per cent), *Andhra Jyoti* (15.8 per cent) and *Eenadu* (12.5 per cent). Such a late completion of the reading might be partly because of the late delivery of the papers and partly because of habitual reasons.

Table 6.12

Prime Time Preferences of Readers: Paper-wise

Prime time Preference	*Eenadu*	*Andhra Jyoti*	*Andhra Prabha*	*Udayam*	*Total*
	No. of readers (per cent)				
Before 6 am	5.8	7.5	2.5	5.8	5.4
6 to 8 am	61.7	58.4	46.7	52.6	54.8
8 to 10 am	14.2	18.3	23.3	15.0	17.8
10 to 12 noon	7.5	6.7	5.8	9.1	7.3
12 to 2 pm	1.7	5.8	10.0	6.7	6.0
After 2 pm	3.3	3.3	11.7	5.8	6.0
No response	5.8	-	-	5.0	2.7
Total	100.0	100.0	100.0	100.0	100.0

n = 480

Advancing prime time preferences are suggestive of the life of the daily getting shorter than what is usually thought of. The foregoing analysis makes it clear that for all practical purposes the life of the Telugu daily is ending around 10 o'clock. Such a characteristic as this may adversely affect the loose sales on newspaper stands, which are estimated to be about 15 per cent on weekdays and about 25 per cent on Sundays. Some sort of innovation to speed up such loose sales during the earlier part of the day is to be thought of.

3. What Papers They Read

Though the survey covered only 120 readers each of the four select Telugu dailies, vast differences were found in their consumption habits relating to the frequency of buying and reading and also relating to their habit of reading other Telugu dailies, besides their main newspaper.

In addition to variations in consumption habits, there was an element of overlapping newspaper interests among the readers. To make it more clear, the 480 readers under the survey did not merely read 480 papers only. Many of them were multipaper readers, may be buying or without buying those papers. The 480 respondents' buying and reading habits of the select Telugu dailies are shown in Tables 6.13 and 6.14.

Irrespective of buying it or not, nearly 70 per cent of the sample respondents (335 out of 480 readers) read *Eenadu,* either regularly or frequently. Similarly, *Andhra Jyoti* was read by about half of them, whereas *Udayam* and *Andhra Prabha* enjoyed the readership of 40.4 and 37.7 per cent, respectively. Frequent readership implies reading it at least thrice a week.

On the whole, 352 respondents (73.3 per cent) were regular buyers of at least one Telugu daily. Of them, 324 bought one paper each, 23 two each and 5 three each, totalling 385 papers in all. *Eenadu* and *Andhra Jyoti* were regularly bought by 23.3 and 21 per cent of them, respectively. More or less, the regular subscribers of *Udayam* (17.1 per cent) and *Andhra Prabha* (16.7 per cent) were equal.

Coming to readership, regularly or frequently, without buying, 42 per cent of the respondents read *Eenadu,* followed by *Andhra Jyoti* (25.2 per cent), *Andhra Prabha* (19.2 per cent) and *Udayam* (17.3 per cent). These non-buyer readers should not be mistaken as non-buyers of any one of the Telugu papers under the study. Much of such non-buyer readership was supplemental paper reading. It was supplemental to the

Table 6.13

Buying and Reading Habits of the Respondents

Newspaper	*Buying*			*Reading without buying*		*Grand*	*Per cent*	
	Regularly	*Frequently*	*Total*	*Regularly*	*Frequently*	*Total*	*Total*	
Eenadu	112	21	133	91	111	202	335	69.7
Andhra Jyoti	101	15	116	50	71	121	237	49.3
Andhra Prabha	80	9	89	46	46	92	181	37.7
Udayam	82	29	111	32	51	83	194	40.4
Total	385*							

n = 480

* Altogether, 352 respondents bought 385 papers: 324 one each, 23 two each and 5 three each. The remaining 128 respondents were nonbuyers.

Note: Of the 480 respondents, 352 were buyers; 152 of them were single newspaper readers and 328 read multiple newspapers.

Table 6.14

Buying and Reading Habits of the Respondents (Per cent)

Newspaper	No. of respondents (per cent)						
	Buying			Reading without buying			Grand Total
	Regularly	Frequently	Total	Regularly	Frequently	Total	
Eenadu	23.3	4.4	27.7	18.9	23.1	42	69.7
Andhra Jyoti	21	3.1	24.1	10.4	14.8	25.2	49.3
Andhra Prabha	16.7	1.8	18.5	9.6	9.6	19.2	37.7
Udayam	17.1	6.0	23.1	6.7	10.6	17.3	40.4

n=480

paper to which they have subscribed to, keeping in mind that 73.3 per cent of the sample readers were subscribing to at least one daily.

An attempt is also made to know, paper-wise, the select Telugu newspaper buyers' reading habits of other Telugu dailies (Table 6.15). 62.7 per cent of *Andhra Jyoti,* 51.8 per cent of *Udayam* and 44.3 per cent of *Andhra Prabha* buyers also read *Eenadu* respectively. This shows the popularity *of Eenadu* even among the buyers of other Telugu newspapers. Its high readership might be due to its easy accessibility to other readers since it is the largest circulated daily.

Table 6.15

Buyers' Habit of Reading other Telugu Dailies*

Main Newspaper	*No. of buyers*	*Per cent of buyers reading other dailies*			
		Eenadu	*Andhra Jyoti*	*Andhra Prabha*	*Udayam*
Eenadu	97	—	39.1	19.5	30.9
Andhra Jyoti	95	62.1	—	17.8	22.1
Andhra Prabha	79	44.3	25.3	—	7.7
Udayam	81	51.8	33.3	19.7	—
Total	352				

n = 352 buyers.

* Includes both regular and frequent reading.

Similarly, *Eenadu* buyers were also in the habit of reading other dailies. *Andhra Jyoti* was the popular daily among the *Eenadu* buyers as 39 per cent of them read it, either regularly or frequently. *Udayam* was read by 31 per cent of *Eenadu* buyers. Nearly 45 per cent of *Andhra Prabha* buyers also read *Eenadu,* while *Andhra Jyoti* was read by 25 per cent of *Andhra Prabha* buyers. Thus, the reading habits of newspaper buyers show how they were interested in other papers also.

Borrowing from neighbours and friends, public libraries, college and school libraries, offices and commercial establishments were the main sources of readership without buying. Borrowership from neighbours and friends was more prevalent in villages.

Even non-buyer readership is a significant dimension in newspaper business. The advertiser also relies upon readership, besides circulation of a newspaper while buying newspaper space.

Table 6.16

Average Readership per Copy

Newspaper	*No. of buyers*	*Buyers' family readership*	*Borrower readership*	*Total readership*	*Average readership per copy*
Eenadu	97	368	434	802	8.26
Andhra Jyoti	95	338	544	882	9.28
Andhra Prabha	79	258	466	724	9.16
Udayam	81	294	414	708	8.74
Total	352	1258	1858	3116	8.85

n = 352 buyers.

Readership per Copy

It is attempted to assess the average readership of a single copy of newspaper. A distinct feature of Indian readership is that Indians, in general, prefer to read a newspaper without buying it. In the present survey, the 352 copies were read by 3116 people of which 40.3 per cent were the family members of the subscribers as seen from Table 6.16. Interestingly, the average borrower readership per copy was 5.27 readers compared to the average buyer's family readership of 4 per copy. Thus, the average readership per daily worked out to 9 readers. It is to be noted that a newspaper was read by more number of people in rural areas (9.77 per copy), compared to urban areas (8.46 per copy). Such details are not shown in the table.

The multiplicity of readership for every copy of newspaper, both within and outside the family, has its impact on the shape of the newspaper. In contrast to the practice in earlier days, nowadays, a Telugu paper is coming out in three sections or more instead of one. They are: main paper, feature supplement, district supplement, besides Sunday supplement. Though they are all cost driving forces, the multi-sectional presentation enhances the product divisibility, enabling it to be shared among several readers at the same time with lot of ease. Even the main paper usually presented in two broadsheets is made divisible by carrying forward the continuations from the first page to the second page, instead of the first to the third page, for example.

Even if one of the several non-buyer readers per copy, outside the family readers, could be transformed into an actual buyer, the Telugu newspaper industry would be able to catch up with other language dailies in improving its dailies-to-thousand people ratio.

4. Dependency on the Newspaper

What is dealt here is not the dependency on the particular brand of paper, the respondents bought or read. What is dealt here is their dependency on the newspaper as a medium compared to other media of mass communication, radio and TV, for news. Barring one or two, all respondents owned a radio or a two-in-one. Nearly three out of four respondents owned a TV set. More than one out of four of the respondents in rural areas felt buying a TV set was beyond their financial capacity. Some of them, however, viewed TV programmes occasionally at their friends' houses.

Table 6.17

Readers' First Source of News, Usually

First source of News	*Urban*	*Rural*	*Total*	*Urban*	*Rural*	*Total*
	No. of readers			*Per cent*		
Newspaper	190	65	255	39.4	40.6	53.1
Radio	45	50	95	14.0	31.3	19.8
TV	76	43	119	23.8	26.9	24.8
No response	9	2	11	2.8	1.2	2.3
Total	320	160	480	100	100	100

n = 480 readers

The survey revealed that 45 per cent of the readers admitted that TV affected the newspaper reading habit of their family members. Interestingly, 60 per cent of readers in rural areas did not see any threat from TV to their newspaper reading habit.

Using Newspaper as the First Source of News

As seen from Table 6.17, for more than half of the respondents (53.1 per cent) newspaper was the first source of news. The government-controlled television (Doordarshan) which is a late entrant on the Indian media scene has outstripped the older player radio as news medium. While one-fourth of the respondents rated TV as their first source of news, only 20 per cent of the respondents identified radio as the first source of news. However, significant differences persisted between the urban readers and their rural counterparts in this regard. Newspaper was the first source of news for 59.4 per cent of urban readers. But in rural areas newspaper was not that much popular as only 40.6 per cent of the respondents were of the same view. Evidently, radio was somewhat closer to newspaper as news medium in rural areas. About one-third of the rural respondents (31.3 per cent) acknowledged radio as their first source of news as against 14 per cent of the respondents in urban areas.

The Intensity of Consumption: The first source of news need not be the most intensively used medium. Though 45 per cent of the respondents felt that newspaper was not their first source of news, most of them (95 per cent) confessed that they usually rely mostly upon newspaper for news. Interestingly, no difference is visible between the readers of urban areas and those of rural areas on this front.

On the whole, it augurs well to the Telugu newspaper business to find out that the newspaper continues to be the first and the most intensively used source of news even in the face of the invasion by electronic media.

References

1. Victor P. Buell, Marketing Management: A Strategic Planning Approach, Mc Graw- Hill, New York, 1985, p. 90.
2. John O' Shaughnessy, *op. cit.*, p. 61.
3. Cf. Table 3.1, Chapter-III.
4. W. Schramm and D. White, "Age, Education, and Economic Status: Factors in Newspaper Reading", Journalism Quarterly, 26, 1949, pp. 150-158.
5. Gerald Stone, *op. cit.*, p. 39.
6. Cf. Table 2.7 and 2.8.
7. Cf. Table 2.7.
8. G.C. Stone, and R.V. Wetherington, Jr., "Confirming the Newspaper Reading Habit", Journalism Quarterly, 56: 1979, pp. 554-561, 566.
9. *Ibid.*

7
Consumers' Evaluation
(The Impact of Strategies)

Consumers of the Telugu newspapers and their consumption characteristics are identified in the previous chapter. This chapter attempts to find out the buying motives influencing their choice of the daily, and the extent to which they are satisfied of the daily, non-daily and Sunday features of their paper. Comparative evaluation of the select papers by the multipaper readers is also taken up here.

EVALUATION BY BUYING MOTIVES

It is intended to identify the most important factors or buying motives influencing the Telugu reader in the choice of his or her daily newspaper. In terms of unit price, availability and convenience of purchase, though a newspaper appears to have only short term marketing implications as are applicable to convenience goods like matches and wax candles, the newspaper choice decisions have long term marketing implications. Brand loyalties in case of a newspaper are found to be very strong, as observed in Chapter-IV.[1] Though Telugu subscribers were known for their readiness to encourage a new paper, they were not found changing their newspaper frequently. Once they started subscribing to a paper of their choice, they continued to buy it for several years. It is a matter of great concern to the marketers to find out which of the tangible or intangible attributes of a newspaper influence the readers in the choice of their daily. Such attributes include latest news, their adequacy, unbiased and effective presentation, prompt delivery, etc.

The buyers of the select newspapers were asked to rank, in the order of importance, three of the factors listed in Tables 7.1 through 7.4 which they considered responsible for choosing their particular daily. Factors thus ranked are rated by weighted score. The first ranking item carried three points, the second two points and the third one point. Overall ranking is made on the basis of the percentage of total weighted score for each motivating factor. The readers' choices relating to the daily, non-daily features and Sunday features are similarly ranked, weighted, rated and the overall rankings are obtained which will be taken up later in this chapter.

Reverting to ascertainment of factors motivating the choice of the daily, the information is obtained from 352 buyer-respondents only, whose distribution among the four dailies ranged from 71 to 97 buyers.

1. Eenadu

Of all the buying motives, latest news was uppermost in the minds of *Eenadu*'s buyers, influencing their choice of the daily. An overwhelming 82.5 per cent of *Eenadu's*, buyers (80 out of 97) ranked it as either number one, two or three of the factors that motivated them to choose it, thus making it a No. 1 motivator (overall ranking being number one), with a rating score of 33 per cent (Table 7.1). Next to latest news, the buyers of *Eenadu* were influenced by prompt delivery and adequate news, their overall ranking being No. 2 and No. 3, respectively. Nevertheless, prompt delivery and adequate news were not as strong as the latest news in influencing the buyers' choice, as they were assigned the rating score of only 17 per cent and 15.9 per cent respectively.

Table 7.1

Factors Responsible for Choosing *Eenadu*

Factors Responsible	*Readers' ranking Number: One*	*Two*	*Three*	*Weighted score*	*Rating (per cent)*	*Rank*
	No. of Readers					
1. Prompt delivery	27	4	3	92	17.0	2
2. Latest news	32	34	14	178	33.0	1
3. Adequate news	11	20	13	86	15.9	3
4. Unbiased news	1	4	10	21	3.9	7
5. Effective presentation	4	10	20	52	9.6	5
6. Family habit	14	11	7	71	13.2	4
7. Emotional attachment	7	6	7	40	7.4	6
No response	1	8	23	—	—	—
Total	97	97	97	540	100.0	

n = 97 buyers

The three of the product attributes influencing the *Eenadu* customers are related to each other. If the paper contained the latest news is delivered a bit late, it amounts to the latter attribute destroying the former attribute. Thus the twin attributes of latest news and prompt delivery alone are capable of creating time and place utilities in one stroke. But what is equally important is the adequacy of news. The hunger for news is not an easily satisfiable human want as in case of physiological needs. If a paper known for promptness of delivery with latest news does not make a good coverage of news, it is not likely to attract more customers. As such, the market leader *Eenadu* appeared never lost sight of such an important need. It should also be remembered that of these three attributes, prompt delivery is more a maintenance or hygiene factor rather than a motivating factor in terms of

Herzberg's two-factor model.[2] For example, if newspaper is promptly delivered, it may not bring additional satisfaction. But, if it is delayed, it brings a lot of dissatisfaction on that day. Thus, the presence of a maintenance factor is not felt, whereas its absence is felt. At a time when prompt delivery culture was brought into the industry on *Eenadu's* entry, it was a sensation and a motivating factor. Motivating factor brings satisfaction in its presence and its absence is not felt. Prompt delivery culture has come to stay in the Telugu newspaper business nowadays. Resultantly, the prompt delivery that used to be a motivating factor formerly has become a maintenance factor at present. Perhaps such a changed situation might have resulted in *Eenadu* buyers acknowledging it as No.2 motivator instead of as No. 1 motivator that shook the market on entry.

Of the rest of buying motives, family habit significantly influenced the market leader's clients, followed by effective presentation which were assigned the fourth and the fifth overall rankings, in that order. However, *Eenadu's* buyers had least consideration for factors such as unbiased news or emotional attachment in choosing their daily.

2. *Andhra Jyoti*

It is interesting to find that family habit was No. l buying motive which influenced *Andhra Jyoti's* customers (Table 7.2). Over half (49 out of 95) of them ranked it as either number one or two or three of the factors that motivated them to choose it, thus making it the No. l motivator, with a rating score of 23 per cent. Such a motive as this spells immediate danger to the runner-up companies. Patronising a product on the basis of a family habit implies that buyers are aware of the availability of better products in the market. Perhaps the family habit stood on their path in reaching the new brands. Such product loyalties do not last longer in the face of competition.

Table 7.2

Factors Responsible for Choosing *Andhra Jyoti*

Factors Responsible	*Readers' Ranking Number:* One	Two	Three	*Weighted score*	*Rating (per cent)*	*Rank*
	No. of Readers					
1. Prompt delivery	17	8	4	71	13.8	3
2. Latest news	12	19	5	79	15.4	2
3. Adequate news	6	10	29	67	13.0	4
4. Unbiased news	16	9	13	79	15.4	2
5. Effective presentation	8	17	8	66	12.8	5
6. Family habit	28	13	8	118	23.0	1
7. Emotional attachment	8	4	2	34	6.6	6
8. No response	1	15	26	—	—	—
Total	95	95	95	514	100.0	

n = 95 buyers.

Latest news and unbiased news were tied for the second place in the overall ranking of buying motives by *Andhra Jyoti's* customers, closely followed by prompt delivery for the third place. Adequate news and effective presentation were closely behind the prompt delivery in that order. The second place to fifth place motives varied from within the narrow interval of 12.8 to 15.4 per cent in terms of rating scores. Such movements within narrow limits are indicative of the absence of striking product attributes that motivate a newspaper purchase. This cannot be a much desired market position for a runner-up firm. In other words, such a product lacks in competitive advantage in the absence of its distinctive differentiation from the competitive products.

3. *Andhra Prabha*

The buyers of *Andhra Prabha* liked it most because of its

unbiased news. Nearly two-thirds of them (52 out of 79) have assigned it a maximum of 25.3 per cent of rating score, as shown in Table 7.3. No doubt, unbiased news is a distinctive advantage for a newspaper to be proud of. Being the chain of Express group - founded by Ramnath Goenka, the lion of unfettered freedom of the press, *Andhra Prabha* commanded the respect of its readers for its impartial coverage of news since its inception. And it reigned supreme as a market leader till the advent of *Eenadu* as is discussed in Chapter-IV.[3] In a background such as this, it is not surprising to find that its buyers stated the heritage of family habit was motive No. 2 hat influenced them. In terms of rating score, the family habit (23.4 per cent) was closely followed by adequate news (21.1 per cent).

Table 7.3

Factors Responsible for Choosing *Andhra Prabha*

Factors responsible	*Readers' Ranking Number:*			*Weighted Rating*		
	One	*Two*	*Three*	*score*	*(per cent)*	*Rank*
	No. of Reader					
1. Prompt delivery	7	1	1	24	5.6	6
2. Latest news	6	7	4	23	5.3	7
3. Adequate news	14	20	9	91	21.1	3
4. Unbiased news	20	17	15	109	25.3	1
5. Effective presentation	5	12	13	52	12.1	4
6. Family habit	21	15	8	101	23.4	2
7. Emotional attachment	5	5	6	31	7.2	5
8. No response	1	2	23	—	—	—
Total	79	79	79	431	100.0	

n = 79 buyers.

It is unbelievable to find out that the leader of the yester years was grossly underperforming on two important fronts, namely, prompt delivery and the latest news. Their rating scores as buying motives literally touched the rock bottom (5.6 and 5.3 per cent, respectively). It is amazing to find a chain newspaper least performing on such counts. Usually a paper belonging to a chain is supposed to enjoy competitive advantage in gathering latest news and in delivering the paper at the earliest. Expectedly, in the years that followed this survey, *Andhra Prabha* continued to lose its circulation to fall farther behind most of its competitors.

4. Udayam

Adequacy of news seemed to attract *Udayam's* buyers significantly, followed by latest news and unbiased news, as exhibited in Table 7.4. Nevertheless, the thorough disappointment of its buyers on delivery front was glaring. In the overall ranking of the motives influencing the purchase of *Udayam,* prompt delivery was found at the bottom of the table, placed sixth. By the time the reader survey was undertaken the paper was found to be in great difficulties to come out. Expectedly, its end came soon in 1995.

READERS' EVALUATION OF THEIR DAILY

Once the buying motives lead to the selection of a newspaper and its purchase, then it is interesting to find out whether the years of consumption that followed kept the readers satisfied. Self-evaluation by the consumers of respective papers is resorted to for the purpose. The consumers include 352 buyer-consumers that formed the sample in the earlier section to evaluate buying motives, plus 128 non-buyer consumers, making a total of 480 readers. The total of 480 readers represent 120 each of the four dailies. In an attempt to seek an evaluation by intense readers, the survey had to cover such of those non-buyer consumers. In case there are multiple buyers or readers among them following more than one newspaper, such of them were asked to evaluate only one of such papers which they considered as their main paper.

Table 7.4

Factors Responsible for Choosing *Udayam*

Factors responsible	*Readers' Ranking Number:*			*Weighted score*	*Rating (per cent)*	*Rank*
	One	*Two*	*Three*			
	No. of Readers					
1. Prompt delivery	10	4	5	43	9.5	6
2. Latest news	16	13	7	81	17.9	2
3. Adequate news	13	28	19	114	25.2	1
4. Unbiased news	15	10	10	75	16.6	3
5. Effective presentation	5	11	1	148	10.6	5
6. Family habit	15	7	10	69	15.3	4
7. Emotional attachment	4	3	4	22	4.9	7
8. No response	3	5	15	—	—	—
Total	81	81	81	452	100.0	

n= 81 buyers.

The readers were asked to evaluate their paper feature-wise. For the purpose, the contents of the select four newspapers were classified into three categories, namely, daily features, non-daily features and the Sunday features or the features forming part of Sunday supplement. Readers' evaluation of daily features is to be taken up first.

1. Readers' Choicest Daily Features

The items that appeared almost every day in the newspaper were bunched as daily features for this purpose.

They included news, cartoons, editorials, editorial page articles, sports, women's page, cinema, district supplement, etc., as listed in the ensuing Tables 7.6 through 7.9. Readers or newspaper consumers were asked, paper-wise, to rank in order of importance the features they liked most over the years of their reading. At least five years of continuous reading of the concerned paper is taken as a criterion for the purpose.

Readers ranking of the daily features they liked, weighted scores, their rating and the overall ranking are presented in Tables 7.6 through 7.9, paper-wise. A preview account of the overall ranking of the five choicest daily features are shown in Table 7.5 which precedes the aforesaid tables. Irrespective of the readers' brand of the newspaper, their choicest item among the daily features was naturally - news. In terms of rating scores, it was 31-plus per cent (Tables 7.6 through 7.9) in respect of all the four papers. If a newspaper is not for news what for it should be. Most of the readers might have rightly perceived the meaning of a newspaper in this sense.

Table 7.5

Readers' Five Choicest Items among the Daily Features of Their Newspapers

*Rank**	*Eenadu*	*Andhra Jyoti*	*Andhra Prabha*	*Udayam*
1	News	News	News	News
2	Cartoons	Cartoons	Cartoons	Cartoons
3	District supplement	Editorials	Editorials	District supplement
4	Editorials	Editorial page articles	*Telugunadu*	Editorials
5	Editorial page articles	District supplement	Editorial page articles	Editorial page articles

Ranking is given on the basis of the overall rating of daily contents, as calculated in Tables 7.6 through 7.9.

Coming to the second choicest item (Table 7.5), again there was unanimity among readers of the four dailies. This time the choice fell on cartoons. Telugu papers usually carry a pocket cartoon placed in the bottom left hand corner of the front page. Occasionally, they also carry cartoons in other sizes at other places, depending on their importance. It may not take more than a couple of minutes to go through and enjoy such cartoons. Popularising the cartoon culture was initiated by *Eenadu* right on its entry into the market as a nicher. It does not mean that Telugu papers never before carried cartoons. Cartoons are perhaps as old as Telugu papers. But, fanatically positioning it to trigger enormous audience interest continues to be the novel marketing exercise at *Eenadu* even today. Its readers are found to be not only genuinely enjoying its cartoons but they are found to be the subject matter of discussion at public places. Sometimes the reader analysts of *Eenadu* cartoons go to the extent of predicting the topic for next days cartoon, depending on the matter of topical interest. It is not unusual to find reader expectations coming true the next day. Its regular reader missing a daily sometimes may not be unusual. But even one of its casual readers does not like to miss the cartoon. Nowadays, humour is becoming increasingly a scarce commodity. Such features provide a great relief and reading pleasure to the newspaper consumer. That is how Sridhar's cartoons gained immeasurable popularity which might have fetched a significant increase in the sales of the paper. In a competitive environment as this, other papers have also started exploiting the use of this feature, though they might have not fetched a distinct circulation gain. Irrespective of the consequences, cartoon has become a regular item of liking to the newspaper consumer. Such a wider appreciation and fuller understanding of the editorial cartoons' messages in Telugu papers is contrary to the findings of Brinkman[4] and Carl.[5] their studies indicate editorial cartoons are not as influential as editorials and only 15 per cent of readers fully understood editorial cartoons' messages.

District supplement was the third choicest feature both to the readers of *Eenadu* and *Udayam*, whereas those of *Andhra Jyoti* and *Andhra Prabha* liked editorials in that place. Of course, the contents of district supplement are not different from news, the only difference being the news is mostly local. The marketing implications of the district supplement were already taken up in Chapter-V.[6] It is worth-noting to find the editorials of *Andhra Jyoti* and *Andhra Prabha* were more liked by the readers of those papers compared to the liking of the editorials in *Eenadu* and *Udayam* to their readers.

The aforesaid findings reinforce the research findings of Bain and Weaver that readers devote more reading activity to hard news.[7] On the whole, the five choicest daily features, irrespective of their paper-wise ranking, were limited to only five prominent features, though the list subjected to evaluation contained eight specified features plus several other nonspecified features. The prominent features thus emerged were the news, cartoons, district supplement or page, editorials and editorial page articles. Understandably, they are all either news or news-related items as different from magazine features that are found to be increasingly dominating Telugu newspapers nowadays. For example, daily features on cinema, women and health are occupying acres of Telugu papers' space. But the survey results indicate that they are not among the star attractions of a daily paper. This implies contribution of such features to the core value of the product is insignificant. The market leader might be benefited, considering its capability to attract a lion's share of ad revenue. But the trend of the runner-up firms poorly imitating the market leader in providing such features at enormous cost without much impact on ad revenue may lead to marketing disasters in the long run.

Table 7.6

What the Readers Like Most from the Daily Features: *Eenadu*

Daily features	Readers' ranking Number: One	Two	Three	four	five	Weighted score	Rating (per cent)	Rank
1. News	79	30	8	2	—	543	31.3	1
2. Cartoons	11	60	20	6	2	369	21.2	2
3. Editorials	1	13	19	10	8	142	8.2	4
4. Editorial page articles	4	3	9	12	13	101	5.8	7
6. *Vasundhara* (women)	2	5	15	13	11	112	6.4	6
7. Cinema	—	1	4	10	9	45	2.6	9
8. District supplement	18	—	19	23	25	218	12.5	3
9. Other features[a]	—	2	9	15	18	83	4.8	8
No response	—	—	4	10	30			
Total	120	120	120	120	120	1738	100.0	

n= 120 readers.

[a]Other features include: financial news, *Jnananetram* (science), *Tookiga* (human interest) and *Bhubhramanam* (international news)

Table 7.7

What the Readers Like Most from the Daily Features: *Andhra Jyoti*

Daily features	Readers' ranking Number:					Weighted score	Rating (per cent)	Rank
	One	Two	Three	four	five			
1. News	101	12	2	2	—	563	32.8	1
2. Cartoons	7	62	8	4	2	317	18.5	2
3. Editorials	3	12	28	14	4	179	10.4	3
4. Editorial page articles	2	3	17	25	6	129	7.5	4
5. Sports	1	11	6	11	10	99	5.6	7
6. Financial news	1	1	14	8	12	79	4.6	8
7. Film ads	2	8	8	2	5	75	4.4	9
8. *Vividha Bharathi* (national news)	—	1	3	8	8	37	2.1	10
9. District supplement	—	4	7	22	38	119	6.9	6
10. Other features*	2	3	18	17	14	124	7.2	5
No response	1	3	9	9	21			
Total	120	120	120	120	120	1721	100.0	

n = 120 readers.

Other features include: international news. TV news and astrology.

Table 7.8

What the Readers Like Most from the Daily Features: *Andhra Prabha*

Daily features	Readers' ranking Number:					Weighted score	Rating (per cent)	Rank
	One	*Two*	*Three*	*four*	*five*			
1. News	105	13	2	—	—	583	34.8	1
2. Cartoons	3	64	11	2	—	308	18.4	2
3. Editorials	—	17	30	14	3	189	11.3	3
4. Editorial page articles	—	3	18	22	8	118	7.0	5
5. Sports	—	3	9	5	9	58	3.5	8
6. Finaicial news	7	1	7	12	9	93	5.6	6
7. Employment ads	2	—	4	7	4	40	2.3	10
8. *Prapancha netram* (international news)	—	1	6	6	10	44	2.6	9
9. *Chitrakshari* (human) interest)	—	1	2	13	3	39	2.3	11
10. *Telugunadu* (district page)	1	3	15	15	38	130	7.8	4
11. Other features*	—	5	8	9	11	73	4.4	7
No response	2	9	9	15	25			
Total	120	120	120	120	120	1675	100.0	

n = 120 readers.

*Other features include: puzzle, astrology and religion.

Table 7.9

What the Readers Like Most from the Daily Features: *Udayam*

Daily features	*Readers' ranking Number:* One	*Two*	*Three*	*four*	*five*	*Weighted score*	*Rating (per cent)*	*Rank*
1 News	100	16	—	—	1	565	34.6	1
2. Cartoons	3	68	15	3	—	338	20.6	2
3. Editorials	—	5	26	8	1	119	7.3	5
4. Editorial page articles	1	6	13	21	8	118	7.2	6
5. Sports	3	10	9	6	11	105	6.4	7
6. Financial news	1	4	8	19	4	87	5.3	8
7. District supplement	7	3	20	19	32	177	10.8	3
8. Other features*	—	4	15	21	26	129	7.8	4
No response	5	4	14	23	37			
Total	120	120	120	120	120	1638	100.0	

n = 120 readers.

* Other features include: *dhwani* (sound), film news and astrology.

Finally, let the evaluation of the daily features be examined in greater detail, paper-wise. Table 7.6 shows that outside *Eenadu's* star features, namely, news, cartoons and district supplement in that order, there were no distinctively reader attractive daily features. A closer look into the column of rating scores (in per cent) alongside the rank column leads to this inference. None of the remaining six items had a two-digit rating score in terms of reader evaluation. Even the much trumpeted women's page of *Eenadu - Vasundhara,* was not a much sought-after daily feature. It is a startling revelation, even considering that almost all the evaluators were men readers. At any rate it is observed that "one should not miss that page" feeling was not there even among the women readers, though this survey has not taken care of getting the women's page evaluated by women.

Response to *Eenadu's* cinema page also appeared to be lukewarm since it is the least ranked (ninth) among the most liked features. Other daily features that were not specified in the list but which were subjected to reader evaluation included financial news, science column, human interest stories, etc. None of them were found to be significant interest generators to *Eenadu's* readers. Readers skipping the financial columns which are usually spread over two full pages is yet another startling revelation. Nevertheless, financial columns have an advertising angle. Nowadays, Telugu papers are able to attract advertisements relating to public issues, annual and half-yearly corporate results, etc. It may be inferred that most of the people interested in financial columns are capable of following English dailies which are supposed to give a lot more details compared to language dailies. Similar inferences are also applicable to the sports columns of Telugu papers.

Item-wise evaluation of the daily features of the other three papers is presented in Tables 7.7, 7.8 and 7.9. By and large, the reader evaluation of the three papers does not appear to be much different from that of the leader's features. In each of these papers, there were no significant reader attractions outside the three choicest majors, discussed earlier. No feature, outside those three majors, enjoyed a two-digit rating score.

In this connection, it should not be forgotten that in case of most of the daily features the trend setter was the market leader *Eenadu*. While the market leader succeeded in building up circulations in due course, the runner-up firms merely imitated the leader's strategies by adopting its daily features. But only to lose their circulation further and further. The findings of this survey confirmed that solution to competition cannot be found in me-too features. Further, it appears the runner-up firms jumped to the conclusion that every innovative feature of the leader had reader attractiveness. But the findings of this survey negate such of those assumptions. What is required to be imitative is the competitor's strengths or to exploit the competitor's weaknesses. Exploiting the competitor's weaknesses is not possible through poor imitations.

2. Non-daily Features

Newspaper is not only meant for news, but also views. The modern reader wants views on a variety of subjects that concern his or her life. Such special features distinguish a newspaper from those of competitors. Till mid-1970s, an average Telugu daily was a compact paper, focussing mainly the news. Later on, increased competition made the Telugu dailies to pay more attention to features in terms of space and quality as well. By 1990s, Telugu newspapers became one of the most feature-oriented dailies in the language press of India. Sometimes one may feel that these papers publish features at the cost of news. However, Telugu dailies, from time to time, increased the number of pages with an objective to strike a sensible balance between the two.

Non-daily features of one paper are not easily comparable with those of the others. Their range is much wider compared to the daily features. Paper to paper variations are more. Continuous changes take place even among the features of the same daily over a period of time.

The non-daily features of *Eenadu* are listed in Table 7.10. Content labels of the feature titles are given in the parentheses. The non-daily features of *Eenadu* at the time of survey mostly related to satirical articles, development news, career counselling, consumer affairs, investigative news, etc. The three non-daily features which *Eenadu* readers liked most were: *Akshintalu* (satirical), *Pratibha* (career counselling) and *Melukolupu* (consumer column), in that order. Their rating scores were: *Akshintalu* (25.2 per cent), Pratibha (23.8 per cent) and *Melukolupu* (8.5 per cent). *Akshintalu* is a satirical feature authored by D.V.Narasa Raju, a veteran dialogue writer in films. As many as four of the non-daily features of *Eenadu* were satirical in nature. The other three were: *Punyabhoomi, Paradesi Paathalu* and *Kaburlu* that were authored by Dharma Rao, Kondaveeti Venkata Kavi and Chalasani Prasada Rao, respectively. All these four satirical features together accounted for 41.7 per cent rating score. No other paper had that many satirical features. Each of them appear once in a week in the editorial page. Thus satirical features were among the most frequently recurring features during a week. On the whole, such features formed part of the key ingredients aimed at enhancing the core value of the product, ultimately aiming at sustaining and enhancing reader interest and newspaper sales.

The popularity of the feature on career counselling - *Pratibha* (means merit), forced the paper to convert it into a daily feature later. Investigative news at *Eenadu* was also known to be positioned to enhance the core value of the product, readers evaluating it as one of the five non-daily features they liked most.

Table 7.10

What the Readers Like Most from the Non-daily Features: *Eenadu*

Daily features	*Readers' ranking Number:* One	*Two*	*Three*	*four*	*five*	*Weighted score*	*Rating (per cent)*	*Rank*
1. *Punyabhoomi* (satirical)	2	6	3	1	7	52	5.0	9
2. *Paradesi paathalu* (satirical)	3	9	2	2	2	63	6.0	7
3. *Akshintalu* (satirical)	28	15	12	5	7	263	25.2	1
4. *Kaburlu* (satirical)	2	5	3	7	4	57	5.5	8
5. *Pragathi patham* (development)	1	8	6	8	2	73	7.0	6
6. *Prathibha* (career counselling)	25	16	11	10	7	249	23.8	2
7. *Melukolupu* (consumer column)	3	6	10	9	2	89	8.5	3
8. *Vinodini* (TV review)	5	4	7	5	8	80	7.6	4
9. Investigative news	9	5	1	3	4	78	7.5	5
10. Other features*	1	3	5	2	5	41	3.9	10
No response	41	43	60	68	72			
Total	120	120	120	120	120	1045	100.0	

n = 120 readers.

* Other features include: computer chip chat and *loguttu* (inside story).

Compared to the market leader's non-daily features, the rest of the papers were found to be weak reader attractions. Dominating features like satires as in case of *Eenadu* were not there in those papers. It does not mean the other papers should have carried as many satirical features as possible. On the other hand, the other papers should have performed, in a chosen area of reader interests and the paper's capability where the market leader was found to be underperforming. Tables 7.11, 7.12 and 7.13 exhibit the rating scores and their ranks in other dailies. The non-daily features which were liked most by *Andhra Jyoti's* readers were the consumers' column *(Viniyogadarla Hakkulu-chikkulu)*, Man in the News (Vaarthalaloni vyakthi) and the political analysis *(Vuluku-paluku)* features, in that order. But even the first among them failed to carry an impressive rating score (only 19 per cent). The others fell distantly behind it. Though there was a lot of variety in the subjects that were dealt in the non-daily features, *Andhra Jyoti* failed to make reasonable impression on the minds of its readers.

In case of *Andhra Prabha,* investigative news was the most impressive non-daily feature, followed by youth and children features (*Yuva prabha* and *Bala prabha)* and New Delhi News Reel, which accounted for 21 per cent, 17.6 per cent and 17.4 per cent of rating scores, respectively.

The feature on career counselling *(Diksuchi)*, investigative news and personal investment column (Siri) were the top three favourite features for *Udayam* readers.

On the whole, the market leader banked upon the use of satire in news related features at regular intervals. But its competitors, though provided a lot more variety in non-daily features compared to the leader, they have failed to design a strategy that is capable of driving home any competitive advantage in the marketplace.

Table 7.11
What the Readers Like Most from the Non-daily Features: *Andhra Jyoti*

Non-Daily features	Readers' ranking Number: One	Two	Three	four	five	Weighted score	Rating (per cent)	Rankk
1. *Vuluku-paluku* (political)	7	15	11	9	5	151	11.0	3
2. *Sahitya vedika* (literature)	8	5	3	2	4	77	5.6	9
3. Cinema	10	12	11	6	6	149	10.9	4
4. *Jeevana kalam* (satirical)	5	4	6	6	6	77	5.6	9
5. *Vignana deepika* (science)	—	1	7	17	5	64	4.7	10
6. *Vaarthalaloni vyakti* (Man in the news)	17	17	13	8	5	213	15.5	2
7. *Courtulu-chattalu* (legal)	6	7	3	3	7	80	5.8	8
8. *New Delhi lekha* (political)	2	10	14	9	4	114	8.3	5
9. *Viniyogadarla hakkulu-chikkulu* (consumers' column)	32	10	7	13	13	260	19.0	1
10. *Vidyarangam* (education)	6	3	8	9	7	91	6.6	7
11. Other features*	4	10	7	7	1	96	7.0	6
No response	23	26	30	31	57			
Total	120	120	120	120	120	1372	100.0	

n = 120 readers.

* Other features include: agriculture and local problems.

Table 7.12

What the Readers Like Most from the Non-daily Features: *Andhra Prabha*

Non-Daily features	*Readers' ranking Number:*					*Weighted*	*Rating*	
	One	*Two*	*Three*	*four*	*five*	*score*	*(per cent)*	*Rankk*
1. *Aardhika rangam* (economy)	11	14	8	7	1	150	12.0	4
2. *Sahitya prabha* (literature)	4	7	6	2	5	75	6.0	7
3. *Yuva prabha/Bala prabha* (youth/children)	8	18	22	14	13	219	17.6	2
4. Cinema	10	7	13	12	3	144	11.6	5
5. *New Delhi news reel* (political)	17	12	18	11	7	216	17.4	3
6. Job opportunities	13	10	6	2	2	129	10.4	6
7. Investigative news	29	16	8	8	13	262	21.0	1
8. Other features*	3	6	4	4	1	50	4.0	8
No response	25	30	35	60	75			
Total	120	120	120	120	120	1245	100:0	

n= 120 readers.

* Other features include: district news letter and *aalokana* (analysis).

Table 7.13

What the Readers Like Most from the Non-daily Features: *Udayam*

Non-Daily features	*Readers' ranking Number:*					*Weighted score*	*Rating (per cent)*	*Rankk*
	One	*Two*	*Three*	*four*	*five*			
1. *Diksuchi* (career counselling))	39	10	8	6	6	277	22.8	1
2. *Videsi netram* (international news)	6	19	12	7	4	160	13.2	4
3. *Nyayanyayalu* (legal)	—	2	4	3	3	29	2.4	9
4. *Vignaana veechikalu* (science)	3	8	5	5	3	75	6.2	7
5. *Chaduvu* (literature)	7	7	8	10	2	109	9.0	6
6. *Saadhana* (youth)	1	4	10	5	10	71	5.9	8
7. *Siri* (personal investment)	12	13	11	11	15	182	15.0	3
8 Investigative news	14	10	13	18	7	192	15.8	2
9. Other features*	5	9	8	14	5	118	9.7	5
No response	33	38	41	41	65			
Total	120	120	120	120	120	1213	100.0	

n = 120 readers.

* Other features include: *palukubadi* (satirical), *avalokanam* (satirical) and religion.

3. Sunday Supplement

At the time of survey, Sunday supplement in a magazine form was brought out by *Andhra Prabha,* besides its innovator *Eenadu.* The remaining two players were bringing it in a tabloid form. Irrespective of the format, there was uniformity in the contents of all the supplements. They included cartoons, a crime story, a short story, a human interest or an achievement story, etc., in addition to the cover story. Here again the market leader was imitated by others.

The top three reader interests of all the Sunday supplements were confined to seven features (Tables 7.14 through 7.17). They included cartoons, the cover story, crime story, human interest feature, short story, consumer column and health. The crime story was common among such top interests in all the supplements, besides the cover story in three.

Eenadu's readers' top three interests were cartoons, crime story and the cover story, in that order. In case of *Andhra Jyoti* supplement, the corresponding positions were taken by the cover story, crime story and short story. Health, crime story and consumers' column of *Andhra Prabha* were the top interests of their readers in the order given, whereas the corresponding strengths of *Udayam* were the cover story, followed by human interests feature and crime story. Of all such features, cartoons of *Eenadu,* the cover story of *Andhra Jyoti,* and *Udayam* and the health feature of *Andhra Prabha* were No. 1 preference of their readers. But it is surprising to find lack of adequate response from the readers in evaluating Sunday supplements. Even in respect of the market leader's product, as high as 40 per cent of the readers (49 out of 120) did not respond. Lack of response was much higher in case of the supplements of the other papers. For example, as high as 59 per cent (71 out of 120) of *Andhra Prabha's* readers did not respond. This leads to yet another startling revelation that most of the readers of Sunday supplement including those of the market leader did not have adequate reader interest in it. It is to be noted that this survey did not attempt to find out other family members' interest of its reading. However, the reported 15 to 20 per cent surge in the sales of the Sunday papers is indicative of their readership among the women and the youth and those of the magazine lovers as different from the newspaper lovers. Nevertheless, the voracious Telugu newspaper readers were not serious readers of Sunday supplement. Because they read more of the daily features plus more of the other papers, finding less time to go through Sunday supplements. Increased readership of the Sunday supplement might be further restricted because of the difficulty in borrowing it compared to the main paper. It is noticed that the family members are less inclined to lend the supplement outside the family compared to the main paper.

The reported Sunday's surge in sales of papers attributable to the supplement in the magazine form leads to several inferences: (1) The surge is suggestive of a sales potential for weekly magazines; (2) the supplement is capable of augmenting ad revenue; (3) besides the supplement, the main paper on Sundays is also capable of augmenting ad revenue; (4) the constituency of Sunday buyers are potential regular buyers in future; and (5) regular buyers cannot easily change their paper because of the family members' attachment to it. Such inferences are based on the assumption that the supplement possesses the attribute of real reader attractiveness. The advertising implications of the Sunday supplement are deferred to the ensuing chapter.

4. Generic Features

Generic features are the overall attributes of a newspaper which are applicable to the whole of a newspaper as such. Important among them are news-to-advertisements

Table 7.14

What the Readers Like Most from the Sunday Supplement: *Eenadu*

Features from the supplement	*Readers' ranking Number:*					*Weighted Rating*		
	One	*Two*	*Three*	*four*	*five*	*score*	*(per cent)*	*Rank*
1. Cartoons	40	15	5	1	4	281	28.0	1
2. *Vichithra viswam* (human interest)	4	15	6	8	3	117	11.7	4
3. Short story	5	12	5	9	9	115	11.5	5
4. Homeo *vydyam* (health)	5	5	7	3	1	73	7.3	6
5. *Idi kadha kaadu* (crime story)	10	8	14	14	10	162	16.1	2
6. Cover story	5	4	17	10	11	123	12.3	3
7. Literary reviews	2	6	1	6	5	54	5.3	8
8. Other features*	—	14	10	8	12	78	7.8	9
No response	49	50	55	61	65			
Total	120	120	120	120	120	1003	100.0	

n= 120 readers.

* Other features include: *bala vinodini* (children) and *mee maata* (letters to the editor)

Table 7.15

What the Readers Like Most from the Sunday Supplement: *Andhra Jyoti*

Features from the supplement	*Readers' ranking Number:*					*Weighted*	*Rating*	
	One	*Two*	*Three*	*four*	*five*	*score*	*(per cent)*	*Rank*
1. Cover story	36	11	4	8	3	255	26.5	1
2. Science	4	14	6	1	6	102	10.6	5
3. Literary	—	4	9	1	1	46	4.7	7
4. Serial novel, short story	9	11	8	6	—	125	13.0	3
5. Personal counselling	2	10	15	11	6	123	12.8	4
6 Police file	15	14	15	7	2	192	19.9	2
7. Health	4	3	7	13	17	96	10.0	6
8. Children's feature	—	1	2	5	5	25	2.5	8
No response	50	52	54	68	80			
Total	120	120	120	120	120	964	100.0	

n = 120 readers.

Table 7.16

What the Readers Like Most from the Sunday Supplement: *Andhra Prabha*

Features from the supplement	*Readers' ranking Number:*					*Weighted*	*Rating*	
	One	*Two*	*Three*	*four*	*five*	*score*	*(per cent)*	*Rank*
1. Cover story	8	1	7	4	8	81	11.9	4
2. Crime story	9	10	4	5	2	109	16.0	2
3. Science column	5	6	10	1	—	81	11.9	4
4. Health	9	11	12	2	1	130	19.0	1
5. Women's feature	5	3	3	4	2	56	8.1	6
6. Literature	6	5	2	6	—	68	10.0	5
7. Youth feature	1	7	1	3	6	48	7.0	8
8. Consumers' column	6	4	6	10	8	92	13.5	3
9. Other features*	—	2	1	2	3	18	2.6	7
No response	71	71	74	83	90			
Total	120	120	120	120	120	683	100.0	

*Other features include: children's feature and TV review.

n = 120 readers.

Table 7.17

What the Readers Like Most from the Sunday Supplement: *Udayam*

Features from the supplement	*Readers' ranking Number:*					*Weighted*	*Rating*	
	One	*Two*	*Three*	*four*	*five*	*score*	*(per cent)*	*Rank*
1. Cover story	14	13	5	6	2	151	18.1	1
2. *Vinthavintha lokamulo*	19	8	3	3	2	144	17.2	2
3. *Yadardha neram* (crime story)	6	9	13	7	4	123	14.7	3
4. *Siri muvvalu* (personal investment)	5	4	7	8	4	82	9.8	4
5. Cinema	3	4	10	4	3	72	8.6	6
6. Science column	2	3	4	6	6	43	5.2	8
7. *Vaasthu saastram*	3	1	6	2	2	43	5.2	8
8. Short story and poetry	3	7	1	6	4	62	7.4	7
9. Health	4	7	4	3	9	75	9.0	5
9 Other features*	—	3	6	2	6	40	4.8	9
No response	61	61	61	73	78			
Total	120	120	120	120	120	835	100.0	

n = 120 readers.

*Other features include: *balala* page (children) and *spoorthi* (achievement story).

ratio, price and colour printing. The survey also covered the evaluation of such features.

(i) Ratio of News to Advertisements

Newspaper consumers are equally concerned with the quantity and the quality of news. If a paper contains acres of advertisements at the cost of news, the circulation of that paper is likely to go down, despite the paper earning a lot of ad revenue. Continued circulation decline ultimately leads to reduced advertiser interest, thus threatening the survival of the paper. Hence, apportioning space between news and advertisements is an area which deserves continuous attention in newspaper business management. The market leader attracts more than a proportionate share in advertisements. The opposite is true in case of other papers, attracting much less than a proportionate share in advertisements. This leads to imbalances in the ratio of news-to-advertisements and customer dissatisfaction.

It is commonly thought that the runner-up papers have less of such problems as they are free from the pressure for news space in view of the less demand for advertising space. But findings of this survey are contrary to this common belief, as shown in Table 7.18. The market leader *Eenadu* provided a better coverage of news to their readers compared to its competitors. 60.9 per cent of *Eenadu* readers felt that their newspaper maintained either a balanced proportion between news and advertisements or provided more news. The readers of no other paper were so much satisfied on this front. Only 50 per cent of *Andhra Jyoti* readers, and about 53 per cent of *Andhra Prabha* and *Udayam* readers felt that their papers maintained a balance between news and advertisements or provided more news. But all the papers were more or less of the same size and the leader paper devoted more space to advertisements compared to other papers. This implies other papers devoted more space to news compared to the market leader. But in terms of reader satisfaction, the paper devoting lesser space to news provided more satisfaction.

Table 7.18

Ratio of News to Advertisements : Evaluation by Readers

Evaluation	*Eenadu*	*Andhra Jyoti*	*Andhra Prabha*	*Udayam*
	No. of readers (per cent)			
1. More news	8.3	10.0	20.0	17.5
2. Balanced proportion	52.6	40.0	32.6	35.9
3. Less news	10.8	24.2	5.8	10.0
4. No idea	22.5	25.0	40.8	35.8
5. No response	5.8	0.8	0.8	0.8
Total	100.0	100.0	100.0	100.0

n = 420 readers

Adequacy of space to news and adequacy of news are two different attributes. They need not necessarily move in the same direction. Adequacy in terms of physical space need not bring customer satisfaction in the same measure. Adequacy implies adequacy in terms of the news items, their breadth and depth only to the extent as required by the customers, not more not less. If such a balance is maintained, it is possible for a newspaper to provide more news in less space. The market leader in the Telugu newspaper scene might have performed such a balancing exercise better than its competitors. The competitors, it is observed, devoted more columns and pages of the precious space in their papers to fewer and fewer news stories but of unlimited nature in their details and length. Extra length and extra details kill readers' interest and time.

But all was not well with the market leader. As many as 39.1 per cent of readers expressed dissatisfaction of the news coverage either directly or indirectly by not responding to such a question positively. If the leader leaves so large a proportion of its customers unsatisfied, its competitors may step in even to wrest the leadership which *Eenadu* did exactly two decades ago.

Let the results here be corroborated with the buying motives dealt in the earlier section. *Udayam's* buyers have chosen that paper expecting it to be good in providing adequate news. It was No. 1 motive that influenced them. But the reality was contrary to it, as mentioned earlier. For the buyers of *Andhra Prabha* also the same motive was instrumental (ranked No.3) in choosing it, of course, only to result in bringing less than expected satisfaction.

(ii) Printing in Colour

Telugu dailies were accredited as the first newspapers in the country to start publishing the front and back pages in multi-colour every day. A casual look at the front page of any Telugu newspaper reveals the way the musthead, headlines, photographs, advertisements and even pocket cartoon were published in colour. Barring one or two other language dailies, colour printing is the unique feature of Telugu dailies in the country. Moving one step ahead, the papers started publishing the tabloid district supplements in colour. Colour printing has also been extended to the Sunday supplement and film photographs. Media observers raised their eyebrows over the Telugu newspaper industry's massive investment in modern printing technology in this regard. It is to be noted that the giant English newspapers which command nationwide circulation and readership still not extended colour printing beyond their week-end or other supplements. In this backdrop, it is felt necessary to know the importance attached by the respondents to printing their newspaper in colour.

Table 7.19

Importance of Printing the Newspaper in Colour to the Readers

Degree of importance	*Eenadu*	*Andhra Jyoti*	*Andhra Prabha*	*Udayam*	*Total*
	No. of readers (per cent)				
Very important	20.0	20.8	11.7	12.5	16.2
Important	47.5	35.1	42.5	50.9	44.0
Not so important	17.5	27.5	29.2	19.2	23.3
Unimportant	2.5	3.3	6.6	3.3	4.0
No idea	8.3	10.0	10.0	10.8	9.8
No response	4.2	3.3	—	3.3	2.7
Total	100.0	100.0	100.0	100.0	100.0

n = 480 readers.

Printing in colour is found to be very important or important only to three-fifth of readers of all the papers, as shown in Table 7.19. For the rest of them it was not a serious interest. Paper-wise, readers of *Eenadu* and *Udayam* were more interested in colour compared to others. Nevertheless, some readers also suggested the newspaper managements to dispense with the colour printing so as to benefit the subscribers by lowering the cover price of the papers.

Such a suggestion is worth considering in all seriousness it deserves. In matters such as this, better if the market leader takes the initiative to test the idea at least on experimental basis. If the idea is put into practice, it may lead to substantial reduction in costs, further leading to reduction in cover price of the paper. Reduced paper price may result in substantial enlargement of industry sales, if all the players conceitedly act upon it. But the reversal of the industry trend is like putting the clock back. All the players going colour and even the new player *Vaartha* coming out in colour since its inception speak of this. But *Udayam* coming to the end while in colour reminds the necessity of rethinking on the issue of colour at least in case of runner-up papers. But exploiting the colour for advertising reasons appears to be a good proposition in the face of competition from colour TV. Hence, what is suggested is avoidance of bringing out paper in colour, certainly not the avoidance of advertising in colour.

(iii) Price of the Paper

The Telugu papers were not used to indulge in any price wars as such, as is currently experienced by the English press in India. *Eenadu, Udayam* and *Vaartha* all pricing their product on entry on par with the competition supports this view. Even in the years that followed, the same pricing policy was adopted by them. However, *Andhra Prabha* was found to be offering at a price lesser than its competitors. Perhaps they could afford it because the paper belonged to a chain. Nevertheless, association between the cover price and the circulation of *Andhra Prabha* could not be established. Realising this *Andhra Prabha* fall in line with other competitors in its pricing policy from 1997 onwards. Thus nonprice competition and product differentiation have to come to stay in Telugu newspaper market.

At the time of conducting this survey, *Eenadu, Andhra Jyoti* and *Udayam* charged the same cover price of Rs.2.30 per copy whereas *Andhra Prabha* was priced at Rs.1.50 on weekdays. On Sundays, the former three papers were priced at Rs.2.75 and *Andhra Prabha* was priced at Rs.2.00. In such a price scenario as this, over one half of *Udayam* subscribers, a third of those of *Eenadu* and *Andhra Jyoti* and a sixth of *Andhra Prabha* felt the cover price of their paper was on the high side on weekdays. But their complaints on the price of Sunday issues were far fewer compared to weekdays. At that time, only the readers of *Eenadu* and *Andhra Prabha* were getting the Sunday supplement in a magazine form.

COMPARATIVE EVALUATION

What is analysed so far is confined to the consumer's evaluation of the paper read by him or her as the main paper. But the real strengths or weaknesses of a product could be brought to light more clearly only through a comparative evaluation. To fulfil this objective, 328 readers following more than one newspaper,[8] hereafter called multi paper or multiple newspaper readers, are asked to evaluate them by comparison. To put it differently, to find out which paper excels in which feature or attribute is the goal of comparative evaluation. Multipaper readership experience for a duration of at least two years is taken as the criterion for this purpose.

1. Choice for News and Views

For the purpose of the multipaper evaluation of the news and views carried by Telugu dailies, the item was categorised into nine heads, as listed in Table 7.20. The readers' choice of the daily for a particular category of news or views was solicited on a one-reader one-choice basis. In other words, it was some sort of multipaper readers voting for one daily in the matter of reading the specified item of news or views. Thus, the daily mostly favoured by the multipaper readers for reading the specified item is designated - the best, so far as that item is concerned. The daily placed behind the best is labelled — the next best. Paper securing other lower positions are not shown in the table.

Category-wise evaluation of news and views reveals that *Eenadu* emerged the best choice in respect of six of the nine categories. local; financial; international; national; state; and sports news. The paper emerged the next best choice in two categories: editorials; and editorial page articles. The category of news where it has failed to secure a top position

Table 7.20

Multipaper Readers' Choice of the Telugu Daily for News and Views

News and Views	*Readers' Choice of the Daily*				
	The best	*Per cent of readers*	*The next best*	*Per cent of readers*	*No response per cent*
1. International news	*Eenadu*	38.4	*Andhra Prabha*	28.6	3.9
2. National news	*Eenadu*	35.6	*Andhra Prabha*	26.8	3.6
3. State news	*Eenadu*	35.3	*Andhra Jyoti*	26.2	6.4
4. Local news	*Eenadu*	58.8	*Andhra Jyoti*	14.0	10.6
5. Investigative news	*Andhra Prabha*	21.3	*Udayam*	10.3	57.0
6. Financial news	*Eenadu*	46.6	*Andhra Prabha*	7.0	41.4
7. Sports	*Eenadu*	32.3	*Udayam*	9.1	45.7
8. Editorials	*Andhra Prabha*	22.2	*Eenadu*	20.7	31.0
9. Editorial page articles	*Andhra Jyoti*	21.3	*Eenadu*	20.7	29.5

n = 328 multipaper readers.

was investigative news. In investigative *news Andhra Prabha* was the best of the lot (Table 7.20).

In addition to investigative news, *Andhra Prabha* emerged the best in editorials. And this paper was the next best in international, national and financial news. *Andhra Jyoti* emerged the best in editorial page articles and the next best both in state and local news. *Udayam* was no winner in any of these segments, remaining the next best in sports, besides investigative news.

On the whole, these findings establish that *Eenadu* lived upto its buyers' expectations in providing adequate news as it was their No.3 buying motive, as discussed earlier. In contrast, similar expectations of buyers of *Udayam* and *Andhra Prabha* for whom adequacy of news was No.1 and 3 buying motives, respectively, were frustrated. This may be described as expectancy-actuals gap. *Eenadu* appeared to have particularly excelled others in the segment of local news for which nearly three-fifth (58.8 per cent) of the multipaper readers opted it. Other segment of news where it stood miles ahead of others was financial news (46.6 per cent), besides sports.

Eenadu's strategy of positioning itself to provide local news matched well its customer need satisfaction and made a good harvest of it. Whatever other strategies they have designed in getting closer to the customer in the form of district supplement and in moving to many number of places to achieve such an objective were all intended to provide more and more of local news. At the same time, it has not neglected either in providing international, national or state news as the comparative evaluation by multipaper readers indicates.

These findings further establish the overdelayed reactions of the runner-up papers resulting in only me-too poor imitations, which have taken them no where near the lead performer. The vast difference between *Eenadu* and

Andhra Jyoti in reader preferences to read local news in them illustrates this. As against 58.8 per cent of readers preferring to read *Eenadu* for local news, only 14 per cent preferred *Andhra Jyoti*, the next best choice in this segment. Such differences were also glaring in financial news and sports news between the lead performer *Eenadu* and the next best paper.

Hypothesis of Underperformance or Unwanted Performance

On the basis of the above inferences, one should not be hasty in jumping to the conclusion that all appears rosy in the performance of the market leader. The no-response figures (in per cent) in Table 7.20 very clearly indicate where the industry in general, and the leader in particular, were underperforming. For five out of nine news items, no-responses varied from 29.5 to 57 per cent. If significant responses are not forthcoming from the evaluators, such responses are either indicative of their negative feelings or their lack of positive interest, may be in the newspaper as a product or in that segment of the newspaper. Here it cannot be assumed the readers have no newspaper interest as such, since all of them are fanatic readers, reading several papers for several years. Then coming to the cause of the negative feelings, such of these readers may not be interested in that particular segment of the news or they may be depending on an English paper or other media like radio or TV. Either of these two causes has marketing implications. It is a futile exercise for a newspaper to carry a segment of news in which there is no reader interest, or where the other media or the competitors from other languages known to the customer are exceedingly doing well. For example, sports and finance are such columns which are supposed to be the forte of English dailies. Nowadays, financial dailies are able to reach even small towns of Andhra Pradesh. Specialised sports magazines are not uncommon. Live coverage of the sporting events has become a regular phenomenon of the electronic media. TV viewers are getting updated of the stock prices the same day instead of depending on tomorrow's paper. In such a competitive intra and inter media scene, Telugu papers devoting acres of most precious reading space to such segments does not lead to building up good circulation or readership. The fact that mostly the readers of sports and finance columns are capable of following the English papers or TV should be remembered while designing content strategies. What is suggested certainly is not dropping such features, but limiting them to the lengths and depths as desired by the customers, so that the space thus saved could be otherwise utilised to build up customer satisfaction, circulation and ultimately the ad revenue.

No-response figures in Table 7.20 adequately supports the aforesaid point of view relating to financial and sports news where such figures were staggering 41.4 and 45.7 per cent, respectively. The figures are reflective of the aggregated underperformance or unwanted performance of the Telugu newspaper industry. Unwanted performance has more marketing implications compared to underperformance. Unwanted performance warrants remarketing efforts, whereas underperformance warrants product enrichment so far as that segment of news is concerned. If the customer need-satisfaction profile is not properly analysed and if unwanted performance is wrongly diagnosed as underperformance and whatever remedial action is taken, it may lead to greater marketing catastrophy. Remarketing efforts relating to a particular segment of news are a matter of conviction, courage, and strong determination requiring bold decisions.

Telugu newspapers appeared to be providing unwanted performance in the area of investigative news where the no-response level was of unbelievable heights measuring 57 per cent of multipaper readers. This is one area where almost all the Telugu papers along with their counterparts in English were bringing out a series of news stories on most of the days in a week. The stories mostly related to the corruption at high places at various levels, national, state and local. At the time of this survey, the papers were found to be publishing unending accounts of such issues. They were innumerable to enumerate. They were like serials without any end in the sight. They looked like stretching into the 21st century even. Perhaps people were fed up in reading into such news. It was found to be difficult for the readers to gather the thread of continuity even. Despite such commitment of the papers to expose the people at high places, concrete action was not found to be forthcoming against such offenders, in any form. Better if the newspapers change their space use priorities, properly assessing the customer need- satisfaction profile. It is not asking the papers not to effectively play their social role. At any cost the people expect them to discharge their social responsibility. But what is less desired is their playing without any purpose or direction or fruitful agenda-setting.

To sum up, the foregoing analysis proves hypothesis of underperformance or unwanted performance of Telugu papers, including the leader, in several segments of news. Scanty readership of underperforming or unwanted segments of news are not capable of attracting sufficient ad revenues in the long run, justifying their costs. In the process, the customers are denied of an opportunity to satisfy their other pressing newspaper needs.

2. Choice for Major Features

If news and views make the core of the product, its other major features consist of cartoons, features relating to literature, children, youth, women, science and technology, agriculture, etc., as are listed in Table 7.21. The results of comparative evaluation of such major features are also shown in the table.

Table 7.21

Multipaper Readers' Choice of the Telugu Daily for Major Features

Features	Readers' Choice of the Daily				
	The best	*Per cent of readers*	*The next best*	*Per cent of readers*	*No response per cent*
1. Cartoons	*Eenadu*	53.6	*Udayam*	15.8	6.0
2. Literary features	*Andhra Jyoti*	20.1	*Udayam*	12.8	53.9
3. Children's features	*Udayam*	14.6	*Andhra Prabha*	9.7	61.8
4. Youth features	*Udayam*	25.9	*Andhra Prabha*	13.4	44.5
5. Women's features	*Eenadu*	16.7	*Udayam*	8.5	65.8
6. Science and technology	*Eenadu*	13.1	*Udayam* and *Andhra Jyoti*	10.3	61.8
7. Agriculture	*Eenadu*	7.6	*Andhra Jyoti* and *Udayam*	2.7	84.7

n = 328 multipaper readers.

Of seven of the major features, *Eenadu* was the winner in four of them namely, cartoons, women's features, science and technology, and agriculture. *Udayam* topped the choices in youth and also children's features, and *Ahdhra Jyoti* in literary features. Among such choices of multireaders, cartoons of *Eenadu* were liked by most of them (53.6 per cent). No feature among the four papers, be it news or views (Table 7.20) or major features or other features (listed in Table 7.22) equalled *Eenadu's* cartoons in providing customer satisfaction to multireaders with one exception. That exceptional feature also belonged to the market leader. Such an exceptional feature exceeding the cartoons in providing consumer satisfaction was its local news gaining 58.8 per cent of multireader acceptance, as noticed earlier. Positioning a cartoon, mostly a pocket one, for extracting such an extraordinary marketing mileage is particularly noteworthy among the strategies of *Eenadu*.

No other major feature was found to be strikingly attractive to the multipaper readers. The reader patronage for them ranged from 7.6 per cent (agriculture) to 25.9 per cent (youth features), even in respect of the papers that are labelled the best choice. No response reader reactions were of alarming proportions for six out of seven of such features ranging from 44.5 per cent (youth features) to 84.7 per cent (agriculture). Such negative or indifferent responses warrant the invoking of underperformance or unwanted performance hypothesis discussed earlier. The hypothesis spells danger to the industry, including the leader. The runner-up papers should think twice before undertaking the imitation exercises of the leader. An ounce of prevention may be able to dispense with a pound of cure. Misconceiving the leader's weaknesses as its strengths and imitating them illogically is blindfold marketing.

3. Choice for Other Features

Other features outside news and views and the major

Table 7.22

Multipaper Readers' Choice of the Telugu Daily for Other Features

Features	*Readers' Choice of the Daily*				
	The best	*Per cent of readers*	*The next best*	*Per cent of readers*	*No response per cent*
1. Sunday supplement	*Eenadu*	26.5	*Andhra Prabha*	7.9	53.3
2. Film news *Jyoti*	*Andhra Jyoti*	35.0	*Andhra Prabha*	20.1	47.5
3. Health counselling	*Andhra Jyoti*	11.5	*Udayam*	10.9	65.2
4. TV Reviews	*Andhra Jyoti*	28.9	*Eenadu*	5.4	59.1
5. Advertisements	*Eenadu*	35.9	*Andhra Jyoti*	7.6	50.0

n = 328 multipaper readers.

features discussed earlier, included Sunday supplement, film news, health counselling, TV reviews and advertisements. Table 7.22 shows the results of comparative evaluation. *Eenadu* emerged the best choice in Sunday supplement and advertisements, conceding all other features to *Andhra Jyoti.* Once again, the next best papers were far distantly placed from the best paper, leaving a large no-response gap. The no-response gap varied from 47.5 per cent to 65.2 per cent. The situation once again warrants the invoking of underperformance or unwanted performance hypothesis.

On the whole, feature-wise analysis reveals the existence of several gray areas of marketing performance. The market leader is no exception. Facing such uncertainties of customer acceptance, *Vaartha* preferring to enter more or less with the same features in a copy book fashion is debatable. Their genuineness in committing huge amount of funds right on entry, going for new technology, etc., no doubt, were all innovative moves. But if such moves were preceded by meaningful research into the customer desired features that might have enabled them to enter the market with a better product. It is not too late for the runner-up firms to look ahead in this direction.

4. Evaluation by Values

This time the evaluation is on the basis of the values for which the Telugu papers were striving for, as perceived by their readers. According to Thomas Peters and Robert Waterman Jr., values were found to be one of the attributes shaping America's business companies.[9] Any organisation in order to survive and achieve success, must have a sound set of beliefs on which it premises all its policies and actions. The most important single factor in corporate success is faithful adherence to those beliefs. In other words, the basic philosophy, spirit and drive of an organisation have far more to do with its relative achievements than do technological or economic resources, organisational structure, innovation and timing. All these things weigh heavily in success.[10] Such of those considerations have added significance in media business, considering they are basically viewed as vehicles of certain values. Historically, the newspapers, as different from other media came into existence to live for certain values.

The multipaper readers were asked to evaluate the papers around certain value premises. The values chosen for the purpose are listed in Table 7.23. They include: the paper's role in educating and moulding public opinion, in upholding the democratic values, in fighting against corruption, etc., For the purpose of evaluation, 13 of such values were chosen. And the multipaper readers were asked to name the paper excelling the other papers around the specified value premises.

The scores, in per cent, are given in Table 7.23 for the chosen values. The multipaper readers perceived that the market leader excelled all other papers in six out of 13 items of the value premises. Such value premises in which it excelled were: 1. Highlighting the problems of farm sector and villages; 2. Educating and moulding public opinion; 3. Providing entertainment; 4. Upholding democratic values; 5. Highlighting developmental issues; and 6. Expressing concern at human misery or deterioration of human values, in that order, in terms of the readers' support they have mustered. *Andhra Jyoti* was found excelling around three values: in promoting cultural and literary values; in highlighting consumer problems; and in journalistic standards, in that order. *Andhra Prabhu* excelled around two values, namely, in fighting corruption in high places, and in promoting national integration. Strangely, *Udayam* was not found to excel in any of the selected values. It is interesting to note that none of the Telugu papers excelled either in promoting scientific temper or in highlighting the problems of the poorest of the poor, 46 and 39.3 per cent of the readers, respectively, stating

Table 7.23

Which Telugu Daily Excells Others around Certain Value Premises: Multipaper Readers' Evaluation

Value Premise	*Readers' Choice of the Daily Excelling others*					
	Eenadu	*Andhra Jyoti*	*Andhra Prabha*	*Udayam*	*None of these*	*No response*
Which daily excells others:	*No. of readers (per cent)*					*(per cent)*
1. In educating and moulding public opinion	38.7	10.1	14.3	14.3	10.7	11.9
2. In upholding democratic values	34.5	7.9	20.4	11.9	12.8	12.5
3. In expressing concern at human misery or deterioration of human values	24.1	18.9	18.3	21.3	5.8	11.6
4. In promoting national integration and universal brotherhood	18.0	17.7	21.6	15.5	13.5	13.7
5. In highlighting developmental issues	26.8	11.6	12.2	22.6	15.9	10.9
6. In highlighting problems of farm sector and villages	39.1	14.0	4.3	7.9	21.3	13.4
7. In promoting scientific temper	22.3	7.6	3.6	4.3	46.0	16.2
8. In highlighting consumer problems and supporting consumer movement	20.2	32.6	12.8	14.6	7.3	12.5

9. In highlighting the problems of the poorest of the poor	9.4	6.4	3.4	25.3	39.3	16.2
10. In fighting against corruption in high places	13.4	5.5	32.3	17.1	18.6	13.1
11. In promoting cultural and literary values	14.6	34.5	19.2	14.0	5.2	12.5
12. In providing entertainment	34.8	20.4	14.9	16.5	4.6	8.8
13. In maintaining high standards in journalism without any bias or sensationalism	18.0	23.8	19.5	15.9	10.6	12.2
Rating on 13 -point scale	3.15	2.11	1.95	2.00	2.14	1.65

n = 328 multipaper readers.

Note on 13-point Combined Rating Scale: 1. Totalled horizontally, each of the rows in the table makes 100. 2. The figures (in per cent) in each of the horizontal rows are converted into equivalents of one. 3. Then if the equivalents of one are totalled vertically, it gives the measure on 13-point combined rating scale, paper-wise.

so emphatically. No-response reaction varied from 8.8 (providing entertainment) to 16.2 (promoting scientific temper and highlighting consumer problems) per cent.

13-Point Combined Rating Scale

The aforesaid reader preferences (in per cent) are taken as proportions of 1, item-wise. Thus, for each of the value premises the maximum possible score becomes 1, making an aggregate of 13 points for all the items. Then paper-wise totals become the combined rating of that paper on a 13-point scale. On such a 13-point combined rating scale, *Eenadu's* total value premises measured 3.15 points, naturally the maximum for the leader. *Andhra Prabha* was at the bottom measuring only 1.95 points, despite the paper taking the lead in two values. Though *Udayam* did not excel in any of these values, it was marginally ahead of *Andhra Prabha* measuring 2 points. Expectedly, the market challenger, at the time of the survey, *Andhra Jyoti* was far distantly placed behind the leader, measuring 2.11 points, despite holding the second place on the rating scale. This accounted for a difference of 1.04 points between the leader and the challenger.

But it is intriguing to find that the constituency of readers believing that none of these papers excelled in such and such values measured 2.14 points, larger than any of the individual scores of runner-up papers. It is further intriguing to find out that another constituency of no-response readers measured as high as 1.65 points. Together both of them measured a staggering 3.79 points, which may be labelled a tally of the dissent readers' constituency. Gray area of 3.79 points on a 13-point rating scale represents the extent to which the industry was underperforming on value front.

Satisfying media audience in general and newspaper consumers in particular, are vastly different from satisfying other customers. Whether it is news or views, daily feature or non-daily feature, major one or minor one, cartoon or a literary feature, or designing a value system all required constant attention and continuous innovation. To quote Ramoji Rao, "For a newspaper, the reader is its master. The answer book of a student is valued by one single examiner. But a newspaper has lakhs of critical examiners of differing intellectual backgrounds and varying tastes. It is difficult to bring out a newspaper which would pass with distinction every day. This is more true of language newspapers than others. For the language newspaper, reader looks at the paper from his native view point, his dialect and environment."[11] The most important of all these variables is the everchanging profile of Telugu newspaper consumer, being the causal variable and the starting point of all marketing efforts.

References

1. See Chapter - IV
2. See Frederick Herzberg, *Work and the Nature of Man*, William Collins, Cleveland, 1966.
3. Cf. Table 4.2.
4. D. Brinkman, "Do Editorial Cartoons and Editorials Change Opinions?" *Journalism Quarterly*, 44, (1968), pp. 724-726.
5. L.M. Carl, "Editorial Cartoons Fail to Reach Many Readers", *Journalism Quarterly*, 44, (1968), pp. 533-535.
6. See Chapter - V.
7. C. Bain and D. Weaver, "Readers' Reactions to Newspaper Design", *Newspaper Research Design*, *1 (1)*, 1978, p. 48.
8. Cf. table 6.2 Chapter — VI.
9. Thomas J. Peters and Robert H. Waterman Jr., *op. cit.*, p. 815.
10. *Ibid.*, p. 280.
11. Quoted from: *Interface*, a half-yearly journal published by the Dept. of Communication and Journalism, Osmania University in 1979.

8
Marketing the Space

Marketing strategies targeted at the delivery of customer want-satisfaction through designing a product excelling in journalistic standards alone will not guarantee the survival of a newspaper. Besides serving the needs of the subscriber market, the paper has to necessarily serve the needs of its second market i.e., advertisers, as is already learnt in Chapter-I.[1] This chapter, as a concluding part of this dissertation, highlights the space selling strategies emerging in the Telugu newspaper market. As a prelude to such strategies, the rationale of space marketing and the competitive context that surrounds it are taken up first.

(A) Advertising, the Financial Heart

There are strong links and dependencies between the news, circulation and advertising functions of the newspaper. News is the soul of a newspaper, its historic rationale. From the business perspective, a newspaper's financial foundations rest on news—the quantity and quality of news sold to readers who, in turn, are sold to advertisers. News development remains the key to circulation growth. But even a superior news product may not attract advertisers,[2] unless a newspaper reaches its circulation marketing potential. It is worth emphasising that the marketing concept requires tightly coordinated and interdependent effort by the news, circulation and advertising departments.

Obviously, the larger the circulation a newspaper has, the more advertising it will attract, provided the demographics of its readership interest advertisers. If simply selling more papers had been the only newspaper game, the newspaper death list would have been considerably shorter in the USA, in the early 1980s. The *Washington Star,* for example, had a very substantial 3,40,000 circulation when it failed. The *Cleveland Press* claimed 3,16,000, nineteenth largest in the nation, just before it died. The *Philadelphia Bulletin* went down with close to 4,00,000, fourth largest for any afternoon paper in the country. Reader loyalty in those cities was translated into millions of dollars in circulation revenue each year. In other cities, in different competitive and cost environments, circulation of that magnitude would mean immensely profitable operations. Thus newspapers could fail financially even when thousands and thousands of subscribers shell down cash to buy them each day.[3]

The equation of failure in newspaper publishing is extremely complex and disaster wore many faces when it struck in *Washington, Philadelphia* and *Cleveland.* Yet a common theme ran through those sad stories : Each failed newspaper lost advertiser loyalty and share of advertising market. For each, there came a time when revenue would not cover out-of-control costs, management error, journalistic weakness, onrushing competitors—all the ills that can afflict a newspaper. And those papers were starved to death financially. Loss of advertising market share is a manifestation of ills, not the cause; often, when share deterioration becomes glaringly visible, the newspaper's situation is already precarious.[4]

Circulation has an additional dimension. It is not enough for a newspaper to have a build-up of sizable circulation in absolute figures. A distinctive circulation lead over its rivals is capable of driving home a competitive advantage in attracting adequate ad revenue in newspaper business.

Newspaper analyst John Morton asserts that if one of the two competing dailies has a significant circulation lead it can charge higher advertising rates than its competitor and still offer advertisers a lower cost per thousand figure. To quote John Morton, "Advertisers respond to these circumstances by placing a disproportionate share of their spending with the larger paper. The paper with 60 per cent of the circulation in the market might get 70 to 75 per cent of the advertising. Thus the newspaper with 40 per cent of the circulation gets a small share of the advertising, and this ... often means that not enough revenue comes in to cover operating costs. The small paper's operating costs will be less than the big paper's, but not greatly so. The small paper does not skimp on staff and news-hole if it hopes to remain competitive."[5]

Thus advertising is the financial heart of the newspaper. The newspaper is to be created as a successful advertising medium, because readers alone do not come close to fully supporting it. It is advertisers, contributing 80 per cent or more of total revenue, who determine whether a newspaper will succeed financially.[6] Unless reader loyalty can be translated into advertiser support a newspaper is doomed. A circulation-advertising imbalance - high circulation costs, low ad revenue—creates a cost structure so high that the newspaper is vulnerable to disruptions in internal operations or external environment.[7]

Advertising in Newspapers

One way to determine the popularity of media as advertising vehicles is to count the advertising expenditure spent on each of them. In 1995, the print media in India accounted for 61.2 per cent of advertising expenditure followed by television with 26.4 per cent (Table 8.1, infra). Some of the reasons newspapers are such good advertising vehicles are the following:

Universal Appeal: Newspaper advertising has rightly been called the foundation of all advertising. Its appeal is so general, the dependence upon it so widespread and the acceptance of it so universal that its place as a social and economic force in modern life is assured and permanent.[8]

Flexibility: Newspapers typically offer national advertisers more territorial flexibility than other media do. With newspapers the advertiser can place his advertising where the potential market looks best. Territorial flexibility has special appeal to national advertisers who want to test a new product. They can advertise it in certain test markets and save the time, trouble and expense of a national campaign. Also, the mass coverage most newspapers provide, the chance to put the new product ad in a news context, and the opportunity of getting fairly immediate action all enhance the desirability of newspapers for introducing new products.[9]

The newspaper enables the advertiser to change his plans overnight to take advantage of changed conditions. The advertisement may be changed upto a few hours before the paper goes to press.

Newspaper ads are available in a variety of sizes. The smallest advertising unit is an agate line[10] of classified advertising, and the largest is a full page ad. This flexibility gives newspapers an advantage over TV, which can generally offer only 10 second commercial spots.

Interdependency: A particular advantage of the newspaper as an advertising medium is the inherent relationship between its news and its advertising contents. Neither could exist satisfactorily without the other. A publication that was all news and no advertising would be prohibitive in price and would be lacking in a vital element. Similarly, a publication that is nothing but advertising would get relatively scant attention from the consuming public. The newspaper combines these two essential elements economically and conveniently as no other medium does.[11]

Community Prestige: Newspapers are local and their strong suit is local news and local advertising. Both retail and national advertisers like to associate themselves with the prestige most papers enjoy in a community. One of the best indicators of how people feel towards their newspaper is their behaviour when they are without it. Several studies have been made world over which have indicated the deep impact a newspaper has on a community.

Intense Coverage: Newspaper readers are well educated. They have higher mean incomes than people who do not read newspaper regularly. The Indian National Readership Survey-95 shows 75 per cent of households with a monthly income in excess of Rs. 10,000 are exposed to press. Almost every newspaper includes news of interest to all segments of the population—sports fans, film lovers, business people and women. The advertiser car select customers of a particular segment by placing his ad in a special-interest section.

But newspaper advertising is not free from drawbacks. Its life span is very short. Nothing is alive as today's newspaper, and nothing is stale as yesterday's newspaper. Even in the USA, except a few, there are no truly national newspapers. Thus, the very fact that the newspaper is so essentially, or at most, local or regional in character is sometimes a deterrent to advertisers who are looking for nationwide circulation. This objection can be met, of course, by using in a combination of strong regional newspapers.

With the importance of advertising in mind, it is easy to see why newspaper managements spend so much effort and time worrying about dips in advertising revenue. Sometimes the causes of these dips can vary, and that makes the job of shoring up the erosion more difficult. Some of these causes include failing business in a local economy; insufficient penetration into the market; defection of advertisers to other non-traditional media; mismanaged sales staff; inadequate sales promotion; defection of an important target reader group; a declining editorial product; poor image building by the newspaper's marketing department; a bad fit between the market and the kind of product offered; or all of the above.[12] The management has to isolate those causes for their newspaper, because whatever the reason, the level of advertising revenue will influence the success or failure of every department in the newspaper. Thus, meaningful marketing strategies imply newspaper circulation build-up —as well as advertising revenue—though marketing the total newspaper.

(B) The Competitive Context

The foregoing analysis emphasises the importance of advertising revenue to the newspapers. Nevertheless, such a cake of ad revenue is chased by several other media for their survival, along with newspapers. The TV, radio, cinema, outdoor advertising, etc., are also there in a race of intermedia competition. Again print advertising is not the exclusive domain of newspapers. It has to be shared among other print media like magazines and other periodicals, resulting in a situation of intramedia competition including the competition among newspapers of different languages or of the same language.

1. Intermedia Competition

Newspapers are the oldest medium as far as advertising. Yet, they continue to claim the largest share in advertising even in the highly developed markets of the USA, facing severe competition from the electronic media. Thus the newspapers have akeady taken many of the marketing steps they need to remain on the top. That is good news. But there is bad news, too. The much discussed historical decline in share of ad dollars captured by the newspapers is continuing.[13] Similar situation of lesser magnitude has also started emerging in India with a phenomenal expansion of government-owned Doordarshan in 1980s. Further, a plethora of private channels came into existence in 1990s with the advent of satellite TV. In 1997, there were 18 Doordarshan channels, two of them national channels and 16 regional, whereas there were 28 private TV channels, regional or national.[14] One estimate shows they deliver a total of 750 hours or more of TV footage everyday.[15] The recent Indian Readership Survey, 1998 shows that 54.5 million homes had television sets in 1997. Of them, 34 per cent had cable connections. From advertising point of view, radio as a medium became available in 1967 when the first Vividh Bharathi station started. Today there are 30 Vividh Bharathi centres and 61 primary channels. In 1994, F M channel was introduced and today there are five F M centres broadcasting in India.

The Indian Readership Survey (IRS), 1997 puts the overall media reach at: TV 76 per cent, press 59 per cent and radio 23 per cent.[16] Thus the intermedia competition, particularly the contest between the press and TV is getting keener, in terms of the overall reach and also in attracting advertising. Advertising revenue by medium is shown in Table 8.1, relating to the years 1991-95. During these years the total advertising revenue grew from Rs. 1,700 crores to Rs.4,600 crores, registering a 270 per cent growth. The share of TV grew from 18 per cent to 26.4 per cent, while the press was a loser coming down from 68 per cent in 1991 to 61 per cent in 1995. As such, the problem is one of a rising market but a declining share in ad revenue so far as press is concerned, despite the share of the newspapers remaining predominant. Ad revenue in 1996 was over Rs.5,000 crore,[17] slated to become Rs.10,000 crore in the next five years.[18]

Table 8.1

Advertising Expenditure by Medium in India: 1991-95

(Rs. Crores)

Year	*Press*	*TV*	*Radio*	*Cinema*	*Outdoor*	*Total*
1991	1156(68)	306(18)	51(3)	34(2)	153(9)	1770(100)
1992	1386(66)	42(20)	63(3)	46(2.2)	189(9)	2104(100)
1993	1820(64.7)	560(20)	84(3)	30(1.0)	320(11.3)	2814(100)
1994	2255(64.4)	750(21.4)	110(3.1)	25(0.7)	360 (10.3)	3500(100)
1995	2815(61.2)	1215(26.4)	136(0.5)	24(0.5)	410(8.9)	4600(100)

Note: Figures in parentheses are percentages indicating share of advertising.

Source: Operations Research Group (adapted from *Media Market Guide 1996-97,* Media Direction—A division of R.K.Swamy/BBDO, August 1996, New Delhi, p. 14).

The findings of NRS-VI (1997) augur well to the newspapers, establishing that the newspapers were not losing their readership, despite the viewership of the television mounting up.[19] The findings of the Scarborough Research Corp.,[20] relating to the years 1996-97 also strengthen such a view on a wider scale. Their research into the newspapers in 50 largest markets in the US confirm that the newspapers there outperformed TV and cable in audience retention. The first Competitive Media Index (CMI)[21] shows that the newspapers there gained seven lakh new readers, while prime time TV viewership fell by three per cent and cable by 0.6 per cent between 1996 and 1997. Moreover, in 1997, daily newspapers reached more adults than any other medium studied—an average 58.7 per cent, compared to 48.4 per cent for prime time television, 25.4 per cent for morning-drive radio stations and 10.4 per cent for prime time cable. On the basis of this analysis, John Sturm, president and chief executive of the Newspaper Association of America (NAA) asserts, "This analysis dispels the notion that the newspapers are losing readers, while reaffirming the industry's vitality. Newspapers continued to provide advertisers an effective medium to reach a highly educated and high income audience."[22] Further, William B. Drewry, managing director, Paine Webber infers that the belief held by the investment community over the past several years that newspapers have come to be regarded as an eroding medium is proved to be a myth, considering the consumer penetration perspective.[23]

2. Intramedia Competition

Apart from intermedia competition, imbalances existed in the distribution of the advertising cake belonging to the print media among its various constituents. The Centre for Media Studies (CMS) analysed the ads in a sample of 400 publications of all types in 1987- 88 which together accounted for 85-88 per cent of all advertising through press in the country.[24] The Centre's findings showed that English publications continued to get a major cake of ads disproportionate to their circulation and readership even compared to Hindi publications with a much higher circulation and readership. The English press shared 51 per cent of the total press ad revenue, whereas a total of eight language publications together accounted for only 46.5 per cent. Language-wise shares were (in per cent): Hindi 12.7, Gujarati 7.1, Marathi 6.4, Bengali 5.4, Tamil 5.3, Malayalam 4.6, Kannada 2.9 and Telugu 2.1. It is paradoxical to find out that the English dailies comprising of only 12.8 per cent of total circulation of all languages in India, claiming such a high share in ad revenue.[25] In contrast, the proportion of Hindi dailies was as high as 38.3 per cent but claiming only a low share in ad revenue.

Such imbalances lead to further inequities considering the number of publications are much fewer in English compared to the regional languages. To illustrate the point, there were 122 dailies in 1996 in all languages put together as ABC members. Of them, only 22 were in English the rest representing all other languages.[26]

A fewer English dailies thus are taking a lion's share in ad revenue, leaving the rest to a very large number of language dailies. Coming to each language segment, the leader takes away the bulk of it, as is already learnt. In such a context as this, the survival of a language newspaper in general, and the Telugu one in particular, looks like a feat of treading a camel through the needle's eye so far as securing the ad revenue.

Regional Language Papers set to be Competitive

Despite such desperation in chasing very limited ad cake, advertisers in recent years began to change their perceptions as more people are reading papers in regional languages. And such readers are found to be having more disposable income to be spent on consumer durables and to invest in financial markets. In general, people who read are getting richer. Economic opportunity has reached beyond the elite of the pre-liberalisation days. Consequently, mothertongue pride has risen (even in the North), so fewer families take English papers purely as a signal of social status.[27]

Between NRS-V (1995) and VI (1997), Indian language dailies have shown a sharp increase in readership figures even in urban India. According to NRS-VI, among the top 10 newspapers, language dailies ruled the roost in terms of readership with only one English newspaper at No. 10, i.e., *The Times of India*. This phenomenon is reflected in metros too. This shows that urban people today have no qualms about reading in their mother tongue.[28]

For example, in Kerala, the state with the highest literacy, English dailies can barely match their Malayalam counterparts. *Malayala Manorama* claimed ad revenues of Rs. 78.7 crore in 1996, the envy of any English media house.[29] Some of the language dailies that have made significant gains in readership in 1990s are: *Punjab Kesari, Nava Bharat, Dainik Bhaskar, Amar Ujala* and *Rashtriya Sahara* in Hindu, *Gunjarat Samachar* and *Sandesh* in Gujarati, *Bartaman* in Bengali, apart from *Dina Thanthi* (Tamil), *Eenadu, Malayala Manorama* and *Mathrubhumi* (both in Malayalam) in the South.

On the other hand, English newspaper readers are not of uniform worth to advertisers. They show sharp differences in terms of global exposure, interest areas, disposable income and propensity to splurge.[30] Nevertheless, according to an estimate, English dailies are attracting five million new readers every year. In mid-income households of semi-urban pockets, for instance, English papers are being bought to complement language ones.[31] Between NRS-IV and V, the aggregate circulation of English dailies has risen by nearly 25 per cent, but there has not been a proportional increase in readership.

Thus, in 1990s newspapers whether English or language ones been merrily invading one another's turf. Geographical expansionism, aggressive cover pricing, content enrichment and reader targeting strategies are all part of the game.

3. The Cost Compulsions and Competition

The Indian newspaper is passing through the era of satellite technology and paperless newsrooms involving massive investments. Telugu newspapers or regional newspapers are never behind their English counterparts in this regard.

Mere technological upgradation is not enough to attract new readership and thereby advertising. The newspaper marketer has to look beyond the present geographical boundaries. *Dainik Jagran*, for example, has added on six new editions. *Dina Thanthi, Eenadu* and *Vaartha* have launched many more editions. In olden days, no big infrastructural investments were needed. Most of the running costs were incurred on newsprint, journalists, printing and office overheads. Nowadays most of the editorial work (story creation and page designing) is done through sophisticated computers. So is the processing and printing. According to one estimate,[32] one printing unit to deliver top-end quality would cost between Rs.20 and Rs.30 crore. The risk is that the whole system could be rendered obsolete in only two years. This implies that the publisher should be able to not only recover the costs before it happens but also have enough resources to reinvest. In newspapers, where "lead time" is a matter of hours and speed of news delivery is a sought-after competitive advantage, high speed links are often needed. That is why new daily *Vaartha's* initial investment was Rs.50 crore when it used satellite connections to bring out the paper from nine centres simultaneously. According to a conservative estimate, for classy newspaper, a publisher should be willing to lose Rs.35 crore during the first three years without returns.[33] The Lucknow edition of *The Pioneer* broke-even in the fourth year of its operations, while the Delhi one is still to turn in operating profits.[34] This speaks of how the barriers to entry are rising as never before. According to N.Bhaskara Rao, Chairman of CMS, of every 20 aspirants who attempt to enter the print media industry, 10 actually bring out a publication, and of these only one succeeds.[35]

All that makes newspaper publishing a peculiarly risky business in India. The non-manpower costs are almost as high as in the West, but the circulation figures (and thus ad revenues) are pathetically low. The Indian newspapers cannot command the same kind of prices for its ad space in the market. This does not mean that traditional cost burdens are lower. Newsprint prices have been soaring. For one lakh copies of a daily, it could take Rs. 1.5 crore every month for a 16-page daily. An average wage bill would be a tenth of that.[36] In fact, the rising cost of newsprint is compelling the newspaper marketers to sell space at higher rates. Y.M.Gupta, managing director, *Dainik Jagran*, the largest circulated daily in Uttar Pradesh, says that he could raise circulation, but it results in reduced profitability in the face of limited avenues of advertising.[37] Many newspapers, particularly the runner-up ones in language segments are facing more or less the same situation in all parts of the country.

Hence, printing more copies is expensive. As such, it is required to attract advertisers, unless the paper is priced abnormally high on the stands. Satish K.Mehta, a media consultant said that the marketer starts losing heaps beyond 25,000 copies without advertising.[38] As per his estimate, overheads form about a fifth of the costs. 60 per cent of the cost is on newsprint. Its average price rose from Rs. 14,000 per ton in 1994 to Rs.28,000 per ton in 1995 before settling at about Rs.20,000. The daily uses about 150 gms. of paper on

22-24 pages. Considering all costs, the production cost works out to more than Rs.5 per copy. It is advertising revenue which makes up the gap thus supporting the whole of the organisation.

4. Competing to Become the First or Near-First

Being No. 1 player involves an enormous competitive advantage in terms of attracting ad revenue. If No.l newspaper outsells No.2 three copies to two, it will draw thrice the ad revenue. Even in a city with high local ad spend, being second can be painful unless the circulation is close to the market leader's. Media consultants caution that No. 2 newspaper should be closer to No.l than No. 3. For example, *The Times of India,* the leader in Mumbai for decades was placed in a poor No. 2 position in Delhi market in the 1980s. At that time, The Times of India was closer to *Indian Express,* No. 3 paper whereas *The Hindustan Times,* the market leader, was far ahead of its rivals, hi the 1990s *The Times of India's* well carved out reader targeting strategies enabled it very close to the market leader in terms of circulation and this No. 2 player emerged as the successful advertising vehicle for the marketers of premium products and services. Instead of looking for local tenders and retail ads, *The Times of India* attempted to reach the well educated, upend customers. In Mumbai *The Times of India* (the market leader) out-sells *Indian Express* (its closest rival) two copies to one, but draws six times the ad revenue. This is primarily because *The Times of India* is perceived as an upmarket read, a paper that reaches some of the country's richest families.[39]

The runner-up companies face still worse situations whenever a hike in ad tariffs is initiated by the market leader. The advertisers hitherto patronising some of the runner-up papers in issuing ads to them to some extent are compelled to confine only to the leader paper in view of the budget constraints.

Thus, safety-loving space buyers, with little proven information on whether one brand's audience has greater disposable income than the other's, prefer to stick to the big circulation figures. Mainstream brands, therefore, try to reach as many people as possible.

It does not mean the players in the lower order have no chance of survival. There are, provided they continue playing holding the cards close to their chest. The best play should be such, that at any cost, the competitors in newspaper business should not allow the market to become a game of musical chairs, where only one finalist occupies the chair edging out all others. Newspaper is not a one market business just like any other product. For example, a player in the Telugu newspaper business need not consider the whole state of Andhra Pradesh, where Telugu is spoken, as one market. If the player has no chance of staying first or near-first in the entire market as such, then better if he strives to become a leader in a chosen segment instead of the whole market. The secret of success of *Deccan Chronicle,* the leader in the city market of Hyderabad is that. Such examples should become a good lesson to the runner-up firms wherever they are. Instead of being No. 2, No. 3 or No. 4 in a state or larger geographical market, better if each of them play to become a leader in a much smaller segment, may be a city or a region. Marathi newspapers abound in such successes where the players were positioned to lead in the chosen segments leaving only 19.8 per cent of market share to the leader *Lokmat*, as is already mentioned in Chapter-V. Most of the English dailies also succeeded like that in the Indian markets.[40] In the Telugu newspaper scene, *Eenadu* on entry employed this strategy to be strongly entrenched in the markets where it entered first, namely, Visakhapatnam and Hyderabad regions, particularly where large ad markets exist. To begin with, such strategies alone could guarantee ad revenue and the survival of the newspaper. Better if the paper moves into a new market, only after capturing one market.

In the overcast sky of such competitive predicaments, the good news for the language dailies is that space buyers are now open to the proposition that there is more to print than just English. The ad revenue split between the English and language dailies has changed, from about 85:15 in the early 1990s to 75:25 in 1996. Analysts expect that this will change to 60:40 by the year 2000 as small towns come into the media plans of big advertisers.[41]

(C) Contemporary Strategies of Telugu Papers

It is amply clear that the circulation laurels do not automatically lead to the ad revenue laurels and the success of the newspaper. The grandiose product, promotion, pricing, and distribution strategies targeted at increased circulation are all exercises in marketing the paper, only to one of its two audiences i.e., the subscribers or readers. In newspaper business, Peter has to be robbed to pay Paul. Reader support could be sustained only if the advertiser comes forward to buy advertising in the paper. Robbing Peter is not as easy as luring Paul. Marketing the product to the second audience, advertisers, is much tougher than marketing it to the primary audience, the readers. The subscriber merrily takes the paper considering the heavy subsidy it carries and the insignificance of price and the unit of purchase. In contrast, ad space has to be sold in column-centimetres or agate lines or even words sometimes, at unbelievably high rates. The columns may be broader or narrower and the agate lines may be lengthier or shorter. For selling every column-centimetre of space, the newspaper has to struggle really hard. Finding out the advertisers, approaching and convincing them to buy space is not as easy as convincing the paper buyers. Nevertheless, advertiser loyalties melt away very easily, unlike subscriber loyalties which may last even several years, if the product is good enough. On the whole, the ad revenue trickles in drops, unlike the possibility of circulation support coming like a rain. Everyday the paper has to search for advertisers afresh, unlike securing subscribers with whom an unwritten contractual obligation exists at least for a month or so.

Yet, marketing the newspaper in securing the reader support has arrived much earlier than marketing it to the advertiser. To put it differently, marketing concept in news was recognised earlier than in advertising. Unfortunately, some players in the Telugu newspaper market have not recognised the importance of either of them, particularly even in the face of severe competition and they have paid the penalty. Had they realised the importance of marketing the total newspaper, selling it both to the reader and advertiser, things would have been different today. The oldest of the Telugu newspapers and a champion of the freedom struggle *Andhra Patrika* should not have come to the end. And the far behind runner-up papers should have been revived to do much better today. The contemporary space selling strategies that are either sustaining the Telugu papers or failing to support them are to be analysed now.

During the early years the Telugu daily market was confined to one or two players i.e., *Andhra Patrika* and *Andhra Prabha*. The third serious player *Andhra Jyoti* emerged only in 1960. During those years advertising used to be a one paper one advertisement affair implying run of the paper (ROP). It meant the entire print order carrying the advertiser's message. The advent of multi-publication centres and the new papers, particularly *Eenadu* brought in spectacular changes on the advertising front, besides the product front. As a matter of fact, the product strategies and ad sales strategies looked like two sides of the same coin. The product was so meticulously designed that it suits the requirements of the reader and the advertiser simultaneously. The market leader took the initiative in designing such a two-in-one strategy. Now the days of one advertisement running through all the copies state-wise have gone, unless the advertiser desires it so. What the leader did has come to be adopted by the other players. Consequently, more or less similar space marketing strategies are employed by all the players as they are found to be following identical product strategies. Let it be examined how they are related to each other in the Telugu newspaper market.

1. Transforming Segmentation-for-Circulation into Segmentation-for-Advertising

How the product strategies tailored to suit the requirements of the reader also suit the size and taste of the advertiser is depicted in Figure 8.1, with reference to *Eenadu*, the trendsetter of such dual exercise—the master strategy. No Telugu paper is published from just one centre as a state wise edition as *Ananda Bazar Patrika* (Bengali) from Calcutta. For example, *Eenadu* comes out from 10 centres as 10 editions, thus segmenting the paper for advertisers as well as readers into 10 zones. The advertiser interested in sending his message to the audience in just one or two or few zones need not unnecessarily waste his money on other audiences in other zones. This segmentation enables the advertiser to reach the desired audience at desired cost. Such cost-effective strategies are made more meaningful by further segmentation of edition or zone through the introduction of district supplements in tabloid form. Depending upon the number of districts served by each edition, as many supplements are brought out. Such district supplements, in turn, are used as vehicles of district level advertising. The main edition as such serves as a vehicle of advertising in a larger area, the district supplement serving the smaller segment. The district is further fragmented into towns or intra-city zones in the form of slip pages. For example, Hyderabad city edition carries as many as nine slip pages in case of *Eenadu*. Thus a three-tier geographic segmentation is at work at *Eenadu*. This enables the readers to gather news at various levels and at the same time the three-tiers enable the advertisers to reach the target audiences at such levels.

In essence, the paper brought advertising within the reach of even a small individual or a retailer. Advertisers, needless to say are delighted with the range of options *Eenadu* offers them" Adds Suresh Kumar, a media planner of Mudra Communications, "*Eenadu*'s district editions allow advertisers to focus on sharply defined target consumers."[42] An advertiser has the option of choosing a district, a combination of the districts, a unit, a combination of units and all the editions. This is how segmentation-for-circulation strategy is transformed into segmentation-for-advertising, the master strategy innovated by the market leader, which has become a norm for every player now in the market.

On introduction, the district supplement appeared to be one case of overambition finally distorting a successful newspaper's better judgement. Nevertheless, Ramoji Rao was very optimistic of the outcome. "Success goes to those who dare and act," as he puts it. And he adds, "I am prepared to wait. The day these district supplements stabilise, I have a fantastic weapon in my hands."[43] His optimism paid off. It took only two years to break-even the costs of those supplements.[44] Two years later the districts brought in two-thirds of their revenues, as confirmed by their advertising director, Venkat.[45] Consider this: If you add up the column-centimetre rates of all district supplements put together, the total works out to much more than the combined rate of all the main editions that most national advertisers use. So the paper actually needs more money from those smaller papers, than from all its main editions put together, besides having virtually created a whole new segment of very small

Figure 8.1

Three-tier Geographic Segmentation of *Eenadu* by Editions, District Supplements and Slip Pages

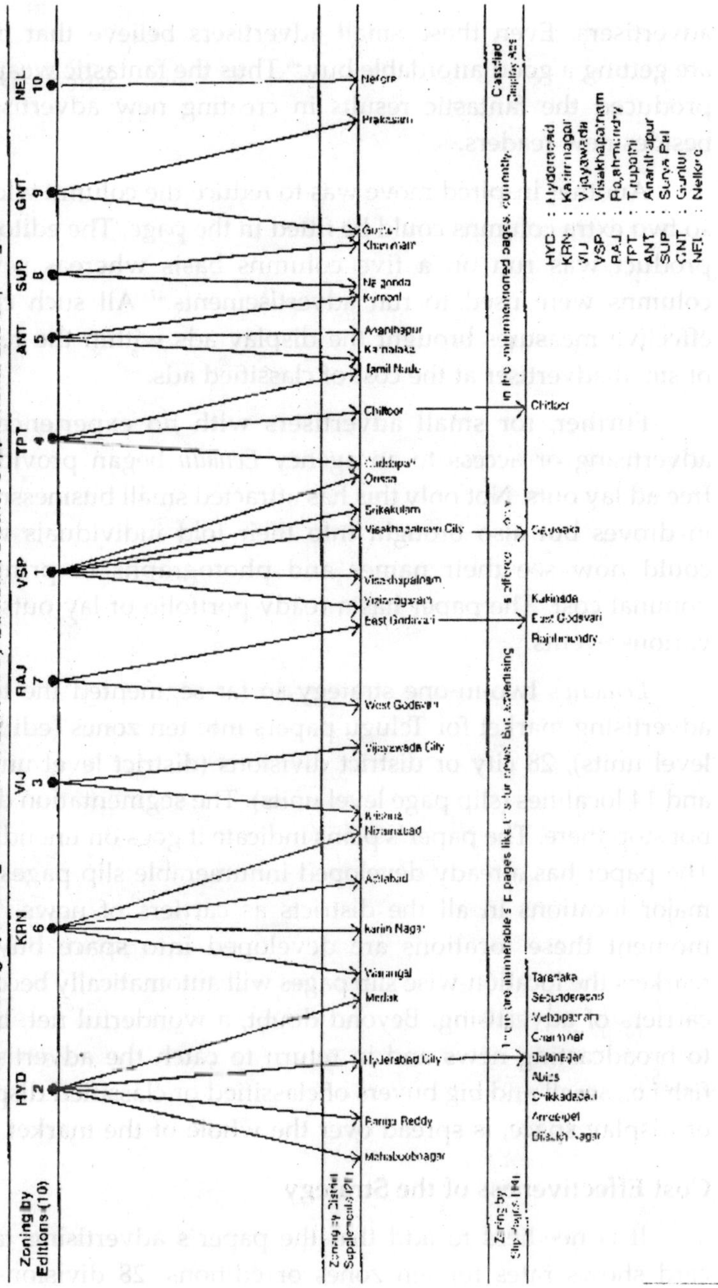

advertisers. Even these small advertisers believe that they are getting a good affordable buy.[46] Thus the fantastic weapon produced the fantastic results in creating new advertisers, besides new readers.

Another inspired move was to reduce the column width, so two extra columns could be fitted in the page. The editorial product was run on a five columns basis whereas seven columns were used to run advertisements.[47] All such cost-effective measures brought the display ads within the reach of small advertiser at the cost of classified ads.

Further, for small advertisers with no experience of advertising or access to an agency *Eenadu* began providing free ad lay outs. Not only this has attracted small businessmen in droves but also brought into their fold individuals who could now see their names and photographs in print at nominal cost. The paper has a ready portfolio of lay outs for various events.

Eenadu's two-in-one strategy so far segmented the total advertising market for Telugu papers into ten zones (edition-level units), 28 city or district divisions (district level units), and 14 localities (slip page level units). The segmentation does not stop there. The paper's plans indicate it goes on unending. The paper has already developed innumerable slip pages for major locations in all the districts as carriers of news. The moment these locations are developed into space buying markets the location-wise slip pages will automatically become carriers of advertising. Beyond doubt, a wonderful net, both to broadcasting news and in return to catch the advertising fish i.e., small and big buyers of classified or classified display or display space, is spread over the whole of the market.

Cost Effectiveness of the Strategy

It is needless to add that the paper's advertising tariff card shows rates for ten zones or editions, 28 divisions or

Table 8.2

Cost-per Thousand Copies of Advertising Tariff, by Type of Advertisement, 1997

(Combined Rate Covering All Editions During Weekdays in Black and White)

	Circulation	*Display (cc)* Rs.	*CPT* Rs.	*Financial (cc)* Rs.	*CPT* Rs.	*Ear Panels* Rs.	*CPT* Rs.
Eenadu	6,53,582	963	1.47	1,106	1.69	21,185	32.41
Vaartha	1,62,594	579	33.56	637	3.92	4,250	26.14
Andhara Jyoti	1,15,438	436	3.78	500	4.33	4,300	37.25
Andhara Prabha	31,906	175	5.48	200	6.27	N.A.	N.A.
Andhra Bhoomi	19,716[a]	300	15.22	450	22.82	3,500	177.52

cc = column-centimetre CPT = Cost-per-thousand copies N.A. Not acceptable a. Estimated circulation

Notes: 1. Circulations are based on the average of ABC data for the two half-years in 1997, (Audit Bureau of Circulations. Mumbai).

2. Rates are based on Tariff Cards of the respective papers, then in force.

districts/cities and 14 localities. Besides, the card specified combined rates for several options. The tariffs are related to circulation strengths in the respective segments. The more the circulation the higher the ad rate per column-centimetre. If *Eenadu's* tariff is compared with those of its competitors, the former's rates appear to be far on a high side. For example, the combined (statewide) display rate per column-centimetre in *Eenadu* was Rs.963 in 1997, whereas that of *Vaartha* stood at only Rs.579, as are shown in Table 8.2. But in terms of cost-per-thousand (CPT) copies circulated works out to a mere Rs.1.47 for *Eenadu*, the lowest of all papers. For *Vaartha*, the CPT per column-centimetre was 142 per cent extra at Rs.3.56. For other papers the CPT per column-centimetre was still higher. In case of *Andhra Bhoomi* , it was over ten times to that of the market leader. Resultantly, what appeared to be the premium tariff in case of the market leader, in fact, is a cost-effective minimum rate to the advertiser. This is how the superior performance of the market leader brings in value both to the marketer and the customer through competitive advantage. In contrast, what appeared to be discount rates of runner-up papers work out to be super-premium rates in terms of CPT per column-centimetre, overburdening the advertiser. This is the cost of the market players' underperformance. Thus, why advertisers do not prefer to bear such costs is justifiable.

Advertising, the Advertising

The capability to provide larger audiences at lesser CPT per column-centimetre alone does not automatically bring value to the doorstep of the advertiser. Success lies in advertisers' acceptance of it. Advertisers' acceptance is not automatic. Sometimes, their acceptance requires a lot of persuasive efforts. Otherwise, marketers and customers remain where they are, thousands of miles apart. Marketing does not stop with creation of standard of living, it is both creation and delivery of standard of living. The market leader's promotion efforts in advertising the advertising are quite imaginative, well-planned and meticulously designed and executed. Their promotion material, particularly targeted at display advertisers—the mainstay of Telugu papers, in the form of highly attractive multicolour booklets tastefully designed in various shapes and the well illustrated contents speak volumes of their ingenuity in space marketing efforts. Some of them are in the form of spiral magazines or a bird sprawling its wings, or a maze or a wedding card and more. Particularly wedding card format is chosen to promote matrimonial advertising. Whatever they may be, their very appearance tempts everyone to go through their contents. The presentation of their contents look like the presentation of findings of a research study. In fact, they are such findings too. They employed marketing research agencies like MARG (Marketing and Research Group). Sometimes they contained the analysis of NRS, IRS and ABC data. The titles of such booklets are quite stimulating. Sometimes they contain a large number of tables or charts. At the same time too simple to read and grasp. Each one of them is found to explain the prospective advertiser how it would be advantageous to advertise in their paper compared to other media options. They never miss to present the updated reader profile in right perspective. To name a few, the promotion material includes: *The Verdict; From Strength to Strength; Andhra is not Andhra ... without Eenadu; Eenadu Weekend Magazine Vs TV; We Knew It, MARG Confirmed It; Andhra's Most Influential Business Page; Now the Festival Season is Over; One million New Prospects; Srirasthu, Subhamasthu, Kalyanamasthu; Eenadu Spreads its Wings;* etc. All such imaginative material plus the untiring efforts of over 1,000 ad sales force are pressed into service to catch the advertiser, small or big, wherever they may be present or potential. Tireless campaigning through TV commercials in E-TV (the group's channel), particularly for their classifieds and matrimonials, speaks of the advantage the paper enjoys in promoting space selling. Space selling efforts of other Telugu papers are found to be no match to those *of Eenadu's*. Marketing is yet to arrive there, to say the least.

Then one wonders whether *Eenadu* is an ad product or a news product. Interestingly, it is both, all such marketing efforts culminating in product differentiation and development marketing.

Product Differentiation, the Heart of *Eenadu's* Performance

Product differentiation implies making a product different from those of the competitors in anticipation of a premium price. Let it be analysed how *Eenadu* could capitalise on it.

How *Eenadu* could differentiate the product simultaneously to both the publics, readers and advertisers, through the master strategy at enormous costs is already discussed. Michael Porter clearly analyses the implications of differentiation. A firm that can achieve and sustain differentiation will be an above-average performer in its industry if its price premium exceeds the extra costs incurred is being unique. A differentiator, therefore, must always seek ways of differentiating that lead to a price premium greater than the cost of differentiating.[48] But the product newspaper being heavily subsidised by another public cannot expect a price premium excepting very marginally from the readers, in the face of competition from other papers and other media. Naturally the advertisers have to bear it. *Eenadu's* premium ad tariffs substantiate this, which work out to be cost-effective to advertisers in terms of cost-per-thousand copies, as is already illustrated (Table 8.2). This is the competitive advantage at the heart of *Eenadu's* performance. Had the paper failed to retain its market leadership after such extreme indulgence in differentiation, it would have resulted in a major marketing disaster. It should be remembered *Eenadu* embarked on heavy differentiation process after firmly securing its place as a leader.

Hypothesis of Imitation Trap

Let the implications of me-too imitations in differentiation be examined now. Like their leader, the imitators have to bear the costs of differentiation. Perhaps they have to bear extra even, considering scale of operation and the time-lag between the leader introducing them and the followers imitating them, inflation interfering. But the far behind followers have no chance of levying premium tariffs on advertisers because of the low circulation of their papers. Even the followers' much low ad tariffs work out to be much high rates in terms of cost-per-thousand copies. This is the competitive disadvantage to which runner-up papers are subjected to in getting into the self-imposed trap of thoughtless imitations, sailing in rough weather of continuously declining circulation. Thus things changed from bad to worse at the follower papers. A situation as this confirms the hypothesis of imitation trap indulged in by the runner-up firms in Telugu newspaper market scene.

Developmental Marketing at Work

Further, product differentiation, both for circulation and advertising at *Eenadu* and the paper's other marketing efforts also culminated in bringing developmental marketing to the fore. Developmental marketing is associated with a state of demand which Philip Kotler calls—latent demand. A state of *latent demand* exists *when a substantial number of people share a strong need for something that does not exist in the form of an actual product or service.* The latent demand represents an opportunity for the marketing innovator to develop the product or service that people have been wanting.[49] For example, nicotine and tar-free cigarettes and pollution-free cars are in latent demand. *Eenadu* sensed the latent demand for district supplements and slip pages both from the readers and advertisers. Hence they innovated them and successfully marketing, converting latent demand into actual demand. The process of effectively converting latent demand into actual demand is that of development marketing.[50] Development marketing leads to enlargement of industry size as it happened to Telugu newspaper market as a result of *Eenadu's* innovations.

Pitfalls in the Master Strategy

The two-in-one master strategy is not without some serious limitations from the view point of both the leader—its innovator, and the followers - its me-too imitators. The news net thus cast statewide or more covering all the lanes and by-lanes in anticipation of a reasonable catch of advertising may draw a blank at times or seasonally or even mostly in pockets where the industry in general is not able to do well. Such problems are not uncommon even to the market leader. In such situations, the unused ad space is found to be filled in by overstretched local news stories even at ward level, sometimes intruding into the rights of privacy of individuals. Unmindful of the sensitivity of the problem, nowadays, Telugu papers are found to give even the minutest of the details relating to rape victims or high school students that are debarred from taking examinations for their indulgence in copying. Papers' failure to keep the identity of such victims or such juvenile wrong doers in anonymity sometimes lead to suicides. Papers should keep off adding insults to injuries. These are more a problem of overstretching the news when ads are less forthcoming.

Further, either overcoverage of local news or its undercoverage results in undesirable news mix. A feeling is already growing at least in some quarters that district supplements need not be read or it is a light weight product.

What is important is quality of the news rather than quantity. The excess of the latter dilutes the former.

The follower players are more prone to such overdoings, considering the scanty advertising the papers carry. The design that suits the leader need not suit the followers. What is tailored to one's needs becomes only a readymade wear to others and problems of maladjustments arise. The multi-centre editions, district supplements or slip papers are all developed at enormous costs. Unless the paper is capable of raising ad revenue justifying such costs, a mere me-too imitations have dangerous implications. Further, the followers should not allow themselves to become the prototypes of the leader. Better if a newspaper develops its own personality, its own product, and advertising strategies and ultimately its own image chasing a competitive advantage of some form or other.

Michael Porter asserts, "Competitive advantage is at the heart of any strategy, and achieving competitive advantage requires a firm to make a choice—if a firm is to attain competitive advantage, it must make a choice about the type of competitive advantage it seeks to attain and the scope within which it will attain. Being 'all things to all people' is a recipe for strategic mediocrity and below-average performance, because it often means that a firm has no competitive advantage at all."[51] Thus merely imitating the leader's strategy does not automatically bring in its competitive advantages to the follower firms. It is marketing blindfold resulting in disastrous consequences to the followers. Unfortunately this is the phobia gripping the runner-up firms in Telugu newspaper market, either in relation to circulation or advertising strategies. The earlier such imitations are given up the better it would be for the industry. A firm must compete aggressively, but not indiscriminately.[52] *Vaartha's* encirclement attack imitating the leader in every minute detail looks like an example of colossal indiscrimination, apart from what other competitors did.

2. Other Dual Exercises

Besides the master strategy, the linkage between other product strategies and ad sales strategies is summed up in Table 8.3. Other product strategies include Sunday supplement, interest-zoning, the use of colour, matrimonial and classified advertising. Each of them is again a dual exercise fostering both circulation and advertising. Let each of them be examined as a vehicle of advertising.

(i) The Sunday's Special Vehicle

The Sunday supplement in a magazine format has several implications relating to space marketing. The supplement stretches the life of an ad from one day to one week or even more thus stretching its shelf life. The magazine features further stretch the circulation and reader bases in which the advertiser is intensely interested. The supplement enlarges reader involvement too. It is a "super way"[53] to sample new products, get consumer trial and feedback. The advertiser could conveniently use the supplement as a carrier of such sample sachets, pinning them on the cover page. Unlike the usual main paper, it has the capability to incorporate revolutionary layouts and designs forming part of the advertisements. All such strengths enable to position itself as a competitor to the well-entrenched magazines in attracting advertisements. *Eenadu* has gone to the extent of positioning their Sunday supplement as a meaningful competitor to the TV in offering colour advertising opportunities.[54]

The Super way Becoming a Subway

On the circulation front, *Eenadu's* Sunday supplement succeeded in terms of much enlarged sales on Sundays as discussed earlier in Chapter-VII.[55] But its performance is directly attracting ad revenue so far appeared to be dismal. Ads are found to be very scanty in Sunday supplement. Nevertheless, it is found to be indirectly attracting volumes

Table 8.3

Market Leader's Innovativeness in Relating Product Strategies to Advertising Sales Strategies.

Product Strategy	*How it is Related to Space Selling Strategy*
1	2
1. The three-tier master strategy of segmentation-for-circulation (1989). Gets closer to one audience i.e., readers.	1. Also becomes the three-tier master strategy of segmentation-for-advertising. Gets closer to another audience i.e., advertisers in attracting space buying from them.
	Advertising could be brought within the reach of small advertiser.
Such intense coverage of local news creates new circulation and readers.	Such new circulation and new readers create new advertisers too.
2. Other Such Dual Exercises	
(i) Bringing out Sunday supplement in a magazine form with magazine features (1988).	(i) Magazine features stretch the life of an advertisement from one day to one week or even more.
	Stretch the reader and circulation bases.

1	2
	Enlarge reader involvement. All such strengths enable to position it as a competitor to the well-entrenched magazines in attracting advertisements.
(ii) Interest-zoning of the newspaper by introducing a page for finance (1990), cinema (1991), the women (1992), career counselling, etc., as daily features.	(ii) Such zoning is also an exercise to create appropriate audiences to suit the requirements of advertisers of varied interests. It may further lead to creation of premium zones of ad space as in case of business sections of *Eenadu* and *Andhra Jyoti*.
(iii) Initiating and popularising matrimonial advertising column -*Pelli Pandiri* (means marriage pendal).	(iii) Besides creating new subscribers, creates new class of advertisers too. Enhances the paper's competitiveness in relation to English dailies in attracting such ads.
(iv) Bringing out the culture of other	(iv) Precisely, advertisers need such audiences

1	2
classifieds to the fore. Classifieds are an index of the paper's popularity among readers, who are adults and whose educational and income levels are high. Classifieds evoke both reader interest and response and thus a potential circulation bastion.	to spread their messages.
(v) Exploiting the use of colour in printing, earlier than any daily newspaper in India.	(v) It creates an audience to receive ads in colour. Using colour, the daily newspaper could position itself favourably in competition with colour TV and glossy magazines.
(vi) Newspapers image building strategies attract quality readers in large measure.	(vi) Advertisers will be too happy to reach such audiences through such papers.

of advertising. Because *Eenadu* was selling extra copies in large number on Sundays (attributable to the attraction of the supplement), advertisers were preferring to advertise on that day but in the main paper, quite unexpectedly. *Eenadu* charging premium rates for Sunday advertising speaks of the significance of the Sunday supplement in that direction. But what was proved to be a distinctive advantage to the leader appears to have become a distinctive disadvantage to runner-up papers. They were forced to imitate the leader's strategy triggering extra sales and thus extra costs but leaving no extra ad revenue. The fact that they are not able to quote premium rates on Sunday ads establishes this fact. The leader's success is also limited in this area considering their Sunday supplement as such has failed to make significant inroads in capturing ad revenue into its pages. This requires serious attention of the paper in revitalising and repositioning it as a direct vehicle of advertising.

(ii) Interest-Zoning

Mere circulation build-up of the newspaper may not attract adequate advertisers. The need of the advertisers is not simply the audience numbers. The social composition of the audience, rather than its size, is the basic criterion influencing the media planning. Sometimes the advertiser's target audience is youth. At other times it may be women or investing public or highly educated or sports lovers, depending upon what they intend to sell them. Philanthropic or religious communities, art lovers or film-goers, middle income or top income segments may be the advertisers' required audience. In an attempt to attract readers representing such socio-economic and psychographic segments, newspapers create several interest-zones. They serve the dual purpose of circulation as well as ad revenue enlargement.

Exclusive women's page or business section or youth features like career counselling or educational features like computer chip chat creeped into almost all Telugu papers. Some of the papers used such interest-zones even to create premium advertising zones. For example, *Eenadu* and *Andhra Jyoti* charged premium tariff for the financial ads in business section. The equity culture that has been newly invading the Telugu households boosted the potential of the business section as an advertising vehicle in Telugu newspapers. But there is a danger of such a premium advertising zones becoming discount or desert zones in the eventuality of depressed stock markets caused by the declining economic conditions, resulting in the dampening of equity culture. The Indian economy and the Indian stock markets are currently passing through such a difficult phase and the papers have to bear the brunt of it, both in terms reader interest and advertising.

The dangers of the paper's inability to create the right type of audiences could be well understood by Australian publisher Rupert Murdoch's experiences with his *New York Post*. When he bought it he laid down a news strategy featuring highly sensational coverage—rape, murder, pillage and arson were standard fare. His circulation strategy aimed at reaching new heights overshadowing the *Daily News* and the high-toned *New York Times* and *Wall Street Journal*. The *Post* succeeded in pushing its circulation from 4,00,000 to 9,60,000 in just six years. But the paper was a failure in advertising strategy. A story (perhaps apocryphal) illustrating the paradox made the rounds. At that time, the *Post* was delivering more readers then the *Times*. Then Murdoch approached an executive of an upscale New York city department store to convince to switch over advertising to his Post from the *Times*. The reaction from the executive was shocking, "Mr. Murdoch, the *Times'* readers are our shoppers. The *Post's* readers are our shoplifters."[56] Thus, the *Post's* strategy of creating a sensational newspaper of the readers and trying to sell it to advertisers proved to be self-defeating. For years, this inconsistent policy reportedly cost Murdoch some $ 1,000,000 or more, monthly, in operating losses.[57]

(iii) Nurturing Matrimonial Advertising Culture

Matrimonials are by far the most popular form of classifieds. Matrimonial and classified advertising look like advertising strategies rather than product strategies. But they evoke a lot of reader interest and response. Such reader interests are very significant newspaper subscription bases too. For example, job seekers interest in the appointments column of classified ads and it is traditionally a very strong base of paper sales. Considering this, matrimonial and classified advertising are taken as a part of the product too for the purpose of this analysis. Though matrimonial is also part of classified ads, in view of its growing importance in Telugu papers, it is dealt as a separate item.

Serving the metropolitan and urban readers, matrimonial advertising was not new to the English papers even from the earliest of their times. But the papers in regional languages finding their readers mostly in small towns and rural India had no such opportunity of capitalising on matrimonial advertising till recently. Growing employment and business opportunities resulted in population shifts from rural India to urban India. Andhra Pradesh is no exception. Urbanisation is found to be ever increasing. Communities exclusively depending on agriculture formerly started moving into the near and far-off towns and cities. Having uprooted from the village homes intra-community interaction and communication are getting weakened. The changing situation as this naturally poses problems in securing matrimonial alliances through traditional channels or intermediaries.

Eenadu was the first to recognise this marketing opportunity and they lost no time in initiating matrimonial advertising. In a tradition bound Indian society, securing matrimonial alliances through press advertising used to be considered a taboo. A feeling that only the disadvantaged brides and grooms prefer matrimonial advertising prevailed widely. But the imperatives of growing urbanisation and the changing attitudes made the people to realise its advantages. Precisely, *Eenadu* stepped in there to mobilise public opinion in favour of matrimonial advertising by positioning its campaign suitably. They have given matrimonial advertising an attractive and well sounding caption *Pellli Pandiri.* It sounds so sweetly in Telugu which means marriage *pendal.* The paper had the foresight, courage and conviction to run a why-to campaign. It was not an ordinary campaign with a series of three unpaid ads, over and out. But a fullfledged multi-media campaign consisting of television commercials, colour press ads, outdoor posters and even a booklet inserted in the paper on why matrimonials work and how they could be made to work better. And all this because the Telugu reader was traditionally wary of this form of contacting prospective partners for their children. It must have cost a great deal. *Eenadu* succeeded in changing the readers' attitudes. But it took them a lot of time and marketing effort. To begin with, it was a Friday weekly column, now becoming a Sunday full page in the main paper. And it is a statewide advertising feature too at a nominal cost, Rs. 516 a piece. Initially it used to cost not even half of that. No ad is so specially positioned for such a low fare. Beginning with 25 pieces a week, today the paper is able to sell on broad-sheet full of matrimonial advertising. This is how the paper succeeded in creating customers—this time fully paying advertiser customers, hitherto nonexisting.

Their ad copy in a fill-in-and-post-it form is so tempting that *Eenadu*'s *Pelli Pandiri* has become a household term, the middle class and upper class households inclining to use it more and more. A free computerised horoscope is an added temptation. Alliance seekers in Andhra Pradesh are least depending on the English papers and thus, *Eenadu* emerged as their strong competitor.

Envying the trend-setter's performance, the other players too imitated it. But only to lose the battle on that front. In a front as this what the advertiser requires is the widest circulation and effective response. If the paper is on the internet even the global responses may be forthcoming on such matters. So the possibility of depending on a No. 2 paper or the papers in the still lower order does not arise at all. As such even the best efforts of other papers did not bear fruit in selling space for matrimonial advertising. This is one competitive advantage to a player in the leader's position. Reach and response are the essence of matrimonial advertising.

Conversional Marketing Arrives

Eenadu could clinch the competitive advantage in matrimonial advertising not merely by virtue of its market leadership. If it is that easy, the earlier leaders or its counterparts could have easily taken an advantage of it. Matrimonial advertising culture was very carefully tended at *Eenadu* and it is still going on even today through what Philip Kotler calls *conversional marketing*.

Conversional marketing grows out of the state of negative demand. *Negative demand is a state in which all or most of the important segments of potential market dislike the product or service and in fact might conceivably pay a price to avoid it.* Negative demand, far from being a rare condition, applied to many products or services. For example, vegetarians feel negative demand for meat, and atheism is in negative demand by certain groups. The challenge of negative demand to marketing management, especially in the face of positive supply, is to develop a plan that will cause demand to rise from negative to positive and eventually equal the positive supply level. This marketing task is conversional marketing.[58] *Eenadu* is busily engaged in translating this philosophy, slowly but surely and steadily, into reality insofar as matrimonial advertising which was found to be in negative demand sometime back in Telugu papers. There is a possibility of even No.2 player getting benefitted provided the paper's circulation gets closer to No. 1 player rather to No. 3 player,

(iv) Marketing the Other Classifieds

All ads were originally of the classified form—bought directly by the advertisers on a cost per word basis, and typeset by the publication. Historically, newspapers used to carry classifieds on their front page. The *Times* did so till 1966. Today classifieds and display are clearly segregated. Classifieds are non-intrusive and response-oriented. Readers search them out rather than the other way round, and to help them, the ads are all gathered together in fixed locations and arranged—hence classified into different categories. Readers of classifieds usually have a way of contacting the advertisers, either directly, or through newspaper box numbers.

"There are sociological as well as economic reasons for having classifieds, Bhaskar Das, vice-president (West), *The Times of India* group points out.[59] Classifieds are advertising in a most democratic way. Anyone can place or respond to one. As such, they are an important service to the readers. For the reader, classified pages are an index of the paper's popularity. In particular, classifieds made a difference in competitive situations. *The Hindustan Times,* for example, has withstood *The Times of India*'s, Delhi's onslaught at least partly because of the pull of its classifieds. Despite *The Telegraph*'s, success in Calcutta, people continue to use *The Statesman* for placing and accessing classifieds. Given this reason for retaining them, publishers are now trying to increase their returns from classifieds. Marketing classifieds involves three activities—getting the advertiser to place ads, simplifying the procedures for them to do so and getting readers to refer them.

All large publications carry classifieds especially on Sundays. "Any publication with a circulation of over 1,00,000 has about 8-columns of classifieds", says K.K.Sibbal, marketing manager Hind Samachar group.[60] In Mumbai, *The Times of India* publishes an average of 16-17 pages of classifieds a week, while *Punjab Kesari* (Hindi) in Delhi has two pages of classifieds during the weekend, tapering down to five columns on weekdays. Classified share of the total revenue relating to 190 members of the Indian Newspaper Society (INS) was only 4.6 per cent in 1995. But in the developed countries, classifieds continue to be the newspaper's forte. For example, in the USA classifieds yield the highest per-page-profit for most newspapers with more than 50 per cent of incremental revenue sometimes going directly to operating profit.[61] There it comprised 31-33 per cent of total newspaper ad revenue, industrywide.[62] On an average, 53 per cent of all readers see some classifieds on a weekday and 54 per cent on Sunday.[63] There if the local economy sneezes, classified gets pneumonia.[64] It appears the business in classifieds is strongly associated with the levels of the economic development, leaving India's classified business in a primitive stage.

Yet, *Eenadu* picked up the courage to accept the challenge of designing the strategy to create advertisers for its classifieds. Tasting or smelling success in matrimonials, *Eenadu* started targeting on other forms of classifieds, making a small beginning with a Real Estate page (every Saturday) in the city supplements of Hyderabad, Visakhapatnam and Vijayawada simultaneously in 1992. As in case of matrimonials they made the classifieds easier to customer by providing fill-in-and-drop-it coupons in their ad copies. And the initial piece rate was a mere Rs.143. They made it still easier to the small advertiser by throwing open a large network of zonal offices. For example, as many as 10 zonal offices in Hyderabad city alone were put to work which were of immense use in collecting the ads and rendering the necessary service to the advertiser. The long-term strategy has yet to bear fruit in a big way but the pursuit is not given up. No other Telugu newspaper is found to be so vigorous as *Eenadu* in campaigning for its classifieds. The classified culture has started creeping into the Telugu newspaper market. The day the classified ads business grows in stature, *Eenadu* will be a major beneficiary, assuming its marketing aggressiveness continues. Unlike the battle for matrimonials, the battle for classifieds is not yet over. It is still on.

Stimulational Marketing is On

Eenadu's continued efforts to build-up a market for its classifieds is an exercise in *stimulational marketing,* in the terminology of Philip Kotler.

There is a whole range of products and services for which there is no demand. Instead of people having negative or positive feelings towards the offering, they are indifferent or uninterested. *No demand is a state in which all or important segments of a potential market are uninterested in or indifferent to a particular offering.* The task of converting no demand into positive demand is called *stimulational marketing.* Stimulational marketing is a tough task because the marketer does not start with a semblance of latent demand for the offering. One way to create a positive demand is to try to connect the product or service with some existing need in the marketplace. *Eenadu* starting the real estate page in Hyderabad city supplement was in that direction. Another way to create positive demand is to distribute information or the object itself in more places in the hope that people's lack of demand is only lack of exposure.[65] *Eenadu* is vigorously moving in this direction in exposing their classifieds, through TV commercials and throwing open a large network of zonal offices.

(v) The Colour Dimension

The colour dimension is yet another example of inseparability of a circulation strategy and the advertising strategy in newspaper business. *Eenadu* was very tactful in putting colour to its advantage in creating and sustaining its circulation. Even without using colour the paper succeeded in achieving market leadership. Even after becoming the leader the paper continued without colour for a long time. Till a distantly behind competitor *Andhra Jyoti* triggered the colour war (1987), *Eenadu* has no colour designs. Then it had no option except retaliating with the same stick. This brought in rich returns in the form of safeguarding the competitive advantage it was enjoying by then, having very firmly saddled in a position of far superior strength of the leader. Then the colour became handy in creating premium zones of advertising, thus compensating the extra efforts and costs involved in it. It was also a time the colour TV invading the Indian markets. The situation was thus ripe for the Telugu papers to offer advertising in multicolour. Resultantly, a circulation strategy has come to stay as an advertising strategy too.

The fact that *Eenadu* could quote an extra premium of 100-150 per cent for its multicolour ads depending on their location speaks of the competitive strength of this strategy. Its rivals' premium rates were only marginally higher compared to their black and white category.

What is advantageous to a leader paper need not be so to the others. Strategies such as colour could only strengthen a paper provided if it is otherwise good enough. Players whose circulations were found to be continuously plummeting may not be able to drive home any advantage either by offering a paper or an ad in colour. The experiences of other Telugu papers proved it.

Andhra Jyoti indulging in colour war is an instance of attacking a good leader, who had no intentions of a battle on that front. Michael Porter cautions, "Followers sometimes commit the fatal error of attacking a good leader. The leader is then forced to retaliate, and what has been a profitable position for the follower turns into a marginal one."[66] Thus *Andhra Jyoti* paid the penalty.

(vi) Newspaper's Image Building Strategies

The issue of newspaper image building was, for a very long tune, taken very lightly among publishers and editors. Not many managers got excited about image and was neglected by the industry and individual newspapers alike. But tunes have changed. Image building today is an extremely important managerial responsibility and must be integrated into every newspaper's marketing effort. Image in the marketplace must be built carefully and protected devotedly. First one should look at the wider newspaper industry image to organise and manage a promotion effort to improve the newspaper's general image, increase circulation and augment advertising sales.[67]

It is a difficult to define the concept. It includes credibility, believability, public confidence, accurate reportage and many more things. Building it requires long-range planning process. It takes generations to build and unceasing vigilance to protect. But in a flash, despite constant watchfulness, grievous damage can be done to it. A single hoax or error might not destroy credibility. But it can draw down the reservoir of public confidence to dangerous levels. Probably more serious over the long haul is gradual erosion of public confidence due to errors in fact or to perceived bias in handing news, lack of good taste, or intensive or unfair invasions of privacy. All find their way into papers, large and small, and though each may seem insignificant, their cumulative impact can be devastating and long-lasting.[68]

Image is the invisible but most precious attribute of the newspaper that is constantly sold to its readers and advertisers. If the credibility of a paper is low, readers do not like to read it. If so, the advertisers do not like to buy space in such papers. Mere circulation jumps are no index of a growing image or reliability. The lesser the credibility of a paper, the faster the circulations melt away in competitive situations. *Udayam,* though produced short-time upward jumps in circulation, the performance did not last longer because it could not project better image in the minds of its clientele. Even in the face of competitive onslaughts it took *Andhra Patrika* very long time to reach the dead end. The image it built over the years might have protected it from early exit. Despite *Vaartha* indulging in encirclement attack it could neither secure the support of the readers nor advertisers on that scale because image building cannot be achieved overnight that instantly and in such a big way.

Andhra Prabha accepts public service advertising free of cost. *Eenadu's* unwillingness to accept the ads relating to alcohol and cigarettes is an exercise in image building activity. They are also unwilling to sacrifice reader interest to accommodate the advertiser's unreasonable demands. The paper refused to sell Tata Cellular the whole of the first four pages space in Hyderabad edition on their launching the phone on 13thDecember, 1996. But *Deccan Chronicle* obliged the advertiser. It involved an advertising tariff of Rs.7.6 lakh. Nevertheless, *Eenadu* obliged them in a different way. On that day, they sold all their advertising space including ear panels to Tata Cellular without making any sacrifice of their news space in usual locations but without accommodating no other advertiser. The tariff involved was Rs.5.58 lakh.[69] *Eenadu* had rescheduled the ads booked for that day duly requesting its advertisers. *Deccan Chronicle* attracted criticism from the readers, whereas *Eenadu* escaped it. This is how images are made and unmade in newspaper business.

Summing up, it is thought appropriate to bring to the fore the recommendations discussed by the participants in a

1985 American Press Institute seminar on advertising sales strategies[70]

- If newspapers are to continue their appeal as a mass medium, they must build new product lines that will attract more readers.
- Newspapers need to identify their true competition, and define it precisely to compete more effectively.
- Newspapers need to become more sensitive to the needs of the advertiser.
- Segmentation of advertising needs to be sharpened down to such a fine level as zoning the zones.
- Networking (several regional newspapers offering a multimarket buy) is a necessity to make it easier for the advertiser to buy in regional patterns.
- Newspapers must be affordable to the small advertiser.
- Advertisers want standardised market research. They are seeking national "trend information" about newspapers and their readers.
- Publishers should become more active with key advertising accounts and should occasionally accompany the newspaper's advertising sales people to lunches or events in the local advertising community.
- Newspapers should invest in classified as a business centre that will always provide an outlet for the small advertiser and that will prosper with the right promotion.
- Publishers making business trips to major media-buying centres should build in brief visits to advertising agencies, national rep firms, or client accounts of their newspapers.

It appears as though most of such recommendations by the American Press Institute's seminar are carried out by the market leader *Eenadu* both in letter and spirit.

References

1. See Chapter-I.
2. George W. Trotter, "Marketing the Newspaper," in D. Earl Newsom (ed.), *The Newspaper: Everything You Need to Know to Make it in the Newspaper Business*, Prentice-Hall, New Jersey, 1981, p. 151.
3. Conrad C. Fink, *op. cit.*, p. 210.
4. *Ibid.*
5. John Morton, "Singleton: Hedging the Risks", *WJR*, November 1987, p. 52.
6. Conrad C.Fink, *op. cit.*, p. 209.
7. *Ibid.*, p. 211.
8. James E.Pollard, *Principles of Newspaper Management*, McGraw-Hill, New York, 1937, p. 122.
9. S. Watson Dunn and Arnold M. Barban, *Advertising: Its Role in Modern Marketing,* Holt-Saunders, New York, (5th ed.), 1982, p. 515.
10. Unit of measuring advertising space, one column wide and 1/14 inch deep, regardless of column width.
11. James E.Pollard, *op. cit.*, pp. 129-130.
12. Jim Willis, *op. cit.*, p. 68.
13. Mark Fitzgerald, "Advice to Newspapers: Marketing Better", *Editor and Publisher,* September 28, 1985, p. 18.
14. Ravi Shankar, "Trends in Indian Advertising and Media", *Indian Journal of Commerce* (Vol. 51, No. l), March 1998, pp. 25-27.
15. Bhanu Pande, "Survey on Media", *A&M,* 31 May 1996, p. 44.
16. Quoted from: Paulomi Dhawan, "Marketing Ammo", *A & M,* 15 May, 1998, p. 60.

17. Gopinath Menon, "How the English Press Scores", *Vidura*, April-June, 1997, p. 7.
18. An Indian Newspaper Society (INS) seminar on "Advertising —New Media Directions," in Mumbai, [n.d.].
19. Paulomi Dhawan, *op. cit.*, p. 60.
20. The Scarborough Research Corp., is a leading market research firm, which compiles market-by-market data for various media. Scarborough conducted telephone surveys and followed up written questionnaires by mail with 1,63,439 adults in the top 50 media markets in the USA over a twelve month period ending in August 1997.
21. The CMI, based on audience research conducted by Scarborough Research Corp., assessed market penetration by each medium looking at total adult readership, viewership and listenership in the top 50 markets for 1996 and 1997.
22. The Newspaper Association of America's release, published in *The Times of India*, dated 20 July, 1998.
23. *Ibid.*
24. N. Bhaskara Rao, "The Indian Ad Scene: Some Perspectives", The *Economic Times*, February 9, 1989, p. 10.
25. The Circulations relating to the year 1991, Cf. Table 2.6, Chapter-II.
26. Cf. Table 5.3, Chapter-V.
27. Bhanu Pande, "News Dailies", *A & M*, 16-31 July 1997, p. 49.
28. Paulomi Dhawan, *op. cit.*, p. 60.
29. Bhanu Pande, *op. cit.*, p. 58.
30. *Ibid.*, pp. 48-49.
31. *Ibid.*, p. 49.
32. By Pradeep Guha, director, Response, The *Times of India* group (Bhanu Pande, "Survey on Media", *op. cit.*, p. 46).
33. *Ibid.*, p. 48.
34. *Ibid.*
35. *Ibid.*

36. *Ibid.*, p. 46..
37. Bhanu Pande, "News Dailies", *op. cit.*, p. 58.
38. *Ibid.*, p. 56.
39. *Ibid.*, p. 57.
40. Cf. Table 5.3, Chapter-V.
41. Bhanu Pande, "News Dailies," *op. cit.*, p. 58.
42. Vinay Kamath, *op. cit.*, pp. 102-103.
43. K. Sai and Brij Bhushan Sahani, *op. cit.*, p. 28.
44. Lynn de Souza, *op. cit.*, p. 23.
45. Vinay Kamath, *op. cit.*, p. 102.
46. Lynn de Souza, *loc. cit.*
47. Similarly the traditional 6-column format was changed to 8-column in the main paper.
48. Michael E.Porter, *Competitive Advantage: Creating and Sustaining Superior Performance, op. cit.*, p. 14.
49. Philip Kotler, "The Major Tasks of Marketing Management," *Journal of Marketing*, October, 1973, pp. 42-49. (Also see Philip Kotler, *Marketing Management: Analysis. Planning and Control,* Prentice-Hall of India, New Delhi, 1979, (3rd ed.), pp. 9-10).
50. *Ibid.*
51. Michael E.Porter, *Competitive Advantage: Creating and Sustaining Superior Performance, op. cit.*, p. 12.
52. *Ibid.*, p. 228.
53. *Eenadu's* promotion material claims and positions it so. (*Eenadu Weekend Magazine Vs. Television*, 3rd cover).
54. *Ibid.*, round 6.
55. See Chapter-VII.
56. "Post Has The Numbers, But Lineage Trails", *Advertising Age*, November 29, 1982, p. 26.
57. Conrad C. Fink, *op. cit.*, p. 217.
58. Philip Kotler, "The Major Tasks of Marketing Management," *op.cit.*, pp. 42-49. (Also see, the same

author's *Marketing Management: Analysis, Planning and Control,* Prentice-Hall of India, New Delhi, 1979, (3rd ed.), pp. 8-9).

59. Bhakti Chuganee and Ganga Subramaniam, "Selling It Small", *Business India,* September 9-22, 1996, p. 124.

60. *Ibid.*

61. Conrad C. Fink, *op. cit.,* p. 228.

62. "Managers View Behind—The-Pages Scene", *International Newspaper Advertising and Marketing Executives News,* December 1982, p. 4.

63. "Classified Receives High Performance Rating", *International Newspaper Advertising and Marketing Executives' News,* December 1982, p. II.

64. Conrad C. Fink, *op. cit.,* p. 228.

65. Philip Kotler, "The Major Task of Marketing Management," *op. cit.,* pp. 42-49 (Also see, the same author's, *Marketing Management: Analysis, Planning and Control,* Prentice-Hall of India, New Delhi, 1979 (3rd ed.) p. 9).

66. Michael E.Porter, *Competitive Advantage: Creating and Sustaining Superior Performance, op. cit.,* p. 227.

67. Conrad C.Fink, *op. cit.,* p. 228.

68. *Ibid.,* p. 257.

69. K. Suresh, "*Deccan Chronicle*: The Straight Spulrge", *A & M,* 16-31 January 1997, p. 52.

70. *New Strategies for Advertising Sales,* American Press Institute, Reston, Virginia, 1985, pp. 7-8.

9
Evaluation and Suggestions

The need for news is universal. News-hunger is fundamental in human nature. Of all the news media, the newspaper enjoys the premier position. Basically, the need for news and newspaper arises out of the need for information or communication. In turn, all sorts of communication needs are concerned about bringing prosperity and happiness to the mankind.

The Newspaper and Its Marketing

Chapter-I intends to bring out the inter-relationship between the newspaper, communication and development. The conceptual framework relating to the newspaper and its marketing are discussed therein, since marketing strategies of Telugu newspapers make central theme of the study.

It is communication that brings all organisations to life. Communication is an extremely broad topic and, of course, is not restricted to one or few fields of knowledge. If communication is directed at the masses, it becomes mass communication. Besides newspapers or magazines, media firms specialise in products like books and cinema, radio broadcasting and telecasting, dance and drama, song and music and several other forms of this nature.

Communication aimed at accelerating development process is development communication. Interest in communication in general and mass communication in particular are the offsprings of concern for development. Development communication is intended to awaken people; mobilise and educate them to be democratic citizens; safeguard national values; preserve unity and diversity; promote development and accepted national goals; and more. According to Singhal and Rogers, development communication refers to the uses to which communication is put to in order to further development. Such applications are intended to either further development in a general way, such as by increasing the level of mass media exposure among a nation's citizens in order to create a favourable climate for development or to support a specific development programme or project. Mass communication is considered a powerful and direct force for development. The influential works of Lerner and Schramm led communications scholars to expect the mass media to be a "magic multiplier"of development in developing nations. The development of mass media and the related media firms runs parallel to the development of other institutions of modern society such as schools and industry, and is closely related to some of the indices of general, social and economic growth like literacy, per capita income and urbanisation.

In view of the aforesaid reasons, newspapers have a great social responsibility on their shoulders as vehicles of development communication. The first man to envisage the modern newspaper was James Gordon Bennett who founded the *New York Herald*. Then its twin technological knowledge bases were the telegraph and high-speed printing. Subsequent innovation of highspeed typesetting, the spread of mass literacy and mass advertising created mass circulation for a newspaper and at the same time made it cheaper. Invention of a chain further benefited the modern newspaper.

The purpose for which the newspapers exist is dissemination of information. Newspaper is a communications leader. They persuade, motivate the people and mould the public opinion to be integrated into one community, one nation and one people. They are guardians of the democratic fabric and thus acclaimed as the fourth estate. The newspaper, the oldest and the most widely used medium, continues to retain its pre-eminent position all over the world even in the face of the onslaughts from television.

Besides producing news, the newspaper, produces advertising. Advertising is a force that has revolutionised industry and trade by stimulating competition. The newspaper builds regional business. In the modern living, it is the newspaper which awakens everybody early in the morning.

Newspaper, as a product, has some special characteristics. It serves two markets, one the readers and the other the advertisers. It has an all round impact—social, political, economic and cultural, on the ultimate user of the product as different from other consumer products. Speed is of critical importance in the production of a newspaper since news is a perishable commodity. Each edition of a newspaper each day results in additional design and production costs. Resultantly, the argument of the scale of economies is inoperative in the production of a newspaper. Newspaper is a product which can be used even without possessing it. Its non-buyer readership counts for raising advertising tariff. The newspaper industry is a peculiar one in which one group, the advertisers, subsidises another group, the readers. Brand loyalties are irrationally strong in newspaper market. All such peculiarities influence the marketing considerations.

The central thrust of marketing is to identify customer wants and needs and to satisfy them. This holds good for newspapers as in case of other products. In contrast to other products, a newspaper can cause a great deal of harm if it is not good enough. As such, the newspaper should conform to sound journalistic standards. Newspaper is a two-in-one institution. It is on an altruistic mission in informing and enlightening its readers and at the same time it is a business venture too in search of a healthy profit. One without the other brings disaster to the newspaper. Before independence the newspapers in India contented with their missionary role and yet survived. With the opening up of the economy, the media has grown enormously in size and reach. The newspaper transitioned from a mission or a profession to a business. The media-mix in India is also changing rapidly. The liberalisation policies of the government have opened up many avenues for the electronic media, thus stepping up intermedia competition, besides intramedia competition among the newspapers. The old concept of a major industrial group running a newspaper as a side business has gone. Thus newspaper moved into the era of marketing-orientation from production-orientation. In the face of such competitive environment some firms are making mega profits and some are finding it difficult even to survive.

To be effective and efficient, a newspaper's various departments must communicate, cooperate and coordinate efforts at becoming a superior newspaper ready to meet the challenges of the changing market. To meet these challenges—a newspaper must be concerned about—and respond to—the needs of four external target groups: its readers and non-readers, advertisers and nonadvertisers. In fact, many newspaper marketers are even more concerned with the infrequent reader and infrequent advertiser than the people not reading or advertising in the newspaper at all.

Philip Kotler emphasises that successful companies and high performance businesses know how to adapt to a continuously changing marketplace. They practice the art of market-oriented strategic planning. Market-oriented strategic planning is the managerial process of developing and maintaining a viable fit between the organisation's objectives, skills, and resources and its changing market opportunities. Marketing plays a critical role in the company's strategic planning process. Thus, the chief marketing executive's strategic planning responsibility includes: (1) participating in corporate strategy formulation, and (2) developing business unit marketing strategies in accordance with corporate priorities. Michael Porter uses the evolutionary stages of an industry to suggest suitable strategies. Porter identified five forces which are universal that determine the state of competition and ultimately the profit potential of the industry. They are: threat of entry; rivalry among existing firms; threat of substitute products or services; bargaining power of buyers; and bargaining power of suppliers. Porter suggested three generic strategies for coping with the five competitive forces. They are: overall cost leadership; differentiation and focus (segmentation). It is to be noted that a clear strategy and a well thought out supporting programme may be useless if the firm fails to implement them carefully. Indeed, strategy is only one of seven elements (7-S) according to the McKinsey consulting firm, that the best-managed companies exhibit. The other six elements for business success are structure, systems, style, staff, skills and shared values.

The Indian Newspapers

Chapter-II analyses the historic relevance and comparative growth of the Indian newspapers, overall and language-wise, in terms of circulation. Further, it ascertains the status of the Telugu daily in this regard.

Historically newspapers in India, irrespective of their language or region, were a mission to awaken the masses and to build public opinion against social evils like *sati*, untouchability, child marriages and illiteracy. Newspapers were a movement and an upheaval to fight against the alien rulers.

Though the newspaper came to India as one of the benefits of British rule, it came in handy to the great social reformers and patriots in using it effectively in furtherance of the much cherished public causes. Consequently, the nineteenth century and the early years of twentieth century witnessed highly equipped intellectuals, powerful writers, able controversialists, men of integrity and character founding newspapers in Calcutta, Mumbai, Chennai, Chandigarh, New Delhi and elsewhere. To name a few, Raja Ram Mohun Roy, Bal Gangadhara Tilak, Dadabhai Naoroji, G. Subrahmanya Aiyer, Surendranadh Benerjee, Mahatma Gandhi and Jawaharlal Nehru were among them. Regional newspapers and regional stalwarts looked no different from the national scene, all chasing the service ethic. Newspaper was never a serious business proposition in those days. But the post-independence realities were different. Slowly newspapers started realising that in order to succeed they must first survive.

From a mere two million daily circulation in 1951, the Indian daily newspapers registered a twelve-fold change, increasing it to 24.29 million copies in 1991. Nevertheless, the circulations were increasing at a rapidly decreasing rate. The circulation jump between 1951 and 1961 was as high as 162.5 per cent. The corresponding increase for the next 10-year period ending in 1971 was only 73.3 per cent, followed by 67.6 per cent by 1981 and 59.1 per cent by 1991.

Such a phenomenon accompanied by population increases at increased rates during those years, naturally did not allow dailies-to-thousand people ratio (DTP) to go beyond 29 copies in 1991 from six in 1951. On the whole, the DTP ratio was also increasing but at a decreasing rate, more or less. In terms of dailies-to-thousand literate people (DTLP), the growth of dailies was more disappointing from 33 copies in 1951 to 55 copies in 1991, which was less than what it was in 1971 (57 copies), implying a negative growth rate. This analysis disproves the hypothesis that increased literacy leads to increased circulation of dailies.

Robin Jeffrey's series of essays on Indian languages-newspapers evoked a lot of interest in the subject. Analysis of the growth of the newspapers by languages shows that large language segments need not create large circulation. For example, though Hindi was the largest of all language segments, in 1971 its circulation was much behind the circulation of the English daily, the smallest segment. Of course, from 1981 onwards the Hindi daily was in limelight claiming the largest circulation. Malayalam, though the second smallest language segment, its daily was firmly saddled for the third place in circulation all through, besides being a topper in the DTP (71 copies) next only to English (183 copies). For all the languages put together, the DTP ratio was only 29 copies in 1991, as against 22 copies in 1981 and 17 copies in 1971. It implies newspaper culture is determined not by numbers. May be it is a product of literacy, urbanisation, per capita income, etc., variables.

The dailies in the Indian languages started overpowering the English daily in a small way since 1951. Till then the advertisers considered that the readers of the dailies in regional languages did not have much purchasing power for their goods and services. Robin Jeffrey attributed the surge of the dailies in regional languages to six factors. They are: improved technology; expanded literacy; adequate purchasing power; aggressive publishers; increased political excitement and awareness and governmental and social support to the Indian languages.

Literacy is considered as one of the bases on which the newspaper grew. Increased per capita incomes and urbanisation are expected to promote daily circulation. The English daily commanding the highest dailies-to-people ratio indicates this. All the English-knowing people in India were not only literate, their educational, income and urbanisation levels were also high. Next to English, literacy levels were high in Malayalam segment (89.9 per cent) and so also the dailies-to-thousand people ratio (71 copies). Such a tendency suggests that the more the literacy rate, the larger the newspaper circulation. But this does not hold good in other language segments. In essence, there is no relation between literacy, per capita income and urbanisation on the one hand and circulation on the other. This leads to the basic question—what creates a newspaper culture?

The story of Telugu daily is a story of the bottoms compared to other Indian-language dailies. Only in 1991 its DTP reached the double digit, 10 copies. Andhra Pradesh, the linguistic State of Telugu people, did not compare that much unfavourably with other states in terms of literacy, per capita income and urbanisation as it appears from the DTP figures. An attempt is also made to compare the Telugu daily with the Hindi daily. The Hindi belt mostly comprised the population with literacy rates less than Andhra Pradesh. However, all Hindi states put together had a circulation of 25 copies per-1000-people against 10 copies of Telugu. This suggests that a larger proportion of literate people does not necessarily mean proportionately a higher newspaper sales. Though the Hindi belt and Andhra Pradesh experienced political excitement, they appear to be different in intensity and impact. What happened in Andhra Pradesh centred round one regional party i.e., the Telugu Desam and its one leader, in 1980s. But what happened in the Hindi belt centred round several issues, several leaders and several parties, depending on the point of time. Such issues are alive even in 1990s. Thus, the present variation in the DTPs of Hindi and Telugu dailies may further widen.

It is also examined how the Telugu daily compares with the Malayalam, Tamil and Kannada dailies, all South Indian.

On the whole, the inference that higher the literacy rate, the higher the DTP size holds good in respect of all southern languages. But the interlanguage variations were very sharp. Though Andhra Pradesh is having as much literate population as of the size of Kerala (the linguistic state of Malayalis), it was not reflected in newspaper circulation. Either the per capita income of Andhra Pradesh or its urbanisation which were comparable to Kerala could not produce respectable newspaper sales. Thus, the Malayalam and the Telugu dailies represent two extreme positions, indicative of two extreme newspaper cultures, their DTPs were 71 and 10 copies respectively. So newspaper sales is not simply literacy plus incomes plus urbanisation.

Kerala's newspaper culture is deep-rooted in its high social development profile marked by high literacy; small families; intense political awareness; intense passion for newspapers even among agricultural labourers; people's willingness to spend money on newspapers; good network of roads that facilitates transport of papers to the subscribers wherever they live; and the people's habit of reading at commonplaces. Besides, there appears to be very healthy competition among the publishers. *Malayala Manorama*, the largest circulated Indian-language daily, is fiercely contested by several competitors, thus denying a large market share to the leader. The implications of this model are to be analysed carefully and they are worthy of emulation by all other language dailies including Telugu. Telugu dailies have a responsibility in shaping the attitudes of readers, if they have serious intentions of creating a newspaper culture of Kerala type.

The Present Study

Chapter-III depicts the problem of enquiry and the design adopted therefor. During the late 1970s, the Telugu daily has slipped out of the grip of the pioneer *Andhra Patrika* on the one hand and *Andhra Prabha* that belongs to the chain giant *Indian Express* group on the other. The sudden appearance of a new star *Eenadu* made all the difference. *Eenadu,* started in 1974 by a small enterpriser, has emerged as the market leader soon by 1978. Much interesting things followed in later years. *Udayam,* which entered the market towards the fag-end of 1984 occupied the market challenger's position soon in 1985 pushing aside *Andhra Prabha.* By 1987, *Andhra Jyoti* emerged as the challenger relegating *Udayam* to the third position. *Andhra Patrika* ceased publication in its 83rd year of existence, in 1991. The young player *Udayam* ended in 1995. Such shocks did not deter the entry of new paper *Vaartha* soon in January 1996 from as many as nine centres. And right on entry, *Vaartha* emerged No.2 player, though *Eenadu* outsold *Vaartha,* more than four copies to one and thereby taking a two-thirds of the market share.

The study precisely intends to find out an answer to the question of how to account for the difference in the superlative performance of a particular player on the one hand, and the insignificant performance of all other players on the other, in the Telugu newspaper market. Assuming such successes or failures are attributable to the marketing strategies adopted by the players in the field, this study attempts to identify and analyse them. This study intends, *inter alia:* (1) To bring forth the marketing performance of Telugu dailies in terms of their circulation and market share; (2) to identify the competitive strategies to which the success or failure of the individual papers could be attributed; (3) to enquire into the consumer behaviour of Telugu newspapers; and (4) to examine the emerging space selling strategies in the Telugu newspaper market. The study covers all the seven major Telugu newspapers, namely, *Andhra Patrika, Andhra Prabha, Andhra Jyoti, Andhra Bhoomi, Eenadu, Udayam* and *Vaartha,* though *Andhra Patrika* and *Udayam* ceased to exist as mentioned earlier.

The study's special focus is on the period since 1974, the time from which the traces of marketing appear to have arrived to the Telugu newspapers with the entry of *Eenadu*. Nevertheless, the detailed examination is to be preceded by a historical and summary account of the players during the earlier period.

The competitive strategies adopted by the papers are identified from the first-hand observation over the years. To find out the impact of the strategies thus identified on circulation, etc., the study relied upon the data collected from secondary sources like the ABC and the RNI. Besides observation, the study used reader survey as a tool of collecting primary data.

The Rise and Fall of Telugu Dailies

Chapter-IV attempts to make a newspaper-wise analysis of the marketing performance of the Telugu dailies, in terms of their circulation and market share. In a newspaper business, market share as a variable affecting profitability assumes greater importance.

Shifting to Chennai as a daily from Mumbai in 1914, *Andhra Patrika* was in an unquestioned monopoly market for nearly a quarter century till the commencement of *Andhra Prabha*, also from Chennai in 1938. Kasinadhuni Nageswara Rao, the founder of *Andhra Patrika*, ran it in a spirit of service and sacrifice. On his own admission its circulation was about 5,000 copies till 1930. Its sales were doubled due to the impact of the Salt *Satyagraha* and the Quit India Movement in 1942. It received the required financial support from Amrutanjan, their business venture making pain balm. During the freedom struggle, the justification for running a newspaper was to fight against the alien rule. To survive after 1947, the nationalist newspapers had to conduct their affairs more like the long-established English language newspapers which were already well connected to the few sources of existing advertising.

Reaching Vijayawada in 1959, *Andhra Prabha* quickly grew to be the premier Telugu daily outselling *Andhra Patrika* by 1960. At that time, the circulation of *Andhra Prabha* was 53,000 copies, whereas *Andhra Patrika* sold 48,000 copies. The year 1960 saw the birth of two new dailies *Andhra Jyoti* from Vijayawada and *Andhra Bhoomi* of *Deccan Chronicle* from Hyderabad. *Andhra Patrika* was also shifted to Vijayawada in 1965. Thus competition in a small way had come to the Telugu newspaper market from the time they are published from centrally located Vijayawada, allowing the chain publication *Andhra Prabha* to be the front-runner. Despite the availability of more number of newspapers to the customers, the differences they offered to the customers were negligible. The industry remained in production-orientation stage rather than moving towards marketing-orientation.

The last quarter of this century witnessed significant happenings in the Telugu newspaper market. The era of marketing has started taking roots into the Telugu newspaper business with the entry of *Eenadu* in 1974. During the years 1970-75, the total circulation looked very placid, ranging from 1,85,000 to 2,20,000 copies. Nevertheless, in terms of market share, *Eenadu* sprang a surprise in occupying No.3 slot in the second year of its existence claiming a market share of 15.9 per cent. *Andhra Prabha* continued to be the market leader during the years.

Sea-changes swept the Telugu newspaper market during 1976-80. The total circulation was nearly doubled by 1980 (4,35,000 copies) compared to what it was in 1975 (2,20,000 copies). Such a broad jump was mostly caused by the youngest daily *Eenadu*. Out of the total circulation of 4,35,000 copies in 1980, *Eenadu*'s circulation was 2,05,000 copies or 47.1 per cent of market share. In fact, *Eenadu* became the market leader in 1978 itself within four years of the entry, pushing aside *Andhra Prabha* to the second place. It means *Eenadu* virtually succeeded in creating new customers in the real marketing sense, instead of weaning them away from the old firms.

More or less a similar trend continued during the next five years 1981-85. Total circulation continued to gallop to 7,24,000 copies in 1985 from 4,25,000 copies in 1980, but at a marginally decreasing rate, compared to the preceding five years. *Eenadu's* sales were a near three lakh copies in 1985, though they were around three-and-half lakh copies in the earlier two years. *Eenadu* losing its customers is attributable partly to the entry of yet another new paper *Udayam. Eenadu's* market share was slashed to 40.8 per cent and *Udayam* emerged No.2 paper with 27.6 per cent of the market share in 1985. Earlier, *Eenadu's* market share raced to 60.3 per cent in 1983.

What happened during the next 10-year period 1986-95 is not comparable to what happened during the preceding 10 years. The industry started declining in 1986, circulation falling below seven lakh copies. However, the industry never looked back since 1993, going well beyond the new milestone of eight-lakh plus circulation in 1994. The older the competitors, the quicker they lost their circulation during those 10 years, by and large. In the process, the oldest paper *Andhra Patrika* was closed in 1991. The next oldest competitor *Andhra Prabha's* circulation dwindled to a mere 52,000 copies in 1995 and the paper conceded its second place to the youngest daily *Udayam* in 1985. *Andhra Bhoomi* remained a nonserious player as before. *Udayam* was closed in 1995, losing its second place to *Andhra Jyoti* in 1988. *Andhra Jyoti's* market share in 1988 was 25 per cent, the largest ever for that paper. The market leader, *Eenadu's* circulation fell below three lakh mark in 1985. The paper could regain it only in 1989, touching a four-lakh mark in 1993 and a five-lakh mark in the next year. Its market share was 63.9 per cent in 1995. Coming to 1996, *Vaartha* entered into the market straight away taking the second place.

The foregoing analysis proves the existence of tremendous potential for Telugu dailies. Whenever publishers came out with a new daily, keeping in mind the customer-satisfaction, there was overwhelming response in receiving them. *Eenadu* kept on attracting new customers for longer years. This was also reflected in the large inaugural sales of *Udayam* and *Vaartha*. Thus reluctance to buy the existing papers may be an indication of readers' rejecting them. This drives home the importance of researching into the non-readers of the newspapers. Such research brings to light the weaknesses of the existing newspapers. However, it is not to neglect the research into the present readers. Further, the analysis did not establish that the readers dislike easily the papers they were buying already. Even in the face of fierce competition from *Eenadu*, the old papers retained their customers nearly for a decade, though their market shares declined drastically in view of the galloping sales of the new competitor. Initial successes alone do not automatically bring continued patronage of customers to a newspaper. Marketing efforts are to be backed by years of strategic planning and hard work. That is how *Eenadu* succeeded, and in the absence of such efforts *Udayam* faded away.

To sum up, drastic changes took place in the Telugu newspaper market since 1974. The era of either the old players or a chain newspaper dominating the market came to an end, thus the market opened up for new players. Those days of Telugu readers receiving their dailies from outside the state around noon containing more of international or national stories were over. Publication centres were moving much closer to the customers. Telugu dailies are published from 16 places in 1998, compared to four centres till 1974. The Telugu dailies started competing with the English dailies in expanding sales or attracting advertising revenues. Newspaper as a business started transforming into customer-orientation from production-orientation. *Eenadu* playing only since 1974 rising to meteoric heights and some too young dailies willing to compete with the new giant are the result of such a transformation. In the process, the Telugu newspaper circulation registered more than a five-fold increase during 1974-97. Yet a long way to go, considering the dailies-to-thousand ratio of Telugu dailies remained the lowest of all languages.

Business or product failures are as important an area as their success in the field of management and marketing. As such the death of the newspapers should not be viewed lightly. Though *Andhra Patrika* lost the market leadership in 1960, it could retain the customer-loyalty more or less in tact in terms of absolute circulation till 1984. This implies the newspaper lost all the marketing wars with other papers by default rather than by defeat. Defaulting in designing appropriate marketing strategies defensive or offensive spelt disaster to *Andhra Patrika*. *Udayam's* exit also leads to some useful inferences: Customers welcome new papers. But if their expectations are not met in want-satisfaction they do not hesitate to give them up. Obviously, entrepreneurial acumen and managerial expertise are crucial.

The Arthur D.Little management consulting firm sees firms as occupying one of six competitive positions in their industry: dominant; strong; favourable; tenable; weak; and nonviable. Applying such a classification to the Telugu newspaper firms, the leader *Eenadu* is occupying the dominant competitive position. This implies the firm controls the behaviour of other competitors and has a wide choice of strategic options. The runner-up firms fall into one of the five categories last-mentioned. What is significant is competitors' attitudes and their reactions to what happens in the marketplace in the years ahead. What matters most is how they perceive and what they do tomorrow, not what were their competitive strengths yesterday. *Andhra Bhoomi's* competitive position at best may be described as weak, if not nonviable considering the publisher's main interest in *Deccan Chronicle*. No. 2 player *Vaartha's* competitive position could be classified either as strong or favourable, if it could transform its potentiality into a reality. As in case of *Andhra Patrika*, complacency costed *Andhra Prabha* very dearly. Despite losing its market leadership in 1978, its one-lakh plus circulations were retained till 1985. But in 1997, its sales were a mere 32,000 copies, market share being 3.3 per cent. In a situation as this, it cannot be said with confidence that its competitive position is tenable. At best, it is in a weak position, implying the firm has unsatisfactory performance but an opportunity exists for improvement and it must change or else exit. By and large, competition from new entrants did not deter *Andhra Jyoti's* circulation in numbers. Over the years the paper went on to increase its sales steadily compared to other runner-up firms. The paper became No. 2 player in 1988 and retained that position till the entry of *Vaartha* in 1996. Thus *Andhra Jyoti* is in a favourable competitive position. It implies this firm has a strength that is exploitable in particular strategies and has more than average opportunity to improve its position.

The Competitive Strategies and Achieving Leadership

Chapter-V identifies and analyses the marketing strategies in greater detail, which enabled *Eenadu* to become the market leader and a star performer. This chapter also analyses strengths and weaknesses of the strategies adopted by other competitors. Only such of those strategies that are discernible to an outsider as evident from the product form, its features and contents, the distribution system, market expansion, etc., are taken up for consideration.

Ramoji Rao has chosen to launch his paper *Eenadu* in 1974 from Visakhapatnam, located at one end of the state, at a time the newspapers were brought out only from Vijayawada and Hyderabad in the state. The new paper's avowed objective was its delivery at the crack of the dawn, with a particular emphasis on state and local news. In the warfare terminology, it was a flanking attack or strategy. An enemy's army is necessarily less severe in its flanks and rear. Its weak spots (blind sides), therefore, are natural targets for attack by the enemy. The major principle of modern offensive warfare is *concentration of strength against weakness*. At that time the "dak" edition of the newspapers were received in the late hours of the evening in Visakhapatnam. In a situation as this *Eenadu* was bom. What happened at *Eenadu* has three strategic dimensions—all part of a flank attack: (1) Entering the newspaper market from far-flung Visakhapatnam where competitors were underperforming was a geographical flanking; (2) Delivering the newspaper before the sun rise was flanking with distribution—bringing a change in the distribution network to provide a better service; and (3) Changing the news mix to the liking of the readers is an example of flanking with product form. Flanking principles include: (1) moving into an uncontested area; (2) tactical surprise and (3) the pursuit. What *Eenadu* practised was just that. The competitors' failure to defend themselves further strengthened the strategy. Thus the flanking attack proved to be a gateway of entry into the market, to *Eenadu*.

In 1973, *Andhra Prabha,* then market leader sold 1,12,000 copies, followed by *Andhra Patrika* (49,000 copies) *Andhra Jyoti* (31,000 copies) and *Andhra Bhoomi* (17,000 copies). As such they just did not care to block the insignificant attack from an insignificant quarter on an insignificant front with a very meagre initial sales (4,000 copies). Their egos stood in the way of blocking competition. Thus *Eenadu's* mighty competitors slept over dangerously. They have grossly misread the psychological impact of the new paper on the minds of the readers and non-readers of newspapers. *Andhra Prabha, Andhra Bhoomi* and *Andhra Jyoti* appeared in Visakhapatnam only in late 1980s. By that time everything was over. Even in 1984, *Eenadu's* circulation was 3,56,000 copies, the total circulation of all its competitors put together was much less than this.

Tasting the blood of success in Visakhapatnam in 1974 through flanking, *Eenadu* indulged in yet another flank attack in 1975. This time the flank chosen was the ill-served Hyderabad wherefrom only *Andhra Bhoomi* was publishing 15,000 copies, the year before. The earliest delivery of the paper loaded with regional and local news was still their pet theme. *Eenadu*'s experience of continued flanking in Hyderabad was a lesson in pursuit, the strength of a flank. The move was richly rewarded, the paper emerging No. 2 player with 54,000 copies or 23.3 per cent of market share in 1976.

According to Hauser, Shugan and Gaskin, the defender should improve its strong product features even more rather than improving along the lines of attacker's strong product features. But the defender *Andhra Prabha* or other competitors were merely contented with stationary circulation ignoring the declining market share. Such a decline in the face of expanding market size spells danger to the defender. If the leader fails to take cognigence of such positive signs in the marketplace, it is playing the game blindfold. Nevertheless, *Andhra Patrika* was quick to react by bringing out their second edition from Hyderabad in the same year, though the move could not help it to retain its No. 2 position, perhaps failing in delivering as much customer-satisfaction as the leader paper. This strengthens the view that mere strategies do not make miracles. The essence of any strategy should be customer-orientation. *Andhra Prabha* and *Andhra Jyoti* entered Hyderabad leisurely in 1977 and 1986, respectively.

Having become the improved challenger in 1977, *Eenadu* has picked up the courage to indulge in the luxury of frontal attack in 1978 by bringing their third edition from Vijayawada. The attack was not from the flanks as on the earlier two occasions. The attack was heads-on. The battle was confined to almost all the players—really the battle royal. Attacking the market leader is one of the options available to the market challengers to increase their market share, Philip Kotler emphasises. This is a "high-risk" but potentially a "high-payoff strategy and makes good sense if the leader is a "false leader" and not serving the market well. The alternative strategy is to out-innovate the leader across the whole segment. Kotler's assertion proved to be true in *Eenadu's* case. *Andhra Prabha* was a false leader without caring for customer needs and *Eenadu* out-innovated the leader even before reaching Vijayawada. The success was so large that *Eenadu* became the largest selling Telugu newspaper within just six months (by the end of 1978) with 35 per cent of the market share (1,27,000 copies), pushing aside *Andhra Prabha*, the leader for about two decades. *Eenadu*'s cartoons, its sweet language, attractive layouts and its investigative reportage became matters of discussion at commonplaces. Nevertheless, there were no signs of any defensive reaction from the rivals even in the face of such devastating blows into their faces. Perhaps, defensive reaction in the form of delivering more customer-satisfaction compared to new competition was lacking. They were blind to the fast growing market size that was triggered at the initiative and advances of the young player *Eenadu*. Their fastly melting out market share did not bother them at all. Either it was a case of continued complacency, or an example of chronic ego ultimately developing into a crisis of confidence, or both. Any way they have lost not only a crucial battle but also the whole of the marketing war.

The market share steadily growing to 50 per cent and beyond, *Eenadu*, was gaining in stature and self-confidence. At a time of such upbeat, political excitement erupted,

N.T.Rama Rao plunging into politics in 1982, surprising everybody. What happened later was history. The matinee idol's great crowd-pulling capacity, his nine-month long stop-whistle tour of the state enabled his party to come to power to be the first non-Congress government after three and half decades in January 1983. Such electioneering which attracted nationwide attention received the most extensive coverage in *Eenadu,* implying the paper's strategy of setting the people's personal agenda. *Eenadu's* interest and commitment to the agenda was so much that even today people are found to be discussing whether it was NTR creating the TDP wave or *Eenadu* making it. Whatever it may be, *Eenadu* succeeded in marketing it. Its market share soared to 60.3 per cent (3,42,000 copies) in 1983 from 49 per cent (1,97,000 copies) in 1981. The uptrend in circulation continued, the paper pursuing the agenda-setting through the year 1984 covering the events of NTR's dismissal from the chief ministership undemocratically and his reinstatement within an interval of one month. The national press entirely supported NTR in 1984 events. Nevertheless, relating to the political excitement of 1982, *Eenadu's* competitors were either indifferent or misread the people's mood. This proved to be a windfall to *Eenadu.* Their launching the fourth edition from Tirupati in 1982 was handy in furthering the agenda-setting ambition. The euphoria of the TDP dying down, the decline in the circulation of *Eenadu* was set in. The market share steadily declined to 42.2 per cent in 1987, gradually improving to 51 per cent in 1992. *Eenadu's* circulation of 3,39,000 copies in 1992 was still short of 1984 level.

New entrant *Udayam's* frontal attack in 1985 and *Andhra Jyoti's* improved performance in the later years applied breaks to the winning spree of *Eenadu. Udayam's* indulgence in frontal attack with the market leader on entry by launching its editions simultaneously from Vijayawada and Hyderabad fetched the paper the second place and 27.6 per cent of market share straight away. Things hotting up, *Udayam* started its third edition from Tirupati in 1986 and *Andhra Jyoti* did it in 1987. *Andhra Bhoomi* brought out its new edition from Visakhapatnam and Vijayawada in 1986 and 1989, respectively, *Andhra Jyoti* alone succeeded in improving its market share, all others declining including the market leader *Eenadu*, as mentioned earlier.

Entry strategies of *Eenadu* and *Udayam* lead to some useful lessons. *Eenadu* banked on flanking where the leader *Andhra Prabha* was underperforming by 1974, whereas *Udayam* indulged in the luxury of frontal attack where the leader *Eenadu* was performing well by 1984. *Eenadu's*, strategy created new customers in the long run and the lasting impact, whereas *Udayam's* strategy resulted in the expanded market size only to a limited extent, that too during the initial year. It could only wean away the customers of other papers by and large.

Al Ries and Jack Trout emphasise that only the market leader should consider playing the defence. *Eenadu* was on the defensive losing circulation and market share in the face of increased competition. To stage a retrieval, *Eenadu* once again resorted to innovation. The defensive strategies pursued by *Eenadu* may be broadly classified into geographic segmentation and interest-zoning. As is already learnt, *Eenadu*'s special focus on local news earlier received tremendous response. In an attempt to give new shape to its philosophy, the paper launched 28 district or city supplements in tabloid size in January 1989. This idea struck Ramoji Rao when he realised that a lot of local news could not find place in the paper. It is an innovation intended to serve an extreme form of geographic segmentation. Depending on the city or district, the size of the tabloid varied from 8 to 16 pages. The innovation meant 28 papers to as many segments, instead of one paper to the entire market. Serving as a vehicle of local news it could as well serve as a vehicle of local advertising.

Such implications are dealt in greater detail in Chapter-VIII. *Eenadu* launching six more editions in 1990s was complementary to its launching district supplements earlier. Together they formed part of geographic segmentation, making two sides of the same coin. The goal was getting closer to the reader and advertiser. The paper's circulation growth by 18.68 per cent during the first half of 1990 is indicative of the acceptance of its tabloids by readers.

Interest-zoning, another defensive strategy of *Eenadu*, segmented the paper by demographic and psychographic variables. The strategy called for discovering and satisfying the specific-interest groups of readers by adding exclusive features or pages for them. A 32-page Sunday supplement in a magazine form (1988); regular features of a business page (1990); a cinema page (1991); an exclusive women's page (1992); career counselling; matrimonial advertising; and a column on computers once in a week were some of the contents innovated at *Eenadu*. Such interest-zoning meant all things to all people, again getting closer to the customers. Closeness to the customer was thus uppermost in the priorities of *Eenadu* throughout its existence as a new player, a challenger, a market leader and a defender. Research into America's best-run companies by Thomas Peter and Robert Waterman Jr., revealed "close to customer" was one among the eight attributes of such excellent, innovative companies.

Geographic segmentation and interest-zoning put together worked like a pre-emptive defence at *Eenadu*, assuming the proportions of a grand market envelopment. Further, it amounts to the player constantly indulging in self-attacking, the best way to improve the leader's position.

One after another all the other competitors fell in line with the market leader in imitating the product, more or less in every respect, including the new daily *Vaartha*. *Vaartha* employed encirclement attack on entry in 1996 by simultaneously launching the paper from nine centres, outnumbering *Eenadu's* editions.

Comparative evaluation of the entry strategies of *Vaartha* and *Eenadu* leads to some useful lessons. One at a time was *Eenadu's* approach in marketing warfare, in contrast to *Vaartha*'s overambitious strategy of grabbing the whole market at a time. For the purpose, *Eenadu* heavily depended on flanking in contrast to *Vaartha's* encirclement attack on entry. *Eenadu* was abundantly cautious even facing the false leader *Andhra Prabha* in 1974, whereas *Vaartha* was unduly overconfident confronting well-performing leader *Eenadu* in 1996. Added such inherent weaknesses of *Vaartha's strategy, the paper did not realise that Eenadu's defensive* strategies were a great entry barrier. Because *Vaartha*'s other competitors were not so aggressive in defending themselves, they could easily be overtaken. In essence, on entry and during the early phase *Eenadu's* limited resources extracted larger and steadier impact from the market and *Vaarlha's* larger resources could extract only a limited impact.

Other important strategies of the leader *Eenadu* include: credibility; investigative reportage; printing in colour; pre-launch tactics; and effective presentation of news in a sweet language. Such of those strategies permeate through all other features and they are ceaselessly pursued. From the beginning *Eenadu* looked for innovative ways in launching new editions. The most innovative of launches was their Rajahmundry edition in 1992. The edition besides attracting the customers of other papers into its fold, created large number of customers. Continued uptrend of the paper's sales since 1990 speaks of the success of the several defensive strategies pursued.

To put it differently, what happened at *Eenadu* in the name of strategic planning was building customer-satisfaction through which they sustained and improved the paper's performance. Superficially it appears *Eenadu's* strategies were competitor-oriented. But an in-depth analysis shows what all the paper did was customer-oriented. Their focussing on the earliest delivery; coverage of local news; publishing the paper from a place convenient to the customer; trying to be the first in receiving the news and reaching the customer with it; creating different sections to different interest-groups in a systematic way; investigative reportage; exposing the misdeeds at high places; setting up the people's personal agenda; concern for the government's onslaught on democratic institutions; imaginative positioning of the cartoon; and more were all measures intended to build customer-satisfaction, brick by brick. The paper's mission statement interestingly reads: To ceaselessly innovate, upgrade and add value for the reader and the advertiser. Time and again the paper had shown that they mean it and without any ceiling in delivering customer-satisfaction.

Let the leader's performance in the Telugu newspaper market with the leaders in other major language segments of the Indian newspaper industry be compared in 1996. The median of the 13 leaders' average daily circulation stood at 4,44,000 copies in 1996 compared to *Eenadu*'s circulation of 6,04,000 copies in 1996. Only four of the market leaders commanded a higher circulation than *Eenadu*. *Eenadu* stood second in terms of the number of the editions, publishing from nine centres (now ten in 1998) with an average circulation of 67,000 copies per centre. Such an average is on par with the median of an array of average circulations of 62 centres of all leaders. This indicates that *Eenadu*'s publication centres as a lot may not be working at sub-optimum level on the whole. In market shares, the paper was on the top of all the market leaders with 63.5 per cent. Nevertheless, the paper was found to be playing where there were fewer serious players (five), compared to the presence of 16 and 23 players in Gujarati and Marathi markets, respectively. What is desired is the emergence of the competitive industry capable of producing a respectable DTP ratio. In the closely contested markets, the leader commands a low market share facing more stiff competitors. For example, in Marathi market the leader's (*Lokmat*) market share was only 19.8 per cent, several other players following closely behind. The yawning gap in the market share *of Eenadu* (63.5) and *Vaartha* (23.1) signify almost a two-paper market, yet a one-paper show. On the face of it, it appears *Eenadu* was taking undue advantage of its weak competitors. But such a conclusion is hasty and incorrect, considering its closeness to customers and the satisfaction it is delivering to them. The paper withstanding *Vaartha's* encirclement attack proves this. In the circumstances, if such a challenger and other papers could perform well in delivering customer-satisfaction it may be possible to take the industry to the new heights of growth.

Eenadu was found to be enjoying a distinctive advantage in respect of the trade terms offered to its distributors. A perusal of an array of the average trade terms of a sample of 43 dailies of all languages in India shows, such terms ranged from 18.3 to 39.9 per cent in 1996. Unbelievably, *Eenadu's* trade terms were the lowest of all at 18.3 per cent, whereas the median of the trade terms offered by all the papers stood at 29.4 per cent. The paper could drive home such a competitive advantage for two reasons: (1) the pull strategy it has employed in its promotion mix; and (2) the paper's associate Margadarsi Marketing assuming the distributorship of a number of other publications including national magazines such as *India Today* and *The Week*. Such strategies strengthen the earning power of *Eenadu's* agents.

The multiplicity of the problems encountered in Telugu newspaper market include: (1) unwillingness of the trailing firms to revitalise; (2) the challenger's grossly misdirected attacks on the leader, thus leaving large underutilised capacity, despite huge financial commitment; (3) the threat of TV; (4) the unprecedented non-buyer readership; and (5) the imbalances in the social composition of the population of Andhra Pradesh consisting of 40.9 per cent of agricultural labourers.

The Roots of Strategies

The socio-economic profile of the Telugu newspapers' consumers and their consumption characteristics are examined in Chapter - VI. A sample of 480 intense readers, comprising 120 each of the four select papers were chosen for the purpose. Readership experience of five years of a select paper was the criterion of intense readership. The select papers were *Eenadu, Andhra Jyoti, Andhra Prabha* and *Udayam.* Of the sample 480 consumers, 352 were buyers and 128 were non-buyers. The consumers and their behaviour constitute the caused variables in marketing, making the roots of any strategic design.

Age-wise, over three-fifth of the serious newspaper readers were in their 20s and 30s. This speaks of the importance of households that generates newspaper sales. The association between age and intense newspaper readership appeared to be getting weaker beyond 40 years. A twelfth of the readers were in their teens or still younger. Probably the newspaper habit of their parents or the reading habit at commonplaces might have influenced them. Readers in teens are tomorrow's buyers when they grow up. The higher the proportion of such young people, the greater will be prospects for newspaper business. Nearly 70 per cent of the readers were under 40 years. This suggests it makes no sense if the aspirations of the young and middle aged consumers are given a go-by in designing a newspaper.

By educational level, undergraduates (56.1% per cent) far outnumbered the graduates and post-graduates put together (43.9 per cent), implying increased educational levels need not necessarily result in increased newspaper sales in regional languages. Strengthening the newspaper in regional languages along the lines of the English papers may improve the situation. By rural-urban background, graduates and post-graduates put together were more in urban areas (52.8 per cent) compared to rural areas (35 per cent) among the intense newspaper readers.

It is not surprising to find that a majority (51.9 per cent) of the consumers were either white-collared employees (32.5 per cent) or self-employed workmen (19.4 per cent). Traders and students were significant among other readers, representing nearly one-sixth each. It is distressing to find that newspaper was not within the reach of the average Indian farmer. Only 10 per cent of the intense readers were agriculturists. The Telugu newspaper continued to be predominantly a male product, housewives comprising only a paltry 2.5 per cent of the consumers. General readership as different from intense readership may not be that low.

Income and intense newspaper readership moved in the same direction. Only a third of the consumers originated from the segment of less than Rs.25,000/- annual income. On the whole, it is found that age, education, occupation and rural-urban background are closely linked demographics one moving up with the other ultimately resulting in more newspaper sales. Indian newspaper marketers are yet to face the first real television generation - people who had television since their infancy. Consequently the young people under 40 years constituted the largest base (70 per cent) of intense newspaper readership.

Marketing strategies are designed on the tripod of product, production and consumption characteristics. Origins of the newspaper habit, what paper they buy and read, how eagerly they await to receive their newspapers, their prime time preferences, the number of rounds in which they complete their reading, what other papers they read, besides their main papers etc., consumption aspects are examined.

A majority of the readers (55.6 per cent) revealed that their parents exhibited keen interest in the newspaper reading during their childhood. Of them, 60.9 per cent were urban and 45 per cent were rural in background. The major gratification source of such parents' news interest was subscribing to a daily on a regular basis, followed by occasional buying and borrowing including reading at community places.

For a majority of readers (52.5 per cent) the day essentially began with the newspaper reading, including 11.7 per cent awaiting impatiently to receive newspaper. Rest of them read the papers at their convenience depending on the availability of a borrowed paper and leisure time. Even such readers who read at convenience were eager to receive newspapers at the earliest. Basing on such an addiction to newspapers, *Eenadu* on its entry in 1974 capitalised on the weakness of other papers who neglected early delivery. Thus delivering the paper at the earliest has come to stay in the Telugu newspaper market.

An overwhelming 82.3 per cent of respondents completed the paper reading in one or two rounds. This finding suggests Telugu papers are not able to sustain reader interest for longer stretches, compared to English papers. It could be one reason for the underperformance of Telugu dailies in terms of the DTP ratio.

Commencing earlier than 6 o'clock in the morning, the prime time reading of the Telugu dailies appeared to end by 10 AM for 82.5 per cent of rural and 75.6 per cent of urban readers. The peak of the prime time was between 6 AM and 8 AM during which time 52.1 per cent of urban and 60% of rural readers preferred to do their reading. It is worth noting that 7.2 per cent of urban readers were habituated to read it before 6 o'clock in the morning, compared to 2 per cent of such rural readers. Publication centres' closeness to urban readers was the reason. Of one-fifth of the readers completing their reading beyond 10 o'clock, *Eenadu's* readers were fewest (12.5 per cent), implying that paper was delivered at the earliest. For *Andhra Patrika* such proportion of readers was highest (27.5 per cent). Advancing prime time preferences are suggestive of the life of the daily getting shorter than what is usually thought of. For all practical purposes the life of Telugu daily is ending around 10 o'clock, adversely affecting the loose sales on newspaper stands. Some sort of innovation to overcome such a problem is to be thought of.

Whatever their main paper may be, 70 per cent of sample respondents (335 out of 480) read *Eenadu* regularly or frequently. Similarly, *Andhra Jyoti* was read by about half of them, whereas *Udayam and Andhra Prabha* enjoyed readership of 40.4 and 37.7 per cent, respectively. Frequent readership implies at least thrice a week. On the whole, 78 per cent of the readers (328 out of 480) were multipaper readers, others remaining one-paper readers. Borrowing from neighbours and friends, reading at public libraries, college and school libraries, offices and common places were the main sources of readership without buying. Borrowership from neighbours and friends was more prevalent in villages.

On an average there were nine readers per copy. Of them, four were family members and five were borrowers. Even if one of the several non-buyer readers per copy, outside the family, could be transformed into an actual buyer, the Telugu paper would be able to catch up with other language dailies in improving its dailies-to-thousand people ratio.

For more than half of the respondents (53.1 per cent) newspaper was the first source of news, followed by TV (25 per cent) and radio (20 per cent). Nevertheless, for 94.2 per cent of them newspaper was the most intensively used medium for news.

Consumers' Evaluation

Consumers' evaluation of the main paper they read and comparative evaluation of the select papers by multi-newspaper readers is dealt in Chapter - VII. The buyers of the select newspapers (352) were asked to rank, in the order of importance, three of the motives which influenced their purchase decision. Of such buying motives, latest news was uppermost in the minds *of Eenadu* buyers, followed by prompt delivery and adequate news. On a rank order rating scale, latest news measured 33 per cent and the other two motives together measured that much. This implies the twin attributes of latest news and prompt delivery are capable of creating time and place utilities in one stroke. But what is equally important is the adequacy of the news. News-hunger is not easily satisfiable as in case of physiological needs. If a paper known for promptness of delivery with the latest news does not make adequate coverage, it is not likely to attract more customers. As such the market leader *Eenadu* appeared to be doing well in this regard. Of these three attributes, prompt delivery has become a maintenance factor rather than a motivating factor. At a time when prompt delivery culture was brought to the industry by the paper on entry, it was a motivating factor.

It is interesting to find out that family habit was No. 1 buying motive which influenced *Andhra Jyoti*'s customers. Latest news and unbiased news were tied for the second place, closely followed by prompt delivery for the third place. Patronising the product on the basis of family habit (rating score 23 per cent) implies that the buyers were aware of the availability of better products in the market. Family habit stood on their path in reaching the new brands. Such product loyalties do not last longer.

The buyers of *Andhra Prabha* liked it most because of its unbiased news, closely followed by family habit and adequate news. It is unbelievable to find out that a chain paper the leader of the yester years was grossly underperforming on two important fronts, namely, prompt delivery and latest news. Expectedly, in the years that followed the survey, *Andhra Prabha* continued to lose its circulation.

Udayam's buyers were motivated by adequacy of news. But by the time of reader survey, the paper was found to be in great difficulties. As such prompt delivery was the least influencing buying motive.

The readers (120 each of four papers) were asked to evaluate their paper, feature-wise. For the purpose, the contents of the newspapers were classified into three categories, namely, daily, non-daily and the Sunday features.

The readers were asked to rank five choicest daily features they liked most from their paper. The list of the daily features included: news; cartoons; editorials; editorial page articles; women's page; cinema page; district supplement; business page; and several other items depending on the brand of the papers. Irrespective of the readers' brand of the newspaper, their choicest items among the daily features was naturally - news. In terms of rating scores, it was 31-plus per cent in respect of all the four papers. There was unanimity among readers of all the papers in the second choicest item too. This time the choice fell on cartoons. Though cartoons are as old as Telugu papers, *Eenadu*'s positioning it was novel triggering enormous audience interest. Consequently, other papers also started exploiting the use of this feature. Such a wider appreciation and fuller understanding of the editorial cartoons' messages in Telugu paper is contrary to the findings of Brinkman and Carl. Their studies indicate only 15 per cent of readers fully understood editorial cartoons' messages. District supplement was the third choicest feature both for *Eenadu* and *Udayam* readers, whereas those of *Andhra Jyoti* and *Andhra Prabha* liked editorials in that place. The fourth and fifth choicest features of the four papers were also narrowed down to editorials or editorial page articles or district supplement (or page). On the whole, these findings reinforce the research findings of Bain and Weaver that readers devote more reading activity to hard news.

Finally, evaluation of the daily features, paper-wise, has several startling revelations. Even in case of the market leader *Eenadu* there were no distinctively reader attractive daily features outside its three choicest majors—news, cartoons and district suoolement. None of the remaining items secured a two-digit rating score. Even the much trumpeted women's page of *Eenadu—Vasundhara* was not a much sought-after daily feature. Either cinema page or business section or sports columns failed to generate significant interest to *Eenadu* readers. By and large, the reader evaluation of the other three papers does not appear to be much different from that of the leader's features. No feature, outside their three majors, enjoyed a two-digit rating score. Thus the runner-up papers imitating the market leader, feature by feature, proved to be a futile exercise.

Regarding the non-daily features, the market leader, on the whole, banked upon the use of satire in news related features at regular intervals. But its competitors, though provided a lot more variety in non-daily features compared to the leader, they have failed to design a strategy that is capable of driving home any competitive advantage in the marketplace.

The readers' evaluation of the Sunday supplement showed that the top three reader interests were confined to seven features. They were: cartoons; the cover story; crime story; human interest feature; short story; consumer column, and health. The crime story was common among such top interests in all the supplements, besides the cover story in three. But it is surprising to find lack of adequate response from the readers in evaluating Sunday supplements. Even in respect of the market leader's product, as high as 40 per cent of the readers (49 out of 120) did not respond. Lack of response was much higher in case of the supplements of the other papers. However, the reported 15 to 20 per cent surge in the sales of the Sunday papers is indicative of their readership among the women and the youth and those of the magazine lovers as different from the newspaper lovers.

Generic features such as news-to-advertisements ratio, price and colour printing were also evaluated. The market leader attracts more than a proportionate share in ads. This leads to imbalances, the leader paper carrying more ads and less news and the runner-up papers with more news and less ads. Basing on this, it is commonly thought the runner-up papers deliver more customer-satisfaction in the coverage of news compared to the leader. But findings of the survey were contrary to this belief. The market-leader *Eenadu* provided a better coverage of news, over three-fifth of its readers confirming it. Earlier observation that adequacy of news was one of the three purchase motives of its buyers further strengthens the belief. Only half of the readers of other papers felt it so. This implies more acres of news did not deliver more satisfaction. Over stretching of limited news stories in runner-up papers might have dissatisfied their readers. In contrast, coverage of plentiful of items by *Eenadu* in required breadth and depth might have delivered its readers extra satisfaction. In spite of that, two-fifth of the paper's 'readers expressed dissatisfaction of the news coverage directly or indirectly. The leader cannot afford to ignore it.

Colour printing was important only to three-fifth readers of all the papers. *Udayam* coming to the end while in colour reminds the necessity of rethinking on the issue of colour at least in case of runner-up firms. But advertising in colour need not be avoided. Over one-half of *Udayam* subscribers, a third of those *of Eenadu* and *Andhra Jyoti* and a sixth of *Andhra Prabha* felt the cover price of their paper was on the high side on weekdays. Complaints were fewer on the prices of Sunday issues.

What is done so far is evaluation in absolute terms. The reader evaluated various features in his paper only. But the real strengths or weaknesses of a product could be brought to light more clearly only through comparative evaluation. To fulfil this objective, 328 multiple newspaper readers were asked to evaluate the select four dailies by comparison. Multi-paper readership experience of at least three years was the criterion of the sample. To find out which paper excels in which feature or attribute is the goal of comparative evaluation. For the purpose of comparative evaluation, all the papers' features were broadly grouped into: news and views; major features and other features.

On a one-reader one-choice basis, *Eenadu* emerged the best choice in respect of six out of nine categories of news and views, namely, local, financial, international, national, state and sports news, in that order. The paper was the next best choice in two items, namely, editorials and editorial page articles. *Andhra Prabha* emerged the best choice in investigative news and editorials, and *Andhra Jyoti* in editorial page articles. *Udayam* was no best choice anywhere. On the whole, these findings establish that *Eenadu* lived upto its buyers' expectations in providing adequate news as it was their No. 3 buying motive, as discussed earlier. In contrast, similar expectations of *Udayam* and *Andhra Prabha* for whom adequacy of news was No.1 and No.3 buying motives, respectively, were frustrated. This may be described as expectancy-actuals gap. *Eenadu* particularly excelled in local news. 58.8 per cent of readers liking it. On the basis of these inferences, one should not be hasty in jump to the conclusion that all appears rosy in the performance of the market leader. The no-response figures very clearly indicate where the industry in general, and the leader in particular, were underperforming. Relating to investigative news, sports and financial news such figures were staggering 57, 45.7 and 41.4 per cent, respectively. They suggest the aggregated underperformance or unwanted performance of the industry, Unwanted performance warrants remarketing efforts, whereas underperformance warrants product enrichment so far as that segment of news is concerned. Failing to do so, the industry suffers. An indepth analysis of a situation as this proves the hypothesis of underperformance or unwanted performance.

Apart from news items, major features were also subjected to comparative evaluation. Of the seven major features, *Eenadu* was the best choice in four of them, namely, cartoons, women's features, science and technology, and agriculture. *Udayam* topped the choices in youth and also children's features, and *Andhra Jyoti* in literary features. Among such choices of multi-paper readers, cartoons of *Eenadu* were liked by most of them (53.6 per cent). However, no-response reader reactions were of alarming proportions for such features ranging from 44.5 per cent (youth features) to 84.7 per cent (agriculture), covering six out of seven of them.

Other features (outside news and views and the major features discussed earlier) included Sunday supplement, film news, health counselling, TV reviews and advertisements. *Eenadu* emerged the best choice in Sunday supplement and advertisements, conceding all other features to *Andhra Jyoti*. Once again the no response gap covering all the five features varied from 47.5 per cent to 65.2 per cent, invoking the hypothesis of underperformance or unwanted performance.

On the whole, feature-wise analysis reveals the existence of several gray areas of marketing performance. The market leader was no exception. Facing such uncertainties of customer acceptance, *Vaartha* preferrig to enter more or less with the same features in a copybook fashion is debatable.

The multipaper readers were asked to evaluate the papers around certain value premises, making a total of 13 such values. The market leader excelled all other papers in six out of 13 items of the value premises: (1) highlighting the problems of farm sector and villages; (2) educating and moulding public opinion; (3) providing entertainment; (4) upholding democratic values; (5) highlighting developmental issues; and (6) expressing concern at human misery or deterioration of human values, in that order. Strangely, *Udayam* was not found to excel in any of the selected values. *Andhra Jyoti* excelled around three values: in promoting cultural and literary values; in highlighting consumer problems; in maintaining high journalistic standards, in that order. *Andhra Prabha* excelled around two values: in fighting against corruption in high places; and in promoting national integration, in that order. And none of the papers excelled around two items of value premise: in promoting scientific temper; and in highlighting the problems of the poorest of the poor.

The comparative evaluation around selected value premise was reduced to a 13-point combined rating scale. It is intriguing to find that, (1) the constituency of readers believing none of these papers excelled in such values and (2) the constituency of no-response readers together measured a staggering 3.79 points. Such a vast gray area on a 13-point rating scale represents the extent to which the industry was underperforming on value front. *Eenadu's* total value premise measured 3.15 followed by *Andhra Jyoti* 2.11, *Udayam* 2.00 and *Andhra Prabha* 1.95.

Marketing the Space

The last chapter highlights the space selling strategies emerging in the Telugu newspaper market. As a prelude to such strategies, the rationale of space marketing and the competitive context that surrounds it are taken up first. There are strong links and dependencies between the news, circulation and advertising functions of the newspaper. News is the soul of a newspaper, its historic rationale. Yet, advertising is the financial heart of the newspaper, contributing 80 per cent or more of its total revenue. Unless *reader loyalty* can be translated into *advertiser support* a newspaper is doomed. Sizable circulation in absolute figures alone is not enough in newspaper business. A distinctive circulation lead over its rivals is capable of driving home a competitive advantage in attracting adequate ad revenue. Such paper can charge higher advertising rates than its competitors and still offer advertisers a lower cost-per-thousand figure. The paper with 60 per cent of the circulation in the market might get 70 to 75 per cent of the advertising, leaving the balance to the trailing papers thereby making their survival difficult. Being the second could be painful in newspaper business, unless its circulation is close to the market leader. A circulation-advertising imbalance —high circulation costs, low ad revenue—creates a cost structure so high that the newspaper is vulnerable to disruptions in internal operations or external environment.

Newspapers continue to claim the largest share in advertising even in the highly developed market of the USA, facing severe competition from the electronic media. But the problem currently encountered by the newspapers is one of declining share of advertising. Similar situation of lesser magnitude has also started emerging in India with a phenomenal expansion of Doordarshan in 1980s and a plethora of private channels coming into existence in 1990s. Between the years 1991 and 1995, the total advertising revenue grew from Rs. 1,700 crores to Rs.4,600 crores, registering a 270 per cent growth. The share of TV grew from 18 per cent to 26.4 per cent, while the press was a loser coming down from 68 per cent in 1991 to 61 per cent in 1995. As such, the problem of newspapers is one of a declining share, despite a raising market in ad revenue. Ad revenue in 1996 was over Rs.5,000 crore, slated to become Rs. 10,000 crore in the next five years.

Apart from intermedia competition, imbalances existed in the distribution of the print media's advertising cake among various constituents. The findings of the Centre for Media Studies (CMS) showed the English press shared 51 per cent of the total press ad revenue, whereas a total of eight language publications together accounted for only 46.5 per cent in 1987-88. In terms of circulation, English dailies comprised only 12.8 per cent, Hindi dailies 38.3 per cent and the dailies in other languages 48.9 per cent. A fewer English dailies thus are taking a lion's share in ad revenue, leaving the rest to a very large number of language-dailies. However, advertisers in recent years began to change their perception as more people are reading papers in regional languages.

Further, the newspaper business is gripped by severe cost compulsions, considering satellite technology and paperless newsrooms involving massive investments; huge doses of working capital requirements in terms of newsprint and ink; and multicentre publication. According to a conservative estimate, for a classy newspaper, a publisher should be willing to lose Rs.35 crore during the first three years without returns. Considering all costs, the production cost per copy works out to at least three to five times its cover price. It is advertising revenue which makes up the gap thus supporting the whole of the organisation.

Marketing the total newspaper involves selling it both to the reader and advertiser. Marketing concept in news was recognised earlier than in advertising. Unfortunately, some players in Telugu newspaper business have not recognised either of them, particularly even in the face of severe competition and they have perished. The contemporary space selling strategies that are either sustaining or improving the Telugu papers or failing to support them are taken up for analysis.

Segmentation strategies for circulation discussed in Chapter-V were also intended to serve as segmentation strategies for advertising. A three-tier geographic segmentation is at work at *Eenadu,* serving both the target readers and advertisers at the same time. In essence, the paper brought advertising within the reach of even a small individual or a retailer. An advertiser has the option of choosing a district, a combination of the districts, an edition, a combination of editions and all the editions. This is how segmentation-for-circulation strategy is transformed into segmentation-for-advertising. The master strategy innovated by the market leader enabled the advertiser to reach the desired audience at desired cost. Now it has become a norm for every player in the market. The market leader *Eenadu* took only two years to break-even the costs of those supplements. Two years later the districts brought in two-thirds of their revenues. *Eenadu's* two-in-one strategy so far segmented the total advertising market for Telugu papers into ten zones (edition level units), 28 city or district divisions (district level units), and 14 localities (slip page level units). Besides, the paper already developed innumerable slip pages for major locations in all the districts as carriers of news. The moment such locations are developed into space buying markets they will automatically become carriers of advertising. Changing the traditional six-column format to eight-column in the main paper and the five-column format to seven-column in district supplements were other inspired moves. All such cost-effective measures brought the display ads within the reach of small advertiser at the cost of classified ads. Resultantly, the paper created a host of new advertisers as it created new subscribers.

If *Eenadu*'s tariff is compared with those of its competitors, the former's rates appear to be far on a high side. For example, the combined (statewide) display rate per column-centimetre in *Eenadu* was Rs.963 in 1997, whereas that of *Vaartha* stood at only Rs.579. But in terms of cost-per-thousand copies circulated (CPT) works out to a mere Rs. 1.47 for *Eenadu*, the lowest of all papers. For *Vaartha*, the CPT per column centimetre was 142 per cent extra at Rs.3.56. For other papers the CPT per column-centimetre was still higher. Resultantly, what appeared to be the premium tariff in case of the market leader, in fact, is a cost-effective minimum rate to the advertiser. This is how the superior performance of the market leader brings in value both to the marketer and the customer through competitive advantage. Besides, the market leader's promotion efforts in advertising the advertising were quite imaginative, well planned and meticulously designed and executed. Their promotion material speaks volumes of their ingenuity in space marketing efforts. Their contents look like the findings of a research study and at the same time too simple to read and grasp. They never miss to present the updated reader profile in right perspective. Aided by such material, the untiring efforts of over 1,000 ad sales force are pressed into service to catch the advertiser, small or big, wherever they may be, present or potential. Space selling efforts of other Telugu dailies are found to be no match to those of *Eenadu*. Marketing is yet to arrive there in marketing the space. One wonders whether *Eenadu* is an ad product or a news product. Interestingly, it is both, all such marketing efforts culminating in product differentiation and developmental marketing. Product differentiation at such enormous costs implies making a product different from those of the competitors in anticipation of a premium price. But the product newspaper, being a heavily subsidised one by another public, cannot expect a price premium from the buyers. Naturally the advertisers have to bear it. *Eenadu* succeeded in extracting premium ad tariff, at the same time making it cost-effective to advertisers. This was the competitive advantage at the heart *of Eenadu's* performance. Had the paper failed to retain its market leadership after such extreme indulgence in differentiation, it would have resulted in a major marketing disaster.

Runner-up papers also indulged in differentiation by imitating their leader, perhaps at more costs. But they had no chance of levying premium rates on advertisers. This is the competitive disadvantage to which runner-up papers were subjected to in getting into the self-imposed trap of thoughtless imitation, sailing in rough weather of continuously declining circulation. Thus things changed from bad to worse at the follower firms. A situation as this confirms the hypothesis of imitation trap indulged in by the runner-up papers in Telugu newspaper market scene.

Eenadu sensed the latent demand for district supplements and slip pages both from the readers and advertisers. Hence they innovated them and successfully marketed, converting latent demand into actual demand. The process of effectively converting latent demand into actual demand is developmental marketing.

Besides the master strategy, other dual exercises include: Sunday supplement, interest-zoning, the use of colour, matrimonial and classified advertising. Each of them fostered both circulation and advertising. *Eenadu* innovating the Sunday supplement in a magazine format has several implications relating to space marketing. The supplement stretches life of an ad, circulation and reader bases, and reader involvement. It is a "super-way" to sample new products. All such strengths make it a competitor to magazines in attracting ads. However, its performance in directly attracting ad revenue so far appeared to be dismal. Ads were found to be very scanty in the Sunday supplement. But its indirect impact on advertising was tremendous. Because it was selling 20-25 per cent extra copies, advertisers were preferring to advertise on that day but in the main paper. *Eenadu* charging premium rates for Sunday advertising speaks of this. Such a competitive advantage proved to be a competitive disadvantage to other papers. They could not charge premium tariff, though incurring extra costs on the supplements.

Interest-zoning is another dual strategy. Creating the audiences that suit the advertiser's requirement is its goal. Some of the papers used such interest-zones even to create premium advertising zones. For example, *Eenadu* and *Andhra Jyoti* charged premium tariff for the financial ads in business section.

Matrimonial and classified advertising look like advertising strategies rather than product strategies. But they are both, considering a lot of reader interest and response they evoke. In a tradition bound society, the need for matrimonial advertising is less. But the imperatives of growing urbanisation and the changing attitudes made the people to realise its advantages. Precisely, *Eenadu* stepped in there to mobilise public opinion in favour of matrimonial advertising by positioning its campaign suitably. *Eenadu* succeeded in changing 'the readers' attitudes. Matrimonial advertising culture was very carefully tended at *Eenadu* and it is still going on even today through, what Philip Kotler calls, *conversional marketing*—the process of converting negative demand into positive demand. Beginning with 25 pieces a week, today the paper is able to sell one broad-sheet full of matrimonial advertising.

Tasting or smelling success in matrimonials, *Eenadu*

started targeting on other forms of classifieds, making a small beginning with a Real Estate page (every Saturday) in the city supplements of Hyderabad, Visakhapatnam and Vijayawada simultaneously in 1992. They made the classifieds easier to the small advertiser by throwing open a large network of zonal offices. The long-term strategy has yet to bear fruit in a big way but the pursuit is not given up. *Eenadu*'s continued efforts to build-up a market for its classifieds is an exercise in *stimulational marketing*, the task of converting no demand into positive demand. The performance of other papers either in matrimonial or classified advertising was no match to the leader.

The fact that *Eenadu* could quote an extra premium of 100-150 per cent for its multicolour ads, depending on their location, speaks of the competitive strength of this strategy. Strategies such as colour could only strengthen a paper provided if it is otherwise good enough. Players whose circulations were found to be continuously declining may not be able to drive home any advantage either by offering a paper or an ad in colour. The experiences of other Telugu papers proved it.

Image building today is an extremely important managerial responsibility and must be integrated into every newspaper's marketing effort. Image in the marketplace must be built carefully and protected devotedly. The market leader did not lag behind in adopting image building as a strategy.

To sump up, though marketing has started taking roots in the Telugu newspaper business since 1974, it appears such a phenomenon is mostly confined to the market leader, *Eenadu*. The other papers are yet to take on to the marketing orientation in a real sense. *Andhra Patrika* and *Udayam* falling aside, the other papers were languishing, placed far behind the leader. For several years they remained indifferent to the fastly changing market scene, thus losing battle after battle by default rather than by defeat. By the time they have realised the need to retaliate, the war was over. For runner-up papers competitive reaction meant: Merely imitating the leader either in product features or going to new places; and indulging in miscalculated frontal attack *(Udayam)* or sometimes even in encirclement attack (*Vaartha*) right on entry without realising that the leader then was performing well. While the leader was targeting repeatedly to deliver more and more customer-satisfaction, the runner-up papers did not realise that merely imitating the leader will not automatically build customer-satisfaction. Much closer examination revealed that despite the leader enjoying the competitive advantage in advertising sales, the paper made every effort to get close to the advertisers. The runner-up papers have no designs of their own except imitation which proved to be self-imposed traps. The earlier the runner-up papers design the strategies that best suit them, the better it would be for them. Better if they are confined to limited markets rather than thinly stretching over the whole of it, always intending to deliver more customer-satisfaction, securing adequate advertising support and thus ensuring the survival of the paper.

The prospects of the Telugu newspaper may be brightened by researching into related areas such as: Non-reader studies, particularly confining to those whose incomes are high enough to buy newspaper; non-buyer studies, particularly concentrating on those who read a lot of Telugu papers, yet much averse to buy them; intramedia competition between Telugu papers and English papers; studying newspaper business in the state, by major markets in terms of geographic regions, cities or towns, including all languages; studies into women readership; and studies into infrequent advertisers and non-advertisers.

Appendix
Marketing Strategies of Telugu Newspapers

Questionnaire* for Readers

1. General Information

1.1 Name & Address of the Subscriber/Reader:

1.2 Age: 1.3 Education: 1.4 Occupation

1.5 Total annual income of the family:

1.6 What Telugu dailies you buy and read?

Regularly:

Frequently: Duration of subscription:

1.7 What Telugu dailies you read without buying?

Regularly: Frequently:

Duration of readership: Sources of such paper:

1.8 Parent's newspaper interest during the reader's childhood:

Yes/No/Cannot say

---

*Space being the limiting factor, only a condensed version is given here. For a detailed version of the concerned questions, see the tables given in the parentheses.

1.9 How such parent's newspaper interest is gratified during the reader's childhood? (Table 6.8, Chapter-VI)

1.10 Your reading habits:

(a) Awaiting impatiently to receive the newspaper.

(b) Reading soon after waking up.

(c) Reading at convenience.

1.11 Number of rounds in which you complete reading the newspaper: One/Two/Three or more.

1.12 Your prime time preference to complete your newspaper reading:

Before 6 AM/6 - 8 AM/8-10 AM/10-12 Noon/12-2 PM/ After 2 PM.

1.13 Average readership per copy of the Telugu newspaper you buy:

No. of family members: No. of outsiders:

1.14 Do you own (a) a TV? Yes/No (b) a radio or two-in-one set? Yes/No

1.15 Usually, what is your first source of news? Newspaper/ radio/TV

1.16 The impact of TV on the newspaper reading habit of your family members: Yes/No

2. The Readership of Your Main Newspaper

2.1 What factors influenced you in the choice of your daily? Rank *three* of the given factors, in the order of importance. (Table 7.1, Chapter - VII)

2.2 What are the five choicest items among the daily features of your newspaper? Rank *five* of the given features, in the order of importance. (Tables 7.5 through 7.9, Chapter-VII)

2.3 What you like most among the non-daily features of your newspaper? Rank *three* of the given non-daily features, in the order of importance. (Tables 7.10 through 7.13 Chapter - VII).

2.4 What you like most among the features from the Sunday supplement of your newspaper? Rank *three* of the given features in the order of importance. (Tables 7.14 through 7.17 Chapter-VII).

2.5 Your evaluation of the ratio of news to advertisements of your newspaper: More news/Balanced proportion/ Less news/No idea.

2.6 Importance of printing your newspaper in colour: Very important/Important/Not so important/Unimportant/ No idea.

3. Your Multipaper Readership

3.1 What is your choice among the four select Telugu dailies for news and views, item-wise?

(a) International news (b) National news
(c) State news (d) Local news
(e) Investigative news (f) Financial news
(g) Sports (h) Editorials
(i) Editorial page articles

3.2 What is your choice among the four select Telugu dailies for major features, item-wise?

(a) Cartoons (b) Literary features
(c) Children's features (d) Youth features
(e) Women's features (f) Science and technology
(g) Agriculture.

3.3 What is your choice among the four select Telugu dailies for other features?

(a) Sunday supplement b) Film news

(c) Health counselling d) TV reviews

(e) Advertisements

3.4 Which of the select four Telugu dailies excels others around certain value premises?

(a) In educating and moulding public opinion.

(b) In upholding democratic values.

(c) In expressing concern at human misery or deterioration of human values.

(d) In promoting national integration and universal brotherhood.

(e) In highlighting developmental issues.

(f) In highlighting problems of farm sector and villages.

(g) In promoting scientific temper.

(h) In highlighting the problems of the poorest of the poor.

(i) In highlighting consumer problems and supporting consumer movement.

(j) In fighting against corruption in high places.

(k) In promoting cultural and literary values.

(l) In providing entertainment.

(m) In maintaining high standards in journalism without any bias or sensationalism.

Bibliography

Aaker, David A., Batra, Rajeev, and Myers, John G., *Advertising Management*, Prentice-Hall of India, New Delhi, 1995.

Abell, Derek F., *Defining the Business: The Starting Point of Strategic Planning*, Allyn & Bacon, Boston, 1990.

——, "Strategic Windows", *Journal of Marketing*, July 1978, pp. 21-26.

Adams, R.C., and Webber, Gail M., "The Audience for, and Male Vs. Female Reactions to, 'The Day After'" *Journalism Quarterly*, Winter 1984, pp. 812-816.

Agarwal, Amit, "Channels: Star Wars", *India Today*, November 30, 1996, pp. 108-113.

——, "Private Channels: Broadcast Blues", *India Today*, December 31, 1996, pp. 116-117.

Aggarwal, S.K., *Media Credibility*, Mittal Publications, New Delhi, 1989.

Ahuja, B.N., *History of Indian Press: Growth of Newspapers in India*, Surjeet Publications, Delhi, 1988.

——, *Theory and Practice of Journalism*, Surjeet Publications, Delhi, 1979.

Akhileshwari R., and Vishweshwer Rao, P.L., "Readership Dimensions in the Indian Press," *Vidura*, October 1984, pp. 262-264.

Almedia, "A Strategy of Substance," *Business India*, January 30-February 12, 1995, p. 213.

Ananda Bhaskar, Rapolu, *Journalism Charithra—Vyavastha* (Telugu), *Udayam* Publications, Hyderabad, 1988.

Anchan, Helen, "Prey for Tomorrow", *A & M*, May 1992, pp. 68-69.

Andhra Jyoti, Inaugural Issue, July 2, 1960.

Andhra Jyoti, Rajatha Kamalam, editorial, July 1985, pp. 14-15.

Andhra Patrika, April 1, 1914.

Andhra Pradesh Year Book 1993, Data News Features, Hyderabad.

Anjaneyulu, D., "Some Telugu Editors", in K.R. Seshagiri Rao (ed.), *Studies in the History of Telugu Journalism*, Narla Shashtyabdipurti Celebration Committee, Delhi, 1968, pp. 141-146.

Anklesaria Aiyar, Swaminathan, S., "Will The Internet Affect Newspapers, TV and Radio?", *The Economic Times, 1* February 1998, p. 1.

Annuncio, Charubala, and Deb, Sandipan, "The Press Fightback", *A & M*, 31 August, 1994, pp. 39-58.

——, Charubate and Shirali, Aresh, "Is Innovation Enough?", *A & M*, 15 May 1995, pp. 46-51.

Arathoon, Marion, "Crossing the Media Frontiers", *The Economic Times*, Brand Equity, 19-25 July, 1995, pp. 1-2.

Aronson, James, *The Press and the Cold War*, Beacon Press, Boston, 1970.

Arudra, "Beginnings of Telugu Journalism" in K.R. Seshagiri Rao, (ed.), *Studies in the History of Telugu Journalism*, Narla Shashtyabdipurti Celebration Committee, Delhi, 1968.

Astor, J.J., *Art of Modern Journalism*, Akashdeep Publishing, Delhi, 1997.

Audit Bureau of Circulations, *Half Yearly ABC Reports* of the years 1970 to 1997, Mumbai.

Avery, R., "Adolescents' Use of the Mass Media," *American Behavioural Scientist* 23, 1979, pp. 53-70.

Azad, Abul Kalam, *India Wins Freedom*, Orient Longman, Bombay, 1958.

Badrinath, N.D., "Look, the Press is Changing," *The Economic Times*, Brand Equity, 11-17 October 1995, p. 5.

Bagdikian, Ben H., *The Media Monopoly: A Startling Report on the 50 Corporations That Control What America Sees, Hears and Reads*, Beacon Press, Boston, 1983.

Bahl, Sushil, "Press is Still Supreme," *The Economic Times*, September, 1, 1988.

Bain, C., and Weaver, D., "Readers'. Reactions to Newspaper Design", *Newspaper Research Design*, 1(1), 1978.

Balakrishnan, Paran, "The Circulation War," *Sunday*, 3-9 July, 1988, pp. 63-64.

Benerji, Anjan Kumar, "Role of Indian Press in Rural Development", *Kurukshetra*, January-February 1996, pp. 22-24.

Bansal, Shuchi, "A Bleak Picture", *Business World*, 12-25 August, 1992, pp. 118-120.

——, "A New Edition for The Hindi Press," *Business World*, 1 August 1997, pp. 106-107.

——, "Doordarshan is in the Doldrums," *Business World*, 1-14 May, 1996, p. 109.

——, "Price Cuts and the Battle of the Times," *Business World*, 27 July - 9 August 1994, p. 24.

——, "The News, Read by ... Take Your Pick," *Business World*, 19 April - 2 May, 1995, pp. 118-119.

——, and Carvalho, Brian, "India's Murdoch," *Business World*, 7-21 September, 1998, pp. 18-25.

——, and Mukerjea, D.N., "Channel Champ," *Business World*, 26 July- 8 August, 1995, pp. 42-52.

Basu, Anasuya, "Media: The Telegraph Vs. The Asian Age, All Above Board," *The Economic Times*, June 5, 1995.

Basu, Radha, "Readership Survey Breaks New Ground, Explodes Old Myths," *The Times of India*, February 10, 1996.

——, "TV will not Make Newspapers Redundant," *The Times of India*, November 2, 1995.

Bedi, M.S., "Looking at the Fine Print," *The Economic Times*, Brand Equity, 17 November 1993, p. 8.

Behra, Sunil Kanta, "Newspaper Economics and Management," *Vidura*, April, 1985.

Beri, G.C., *Marketing Research*, Tata McGraw-Hill, New Delhi, 1993.

Bhadari, Bhupesh, "Skirmishes Start in Southern Skies," *Business World*, 4-17 September, 1996, pp. 114-116.

——, "Media: Get Ready for The War of the Times," *Business World*, 18-31 October, 1995, pp. 158-160.

Bhargava, Anjali, "Advice From the Competitiveness Guru," *Business World*, 5-18 October, 1994, pp. 129-131.

Bhaskara Rao, N., "The Indian Ad Scene: Some Perspectives," *The Economic Times*, February 9, 1989, p. 10.

——, "The Media: 1990, Ups and Downs," *A & M*, April 1991, pp. 46-51.

——, and Raghavan, G.N.S., *Social Effects of Mass Media in India*, Gyan Publishing House, New Delhi, Undated.

Bhatt, S.C., *Indian Press Since 1955*, Publications Division, Ministry of Information and Broadcasting, Govt. of India, New Delhi, 1997.

Bhattacharjea, Ajit, "The Role of the Press," *The Hindu*, November 6, 1998, p. 12.

Bhattacharjee, Arun, *Indian Press: Profession to Industry*, Vikas Publishing House, New Delhi, 1972.

Biggadike, Ralph, *Entering New Markets: Strategies and Performance*, Marketing Science Institute, Cambridge MA, 1977.

Bist, Raju, "Media Explosion," *Business India*, May 22-June 4, 1995, pp. 54-55.

Blankenburg, William B., "A Newspaper Chain's Prime Behaviour," *Journalism Quarterly*, Summer 1983 pp. 275-280.

Bonoma, Thomas V., *Managing Marketing: Text, Cases and Readings*, The Free Press, New York, 1984.

Boyce, George, Currant, James, and Wingate, Paul, (eds.), *Newspaper History: From The 17th Century to the Present Day*, Constable, 1978.

Boyd, Harper W. Jr., Westfall, Ralph, and Stasch, Stanley F., *Marketing Research: Text and Cases*, All India Traveller Bookseller, New Delhi, 6th ed., 1985.

Brinkman, D., "Do Editorial Cartoons and Editorials Change Opinions?," *Journalism Quarterly*, 44, 1968, pp 724-726.

Bhell, Victor P., *Marketing Management: A Strategic Planning Approach*, McGraw-Hill, Singapore, 1985.

Business India, editorial, March 24-April 6, 1997, p. l.

Busterna, John C., "National Advertising Pricing: Chain Vs. Independent Newspapers," *Journalism Quarterly*, Summer 1988, pp. 307-312, 334.

Buzzell, Robert D., and Gale, Bradley T., *The PIMS Principles: Linking Strategy to Performance*, Free Press, New York, 1987.

——, and Sultan, G.M., "Market Share—A Key to Profitability," *Harvard Business Review*, January-February 1975, pp. 97-106.

Carl, L.M., "Editorial Cartoons Fail to Reach Many Readers" *Journalism Quarterly*, 44, 1968, pp. 533-535.

"Causes of Newspapers' Credibility Gap," *Editor & Publisher*, August 30, 1969, p. 13.

Certo, Samuel C., and Peter, Paul J., *Strategic Management: Concepts and Applications*, McGraw-Hill, New York (2nd ed.), 1991.

Chahal, N., and Kinra, N., "Marketing Evening Newspapers: An Analysis," *Vikalpa*, October-December 1988, pp. 31-35.

"Chain Reaction in Motion," *The Economic Times, Brand Equity*, 6-12 December, 1995, p. 3.

Chakrabharty, Sanjay and Satyamurthy, N.P., "Facing up to the Challenge," *The Economic Times, Brand Equity* 6-12 December, 1995, p. 2.

Chakradhar, Govindaraju, *Meeru Journalist Kaavachu* (Telugu), Jayasri Press, Hyderabad, 1988.

Chakravarthy, Nikhil, "Freedom of the Press," *The Hindu*, April 17, 1995.

——, "The Press: Changing Face of the Watchdog," *India*, August 15, 1997, pp. 63-66.

Chalapatti Rau, M., *Journalism and Politics*, Vikas Publishing House, New Delhi, 1984.

——, *Press in India*, Allied Publishers, Bombay, 1968.

——, *The Romance of the Newspaper*, NCERT, Delhi, 1975.

Chander, "Reppa Vaalchani Kannu Patrika Rachayitha Pennu" (Telugu), Sunday, *Vaartha*, 22 December 1996, pp. 8-11.

Chaney, D., *Processes of Mass Communication*, Macmillan, London, 1972.

Chronicler, "Telugu Journalism—Leaders and Landmarks," published in *The Golden Book*, (n.d.), pp. 120-125.

Chuganee, Bhakti and Subramaniam, Ganga, "Selling It Small," *Business India*, September 9-22, 1966.

"Classified Receives High Performance Rating," *International Newspaper Advertising and Marketing Executives News*, December 1982, p. 11.

"Competition at Home Lacking," *Business World*, 5-18 October, 1994, pp. 124-128.

"Conjuring Junk," *The Financial Express*, June 29, 1996, p. 7.

"Coping with Paper Shortage," *The Economic Times, Brand Equity*, 14-20 June, 1995, p. 6.

Cortada, James W., *TQM for Sales and Marketing Management*, McGraw-Hill, New York, 1993.

Cranfield, G.A., *The Press and Society*, Longman, London, 1978.

Cravens, David W., *Strategic Marketing*, Richard D.Irwin, Homewood Illinois, (2nd ed.), 1987.

Davis, William, *The Innovators: The Essential Guide to Business Thinkers, Achievers and Entrepreneurs*, Ebury Press, London, 1987.

Desai, Ashok, *Economic Aspects of the Indian Press*, Press Institute of India, New Delhi, 1971.

Dhawan, Paulomi, "Indian Readership Survey '95: Clues to Change," *A & M*, 15 March, 1996, pp. 24-26.

——, "Indian Readership Survey '95: The Great Divide," *A & M*, 31 March 1996, pp. 32-34.

——, "Marketing Ammo," *A & M*, 15 May, 1998.

Dhobal, Shailesh, "Fight for the Crown," *The Economic Times, Brand Equity*, 23-29 April, 1997, p. 4.

Doctor, Vikram, "Desert Storm," *Business India*, February 10-23, 1997, p. 124.

"Down Trends in Print Media Deplored," *Indian Express*, November 6, 1995.

Dreze, Jean, and Sen, Amartya, *Hunger and Public Action*, Clarendon Press, Oxford, 1989.

——, *India: Economic Development and Social Opportunity*, Oxford University Press, Delhi, 1995.

Drucker, Peter F., *Innovation and Entrepreneurship: Practice and Principles*, First Affiliated East-West Press, New Delhi, 1991, (First Published in 1986).

——, *Management: Tasks, Responsibilities, Practices*, Harper & Row, New York, 1974.

——, *Managing for the Future: 1990s and Beyond*, Tata McGraw-Hill, New Delhi, 1992.

——, *Managing the Non-profit Organisation: Principles and Practices*, Macmillan India, New Delhi, 1993.

——, *The Practice of Management*, Pan Books, London, 1968.

Dua, M.R., "Wanted: A Media Policy," *The Financial Express*, June 1, 1996, p. 7.

Dube, S.C., *Communication, Innovation and Planned Change in India*, East-West Centre Press, Honolulu, 1964.

Dubey, Chandan, "Designed to Seduce," *The Financial Express, Brand Wagon*, July 8, 1997, pp. 1-2.

Dunn, Watson S., and Barban, Arnold M., *Advertising: Its Role in Modern Marketing*, Holt-Saunders, New York (5th ed.), 1982.

Eapen, K.E., "Daily Newspapers in India: Their Status and Problems," *Journalism Quarterly*, XLIV, 1967.

Edwards, Alien L., *Techniques of Attitude Scale Construction*, Vakils, Feffer and Simons, Bombay, 1969.

Erbring L., Goldenberg, E., and Miller, A., "Frontpage News and Real World Cues: A New Look at Agenda-setting by the Media," *American Journal of Political Science*, 24, 1980, pp. 16-49.

Fejes, F., *Critical Mass Communication Research and Media Effects: Its Uses and Influence*, Faber & Faber, London, 1984.

Fink, Conrad C., *Strategic Newspaper Management*, Southern Illinois University Press, Carbodale, 1988.

Fitzgerald, Mark, "Advice to Newspapers: Market Better," *Editor & Publisher*, September 28, 1985, pp. 18, 33.

Freshly Canned: "The Wisdom of Philip Roller," *Business Today*, November 7, 1998, pp. 119-117.

Gandhi, D.V. (ed.), *Advertisers Handbook, '95*, Indraprastha Prakashan, New Delhi, Undated. Gandhi, M.K., *Young India (1919-27)*, Tagore & Co., Chennai, 1922.

Gameau, "Offering Better Customer Service: Newspaper Executives Agree—It's a Matter of Survival" *Editor & Publisher*, September 23, 1989, pp. 9-10.

Gersh, Debra, "Building a Winning Strategy," *Editor & Publisher*, September 6, 1986, pp. 28-29.

——, "Editor Offers Marketing Advice to Fellow Editors," *Editor & Publisher*, June 28, 1986, p. 38.

——, "Giving The Advertisers What They Want," —*Editor & Publisher*, August 30, 1986, p. 33.

Glasser, T.L., "Play, Pleasure and the Value of Newsreading," *Communication Quarterly*, 30, 1982, pp. 101-107.

Glweck, William F., and Jauch, Lawrence R., *Business Policy and Strategic Management*, McGraw-Hill, Auckland (4th ed), 1984.

Goopta, Pradeep, "The Battle of the Big Four," *The Economic Times, Brand Fruity*, 14 November 1990, p. 4.

Gopalakrishnan, Sunitha, "The Resurgence of Press," *A & M*, 30 May 1994, pp. 99-100.

Goswami, Anupam, "Message for the Media," *Business India*, March 24-April 6, 1997.

Govt. of India, *An Indian Personality for Television*, Volume-I and II, Report of the Working Group on Software for Doordarshan, Ministry of Information and Broadcasting, New Delhi, 1985.

——, *Annaul Report of the Registrar for Newspapers in India*, 1958.

——, *Mass Media in India 1986*, Ministry of Information and Broadcasting, New Delhi, 1987

——, *Mass Media in India 1992*, Ministry of Information and Broadcasting, New Delhi, 1993.

——, *Press in India*, Annual Reports of the Registrar of Newspapers for India of the Years 1986 to 1995, Ministry of Information and Broadcasting, New Delhi.

——, *Report of the Enquiry Committee on the Problems of Small Newspapers*, Ministry of Information and Broadcasting, New Delhi, 1965.

——, *Report of the Fact-Finding Committee on Newspaper Economics*, Ministry of Information and Broadcasting, Govt. of India, 1975.

——, *Report of the Mass Communication Study Team*, Ministry of Information and Broadcasting, New Delhi, 1963.

——, *Report of the Press Commission*, New Delhi, 1954.

——, *Report of the Second Press Commission, Vol. II*, Ministry of Information and Broadcasting, New Delhi, 1982.

——, *Report of the Study Team on Five Year Plan Publicity*, New Delhi, 1963.

——, *Report of Study Group for Newspaper Industry*, National Commission on Labour, New Delhi, 1968.

——, *White Paper on Misuse of Mass Media during the Internal Emergency*, New Delhi, 1977.

Grotta, Gerald L., Larkin, Ernest F., and Plois, Barbara De., "How Readers Perceive and Use a Small Daily Newspaper," *Journalism Quarterly*, Winter 1975, pp. 711-715.

Gujral, I.K., "Mass Communication and Development", *Mainstream*, Annual Number, 1973.

Gupta, Rahul with Dey, Sudipto, "Street-Smart Strategics," *Financial Express*, October 21, 1995, p. 7.

Gurevitch, M., Bennett, T., Curran, J., and Woolacott, J., (eds.), *Culture, Society, and The Media*, Methuen, London, 1982.

Hagner, Paul R., "Newspaper Competition: Isolating Related Market Characteristics," *Journalism Quarterly*, Summer 1983. pp. 281-287.

Hamel, Gary and Prahalad, C.K., *Competing for the Future*, Harvard Business School Press, Boston, 1994.

——, "Strategic Intent," *Harvard Business Review* 67, No. 3, 1989, pp. 63-76.

——, "Strategy as Stretch and Leverage," *Harvard Business Review* 72, No. 4, 1933, pp. 75-84.

"Hard To Digest?," *Financial Express, Brand Wagon*, April 25, 1997, p. 3.

Harrigan, Jane T., *Read All About It: A Day in the Life of a Metropolitan Newspaper*, The Globe Pequot Press, Chester, 1987.

Hartman, Paul, Patil, B.R., and Dighe, Anita, *The Mass Media and Village Life: An Indian Study*, Sage Publications, New Delhi, 1989.

Haskins, Jack B., and Miller, Mark M., "The Effects of Bad News and Good News on a Newspaper's Image," *Journalism Quarterly*, Spring 1984, pp. 3-13, 65.

Hauser, John R., and Gaskin, P., "Application of the 'Defender' Consumer Model," *Marketing Science*, Fall, 1984, pp. 327-351.

——, and Shugan, Steve M., "Defensive Marketing Strategy," *Marketing Science*, Fall 1983, pp. 319-360.

Heimrath, Charles H., *Indian Nationalism and Hindu Social Reforms*, Oxford University Press, Bombay, 1964.

Hemavati, "Indian Languages: A Really Raw Deal," *A & M*. December, 1989, pp. 61-64.

Henry, H., *Readership Research: Theory and Practice, Proceedings of the First Symposium*, Sigmatext, London, 1982.

Herzberg, Frederick, *Work and the Nature of Man*, William Collins, Cleveland, 1966.

Hussain, Sabita, "Rate Race," *The Economic Times, Brand Equity*, 16-22 July, 1997, p. l.

Impact of Newsprint Shortage on Indian Newspapers, IENS, New Delhi, 1974.

Jacob, Smriti, "Reader's Digest: Point to Ponder," *A &M*, 1-15 October, 1997, pp. 84-86.

Jainani, Deepa, "Battles in the Vernacular," *Financial Express*, September 9, 1995, p. 7.

Jayashankar, Mitu, "*The Hindu:* Southern Comfort," *A & M*, 15 September, 1998, pp. 28-29.

Jeffrey, Robin, "Culture and Governments: How Women Made Kerala Literate (And Why It Happened When It Did)" *Pacific Affairs*, 1987.

——, "Culture of Daily Newspapers in India—How it is Grown, What it Means," *Economic and Political Weekly*, April 4, 1987.

——, "Indian Languages Newspapers: 1, Malayalam: The Day-to-Day Social Life of the People...," *Economic and Political Weekly*, January 4-11, 1997.

——, "Indian Languages Newspapers: 2, Hindi: Taking to the 'Punjab Kesari Line'," *Economic and Political Weekly*, January 18, 1997, pp. 77-83.

——, "Indian Languages Newspapers: 3, Bengali: Professional, Somewhat Conservative and Calcuttan," *Economic and Political Weekly*, January 25, 1997.

——, "Indian Languages Newspapers: 4, Telugu: Ingredients of Growth and Failure," *Economic and Political Weekly*, February 1, 1997, pp. 192-195.

——, "Indian Languages Newspapers: 5, Tamil: 'Dominated by Cinema and Politics'," *Economic and Political Weekly*, February 8, 1997.

——, "Indian Languages Newspapers: 6, Gujarati: 'Chequebook Journalism in Reverse ...'," *Economic and Political Weekly*, February 15, 1997.

——, "Indian Languages Newspapers: 7, Marathi: Big Newspapers are Elephants," *Economic and Political Weekly*, February 22, 1997.

——, "Indian Languages Newspapers: 8, Punjabi: The 'Subliminal Charge'," *Economic and Political Weekly*, March 1-8, 1997.

——, "Indian Languages Newspaper: 9, Oriya: 'Identifying ... with Newspapers'," *Economic and Political Weekly*, March 15, 1997.

——, "Indian Languages Newspapers: 10, Kannada: "We Fake it

There is Competition," *Economic and Political Weekly,* March 22, 1997.

——, "Indian Languages Newspapers: 11, Urdu: Waiting for Citizen Kane?," *Economic and Political Weekly* March 29, 1997.

——,"Indian Languages Newspapers and Why They Grow," *Economic and Political Weekly,* September 18, 1993.

——, *Politics, Women and Well-being: Now Kerala Became a Model',* Macmillan, London, 1992.

Joshi, P.C., "Culture Communications and Development," *Mainstream* Republic Day Issue, 1986.

Joshi, Rahul, "David & Goliath Play the Numbers Game," *Business World,* 19 October- 1 November, 1994.

Joshi, Uma and Mehta, Neepa, "Research on Mass Media: Trends Analysis and Challenges for the Future," *University News,* November 4, 1996, pp. 7-10.

Kamath, M.V., *Professional Journalism,* Vikas Publishing House, New Delhi, 1989.

Kamath, Vinay, "The Making of Media Moghul," *Business World,* 15th June, 1994.

Kane, Michael G., "Managing the Promotion Budget," *Editor & Publisher,* January 11, 1986, pp. 9, 19.

Kapadia, Bharat, "Adopting to Flourish," *A & M,* May 1992, p. 71.

Kar, Mitali, "Meteoric Rise," *A & M,* 15 June, 1994.

Karmali, Naazneen and Tak, Devendra, "It's Boom Time, Folks!", *Business India,* January 30-February 12, 1995, pp. 54-60.

Katiyar, Arun, "Indian Express Group: Divide and Rule," *India Today,* March 31, 1995, pp. 142-147.

Kaul, Pummy, "Media Planners Go Radio Ganga," *The Financial Express, Brand Wagon,* April 26, 1996, p. l. Kazmi, Azhar, Business Policy, Tata McGraw-Hill, New Delhi, 1996.

Kelley, Eugene, J. (ed.), *Marketing Strategy and Functions,* Englewood Cliffs, N.J., Prentice-Hall, 1965.

Kerin, Roger A., Mahajan, Vijay and Varadarajan, Rajan P.,

Contemporary Perspective on Strategic Planning, Allyn & Bacon, Boston, 1990.

Khandekar, Sreekant, "Bhaskar Rao: Far From Resigned," *A&M*, March, 1992, pp. 36-37.

——, "Nari Hira: A Deft Touch," *A & M*, March 1990, pp. 24-33.

——, "The Cluster of *Life*," *A & M*, May 1992, pp. 52.58.

Khurana, Rakesh and Ravichandran, A.N., *Strategic Marketing Management: Concepts & Cases—An Indian Context*, Global Business Press, Delhi, 1995.

Kotler, Philip, *Marketing Management: Analysis, Planning, Implementation and Control*, Prentice-Hall, New Delhi, (7th ed.), 1991.

——, (9th ed.), 1997.

——, "Phasing Out Weak Products," *Harvard Business Review*, March-April, 1965.

——, "The Major Tasks of Marketing Management," *Journal of Marketing*, October 1973, pp. 42-49.

——, and Armstrong, Gary, *Principles of Marketing*, Prentice-Hall of India, New Delhi, 6th ed., 1995.

——, and Levy, Sidney J., "Demarketing, Yes Demarketing," *Harvard Business Review*, November-December 1971, pp. 74-80.

Krishnamurthy, Nadig, *Indian Journalism, Origin, Growth and Development of Indian Journalism from Asoka to Nehru*, University of Mysore, Mysore, 1966.

Kulkarni, Neelambika, "Campaign: *Loksatta*, Not Just for the Marathas," *The Financial Express, Brand Wagon*, October 18, 1996.

——, "Putting Media—Buying on Record," *The Financial Express, Brand Wagon*, June 21, 1996, pp. 1-2.

Kulshreshtha, Rajul, "Buying Time on TV," *A & M*, 30 September, 1998, pp. 34-35.

Kumar, Anu, "Stardust: Star Sprinkled Spanner," *A&M*, 1-15 March, 1997, pp. 73-75.

Kumar, Karthik and Dayal, Aarti, "Issues of Readership," *A & M*, May 1992, pp. 59-62.

Kumar, Keval J., *Mass Communication in India,* Jaico Publishing, Mumbai, 1991.

Lacy, Stephen, "The Impact of Intercity Competition on Daily Newspaper Content," *Journalism Quarterly,* Summer 1988, pp. 399-406.

Lain, Laurence B., "Steps Toward A Comprehensive Model of Newspaper Readership," *Journalism Quarterly,* Spring 1986, pp. 69-74, 121.

Lakshmana Rao, Y.V., *Communication and Development,* University of Minnesota Press, Minneapolis, 1966.

Lakshmana Reddy, V., *Telugu Journalism Avatharana—Vikaasam* (Telugu), Gopichand Publications, Vijayawada, 1985.

Lent, John A., (ed.), *The Asian Newspaper 5 Reluctant Revolution,* The Iowa State University Press, Ames, Iowa, 1977.

Lerner, Daniel, *The Passing of Traditional Society: Modernizing in Middle East,* Free Press, Glencol, IL., 1958.

Levitt, Theodore, "Innovative Imitation," *Harvard Business Review,* September-October, 1966.

——, "Marketing Myopia," *Harvard Business Review,* July-August 1960, pp. 45-56.

Lilien, Gary L., and Kotler, Philip, *Marketing Decision Making: A Model Building Approach,* Harper & Row, New York, (2nd Ed.), 1983.

Lingam, *Circulation Problems in Indian Newspapers,* The Press Institute of India, Delhi, 1968.

Luck, David J., and Rubin, Ronald S., *Marketing Research,* Prentice-Hall of India, New Delhi, 1987.

Luthans, Fred, *Organisational Behaviour,* McGraw-Hill, New York, (7th ed.), 1995.

McCarthy, Jerome E., and Perreault, Jr., William D., *Basic Marketing: A Managerial Approach,* Universal Book Stall, New Delhi, (9th ed.), 12987.

McCombs, M.E., and Shaw, D., "The Agenda-setting Function of Mass Media," *Public Opinion Quarterly* 36, 1972, pp. 176-187.

McGann, Anthony F., Russell, Jadith F., and Russell, Thomas J.,

"Variable Pricing in Advertising Space For Regional and Metro Magazines," *Journalism Quarterly*, Summer 1983, pp. 269-274.

Majumdar, Ramanuj, *Marketing Research: Text, Applications and Case Studies*, Wiley Eastern Ltd., New Delhi, 1991.

——, *Marketing Strategies*, Allied Publishers, New Delhi, 1996.

"Managers View Behind—The-Pages Scene," *International Newspaper Advertising and Marketing Executives' News*, December 1982, p. 4.

Mandal, Kohinoor, "Struggle for Survival," *Financial Express*, April 6, 1996, p. 7.

Malik, Amita, "TV in the '80s: The Dangerous Decade," *Express Magazine*, December 17, 1989, pp. 1-2.

Marks, Alexandra, "Writers Up in Arms," *Financial Express*, December 23, 1995, p.7.

"Massive Maneuvering of News by Mulayam Govt.," *The Hindu*, 10 October, 1995.

Media Market Guide 1996-97, Media Direction—A Division of R.K. Swamy/BBDO, August 1996, New Delhi.

"Media Oligopoly Harmful to Democracy, says Sawant," *The Hindu*, December 12, 1995.

Mehta, Prem, "Managing Media in New Millennium," *Financial Express, Brand Wagon*, October 7, 1997, p. 7.

Mehta, Roda, "Media Challenge or Crisis," *The Economic Times, Brand Equity*, December 5, 1990, p. 3.

Menon, Amamath K., "Udayam—Patrika Rangamlo Kotha Samaram," *India Today* (Telugu), May 21-5 June, 1994, p. 44.

Menon, Gopinath, "How The English Press Scores," *Vidura*, April-June, 1997,

——, "The Future of Media," *A & M*, 30 May 1994, pp. 97-98.

——, "The Great Indian Media Bazaar," *The Hindu Business Line, Catalyst*, December 14, 1995, p. 4.

Merchant, Minhaz, "Media: Dramatic Shakeout," *The Week*, December 25, 1994, pp. 103-112.

Merrill, J.C., and Fraser, H.A., *The World's Great Dailies*, Communications Arts Books, New York, 1980.

Mitra, Chandan, "Dainik Bhaskar Goes Gang-Ho," *Vidura*, April-June, 1997, pp. 21-23.

MODE Survey, "The Clutter of Life," *A & M*, May 1992.

Moen, Daryl R., *Newspaper Layout and Design*, The Iowa State University Press, Ames, 1984.

"More Adults Turn to TV Even as Reading Habits Hit a Plateau," *The Times of India*, January 16, 1998, p. 3.

Morton, John, "Singleton: Hedging the Risks," *WJR*, November, 1987.

Mott, Frank Luther, *The News in America*, Harvard University Press, 1952.

Mudgil, Varun, A & M Survey on Big Spenders, *A & M*, 16-31 March 1998, pp. 28-72.

Mukherjee, Alok, "Selling Space and Time," *The Hindu*, February 18, 1996, p. 12.

Mulgaokar, S., "The Magnificent Rebel," *Indian Express*, October 6, 1991, p. l.

Murali, N., "Emerging Trends in Media," Keynote address at the seminar in Bangalore on 26th November, 1988.

Murthy, C.G.K., "Andhra Pradesh—A Blend of Tradition and Modernity," *Yojana*, August 1996, pp. 86-88.

Myers, James H., *Marketing*, McGraw Hill, Singapore, 1986.

NRS-V, *A&M*, 15 November 1995, pp. 51-64.

Nagarajan, Usha, "Boom Times on the Boob Tube," *Business World*, 27 July-9 August 1994, pp. 106-109.

Narayanamoorthy, P.V., "Kinetic Forces," *A & M*, 31 May 1996, pp. 26-28.

——, "Media and Aspirations," A & M, May 1992, pp. 63-66.

Natarajan, J., *History of Indian Journalism*, Ministry of Information and Broadcasting, Govt. of India, New Delhi, 1955.

Natarajan, S., *History of the Press in India*, Asia Publishing House, Bombay, 1962.

Nehru, Jawaharlal, *Discovery of India*, Asia Publishing House, Bombay, 1961.

New Strategies for Advertising Sales, American Press Institute, Reston, Virginia, 1985, pp. 7-8.

Newsom, Earl D., (ed.), *The Newspaper: Everything you Need to know to Make it in the Newspaper Business*, Prentice-Hall, New Jersey, 1981.

Newspaper Distribution Costs: Case Study of a Delhi Newspaper, Indian and Eastern Newspaper Society, New Delhi, 1974.

"Newspapers Should Upgrade Capabilities," *The Hindu*, April 12, 1995.

"Newspapers to Remain Closed on April 27," *The Hindu*, April 21, 1995, p. 13.

Newsprint Industry, *The Economic Times*, February 9, 1989, pp. 7-9.

"Newsprint on OGL, INS Stir Plan Off," *The Hindu*, April 27, 1995.

"Newsprint Production in the Country Comes to a Halt," *The Financial Express*, September 7, 1996.

"Newsprint 'tangible Steps Soon'" *The Hindu*, June 27, 1989.

"Newsprint Units Raided to Track Down Price Cartels," *The Hindu*, April 28, 1995, p. 11.

Ninan, Sevanti, "We Shouldn't Have a Feeble Press," *The Sunday Times of India*, August 13, 1995, p. 12.

O'Shaughnessy, John, *Competitive Marketing: A Strategic Approach*, ELBS, London, 1987.

Ogilvy & Mathur Media, "Rural Media Web Untangled," *The Economic Times, Brand Equity*, 8-14 May, 1996, p. 4.

Ohmae, Kenichi, "Getting Back to Strategy," *Harvard Business Review*, November-December 1988, pp. 149-156.

Ohmae, Kenichi, *The Mind of the Strategist: The Art of Japanese Business*, McGraw-Hill, New York, 1982.

Oxenfeldt, Alfred R., "How to Use Market Share Measurement," *Harvard Business Review*, January-February 1959.

Padmapriya, J., "Victimising the Vernacular," *Financial Express*, December 23, 1995, p. 7.

Pande, Bhanu, "News Dailies," *A & M*, 16-31 July, 1997.

——, "Survey on Media," *A & M*, 31 May 1996.

Parikh, R.D., *The Press and Society: A Sociological Study*, Popular Prakashan, Bombay, 1965.

Parthasarathy, Rangaswami, *Hundred Years of The Hindu*, Kasturi & Sons, Madras, 1978.

——, *Journalism in India: From the Earliest Times to the Present Day*, Sterling Publishers, New Delhi, 1989.

Patel, Meeta, "The Year of Reckoning," *The Economic Times, Brand Equity*, 19-25 February, 1997, p. 4.

Pattabhi Rama Rao, Parakala, "*Telugu Patrikarangamlo Parinamalu*," (Telugu), Communism, July 1992, pp. 55-63.

Peters, Thomas J., and Waterman, Robert H., Jr., *In Search of Excellence: Lessons from America's Best-Run Companies*, Harper & Row, New York, 1982.

Pillay, K.K., "The History of the Tamil Press," Paper presented at the Fourth Annual Conference (1966) of the Institute of Historical Studies, held at the University of Mysore, Mysore.

Pollard, James E., *Principles of Newspaper Management*, McGraw-Hill, New York, 1937.

Porter, Michael, E., *Competitive Advantage: Creating and Sustaining Superior Performance*, The Free Press, New York, 1985.

Porter, Michael, E., *Competitive Strategy: Techniques for Analyzing Industries and Competitors*, Free Press, New York, 1980.

"Post Has Numbers, But Lineage Trails," *Advertising Age*, November 29, 1982.

Prahalad, C.K., and Hamel, Gary, "The Core Competence of the Corporation," *Harvard Business Review* 68, No 3, 1990, pp. 79-91.

Prasad, Sharada H.Y., "A Good Deal of Life Ahead: The Electronic Media Cannot Wholly Displace Newspapers," *Frontline*, August 22, 1997, pp. 86-89.

Hamel Gary and Prahalad, C.K., *Competing for the Future*, Harvard Business School Press, Boston, MA., 1994 (in paperback 1996).

"Press Freedom and The Indian Situation," *The Hindu* editorial, January 13, 1990, p. 8.

Problems of Newspaper Industry in India, IENS, New Delhi, 1957.

Pumpin, Cuno, *The Essence of Corporate Strategy,* Jaico Publishing House, Bombay, 1995.

Radolf, Andrew, "Keys to Circulation Success: Better Service and Training," *Editor & Publisher,* June 22 1995, pp. 18, 38.

Rai, Mona, "Femina: Drop Your Inhibitions," *A & M,* 15 April 1995, pp. 78-80.

Raina, Divya, "Why Not Say it Without Words?," *The Hindu,* Magazine, April 2, 1995.

Rajagopalachari, C, *Towards a Responsible Press: Shri Rajagopalachari's Speeches on the Press Bill in Parliament,* Publications Division, New Delhi, 1952.

Rajan, Ravi, "Space Innovation: Defining the Limits," A & M, December, 1989, pp. 70-72.

Rajeswara Rao, "Telugu Dailies," in K.R. Seshagiri Rao (ed.), *Studies in the History of Telugu Journalism,* Narla Shashtyabdipurti Celebration Committee, Delhi, 1968, pp. 101-111.

Raju, C.V.S.N., "Financial Advertising: Between the SEBI and the Sensex,"*A & M,* 312 May 1996, pp. 60-61.

Raju, R.K., "New York Has its Times," *Indian Express,* Magazine, November 20, 1988, p. 6.

Rahman, M., "Sarikotha T.V. Super Bazar: Meeta Nokkithe Chalu Manollasam," *India Today* (Telugu), November 6-20, 1992, pp. 34-44.

Ram, N., "Foreign Media Entry into the Press: Issues and Implications," *Economic and Political Weekly,* October 22 1994, pp. 2787-2790.

Ramani, V., "Is there Life after Zee?," *The Economic Times, Brand Equity,* 8 September, 1993, p. 5.

Ramnath, Padma, "The Race for Readers," *Business India,* February 10-23, 1997, p.m.

Ramanuj Majumdar, *Marketing Strategies,* Allied Publishers, New Delhi, 1996.

Ranganath, G., "Great Days Ahead," *A & M*, 30 May 1994, pp. 101-102.

Rangarajan, S., "Coming Through Loud and Clear," *The Hindu* Magazine, March 17, 1996, p. 4.

Rao, C.V.H., "The Press in Andhra," in K.R. Seshagiri Rao (ed.), *Studies in the History of Telugu Journalism*, Narla Shashtyabdipurti Celebration Committee, Delhi, 1968.

Rao, K.V., *Research Methodology in Commerce and Management*, Sterling Publishers, New Delhi, 1993.

Rao, S.L., and Natarajan, I., *Indian Market Demographics: The Consumer Classes*, Global Business Press, New Delhi, 1996.

Reagon, Joey, "New Technologies and News Use: Adopters Vs. Non-adopters," *Journalism Quarterly*, Winter 1989 pp. 871-75, 87.

Regani, Sarojini, "The Growth of the Telugu Press," in S.P. Sen (ed.), *The Indian Press*, Indian Institute of Historical Studies, Calcutta, 1967.

Ries, Al., and Trout, Jack, *Marketing Warfare*, McGraw-Hill, New York, 1986.

—— *Positioning: The Battle for Your Mind*, Warner Books, New York, 1982.

Riffe, Daniel and Shaw, Eugene F., "Pricing a Medium Out of the Market: The 25-Cent Daily Newspaper," *Journalism Quarterly*, Autumn, 1980, pp. 385-391.

Rimmer, Tony and Weaver, David, "Different Questions, Different Answers, Media Use and Media Credibility," *Journalism Quarterly*, Spring 1987, pp. 28-36, 44.

Rogers, Everett M., (ed.), *Communication and Development: Critical Perspectives*, Sagar Publications, Newbury Park. 1976.

——, "Communication and Development—The Passing of the Dominant Paradigm" in Everett M. Rogers (ed.), *Communication and Development: Critical Perspectives*, Sage Publications, Newbury Park, 1976.

Rosengren, Karl Erik., Wenner, Lawrence A., and Palmgreen, Philip, (eds.), *Media Gratifications Research: Current Perspectives*, Sage Publications, New Delhi.

Roy, Mahasweta Ghoshi and Mukerjea, D.N., "From Smart Marketing to Dirty Tricks," *Business World*, 27 July-9 August 1994, pp. 22-29.

Sahai, Priya, "The Pioneer: End Game," *A & M*, 1-15 April 1998, pp. 98-103.

Sahai, Priya, et. al., "*A & M*, Survey: Satellite Channels," *A & M*, 16-31 May 1997, pp. 39-52.

Sahni, J.N., *Truth About the Indian Press*, Allied Publishers, Mumbai, 1974.

Sahu, Gopal K., "Communication Strategies for Socio-economic Development," *Kurukshetra*, January-February 1996, pp. 81-83.

Sai, K., and Sahni, Briji Bhushan, "Telugu Press—Colourful Battle," *A & M*, October 1989.

Salmon, Charles T., and Lee, Jung-Sook, "Perceptions of Newspaper Fairness: A Structural Approach," *Journalism Quarterly*, Winter 1983, pp. 663-670.

"Satellite TV Poses no Threat to Print Medium: Survey," *The Hindu*, October 28, 1995.

Satyamurthy, P., and Lakshmaiah, M., "Gadi Thappina Media", *Suprabhatham* (Telugu), 20 November 1995, pp. 2-7.

Sachiffman, Leon G., and Kanuk, Leslie Lazar, *Consumer Behaviour*, Prentice Hall of India, New Delhi, (5th ed.), 1997.

Schramm, Wilber, *Mass Media and National Development*, University Press, Stanford, CA., 1964.

Schramm, W., and White, D., "Age Education and Economic Status: Factors in Newspaper Reading," *Journalism Quarterly*, 26, 1949, pp. 150-158.

Schudson, Michael, *Discovering the News: A Social History of American Newspapers*, Basic Books, New York, 1978.

Schweitzer John C., and Goldman, Elaine, "Does Newspaper Competition Make a Difference to Readers?" *Journalism Quarterly*, Winter 1975, pp. 706-710.

Sen, S.P., *The Indian Press*, Indian Institute of Historical Studies, Calcutta, 1967.

Seshagiri, Rao., (ed.), *Studies in the History of Telugu Journalism*, Narla Shashtyabdipurti Celebration Committee, Delhi, 1968.

Shankar, Ravi, "Trends in Indian Advertising and Media," *Indian Journal of Commerce*, (Vol. 51, No. l), March 1998, p. 25.

Shantaram and Vanaja, "Naadu Visakha Veechika, Eenadu Pathaaka Seershika, (Telugu), *Suprabhatam*, 5-20 December 1993, pp. 2-8.

Sharplin, Arthur, *Strategic Management*, McGraw-Hill, New York, 1985.

Shekar, Meenu, "The Ad Industry Takes Off," *Business World*, 5-18 October, 1994, pp. 98-100.

Shenoy, Meera and Doctor, Vikram, "Advertising: On a Plateau," *Business India*, May 20- June 2, 1996, pp. 116-117.

Shourie, Arun, "Things to do About the Press," *Indian Express*, Sunday Edition, March 25, 1990, pp. 1-2.

Shourie, Deepak, "Why Print is Preferred," *Vidura*, April-June, 1997, pp. 4-5.

Shriram, D., "Dictating One's Business Terms, "*The Economic Times, Brand Equity*, 3-9 April 1996, p. 4.

Shrivastava, K.M., *Media Issues*, Sterling Publishers, New Delhi, 1992.

——, *News Reporting and Editing*, Sterling Publishers, New Delhi, 1991.

——, *Radio and TV Journalism*, Sterling Publishers, New Delhi, 1989.

Silverman, Alvin, *The American Newspaper*, Robert B.Luce, Washington, DC., 1964.

Sindhwani, Trilok, N., *Newspaper Economics and Management*, Ankur Publishing, New Delhi, 1958.

Singh, Sandeep, "On the Sound of Success," *The Economic Times, Brand Equity*, 10-16 April 1996, p. 5.

Singhal, Aravind and Rogers, Everett M., *Indian Information Revolution*, Sage Publications, New Delhi, 1989.

Siva Rao, D.V., "Telugu Journalism—Past and Present," in K.R. Seshagiri Rao (ed.), *Studies in the History of Telugu Journalism*, Narla Shastyabdipurti Celebration Committee, Delhi, 1968.

Smith, Adam, "The Wealth of Nations," Carman ed., *Modem Library*, New York, 1937, First published in 1776.

Soley, Lawrence C., "Does Advertising Lower the Prices of Newspapers to Consumers?," *Journalism Quarterly*, Winter 1989, pp. 801-806.

Sorabjee, Soli J., "Onslaught on Press Freedom," *The Hindu*, April 24, 1995.

Souza, Lynn de, "Horoscopes and Hustle," *A & M*, July 1993.

——, "In Black and White and Bold," *The Economic Times, Brand Equity*, 8-14 November 1995, p. 2.

——, "Power to the Publisher," *A & M*, 15 April 1995, pp. 30-32.

Srinivasa, T.C.A. and Raghavan, "Who Reads, Who Writes, Who Does the Arithmetic?," *Indian Express*, February 14 1988, p. 5.

Srinivasan, V.K., "The Role of Newspapers and Secularism," *The Hindu*, November 8, 1990.

Stack, Neville, "Death by Complacency," *Vidura*, April-June 1997, p. 25.

Stanton, William J., and Futrell, Charles, *Fundamentals of Marketing*, McGraw Hill, New York, (8th ed.), 1987.

Stanton, William J., Etzel, Michael J., and Walker, Bruce J., *Fundamentals of Marketing*, McGraw-Hill Singapore (10th ed.), 1994.

Star, Steven H., Davis, Nancy J., Lovelock, Christopher H., and Shapiro, Benson P., *Problems in Marketing*, McGraw-Hill, Tokyo, (5th ed.), 1977.

Statistical Outline of India 1996-97, Tata Services, Mumbai.

Stone, Gerald, *Examining Newspapers—What Research Reveals About America's Newspapers*, Sage Publications, New Delhi, 1987.

Stone G.C., and Wetherington, R.V., Jr., "Confirming the Newspaper Reading *Habit*," *Journalism Quarterly* 56, 1979, pp. 554-561, 566.

Strentz, Herbert, *New's Reporters and News Sources: Accomplices in Shaping and Misshaping the News*, Prentice-Hall of India, New Delhi, 1992.

Subash, K., "The Big Problems of Small Papers," *Vidura*, October 1984, pp. 273-274.

Subba Rao, K., "Narla's Impact on Telugu Journalism," in K.R. Seshagiri Rao (ed.), *Studies in the History of Telugu Journalism*, Narla Shashtyabdipurti Celebration Committee, Delhi, 1968.

Subrahmaniam, Ganga, "Branching Out," *Business India*, January 13-26, 1997, p. 3, Eenadu.

Suresh, K., "Deccan Chronicle: The Straight Splurge," *A & M*, 16-31 January 1997.

——, "Eenadu TV: Media Switch," *A&M*, December 31, 1995, pp. 11, 14.

Sulton, Howard, *The Marketing Plan in the 1990s*, The Conference Board, New York, 1990.

Swami, Parthasarathi, "The Media Wars," *Business World*, September 14-27, 1988, pp. 29-34.

"Telugu Journalism Theeru Thennulu," *Andhra Jyoti Rajatha Kamalam*, July 1985, pp. 59-62.

Thayar, Frank, *Newspaper Business Management*, Prentice-Hall, New York, 1954.

Theodore, Stanley, "Making News," *The Week*, May 16, 1993.

Thorn, William J., and Pfeil, Mary Pat, *Newspaper Circulation: Marketing the News*, Longman, New York, 1987.

Tikoo, Rajiv, "In Search of Excellence," *Financial Express*, January 27, 1996, p. 7.

Tromer, George W., "Marketing the Newspaper," in D.Earl Newsom (ed.), *The Newspaper: Everything You Need to Know to Make It in the Newspaper Business*, Prentice-Hall, New Jersey, 1981.

Tull, Donald S., and Hawkins Del I., *Marketing Research: Meaning, Measurement and Method, A Text with Cases*, Macmillan, New York, 1976.

Ulrich, David and Lake, David, *Organisational Capability: Competing from the Insideout*, Wiley, New York, 1990.

"U.S. Newspapers Gain Readers Even as TV Loses Viewers," *The Times of India*, July 20, 1998. Vidyanathan, Arun, "A Lot of

Gloss and Gamption," *Business World,* 25 December 1996-7 January 1997, pp. 128-129.

Vallury, Santosh, "Piggyback Papers," *Financial Express,* March 16, 1996, p. 7.

Vasant D. Rao, "The Beginning and Growth of the Marathi Press," paper presented at the Fourth Annual Conference (1966) of the Institute of Historical Studies, held at the University of Mysore.

Vasuki, S.N., "The Ramoji Rao Phenomenon," *Business India,* April 13 - May 6, 1984, pp. 87-94.

Vembuswami, N., *ABC of Mass Media,* Blackie and Sons, Delhi, 1984.

Venugopal, N., "ETV is Ramoji Rao's New Window to the World," *The Economic Times,* 17 September 1995, p. 5.

Vidyadhar Reddy, A., and Shankaraiah, K., "Brand Switching Behaviour of Customers: A Case Study of Telugu Dailies at Karimnagar," *Indian Management,* December 1988, pp. 11-14.

Vilanilam, J.V., *Reporting a Revolution: The Iranian Revolution and NIICO Debate,* Sage Publications, New Delhi, 1989.

Vishweshwer Rao, P.L., *Language Press in India: A Study of Readership, Contents and Language Comprehension with Special Reference to Telugu Daily Newspapers,* Unpublished Ph.D. dissertation, Osmania University, Hyderabad, 1991.

Walker, Martin, *Powers of the Press: Twelve of the World's Influential Newspapers,* The Pilgrim Press, New York, 1983.

Weaver, D.H., "Audience Need for Orientation and Media Effects," *Communication Research* 7, 1980, pp. 361-376.

Weaver, D.H., Graber, D.A., McCombs, M.E., and Eyal, C.H., *Media Agenda—Setting in a Presidential Election: Issues, Images, and Interest,* Praeger, New York, 1981.

Weaver, David H., and Mullins, L.E., "Content and Format Characteristics of Competing Daily Newspapers," *Journalism Quarterly,* Summer 1975, pp. 257-264.

Williams, Herbert Lee, *Newspaper Organisation and Management,*

Surjeet Publications, (The Iowa State University Press, 1978), New Delhi, (5th ed.), 1982.

Willis, Jim, *Surviving in the Newspaper Business*, Praeger, New York, 1988.

Wolseley, Roland E. (ed.), *Journalism in Modem India*, Asia Publishing House, Bombay, 1964.

Wright, John S., Winter, Wills L.Jr., and Zeigler, Sherilyn, K., *Advertising*, Tata McGraw-Hill, New Delhi, 1983.

Wright, Robert V.L., *A System for Managing Diversity*, Arthur D. Little, Cambridge, MA., 1974.

Yadava, J.S., "Mass Media and Development," *Khadi Gramodyog*, October 1998, pp. 62-68.

Yadava, J.S., "Media and Participatory Development," *Kurukshetra*, January-February, pp. 16-20.

Yankel Ovich, Daniel, "New Criteria for Market Segmentation," *Harvard Business Review*, March-April 1964.

Index